Other Information Security Study Guides by Sybex

IAPP AIGP Artificial Intelligence Governance Professional Study Guide — ISBN 978-1-394-36394-0, January 2026

IAPP CIPP/US Certified Information Privacy Professional Study Guide, 2nd Edition — ISBN 978-1-394-28490-0, January 2025

CRISC Certified in Risk and Information Systems Control Study Guide — ISBN 978-1-394-37366-6, May 2026

CISA Certified Information Systems Auditor Study Guide Covering 2024–2029 Exam Objectives — ISBN 978-1-394-28838-0, December 2024

CDPSE

Certified Data Privacy Solutions Engineer

STUDY GUIDE

CDPSE

Certified Data Privacy Solutions Engineer

STUDY GUIDE

PETER H. GREGORY

CDPSE, CRISC, CISM, CISA, CISSP, CIPM, CCSK

Published by John Wiley & Sons, Inc., Hoboken, New Jersey.

For general information on our other products and services or for technical support, please contact our Customer Care Department within the United States at (800) 762-2974, outside the United States at (317) 572-3993 or fax (317) 572-4002. For product technical support, you can find answers to frequently asked questions or reach us via live chat at https://sybexsupport.wiley.com.

Wiley also publishes its books in a variety of electronic formats. Some content that appears in print may not be available in electronic formats. For more information about Wiley products, visit our website at www.wiley.com.

Library of Congress Cataloging-in-Publication Data has been applied for:

Paperback ISBN: 9781394363803
ePDF ISBN: 9781394363827
ePub ISBN: 9781394363810

Cover Design: Wiley
Cover Image: Jeremy Woodhouse/Getty Images

Printed and bound by CPI Group (UK) Ltd, Croydon, CR0 4YY

C9781394363803_250626

To my God, whose grace provided the time, focus, and capability necessary for this and all my prior works.

Acknowledgments

Books like this involve the work of many people, and as an author, I truly appreciate the hard work and dedication that the team at Wiley demonstrates. I want to extend special thanks to my acquisitions editor, Jim Minatel, who worked diligently to make this project possible.

I also greatly appreciated the editing and production team for the book, including Patrick Walsh, the editorial project manager, who kept the train on the tracks; Kezia Endsley, the copy editor, who made sure all of the language and formatting were just right; Pete Gaughan, senior managing editor, who helped out with key questions, Navin Vijayakumar, the managing editor, who managed the various phases of development, and Maduramuthu Krishnaraj, the Content Refinement Specialist, who guided us through layouts, formatting, and final cleanup to produce a great book. Finally, special thanks to John Clark, the technical editor, who provided insightful advice and gave excellent improvement suggestions and feedback throughout the book. I would also like to thank the many behind-the-scenes contributors, including the graphic, production, and technical teams, who helped bring the book and companion materials to fruition.

My long-time literary agent, Carole Jelen of Waterside Productions, continues to provide me with fantastic opportunities, advice, and assistance.

I have difficulty expressing my gratitude to my wife and love of my life, Rebekah, for tolerating my frequent absences (in the home office) while I developed this manuscript. This project could not have been completed without her loyal and unfailing support and encouragement.

About the Author

Peter H. Gregory (CDPSE, CISSP, CISM, CISA, CRISC, CIPM, CCSK, A/CCRF, A/CCRP, A/CRMP) is the author of more than 60 books on security, privacy, and technology, including *Solaris Security* (Prentice Hall, 2000), *The Art of Writing Technical Books* (Waterside, 2022), *CISA Certified Information Systems Auditor Study Guide* (Wiley, 2025), *Chromebook For Dummies* (Wiley, 2023), and *Elementary Information Security* (Jones & Bartlett Learning, 2024). He has spoken at numerous industry conferences, including RSA, Interop, (ISC)^2 Congress, ISACA CACS, SecureWorld Expo, West Coast Security Forum, IP3, ArcticCon, Society for Information Management, the Washington Technology Industry Association, the Inland Northwest Cyber Hub, the Hale Borealis Forum, and InfraGard.

Peter is a recently retired career technologist and cybersecurity executive. He has held security leadership positions at GCI Communications, Optiv Security, and Concur Technologies since the early 2000s, after a celebrated career in software, systems, and security engineering at Bally Gaming, World Vision, and AT&T Wireless. Peter serves on the advisory boards of the University of Washington and Seattle University, with a focus on cybersecurity education programs. He is a 2008 graduate of the FBI Citizens' Academy.

Peter resides in Central Washington State and can be found at `www.peterhgregory.com`.

About the Technical Editor

John Clark, CISSP, CISA, CISM, CDPSE, CIPP/E, CIPT, FIP, is an information security executive advisor with more than 25 years of experience in the information security and privacy field. Over the past eight years, he has worked with CISOs, CIOs, boardrooms, and business leaders to develop practical, business-aligned security and privacy programs built to adapt as regulations evolve. John has contributed to industry publications and spoken at industry conferences on privacy program management. He holds a bachelor's degree in management information systems and an MBA from the University of Houston.

Contents at a Glance

Contents

Introduction

Welcome to the Sybex Study Guide for ISACA's Certified Data Privacy Solutions Engineer (CDPSE) exam! This book will help you study for, and successfully pass, one of ISACA's premier certification exams, the CDPSE exam. This exam is designed to test your knowledge of a wide variety of topics related to privacy engineering and management. The exam focuses on privacy concepts, practices, and technologies.

The information revolution has transformed businesses, governments, and people in profound ways. Virtually all business and government operations are now digital, resulting in everyone's personal details being stored in information systems.

Two issues have arisen from this transformation: safeguarding personal information from criminal organizations and ensuring that it is used only for clearly stated purposes. Difficulties in meeting these challenges have helped create and emphasize the importance of the cybersecurity and information privacy professions. Numerous security and privacy laws, regulations, and standards have been enacted and created, imposing a patchwork of new requirements on organizations and governments to enact specific practices to protect and control the use of our personal information.

These developments continue to drive demand for information privacy, information security professionals, and leaders in both privacy and security. These highly sought-after professionals play a crucial role in developing better information privacy and security programs that result in reduced risk and improved confidence.

This book covers privacy concepts, privacy governance, risk assessments, standards and frameworks, data management, and privacy control design and implementation. I also cover the essential concepts, terminology, and definitions that privacy practitioners need to be effective in these areas. In the book's nine main chapters, I cover all four top-level domains as well as the supporting task statements listed in the official ISACA exam objectives.

While you don't have to be an expert already in all the areas I discuss, having experience in some, such as privacy concepts, helps. A good, broad background of experience and knowledge in information security and/or data management will give you an advantage in your studies for this exam. Of course, you'll get a good background in all these subjects throughout the book.

The Certified Data Privacy Solutions Engineer (CDPSE) certification, established by *ISACA* in 2020, will light the path for tens of thousands of privacy and security professionals who need to demonstrate competence in the privacy field. ISACA, the creator of the Certified Information Systems Auditor (CISA, established in 1978), the Certified Information Security Manager (CISM, established in 2002), and other certifications, is one of the world's leading security, privacy, and IT management and professional development organizations. ISACA has awarded over 300,000 certifications in its ~59-year history,[1] with

[1] ISACA began as an informal group of professionals in 1967, and incorporated in 1969 as the EDP Auditors Association. In 1994, the organization renamed itself to the Information Systems Audit and Control Association (ISACA), and in 2020, the brand name is simply ISACA. (Source: ISACA Overview and History, retrieved from `archive.org`.)

certification holders in 186 countries. More than 90% of certification holders renew their certifications each year—this is a testament to the value of ISACA and its certifications.

Passing the CDPSE exam not only places you in a class of professionals recognized for their experience and expertise in this field, but it also serves to quantify and validate your knowledge of advanced risk management, privacy and data protection topics. After passing this exam, you'll be able to show that not only are you qualified, but you are certified in these areas. This book is designed to help you get there.

Purpose of This Book

Let's get the obvious out of the way: this is a comprehensive study guide for the privacy professional who needs a reliable reference for individual or group-led study for the CDPSE certification. This book contains the information that CDPSE candidates must know. While this book is one source of information to help you prepare for the CDPSE exam, it should not be thought of as the ultimate collection of *all* the knowledge and experience that ISACA expects qualified CDPSE candidates to possess—no one publication covers all this information. The other thing you'll need, just as important as suitable study material in my mind, is experience. There's no substitute for practical, hands-on experience. You should make every effort to learn all aspects of the ISACA CDPSE exam material I discuss in this book.

This book also serves as a reference for aspiring and practicing privacy professionals and leaders. The content required to pass the CDPSE exam is the same content that practicing privacy professionals need to be familiar with in their day-to-day work. This book is an ideal CDPSE exam study guide and a desk reference for those who have already earned their CDPSE certification.

The pace of change in the privacy and information security industries and professions is high. Rather than contain every detail and nuance of every law, practice, standard, and technique in privacy and security, this book shows the reader how to stay current in the profession. Indeed, the pace of change is one of many reasons that ISACA and other associations require continuous learning to retain one's certifications. It is important to understand key facts and practices in privacy and how to stay current as they continue to change.

This book is also invaluable for privacy professionals who are not in a leadership position. You will gain considerable insight into today's privacy challenges. This book is also useful for IT, security, and business management professionals who work with privacy professionals and need a better understanding of what they are doing and why.

Finally, this book is an excellent guide for anyone exploring a career in privacy. The study chapters explain all the relevant technologies, techniques, and processes used to manage a modern privacy program. This is useful if you are wondering what the privacy profession is all about.

How to Use This Book

This book covers everything you'll need to know for ISACA's CDPSE certification examination. Each chapter covers specific objectives and exam details, as defined by ISACA in its job practice areas. The chapters and their sections correspond precisely to the CDPSE job practice that ISACA updates from time to time.

Each chapter has several components designed to effectively communicate the information you'll need for the exam.

The topics covered in each chapter are listed in the first section to help you map out your study.

- The **Summary** section of each chapter briefly explains the chapter, allowing you to easily understand what it covers.
- **Exam Essentials** focus on major exam topics and critical knowledge that you should take into the test. The Exam Essentials focus on the ISACA CDPSE exam objectives.
- **Tips** and **Exam Tips** are included in each chapter that offer great information on how concepts you'll study apply in a place that I like to call "the real world." Often, they give you a bit more information on a topic covered in the text that may appear in the exam.
- **Notes** may be included in a chapter as well. These are bits of information that are relevant to the discussion and that point out extra information.
- **Case Studies** are included to illustrate how an idea, concept, or standard can be put into practice.
- **Twenty practice questions** appear at the end of each chapter and are designed to allow you to attempt some exam questions on the topics covered in the domain.

Benefits of CDPSE Certification

Obtaining the CDPSE certification offers several significant benefits:

- **Expands knowledge and skills and builds confidence** Developing knowledge and skills in privacy and data protection, building and managing a privacy program, and responding to privacy incidents can prepare you for advancement or expand your scope of responsibilities. Personal and professional achievements can boost confidence, which encourages you to move forward and seek new career opportunities.
- **Increases marketability and career options** Because of various legal and regulatory requirements, such as the Health Insurance Portability and Accountability Act (HIPAA), Gramm–Leach–Bliley Act (GLBA), the European General Data Protection Regulation (GDPR), the California Consumer Privacy Act (CCPA), and the California Privacy Rights Act (CPRA), demand is growing for individuals with experience in

developing and running privacy programs. Besides, obtaining your CDPSE certification demonstrates to current and potential employers your willingness and commitment to improve your knowledge and skills in privacy. Having a CDPSE certification can provide a competitive advantage and open many opportunities in various industries and countries.

- **Meets employment requirements** Many government agencies and organizations require certifications for positions involving privacy and information security. Although the CDPSE certification is still somewhat new, it's only a matter of time before government agencies and the privacy industry require a leading privacy certification for their privacy professionals.
- **Builds customer confidence and international credibility** Prospective customers seeking privacy work will have confidence that the quality of the strategies and execution aligns with internationally recognized practices and standards.

Regardless of your current position, demonstrating knowledge and experience in privacy can expand your career options. The certification does not limit you to privacy or privacy management; it can provide additional value and insight to those currently holding or seeking the following positions:

- Executives such as chief privacy officers (CPOs), data protection officers (DPOs), chief operating officers (COOs), chief financial officers (CFOs), chief compliance officers (CCOs), and chief information officers (CIOs)
- Records management executives and practitioners
- Marketing management executives and practitioners
- IT management executives such as chief information officers (CIOs), chief technology officers (CTOs), directors, managers, and staff
- Chief audit executives, audit partners, and audit directors
- Compliance executives and management
- Security and audit consultants

Finally, because privacy and cybersecurity are so closely related, many cybersecurity leaders and professionals see their span of responsibilities expanding to include privacy. Soon, cybersecurity professionals lacking privacy certifications and experience may find themselves at a disadvantage within their organizations and in the job market.

Becoming a CDPSE Professional

To become a CDPSE professional, you are required to pay the exam fee, pass the exam, prove that you have the necessary education and experience, and agree to uphold ethics and standards. To keep your CDPSE certification, you are required to take at least 20 continuing

FIGURE 1 The CDPSE certification lifecycle.

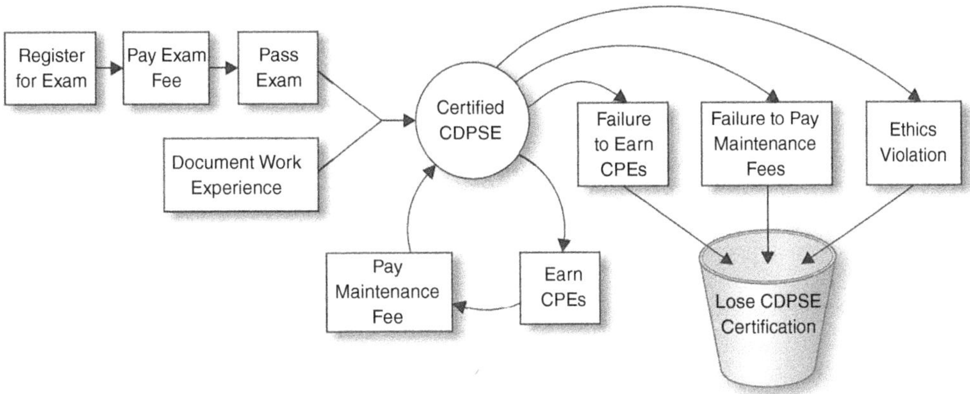

education hours each year (120 hours in three years) and pay annual maintenance fees. This lifecycle is depicted in Figure 1.

The following list outlines the primary requirements for becoming certified:

- **Experience** A CDPSE candidate must submit verifiable evidence of at least three years of professional work experience in data privacy governance, privacy risk management and compliance, privacy engineering, and/or data lifecycle work. Experience must be verified and must be gained within the ten-year period preceding the application date for certification or within five years from the date of passing the exam. No substitution or waiver options are available.
- **Ethics** Candidates must commit to adhering to ISACA's Code of Professional Ethics, which guides the personal and professional conduct of those certified.
- **Exam** Candidates must receive a passing score on the CDPSE exam. A passing score is valid for up to five years, after which the score is void. This means that a CDPSE candidate who passes the exam has a maximum of five years to apply for CDPSE certification; candidates who pass the exam but fail to act within five years will have to retake the exam if they want to become CDPSE certified.
- **Education** Those certified must adhere to the CDPSE Continuing Professional Education Policy, which requires a minimum of 20 continuing professional education (CPE) hours each year, with a total requirement of 120 CPEs over the certification period (three years).
- **Application** After successfully passing the exam, meeting the experience requirements, and having read through the Code of Professional Ethics and Standards, a candidate is ready to apply for certification. An application must be received within five years of passing the exam.

Exam Tip

When preparing for any certification exam, you should routinely refer to the certifying body's website for the latest information about objectives and exam requirements. Visit the ISACA website at `www.isaca.org/cdpse` for up-to-date information on the CDPSE certification and exam requirements.

Experience Requirements

To qualify for CDPSE certification, you must have completed the equivalent of three years of total work experience. These three years can take many forms. Additional details on the minimum certification requirements, substitution options, and various examples are discussed next.

Although not recommended, a CDPSE candidate can take the exam before completing any work experience directly related to privacy management. As long as the candidate passes the exam and meets the work experience requirements within five years of the exam date, and within ten years of the application for certification, the candidate is eligible for certification.

Direct Work Experience

You are required to have at least three years of experience in privacy engineering and/or related fields, such as data management. This is equivalent to 6000 actual work hours, which must be related to one or more of the four CDPSE job practice areas:

- Privacy Governance
- Privacy Risk Management and Compliance
- Data Lifecycle Management
- Privacy Engineering

All work experience must be completed within the ten-year period preceding the certification application or within five years from the date of the initial CDPSE exam. You will need to complete a separate Verification of Work Experience form for each segment of experience.

Substitution of Experience

Unlike most other ISACA certifications, there are no available experience waivers or substitutions. Instead, you must have three or more years of experience in privacy as stated previously.

I recommend that you also read the CDPSE certification qualifications on the ISACA website at `www.isaca.org/cdpse`. From time to time, ISACA changes the qualification rules, and I want you to have the most up-to-date information available.

ISACA Code of Professional Ethics

Becoming a CDPSE professional means you agree to adhere to the ISACA Code of Professional Ethics, a formal document outlining those things you will do to ensure the utmost integrity and to support and represent the organization and certification to the best of your abilities.

Specifically, the ISACA Code of Professional Ethics requires ISACA members and certification holders to do the following:

- Support the implementation of, and encourage compliance with, appropriate standards and procedures for the effective governance and management of enterprise information systems and technology, including audit, control, security, and risk management.
- Perform their duties with objectivity, due diligence, and professional care, in accordance with professional standards.
- Serve in the interest of stakeholders in a lawful manner, while maintaining high standards of conduct and character and not discrediting their profession or the association.
- Maintain the privacy and confidentiality of information obtained in the course of their activities unless disclosure is required by legal authority. Such information shall not be used for personal benefit or released to inappropriate parties.
- Maintain competency in their respective fields and agree to undertake only those activities they can reasonably expect to complete with the necessary skills, knowledge, and competence.
- Inform appropriate parties of the results of work performed, including the disclosure of all significant facts known to them that, if not disclosed, may distort the reporting of the results.
- Support the professional education of stakeholders in enhancing their understanding of the governance and management of enterprise information systems and technology, including audit, control, security, and risk management.

Failure to comply with the ISACA Code of Professional Ethics can result in an investigation into a member's or certification holder's conduct and, ultimately, disciplinary measures, including the forfeiture of their hard-won certification(s).

You can find the full text and terms of enforcement of the ISACA Code of Professional Ethics at `www.isaca.org/code-of-professional-ethics`.

The Certification Exam

The certification exam is offered year-round. You have several ways to register; however, I highly recommend that you plan and register early, regardless of your chosen method.

In mid-2026, the schedule of exam fees in U.S. dollars was:

- CDPSE application fee: $50
- Regular registration: $575 member/$760 nonmember

The ISACA administers the test at testing centers and offers remotely proctored exams for those who prefer remote testing. I discuss both options in this section.

I recommend that you pay close attention to information on ISACA's website regarding testing logistics and locations.

Once registration is complete, you will immediately receive an email acknowledging your registration. Next, you will need to schedule your certification exam. The ISACA website will direct you to the certification registration page, where you will select a date, time, and (optionally) location to take your exam. When you confirm the date, time, and location for your exam, you will receive a confirmation via email. You will need the confirmation letter to enter the test location—make sure to keep it unmarked and in a safe place until test time.

On-site Testing Center

When you arrive at the test site, you will be required to sign in, and may be asked to sign an agreement. Also, you will be required to turn in your smartphone, wallet or purse, and other personal items for safekeeping. The exam proctor will read aloud the rules you are required to follow while you take your exam. These rules will address matters such as breaks, drinking water, and snacks.

While you take your exam, you will be supervised by the proctor, and you will be monitored by video surveillance in the test center to make sure no one can cheat on the exam.

Remote Proctored Testing

If you have registered for a remote proctored exam, make sure you meet all the technical requirements. ISACA has published the "Remote Proctoring Guide," which includes all necessary technical requirements and step-by-step procedures for taking the exam. In the "Exam Candidate Guide," go to the "Online Remote Proctoring" section, where you'll find a link to the Remote Proctoring Guide.

A remote proctored exam means you'll be taking the exam on your own computer in your residence or other location. You'll be in live contact with an exam proctor, and your webcam will be turned on throughout the exam so that the proctor can observe you while taking the exam to ensure you are not cheating with reference materials (books or online). The proctor may ask you to show them the room where you are taking the exam to ensure you do not have reference materials or information anywhere in view.

To be eligible for a remote proctored exam, you must have a supported version of Windows, macOS, ChromeOS, or Linux (Chrome Extension), a current version of Google Chrome, a webcam with at least 640×480 resolution, a microphone, and a stable broadband Internet connection. You must have the ability to install the PSI Secure Browser and modify firewalls and other administrative tasks on the day of the exam (this requires you to have administrative privileges on the computer you are using, which might be a problem if you are using a company-issued computer that often restricts your ability to install software).

You'll be required to log in to your My ISACA account when your exam is scheduled. Next, you'll navigate to your certifications, find the exam you have scheduled, and launch the exam. You'll be directed to perform several tasks, including installing the secure browser and closing several other programs on your computer, including other web browsers and programs like Adobe Reader, Word, Excel, and any others that could include reference material.

You are not permitted to speak or perform gestures at any time during the exam. In short, you cannot be seen to perform any action that might be an indication of aid by an accomplice.

You'll be required to verify your ID by holding it near your webcam so that the proctor can see it to confirm that you are not having someone else take the exam for you. You will also be required to use your webcam to show your proctor the entire room. Note that ISACA does not accept digital IDs.

After all steps have been completed, the proctor will release the exam to you, and you may begin.

Exam Questions

Each registrant has 3.5 hours to take the multiple-choice question exam. There are 120 questions on the exam, representing the four job practice areas. Each question has four answer choices, of which you can select only one best answer. You can skip questions and return to them later, and flag questions you want to review later if time permits. While you are taking your exam, the time remaining will appear on the screen.

When you have completed the exam, you are directed to close it. At that time, the exam will display your pass/fail status, with a reminder that your score and passing status are subject to review.

You will be scored in each job practice area and then provided a final score. All scores are scaled. Scores range from 200 to 800; however, a final score of 450 is required to pass.

Exam questions are derived from a job practice analysis study conducted by ISACA. The selected areas reflect the tasks performed in a CDPSE's day-to-day activities and the background knowledge required to develop and manage a privacy and data protection program. You can find more detailed descriptions of the task and knowledge statements at `www.isaca.org/credentialing/cdpse/cdpse-exam-content-outline`.

Exam Coverage

The CDPSE exam is quite broad in its scope. The exam covers four job practice areas, as shown in Table 1.

TABLE 1 CDPSE Exam Practice Areas

Domain	CDPSE Job Practice Area	Percentage of Exam	Chapters
1	Privacy Governance		
	Part A: Privacy Governance	20%	1
	Part B: Privacy Operations		2
2	Privacy Risk Management & Compliance		
	Part A: Risk Management	18%	3
	Part B: Compliance		4
3	Data Lifecycle Management		
	Part A: Data Collection and Processing	23%	5
	Part B: Data Persistence and Destruction		6
4	Privacy Engineering		
	Part A: Technology Stacks	39%	7
	Part B: Privacy-related Security Controls		8
	Part C: Privacy Controls		9

Independent committees have been established to determine the best questions, review exam results, and statistically analyze them for continuous improvement. Should you come across a horrifically difficult or strange question, do not panic. This question may have been written for another purpose. A few questions on the exam are included for research and analysis purposes and will not be counted against your score. The exam contains no indications in this regard.

Preparing for the Exam

The CDPSE certification requires a significant amount of knowledge and experience from the candidate. You need to develop a long-term study plan to pass the exam. The following sections offer some tips and are intended to help guide you to, through, and beyond exam day.

Before the Exam

Consider the following list of tips on tasks and resources for exam preparation. They are listed in sequential order.

- **Read the candidate's guide** For information on the certification exam and requirements for the current year, see the "ISACA Exam Candidates Information Guide." Go to `www.isaca.org/cdpse` and look for the Exam Candidate Guide download links.
- **Register** If you can, register early to take advantage of any cost savings and solidify your commitment to moving forward with this professional achievement.
- **Schedule your exam** Find a location, date, and time, and commit.
- **Become familiar with the CDPSE job practice areas** The job practice areas serve as the basis for the exam and requirements. Ensure your study materials align with the current list, shown at `www.isaca.org/cdpse`.
- **Know your best learning methods** Everyone has preferred learning styles, whether self-study, a study group, an instructor-led course, or a boot camp. Try to set up a study program that leverages your strengths.
- **Self-assess** Run through practice exam questions available in this book and online. ISACA may offer a free CDPSE self-assessment at `www.isaca.org/cdpse`. There is also a 20-question self-assessment at the end of this chapter.
- **Study iteratively** Depending on how much work experience in information security management you already have, I suggest you plan your study program to take at least two months, but as long as six months. During this time, periodically take practice exams and note your strengths and weaknesses. Once you have identified your weak areas, focus on those areas weekly by rereading the related sections in this book, retaking practice exams, and noting your progress.

- **Avoid cramming** We've all seen the books on the shelves with titles that involve last-minute cramming. Just one look at the Internet reveals various websites that teach individuals how to cram for exams most effectively. Research sites claim that exam cramming can lead to susceptibility to colds and flu, sleep disruptions, overeating, and digestive problems. One thing is sure: many people find that good, steady study habits result in less stress and greater clarity and focus during the exam. Because of the complexity of this exam, I highly recommend the long-term, steady-study option. Study the job practice areas thoroughly. There are many study options. If time permits, investigate the many resources available to you.
- **Find or form a study group** Many ISACA chapters and other organizations have formed specific study groups or offer less expensive exam review courses. Contact your local chapter to see whether these options are available to you. In addition, be sure to keep your eye on the ISACA website. Also, search online or use your local network to find out whether there are other local study groups and other helpful resources.
- **Recheck your confirmation letter** Do not write on or lose your confirmation letter. Put it in a safe place and note what time you will need to arrive at the site. Note this on your calendar. Confirm that the location is the one you selected and is located near you.
- **Check logistics** Check the candidate's guide and your confirmation letter for the exact time you are required to report to the test site (or log in from home if you registered for a remote proctored exam). A few days before the exam, check the site—become familiar with the location and tricks to getting there. If you are taking public transportation, be sure to check the schedule for the day of the exam. If your CDPSE exam is scheduled on a Saturday, public transportation schedules may differ from weekday schedules. If you are driving, know the route and where to park.
- **Pack** Place your confirmation letter and a photo ID in a safe place, ready to go. Your ID must be a current, government-issued photo ID that matches the name on the confirmation letter and must not be handwritten. Examples of acceptable forms of ID are passports, driver's licenses, state IDs, green cards, and national IDs. Note that ISACA does not accept digital IDs. Ensure you leave food, drinks, laptops, cell phones, and other electronic devices behind, as they are not permitted at the test site. For more information on what can and cannot be brought to the exam site, see the CDPSE exam candidate guide at `www.isaca.org/cdpse`.
- **Make a notification decision** Decide whether you want your test results emailed to you. You will have the opportunity to consent to email notification of the exam results. If you are fully paid (zero balance on exam fee) and have agreed to the email notification, you should receive a one-time email approximately eight weeks from the date of the exam with your results.
- **Sleep** Make sure you get a good night's sleep before the exam. Research suggests that you avoid caffeine at least four hours before bedtime, keep a notepad and pen next to the bed to capture late-night thoughts that might keep you awake, eliminate as much noise and light as possible, and keep your room a suitable temperature for sleeping. In the morning, rise early so you don't rush and don't subject yourself to additional stress.

Day of the Exam

On the day of the exam, follow these tips:

- **Arrive early** Check the Bulletin of Information and your confirmation letter for the exact time you are required to report to the test site. The confirmation letter or the candidate's guide explains that you must be at the test site *no later* than approximately 30 minutes *before* testing time. The examiner will begin reading the exam instructions at this time, and any latecomers will be disqualified from taking the test and will *not* receive a refund of fees
- **Observe test center rules** There may be rules about taking breaks. The examiner will discuss the rules and exam instructions. If you need anything during the exam and are unsure of the rules, be sure to ask first. For information on conduct during the exam, see the "ISACA CDPSE Candidate Guide" at `www.isaca.org/cdpse` and look for the Exam Candidate Guide download links. But don't wait until exam day to read this!
- **Answer all exam questions** Read the questions carefully, but do not overanalyze them. Remember to select the *best* solution. There may be several reasonable answers, but one is *better* than the others. If you aren't sure about an answer, you can mark the question and return to it later. After going through all the questions, you can return to the marked questions (and others) to read them and consider them more carefully. Above all, don't try to overanalyze questions, and do trust your instincts. Do not try to rush through the exam, as there is plenty of time to take as long as a few minutes on each question. However, at the same time, do watch the clock so that you don't find yourself going too slowly that you won't be able to answer every question thoughtfully.
- **Note your exam result** When you have completed the exam, you should see your pass/fail result. Your results may not be in large, blinking text; you may need to read the fine print to get your preliminary results. If you passed, congratulations! If you did not pass, please note any remarks about your status; you will be able to retake the exam—information about this is available on the ISACA website.

If You Did Not Pass

Don't lose heart if you did not pass your exam on the first attempt. Instead, remember that failure is a stepping stone to success. Thoughtfully take stock and determine your improvement areas. Go back to this book's practice exams and be honest with yourself regarding those areas where you need to learn more. Reread the chapters or sections where you need more information. If you participated in a study group or training, contact your study group coach or class instructor if you feel you can get any advice from them on how to study up on the topics you need to master. Take at least several weeks to study those topics, refresh yourself on other topics, then give it another go. Success is granted to those who are persistent and determined.

After the Exam

A few weeks from the exam date, you will receive your official exam results by email or postal-service mail. Each job practice area score will be noted in addition to the overall final score. All scores are scaled. Should you receive a passing score, you will also receive the application for certification.

Those who are unsuccessful in passing will also be notified. These individuals will want to closely examine the job practice area scores to identify areas for further study. They may retake the exam as many times as needed on future exam dates, if they have registered and paid the applicable fees. Regardless of pass or fail, exam results will not be disclosed via telephone, fax, or email (except for the consented email notification).

You are *not* permitted to display the CDPSE moniker until you have completed certification. Passing the exam is not sufficient to use the CDPSE designation anywhere, including in email, résumés, CVs, correspondence, or on social media.

Applying for CDPSE Certification

To apply for certification, you must submit evidence of a passing score and related work experience. Keep in mind that you have five years to use this score on a CDPSE certification application once you receive a passing score. After this time, you will need to retake the exam. In addition, all work experience submitted must have been within ten years of your new certification application.

To complete the application process, submit your completed CDPSE application. Note the exam ID number, as found in your exam results letter, list the information security management experience and any experience substitutions, and identify which CDPSE job practice area (or areas) your experience pertains to.

As with the exam, after you've successfully mailed the application, you must wait approximately eight weeks for processing. If your application is approved, you will receive an email notification, followed by a package in the mail containing your letter of certification, certificate, and a copy of the Continuing Professional Education Policy. You can then proudly display your certificate and use the "CDPSE" designation on your résumé, email, social media profiles, and business cards.

You may use the CDPSE moniker *only* after receiving your official certification letter from ISACA.

Retaining Your CDPSE Certification

There is more to becoming a CDPSE professional than merely passing an exam, submitting an application, and receiving a paper certificate. Becoming a CDPSE professional is an ongoing lifestyle. Those with the CDPSE certification must agree to abide by a code of ethics, meet ongoing education requirements, and pay annual certification maintenance fees. This section takes a closer look at the education requirements and explains the costs involved in retaining certification.

Continuing Education

The goal of continuing professional education requirements is to ensure that individuals maintain CDPSE-related knowledge to better develop and manage security management programs. To maintain CDPSE certification, individuals must complete 120 continuing education hours within three years, with a minimum of 20 hours per year. Each CPE hour equals 50 minutes of active participation in educational activities.

What Counts as a Valid CPE Credit?

For training and activities to be used for CPEs, they must involve technical or managerial training directly applicable to information security and information security management. The following list of activities has been approved by the CDPSE certification committee and can count toward your CPE requirements:

- ISACA professional education activities and meetings
- Non-ISACA professional education activities and meetings
- Self-study courses
- Vendor sales or marketing presentations (ten-hour annual limit)
- Teaching, lecturing, or presenting on subjects related to job practice areas
- Publication of articles and books related to the profession
- Exam question development and review for any ISACA certification
- Passing related professional examinations
- Participation in ISACA boards or committees (20-hour annual limit per ISACA certification)
- Contributions to the information security management profession (ten-hour annual limit)
- Mentoring (ten-hour annual limit)

For more information on what is accepted as a valid CPE credit, see the "Continuing Professional Education Policy" (`www.isaca.org/credentialing/how-to-earn-cpe/#cpe-policy`).

ISACA has indicated that changes to its CPE policy will take effect on January 1, 2027. The changes are related to the types of training that can be applied to CPEs.

Tracking and Submitting CPEs

Not only are you required to submit a CPE tracking form for the annual renewal process, but you should also keep detailed records for each activity. Records associated with each activity should have the following:

- Name of attendee
- Name of sponsoring organization
- Activity title
- Activity description
- Activity date
- Number of CPE hours awarded

It is in your best interest to track all CPE information in a single file or worksheet. ISACA has developed a tracking form for your use, which is available in the Continuing Professional Education Policy. To make it easier on yourself, consider keeping all related records, such as receipts, brochures, and certificates, in one place, as shown in Table 2. Documentation should be retained throughout the three-year certification period and for at least one additional year afterward. Evidence retention is essential, as you may be audited at some point. If this happens, you will be required to submit all paperwork. So why not be prepared?

For new CDPSEs, the annual and three-year certification periods begin on January 1 of the year following certification. You are not required to report CPE hours for the first partial year after your certification; however, the hours earned from the time of certification to December 31 can be utilized in the first certification reporting period the following year. Therefore, should you get certified in January, you will have until the following January to accumulate CPEs. You will not have to report them until you report the totals for the following year, in October or November. This is known as the *renewal period*. During this time, you will receive an email directing you to the website to enter CPEs earned over the course of the year. Alternatively, the renewal will be mailed to you, and then CPEs can be recorded on the hardcopy invoice and sent with your maintenance fee payment. CPEs and maintenance fees must be received by January 15 to retain certification.

A notification of compliance from the certification department is sent after all information has been received and processed. Should ISACA have any questions about the information you have submitted, it will contact you directly.

TABLE 2 Sample CPE Records

Name Chris Jacobs

Certification Number 67895787

Certification Period 1/1/2026 to 12/31/2028

Activity Title/Sponsor	Activity Description	Date	CPE Hours	Support Docs Included?
ISACA presentation/lunch	PCI compliance	2/11/2026	1 CPE	Yes (receipt)
ISACA presentation/lunch	Privacy in SDLC	3/21/2026	1 CPE	Yes (receipt)
Regional conference, RIMS	Compliance, risk	1/12–14/2026	6 CPEs	Yes (CPE receipt)
BrightFly webinar	Governance, risk, & compliance	2/16/2026	3 CPEs	Yes (confirmation email)
ISACA board meeting	Chapter board meeting	4/8/2026	2 CPEs	Yes (meeting minutes)
Presented at ISSA meeting	Privacy governance presentation	6/21/2026	1 CPE	Yes (meeting notice)
Published an article in a privacy journal	Journal article on CPRA compliance	4/12/2026	4 CPEs	Yes (article)
Vendor presentation	Learned about GRC tool capability	5/12/2026	2 CPEs	Yes
Employer-offered training	Change management course	3/25/2026	7 CPEs	Yes (certificate of course completion)

CPE Maintenance Fees

To remain CDPSE certified, you must pay CPE maintenance fees each year. These fees are (as of early 2026) $45 for members and $85 for nonmembers each year. These fees are in addition to ISACA membership and local chapter dues (neither of which is required to maintain your CDPSE certification).

Revocation of Certification

A CDPSE-certified individual may have their certification revoked for the following reasons:

- Failure to complete the minimum number of CPEs during the period
- Failure to document and provide evidence of CPEs in an audit
- Failure to submit payment for maintenance fees
- Failure to comply with the Code of Professional Ethics can result in an investigation and, ultimately, the revocation of certification

If you have received a revocation notice, you will need to contact the ISACA Certification Department at `certification@isaca.org` for more information.

Living the CDPSE Lifestyle

Being a CDPSE involves a lot more than passing the exam, participating in continuous learning, and paying the annual maintenance fees. There are numerous opportunities to get involved in local, national, and global activities and events that will help you grow professionally and meet other risk management professionals.

Find a Local Chapter

ISACA has over 200 local chapters in nearly 180 countries worldwide. Chances are, there is a chapter near you. I attended many ISACA chapter meetings and other events in Seattle when I lived there, where engaging speakers covered new topics, and I met many like-minded security and audit professionals over the years.

Local chapters rely entirely on volunteers, and there is room for you to help. Better chapters offer a variety of programs, events, study groups, and other activities that enrich participants professionally. For me, most of my ISACA experience happens in my local chapter.

Attend ISACA Events

ISACA hosts fantastic in-person conferences featuring world-class keynote speakers, expert presentations, vendor demonstrations and exhibits, a bookstore, and opportunities to meet other security, risk, and audit professionals. I find ISACA conferences enriching to the point of being overwhelming. There are so many learning and networking opportunities that I find myself nearly exhausted at the end of an ISACA conference.

Join the Online Community

ISACA has an online community called Engage, where participants can discuss topics related to security, risk, audit, privacy, and IT management. You can read and participate in online discussions, ask questions, help others with their questions, and make new professional connections. You can join Engage at `https://engage.isaca.org/`.

Pay It Forward Through Mentorship

If you are at the point in your career where you qualify for and have a reasonable prospect of passing the CDPSE exam, chances are you have had a mentor or two earlier in your career, and maybe you have one now. As you grow in your professional stature, others will look to you as a potential mentor. Perhaps someone will come out and ask you to consider mentoring them.

The world needs more and better privacy professionals and leaders. Mentoring is a great way to "pay it forward" by helping others get into the profession and grow professionally. You will also find that mentoring enriches you.

Volunteer

As a nonprofit organization, ISACA relies on volunteers to enrich its programs and events. There are many ways to help, and one or more of these volunteer opportunities might be suitable for you:

- **Speaking at an ISACA event** Whether you give a keynote address or a session on a specific topic, it's a mountaintop experience. You can share your knowledge and expertise on a particular topic with attendees, but you'll learn some things, too.
- **Serving as a chapter board member** Local chapters don't run by themselves—they rely on volunteers who are working professionals who want to improve the lot of other professionals in the local community. Board members can serve in various ways, from financial management to membership to events.
- **Starting or helping a CDPSE study group** Whether as a part of a local chapter or at large, consider starting or helping a group of professionals who want to learn the details of the CDPSE job practice. I am a proponent of study groups because study group participants make the best students: they take initiative to tackle big challenges that advance their careers.
- **Writing an article** ISACA publishes online and paper-based publications with articles on a wide variety of subjects, including current developments in security, privacy, risk, and IT management from many perspectives. If you have specialized knowledge on some topic, other ISACA members can benefit from this knowledge if you write an article.

- **Participating in a credential working group** ISACA works hard to ensure that its many certifications remain relevant and up to date. Experts around the world in many industries give their time to ensure that ISACA certifications remain the best in the world. ISACA conducts online and in-person working groups to update certification job practices, write certification exam questions, and publish updated study guides and practice exams. I contributed to the first working group in 2013, when ISACA initially developed the CRISC certification exam, where I met many like-minded professionals, some of whom I am still in regular, meaningful contact with.
- **Participating in ISACA CommunITy Day** ISACA organizes a global effort of local volunteering to make the world a better, safer place for everyone. Learn about the next CommunITy Day at `https://engage.isaca.org/communityday/`.
- **Writing certification exam questions** ISACA needs experienced subject-matter experts willing to take the time to write new certification exam questions. ISACA has a rigorous, high-quality process for exam questions, including training. Who knows—you could even be invited to an in-person workshop on writing exam items. You can find out more about how this works at `www.isaca.org/credentialing/write-an-exam-question`.

You can learn about these and many other volunteer opportunities at `https://engage.isaca.org/volunteeropportunities/about`.

Please take a minute to reflect on the quality and depth of ISACA and its many world-class certifications, publications, and events. These are all fueled by volunteers who made ISACA into what it is today. Only through your contributions of time and expertise will ISACA continue to excel for future security, risk, privacy, and IT professionals. And one last thing you can only experience on your own: volunteering not only helps others but enriches you as well. Will you consider leaving your mark and making ISACA better than you found it?

Continue to Grow Professionally

Continuous improvement is a mindset and a lifestyle that is built into IT service management and information security—it's even a formal requirement in ISO/IEC 27701 and ISO/IEC 27001, the international standards for privacy and security management! I suggest that you periodically take stock of your career status and aspirations, be honest with yourself, and determine what mountain you will climb next. If needed, find a mentor who can guide you and give you solid advice.

While this may not immediately make sense to you, know this: helping others, whether through any of the volunteer opportunities listed previously or in other ways, will enrich you personally and professionally. I'm not talking about feathers in your cap or juicy items on your résumé, but rather the growth in character and wisdom that results from helping and serving others, notably when you initiated the helping and serving.

Professional growth means different things to different people. Whether it's a better job title, more money, a better (or bigger or smaller) employer, a different team, more responsibility, or more certifications, embarking on long-term career planning will pay dividends. Take control of your career and your career path—this is yours to own and shape as you will.

Additional Study Tools

This book comes with a number of additional study tools to help you prepare for the exam. This section explains them all.

Go to www.wiley.com/go/Sybextestprep to register and gain access to this interactive online learning environment and test bank with study tools.

Sybex Test Preparation Software

Sybex's test preparation software lets you prepare with electronic test versions of the review questions from each chapter, the practice exam, and the bonus exam that are included in this book. You can build and take tests on specific domains, by chapter, or cover the entire set of CDPSE exam objectives using randomized tests.

Electronic Flashcards

Our electronic flashcards are designed to help you prepare for the exam. Over 100 flashcards will ensure that you know critical terms and concepts.

Glossary of Terms

Sybex provides a full glossary of terms in PDF format, allowing quick searches and easy reference to materials in this book.

Bonus Practice Exams

In addition to the practice questions for each chapter, this book includes two full 120-question practice exams. I recommend using both to test your preparedness for the certification exam.

Like all exams, the Certified Data Privacy Solutions Engineer (CDPSE) from ISACA is updated periodically and may eventually be retired or replaced. At some point after ISACA no longer offers this exam, the old editions of our books and online tools will be retired. If you have purchased this book after the exam was retired or are attempting to register in the Sybex online learning environment after the exam was retired, please know that we make no guarantees that this exam's online Sybex tools will be available once the exam is no longer available.

How to Contact the Publisher

If you believe you have found a mistake in this book, please bring it to our attention. At John Wiley & Sons, we understand how important it is to provide our customers with accurate content, but even with our best efforts, an error may occur. To submit your possible errata, please email it to our Customer Service Team at `wileysupport@wiley.com` with the subject line "Possible Book Errata Submission."

Assessment Test

Are you wondering how much you already know? Then go ahead and take this quick assessment test. Answers and explanations follow (no peeking) to see how you score.

1. A privacy program defines personal information primarily as which of the following?
   - A. Any data stored electronically
   - B. Any confidential business information
   - C. Only government-issued identifiers
   - D. Information that can identify or be linked to an individual
2. Which privacy principle requires integrating safeguards throughout the system lifecycle?
   - A. Transparency
   - B. Accountability
   - C. Data Minimization
   - D. Privacy by Design
3. A privacy policy and supporting procedures are examples of which of the following?
   - A. Risk treatments
   - B. Privacy documentation
   - C. Operational metrics
   - D. Incident response controls
4. Which activity best reflects privacy operations?
   - A. Responding to data subject access requests
   - B. Drafting legislation
   - C. Defining encryption algorithms
   - D. Building network segmentation
5. A vendor that processes personal data on behalf of an organization should be managed primarily through which of the following?
   - A. Source code review
   - B. Contractual privacy requirements and due diligence
   - C. Patch management policies
   - D. Endpoint configuration baselines

6. A Privacy Impact Assessment (PIA) is primarily used to do which of the following?
   A. Detect malware
   B. Measure encryption strength
   C. Audit financial controls
   D. Identify and evaluate privacy risks of processing activities

7. Which item is an example of a privacy risk response?
   A. Eliminating unnecessary data collection
   B. Creating a data inventory
   C. Conducting awareness training
   D. Drafting privacy principles

8. A privacy framework, such as the NIST Privacy Framework or ISO guidance, primarily supports which of the following?
   A. Encryption implementation
   B. Database normalization
   C. Structured compliance and governance alignment
   D. Log aggregation

9. A data flow diagram (DFD) is most useful for which of the following?
   A. Calculating retention periods
   B. Encrypting data at rest
   C. Mapping data movement between systems
   D. Monitoring user authentication

10. Data use limitation requires organizations to do which of the following?
    A. Retain data indefinitely
    B. Use data only for specified purposes
    C. Encrypt all personal data
    D. Transfer data to trusted vendors

11. Which action best supports data minimization?
    A. Storing raw logs permanently
    B. Collecting optional demographic data
    C. Retaining only necessary attributes for processing
    D. Expanding analytics datasets

12. Secure destruction of personal data is intended to do which of the following?
    - A. Improve performance
    - B. Prevent unauthorized recovery
    - C. Enable analytics
    - D. Reduce network traffic
13. The secure development lifecycle (SDLC) integrates privacy by doing which of the following?
    - A. Eliminating testing
    - B. Removing documentation
    - C. Avoiding change management
    - D. Adding privacy requirements during design and development
14. Identity and access management supports privacy primarily by doing which of the following?
    - A. Improving network speed
    - B. Increasing data retention
    - C. Limiting access to personal data
    - D. Enhancing analytics
15. Encryption protects personal data by doing which of the following?
    - A. Rendering data unreadable without keys
    - B. Removing identifiers
    - C. Reducing storage size
    - D. Eliminating retention requirements
16. Consent tagging in privacy engineering is used to do which of the following?
    - A. Monitor network latency
    - B. Encrypt browser cookies
    - C. Associate processing with user consent preferences
    - D. Classify hardware assets
17. Differential privacy is an example of which of the following?
    - A. Data retention policy
    - B. Privacy-enhancing technology
    - C. Incident response mechanism
    - D. Identity federation protocol

18. Monitoring and logging controls support privacy by doing which of the following?
    - A. Increasing storage costs
    - B. Eliminating encryption
    - C. Detecting unauthorized access to personal data
    - D. Replacing access control
19. Model inversion attacks attempt to do which of the following?
    - A. Delete training data
    - B. Infer sensitive attributes from trained models
    - C. Encrypt AI outputs
    - D. Prevent anonymization
20. Which combination best demonstrates end-to-end privacy engineering?
    - A. Data minimization, access control, logging, and anonymization
    - B. Privacy policy only
    - C. Encryption plus vendor contract
    - D. Incident response plan only

Answers to Assessment Questions

1. D. Personal information refers to any data that identifies or can reasonably be associated with an individual, either directly or indirectly. Direct identifiers include names, email addresses, and government identifiers, while indirect identifiers may include combinations of attributes such as location, device identifiers, or demographic data. Most privacy regulations adopt broad definitions to account for modern analytics capabilities that can re-identify individuals from seemingly innocuous data. This definition forms the foundation of privacy governance because it determines what information must be protected and subject to privacy controls.

2. D. Privacy by Design emphasizes embedding privacy protections into systems, processes, and technologies from the earliest stages of planning through deployment and maintenance. Rather than relying on reactive controls, organizations proactively incorporate requirements such as data minimization, purpose limitation, and access controls into architecture and workflows. This approach reduces risk, improves compliance, and ensures privacy considerations are not overlooked. It also aligns with engineering practices that treat privacy as a core requirement rather than an optional or retrofitted feature.

3. B. Privacy documentation includes formal artifacts such as policies, standards, procedures, guidelines, and playbooks that define how privacy requirements are implemented. These documents establish expectations, assign responsibilities, and provide operational direction. Policies typically define high-level principles, while procedures describe specific steps. Together, they demonstrate governance maturity and support accountability, auditability, and consistent execution of privacy practices across the organization.

4. A. Privacy operations focus on executing privacy program activities, including handling data subject requests (DSRs), coordinating incident response, overseeing vendors, and maintaining records. Responding to DSRs involves verifying identity, locating personal data, and delivering responses within regulatory timelines. This operational work ensures regulatory compliance and demonstrates the organization's ability to operationalize privacy governance requirements.

5. B. Vendor and supply chain privacy management relies heavily on contractual obligations and due diligence. Organizations must ensure that third parties agree to data protection requirements, such as confidentiality, breach notification, and data use limitations. Due diligence assessments evaluate vendor capabilities, security posture, and compliance readiness. Ongoing monitoring ensures continued adherence. These measures help maintain accountability when personal data is processed externally.

6. D. A PIA evaluates how personal data is collected, used, stored, and shared, identifying potential risks to individuals. The assessment analyzes dataflows, purposes, legal bases, and safeguards. It then recommends controls such as minimization, access restrictions, or anonymization. PIAs are typically conducted before new systems or processing activities are introduced, ensuring privacy risks are understood and mitigated early in the lifecycle.

7. A. Eliminating unnecessary data collection reduces the volume of personal information processed, thereby lowering exposure and risk. Risk responses include mitigation strategies that directly reduce likelihood or impact. Data inventories and training help identify or manage risks, but do not directly reduce exposure. Minimizing collection is one of the most effective responses to privacy risks because it reduces both breach risk and potential for misuse.

8. C. Privacy frameworks provide structured guidance for governance, risk management, and operational privacy controls. They help organizations identify responsibilities, implement controls, and measure program effectiveness. By aligning with recognized frameworks, organizations demonstrate due diligence and consistency. Frameworks also support regulatory mapping and continuous improvement of privacy practices.

9. C. DFDs visualize how data enters, moves through, and exits systems, including processing points and transfers. This mapping helps identify where personal data resides and how it flows between components. Understanding dataflows is essential for risk assessments, compliance documentation, and identifying controls such as encryption or access restrictions. DFDs are foundational artifacts in privacy engineering and governance.

10. B. Data use limitation ensures that personal data is processed only for legitimate purposes communicated at the time of collection. This principle prevents secondary uses that were not originally disclosed. It supports transparency, accountability, and regulatory compliance. Organizations enforce this through policies, system controls, and consent management mechanisms.

11. C. Data minimization reduces risk by limiting collection and retention to only necessary information. Retaining only essential attributes reduces exposure in the event of a breach and reduces the impact of misuse. It also simplifies compliance and lowers storage costs. Minimization applies across collection, processing, and retention decisions.

12. B. Secure destruction ensures personal data cannot be reconstructed after disposal. Methods include shredding, overwriting, degaussing, and cryptographic erasure. Proper destruction reduces residual risk and supports retention policies. Without secure destruction, discarded media may expose sensitive information.

13. D. Integrating privacy into the SDLC includes defining requirements, performing threat modeling, implementing controls, and validating privacy protections. This ensures systems are designed to protect personal data. Early integration reduces costly redesigns and strengthens compliance.

14. C. Identity and access management (IAM) enforces authentication and authorization controls to restrict access to personal data. Least privilege and role-based access reduce unauthorized exposure. Proper IAM also supports accountability and auditability.

15. A. Encryption transforms data into unreadable ciphertext. Only authorized parties with keys can access the information. Encryption protects data at rest and in transit, reducing the impact of breaches.

16. C. Consent tagging attaches metadata to data elements indicating permitted processing activities. Systems can enforce consent restrictions automatically. This ensures processing aligns with user choices and regulatory requirements.

17. B. Differential privacy adds controlled statistical noise to outputs. This allows aggregate insights while protecting individual identities. It is widely used in analytics and AI to reduce re-identification risk.

18. C. Logs provide evidence of system activity. They help detect misuse, support investigations, and demonstrate accountability. Monitoring is critical for detecting unauthorized access.

19. B. Model inversion attacks analyze model outputs to infer sensitive information about training data. Attackers may reconstruct features such as images or attributes. Mitigation includes differential privacy, access controls, and output limitation.

20. A. End-to-end privacy engineering integrates layered controls across the lifecycle. Minimization reduces collection, IAM restricts access, logging detects misuse, and anonymization protects analytics. Together, these controls provide comprehensive protection.

Chapter 1

Privacy Governance

This chapter covers CDPSE Domain 1, "Privacy Governance," specifically the "Privacy Governance" subdomain.

This chapter covers these job practice elements:

✔ *A–PRIVACY GOVERNANCE*

1. *Personal Information*
2. *Privacy Principles (e.g., Privacy by Design, Consent, Transparency)*
3. *Privacy Laws and Regulations*
4. *Privacy Documentation (e.g., Policies, Guidelines)*

The other subdomain in Domain 1, Privacy Governance, is:

✔ *B–PRIVACY OPERATIONS*—covered in Chapter 2.

The CDPSE Task Statements relevant to this domain are:

1. *Identify internal and external requirements to develop and maintain the organization's privacy programs.*

6. *Contribute to the integration of privacy principles (e.g., privacy by design) in the development of procedures and operational manuals for organizational needs.*

7. *Collaborate with stakeholders to promote privacy principles (e.g., privacy by design) are followed during the design, development, and implementation of systems, applications, and infrastructure.*

17. *Advocate for advancing privacy posture and maturity as it aligns with the organizational objectives.*

The topics in this chapter and in Chapter 2 account for 20% of the CDPSE examination.

This chapter introduces the foundational concepts of privacy governance, establishing how organizations manage personal information in alignment with legal, regulatory, and business requirements. The chapter begins with governance structures, roles, and accountability models that define oversight and decision-making, including the integration of privacy into enterprise strategy. The chapter then examines the nature of personal information, key privacy principles such as transparency and data minimization, and the legal and regulatory frameworks that shape organizational obligations. It also addresses privacy documentation, including policies, notices, and records that support consistent and compliant operations. Supporting topics such as privacy program strategy, lifecycle management, and the three lines of defense provide additional context on how privacy is operationalized and sustained. Together, these elements form a comprehensive view of how organizations design, implement, and maintain effective privacy governance programs.

While not explicitly a part of the CDPSE job practice, this chapter begins with a comprehensive discussion of governance and the development of a privacy program strategy.

Introduction to Privacy Governance

Privacy governance is a set of established *governance* lifecycle activities that typically focus on several fundamental principles and outcomes, designed to enable management to have a clear understanding of the state of the organization's *privacy* program, its current risks, its direct activities, and its alignment with the organization's business objectives and practices. A goal of the privacy program is to enable the fulfillment of the privacy strategy, which itself will continue to align with the business, business objectives, and evolving regulations. The processes supporting these principles and outcomes include privacy policy, data governance, compliance, risk management, and cybersecurity. Whether the organization has a board of directors, council members, commissioners, or another top-level governing body, governance begins with establishing top-level strategic objectives that are translated into actions, roles, and responsibilities through policies, processes, procedures, and other activities, cascading downward through each level of the organization.

Privacy is a business issue, and organizations that are not yet properly managing or adequately protecting personal information have a business problem. The reason for this is almost always a lack of understanding and commitment by boards of directors and senior executives. For many, privacy is viewed as a security issue that focuses on tactical data protection problems or on data usage problems, and it's not about protection at all. The challenge is that, due to a lack of awareness or experience with privacy, organizations still struggle to organize, manage, and communicate about privacy successfully at the executive leadership and boardroom levels.

To manage privacy successfully, organizations need to understand that privacy is also a people issue. When people at every level of the organization—from board members to individual contributors—understand the importance of privacy and security in their roles and responsibilities, the organization will be at reduced risk. This reduction in risk or identification of potential privacy or security events results in fewer incidents with less impact on the organization's ongoing reputation and operations.

A privacy program operates as a lifecycle to ensure that governance, controls, and practices progress alongside regulatory, technology, and business changes. A privacy program consists of these components:

- **Initiation** Establish the foundation of the privacy program by identifying legal, regulatory, and business requirements. Define scope, objectives, stakeholders, and governance structure.
- **Design** Develop policies, standards, processes, and controls that align with privacy principles and organizational objectives. Architect the program to address data lifecycle activities, risk management, and compliance obligations.
- **Implementation** Deploy the designed controls, processes, and technologies across the organization. Assign roles and responsibilities, conduct training, and integrate privacy into business operations and system development.
- **Monitoring** Continuously assess the effectiveness of privacy controls and processes through metrics, audits, and reviews. Identify gaps, incidents, and compliance issues to ensure ongoing alignment with requirements.
- **Continual improvement** Refine and enhance the privacy program based on monitoring results, regulatory changes, and evolving risks. Implement corrective actions and maturity improvements to strengthen governance and operational effectiveness.

A mature privacy program treats this lifecycle as iterative, ensuring sustained alignment with organizational goals, regulatory constraints, and emerging risks.

Because modern privacy practices are heavily influenced by privacy laws such as the European Union's General Data Protection Regulation (GDPR), the California Consumer Privacy Act (CCPA), and the California Privacy Rights Act (CPRA), organizations should rely on qualified legal counsel as part of their overall governance process. Including legal counsel helps to ensure that the organization's privacy policies and practices comply with these and other laws.

Think of privacy as having two main components: proper data management and usage and data protection—commonly referred to as cybersecurity, data security, or information security. A privacy program cannot succeed without effective cybersecurity. Further, cybersecurity cannot succeed without a solid foundation in IT and IT operations. IT is the enabler and force multiplier that facilitates business processes that fulfill organizational objectives. Without effective IT governance, privacy and *information security governance* will not reach their full potential. The result might be that the IT bus will travel safely, but to the wrong destination. Figure 1.1 shows how the business vision, strategy, and objectives of privacy and information security governance flow downward through an organization's privacy and IT security strategies, policies, standards, and processes.

FIGURE 1.1 In a governance model, vision flows downward, and reporting and metrics flow upward.

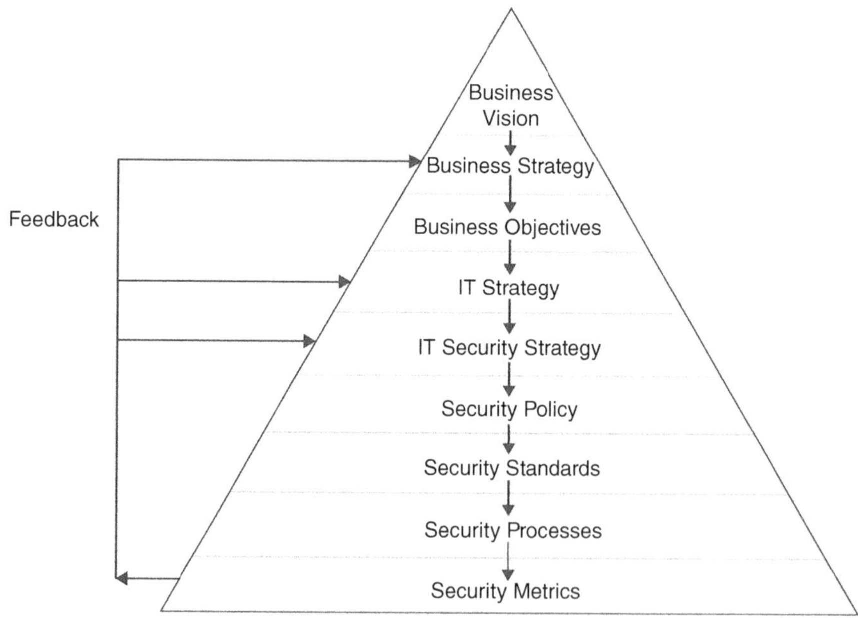

Source: Author.

Although the CDPSE certification is not directly tied to IT governance, this implicit dependence of privacy and security governance on IT governance cannot be understated. IT and security professionals specializing in IT governance might be interested in ISACA's Certified Information Security Manager (CISM) and Certified in the Governance of Enterprise IT (CGEIT) certifications, which focus on these domains.

For privacy governance to succeed, organizations also need effective security, data, and IT governance. Figure 1.2 depicts these dependencies. And while outside the scope of this book, AI governance depends on privacy governance because many organizations train their AI systems on personal information.

While IT governance, information security governance, and privacy governance can be separate activities, in many organizations, these activities will closely resemble or rely on one another. Many issues will span IT, security, and privacy governance bodies, and many individuals will participate actively in all three areas. Some organizations integrate IT, information security, and privacy governance into a single set of participants, activities, and business records. The most important thing is for organizations to establish governance programs that effectively achieve formally established business outcomes.

Privacy governance will enable alignment of the organization's privacy program with customer or constituent expectations, applicable regulations, identified risks, and business needs. An objective of *privacy governance* is to provide, from a strategic perspective, assurance of the proper protection and use of personal information, ensuring that required privacy practices align with business practices. These are some of the artifacts and activities that flow out of sound privacy governance:

FIGURE 1.2 Privacy governance relies upon security and data governance, which in turn rely upon IT governance.

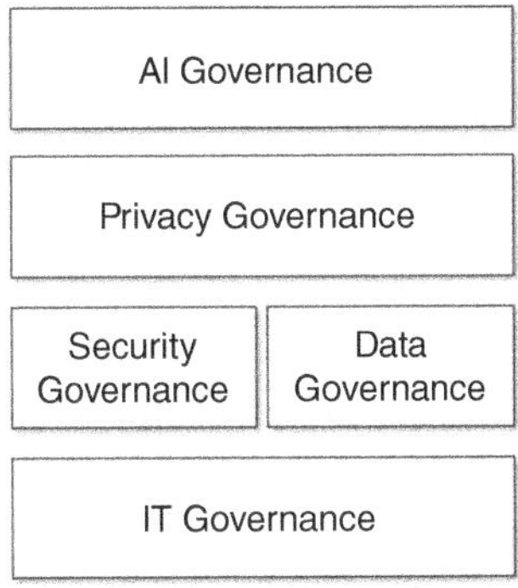

Source: Author.

- **Objectives** The desired capabilities or end states, ideally expressed in achievable, measurable terms.
- **Established legal basis** The way the organization can lawfully collect and process personal information about data subjects.
- **Consent** The mechanism through which the organization directly or indirectly obtains permission from data subjects to collect and process their personal information.
- **Strategy** The plan to achieve one or more objectives.
- **Policy** The mission, objectives, and goals of the overall organization that align with constituent expectations and applicable laws.
- **Priorities** The main concerns of the privacy program, which should flow directly from the organization's mission, objectives, and goals. Whatever is most important to the organization should be relevant to privacy and information security.
- **Standards** The technologies, protocols, and practices used by IT that should reflect the organization's needs. On their own, standards help to drive a consistent approach to solving business challenges; the choice of standards should facilitate solutions that meet the organization's needs cost-effectively and securely.
- **Processes** The formalized descriptions of repeated business activities that include instructions to applicable personnel. Processes consist of one or more procedures, along with definitions of business records and other facts that help workers understand how things are supposed to be done.
- **Controls** The formal descriptions of critical activities performed to ensure desired outcomes.
- **Program and project management** The ways in which the organization's privacy, security, and IT programs and projects are organized and performed, which should be in a consistent manner that reflects business priorities and supports the business.
- **Metrics/reporting** The formal measurement of processes and controls that management can understand and measure.
- **Review/audit** The formal evaluation of processes and controls to determine their effectiveness.

To the greatest extent possible, privacy governance in an organization should be practiced in the same way the organization approaches cybersecurity, IT, and overall corporate governance. Privacy governance should either mimic organizational, security, and/or IT governance processes or be integrated into corporate, cybersecurity, or IT governance processes.

Though privacy governance contains the elements just described, strategic planning is also a key component of governance. Strategy development is discussed in the next section.

Privacy and Security: Together or Separate?

Should privacy and security be managed separately or together? Although there's no right or wrong answer, know this: privacy cannot succeed without information security. The objectives of a privacy program are to protect and properly handle personal information. The protection part is done by information security, and the proper handling part is solely the domain of privacy.

Privacy needs information security to be successful. Security is a prerequisite to privacy, but privacy adds more: the proper *handling* of information and its *protection*.

This is why privacy and security are discussed hand in hand throughout this chapter and throughout most of this book. Discussing privacy alone, without security, tells only half the story.

The Three Lines of Defense

The *three lines of defense* is a governance framework that clarifies accountability for risk management, control, and assurance across an organization. Responsibilities are separated to ensure that risks to personal information are identified, managed, and independently evaluated. The aspects are as follows:

- **First line: Operations** Business units and teams collect, use, and manage personal information. They implement privacy controls and ensure that day-to-day activities comply with legal and organizational policies and requirements. They own risks associated with their processes and are accountable for properly handling data.
- **Second line: Privacy, Compliance, and Risk Management** These groups establish policies, standards, guidelines, and monitor adherence to requirements. They support the first line by interpreting laws and regulations, advising on privacy risks, and overseeing control effectiveness.
- **Third line: Internal Audit** This group provides independent assurance to senior management and the board of directors by performing audits of governance, risk management, processes, and privacy-related controls.

These three functions are assigned to three different persons or teams that operate independently and collaborate extensively. The three lines of defense model is an implementation of the separation of duties, in which essential functions are divided among multiple parties so that no single party can exert excessive control or suffer from groupthink.

Privacy Governance Influencers

An organization's privacy program must focus on several internal and external events and activities. Privacy professionals recognize that some of these factors can be influenced to some degree, while others are entirely outside the privacy professional's sphere of influence. We must be informed and able to react to these influencers.

Much of the information in information systems concerns people. In both government and business, information systems keep track of property owners, taxpayers, voters, patients, clients, customers, and potential customers. Often, the information retained about people is sensitive—even secretive—and all parties have a vested interest in the adequate protection of that information.

In most situations, transactions between individuals and businesses, governments, and healthcare organizations are considered confidential, not to be disclosed, and to be used only for official business purposes.

When this information migrated from paper to information systems and with advancements in information technology, organizations developed numerous techniques to obtain more value from information about their citizens, patients, customers, and constituents. Abuses of these practices have given rise to privacy laws intended to curb these activities.

Privacy laws are discussed in detail in this section. Note that there are many variances among these laws in the following areas:

- **Definitions of personal information** Privacy laws sometimes provide specific, sometimes vague definitions of which types of data are considered sensitive and which are not. Most laws consider the aggregation of someone's name, along with other items such as financial account numbers, medical records, political affiliation, and more, to be personal information that is to be safeguarded and used within stated guidelines.
- **Data subject rights** Privacy laws define many rights that vary somewhat from one regulation to another. These rights include transparency, limitations on use, adequate protection, correction, and removal.
- **Protection of personal information** Laws require organizations to take measures to ensure the adequate protection of personal information, so that it cannot be accessed, altered, stolen, or destroyed by unauthorized parties.
- **Use of personal information** Laws require transparency regarding the use of personal information, so that persons can be aware of these uses.
- **Notification of breach** Laws require organizations to disclose to affected individuals any instances in which their personal information was improperly accessed, used, or compromised.
- **Jurisdiction** Many privacy laws today are "extraterritorial," meaning they are intended to regulate the activities of organizations located outside political boundaries.

Data privacy and data protection laws are being enacted at a relatively fast pace, reflecting the vast expansion of the collection and use of personal information, abuses and breaches by organizations that collect and use personal data, and still-developing social norms regarding the definitions and expectations of privacy.

The Imperfect Lexicon of Privacy

As with any profession, privacy and information security have their own specialized vocabulary. In the privacy profession, we use the terms *personal information* and *data subject request*. Is there really a distinction and a valid reason why "personal information" uses the term *information* while "data subject request" uses the term *data*?

In practical terms, *data* consists of raw values, symbols, or observations (such as numbers, text strings, or timestamps) that, on their own, can lack meaning. *Information* is produced when data is organized, processed, or interpreted in context, enabling understanding and supporting decision-making.

This distinction is important in privacy governance because legal and regulatory obligations generally apply to information about identifiable individuals, even though that information is often stored and processed as data within information systems.

Perhaps this is a clue. The remainder of this exercise is left to the reader.

Reasons for Privacy Governance

Whether you attribute the emergence of sweeping data privacy laws to citizen backlash or to a coming of age, organizations everywhere are becoming aware that people's privacy rights matter and that ignoring them can land an organization in hot water. For the most part, organizations are being forced to change their practices, information systems, and sometimes even their business models to align with the new reality: they must be transparent about how they obtain, collect, process, and share personal information.

Governance is management's sharpest tool for getting things done. Regarding privacy laws such as the GDPR, CCPA, and CPRA, organizations have put governance structures in place to oversee the transformation in their business processes and information systems from practices of opaqueness to practices of transparency. In many cases, this transformation meant an about-face on internal practices. Indeed, this has prompted numerous (dare I say, the majority of) organizations to "discover" how they use personal information internally, as though the proverbial foxes have been in charge of the henhouse.

Simply put, privacy governance is all about keeping organizations out of trouble with regulators, outraged citizens, and the courts. Many organizations have shown no desire to change their business models, and many complain that doing so will hurt them financially. Just as the do-not-call lists have curbed the use of unsolicited "robo-calls" in the United States, privacy laws will forever alter business models that mine and monetize personal data behind the dark curtains of organizations' marketing machines.

While the foregoing portrays the darker side of some organizations, many others were already "doing the right thing" regarding transparency in the management of personal data. For them, the new journey to privacy compliance has been less impactful.

Because privacy governance is driven by emerging privacy laws, many organizations have legal counsel in their governance structure as experts on the law and its interpretation. As more privacy laws are enacted and case law begins to emerge, organizations will monitor their development and adjust processes and systems accordingly.

The flexibility and capabilities of information systems make it all too easy for organizations to exceed the implicit or explicit purposes for which personal information is collected and used, leading to potential abuses and overreach. As a privacy professional, you must understand the business's operations regarding data about natural persons, including how it is collected, used, and protected. These four things should be considered when you're building out a privacy governance structure. Still, the type of information the organization uses will drive the priority given to managing data use and protection. Privacy governance, then, is needed to ensure that the organization's data management and protection activities do not lead to incidents that could harm affected persons or the organization itself.

Privacy and Security Governance Activities and Results

Within effective privacy and security governance programs, an organization's senior management team will ensure that information systems necessary to support business operations are adequately protected and that data about natural persons is properly collected, managed, and used. These are some of the activities required to protect personal data and information:

- **Risk management** Management will ensure that risk assessments are performed to identify risks in business processes and information systems. Follow-up actions will be carried out to reduce the risk of system failure and compromise.
- **Process improvement** Management will ensure that key changes are made to business processes to achieve compliance with privacy laws and improve cybersecurity.
- **Event identification** Management will put technologies and processes in place to ensure that privacy and security events and incidents are recognized and acted upon as quickly as possible.
- **Incident response** Management will implement incident response procedures to help prevent incidents, reduce the likelihood and impact of incidents, and improve response to incidents, thereby minimizing their impact on the organization.
- **Improved compliance** Management will ensure that all applicable laws, regulations, standards, and other legal obligations are identified and that activities are carried out to confirm the organization can attain and maintain compliance.
- **Metrics** Management will establish processes to measure key privacy and security events, including subject requests, complaints, incidents, policy changes, violations, audits, and training.

- **Resource management** Management will *monitor* the allocation of staffing, *budget*, and other resources to meet privacy and security objectives.
- **Improved IT governance** Management will implement an effective privacy governance program that will result in better strategic decisions that keep risks at an acceptably low level.

These and other governance activities are carried out through scripted interactions among key business, privacy, security, and IT executives at regular intervals. Meetings will include a discussion of the impact of regulatory changes, alignment with business objectives, the effectiveness of measurements, recent incidents, recent audits, and risk assessments. Other discussions can include changes to the business, recent business results, and anticipated business events, such as mergers or acquisitions.

There are two key results of an effective privacy governance program:

- **Increased trust** Customers, suppliers, and partners trust the organization to a greater degree when they see that privacy is managed effectively.
- **Improved reputation** The business community, including customers, investors, and regulators, will hold the organization in higher regard.

Business Alignment

An organization's information privacy program needs to fit in with the rest of the organization. This means that the program needs to align with the organization's highest-level guiding principles, including the following:

- **Mission** Why does the organization exist? Who does it serve, and through what products and services?
- **Goals and objectives** What achievements does the organization want to accomplish, and when does it want to achieve them?
- **Strategy** What are the activities that need to take place so that the organization's goals and objectives can be fulfilled?

To be business aligned, privacy and security professionals should be aware of several characteristics of the organization, including the following:

- **Business model and processes** This includes the organization's data flows (particularly flows of personal information), its use of information systems, and its sources of revenue.
- **Sources and uses of personal information** At the core of a privacy program, it's vital that all sanctioned and unsanctioned uses of personal information are understood, documented, rationalized, and managed.
- **Culture** This includes how personnel in the organization work, think, and relate to each other. Of utmost importance is the cultural attitude toward the treatment of personal information.

- **Asset value** This includes information the organization uses to operate. This often includes intellectual property such as designs and source code, as well as sensitive information related not only to the organization's personnel but also to its customers, information-processing infrastructure, and service functions.
- **Risk tolerance** Risk tolerance for the organization's privacy and information security programs needs to align with the organization's overall tolerance for risk.
- **Legal obligations** What external laws and regulations govern what the organization does and how it operates? These laws and regulations include the GLBA, GDPR, CCPA, CPRA, and HIPAA. Also, contractual obligations with other parties often shape the organization's behaviors and practices.
- **Market conditions** How competitive is the marketplace in which the organization operates? What strengths and weaknesses does the organization have in comparison with its competitors? How does the organization want its privacy and security to be differentiated from those of its competitors?
- **Privacy law enforcement** Are regulators and other authorities actively enforcing privacy laws and regulations, or are those laws "paper tigers" that stand unenforced. Organizations are generally reluctant to invest in changing business models, business processes, and information systems to comply with laws that might not be enforced.

Goals and Objectives

An organization's goals and objectives specify the activities that are to take place in support of the organization's overall strategy. Goals and objectives are typically statements in the form of imperatives that describe the development or improvement of business capabilities. For instance, goals and objectives can be related to increases in capacity, improvements in quality, or the development of entirely new capabilities. Goals and objectives further the organization's mission, helping it to continue to attract new customers or constituents, increase market share, and increase revenue and/or profitability.

Risk Appetite, Tolerance, and Capacity

Each organization has a particular "appetite" for risk, though few have documented it. ISACA defines *risk appetite* as "the level of risk that an organization is willing to accept while in pursuit of its mission, strategy, and objectives, and before action is needed to treat the risk."

Risk tolerance is related to risk appetite. ISACA defines *risk tolerance* as "the acceptable level of variation that management is willing to allow for any particular risk as the enterprise pursues its objectives."

Risk capacity is related to risk appetite. ISACA defines *risk capacity* as "the objective amount of loss that an organization can tolerate without its continued existence being called into question."

Generally, only highly risk-averse organizations such as banks, insurance companies, and public utilities will document and define risk appetite in concrete terms. Other organizations are more tolerant of risk and make individual risk decisions based on gut feeling or qualitative risk analysis. However, due to increased regulation, customer influence, and mandates, many organizations are finding it necessary to document and articulate their risk posture and appetite. This is an emerging trend in the marketplace, but it is still relatively new to many organizations.

In a properly functioning risk management program, the chief information security officer (CISO) is rarely the person who makes a risk-treatment decision or is accountable for it. Instead, the CISO is a *facilitator* for risk discussions that eventually lead to risk treatment decisions. The only time the CISO would be the accountable party is when risk treatment decisions directly affect the risk management program itself, such as in selecting a governance, risk, and compliance (GRC) tool for managing and reporting on risk.

The data privacy officer (DPO) plays a role in privacy-related risk decisions. Like the CISO, the DPO is a domain expert and guides the business toward decisions that align with applicable laws, internal policies, and the expectations of its affected constituents. Generally, it is business leaders who will make those decisions.

Privacy Governance Frameworks

It is unnecessary to build a privacy governance framework from scratch when industry-standard privacy frameworks are available for the privacy leader to consider. These frameworks include:

- NIST Privacy Framework
- ISO/IEC 27701

These frameworks are described in detail in Chapter 4.

Privacy Strategy Development

Among business, technology, privacy, and security professionals, there are many different ideas about the meaning of *strategy*, *strategic planning*, and the techniques used to develop one, which can result in general confusion. Although a specific strategy itself can be complex, the concept of a strategy is quite simple. A *strategy* can be defined as *a plan to achieve an objective*.

The effort to build a strategy requires more than saying those six words. Again, however, the idea is not complicated. The concept is this: understand where you are now and where you want to be. The strategy is the path you must follow to get from where you are (current state) to where you want to be (strategic objective).

The remainder of this section explores strategy development in more detail.

This section discusses privacy and security together because privacy depends on security for its information-protection capabilities.

Strategy Objectives

As stated earlier in this section, a strategy is a plan to achieve an objective. The objective (or objectives) is the desired future state of the organization's privacy and security posture and risk level.

There are, in addition, objectives *of* a strategy:

- **Strategic alignment** The desired future state, and the strategy to get there, must align with the organization and *its* strategy and objectives.
- **Effective risk management** Privacy and security programs must include a risk management policy, processes, and procedures. Without risk management, decisions are made blindly without regard to their consequences or level of risk.
- **Value delivery** The desired future state of a privacy or security program should focus on continual improvement and increased efficiency. No organization has unlimited funds for privacy and security; instead, organizations need to reduce the right risks for the lowest reasonable cost.
- **Resource optimization** Similar to value delivery, strategic goals should efficiently utilize available resources. Among other things, this means having only the necessary staff and tools required to meet strategic objectives.
- **Performance measurement** While strategic objectives need to be SMART, the ongoing privacy and privacy-related business operations should themselves be measurable, enabling management to drive continual improvement.
- **Assurance process integration** Organizations typically operate one or more separate assurance processes in silos that are not integrated. An effective strategy would work to break down these silos and consolidate assurance processes, reducing hidden risks.

All of these should be developed in a way that makes them measurable. This is why these six topics were discussed earlier when discussing governance metrics. These components were made to fit together in this way.

Risk Objectives

A vital part of strategy development is determining desired risk levels. One input to strategy development is understanding the current level of risk, and the desired future state can also have a level of risk associated with it.

It is quite difficult to quantify risk, even for the most mature organizations. Getting risk to a reasonable "high-medium-low" is simpler, though less straightforward, and difficult to do consistently across an organization. In specific instances, the costs of individual controls can be known, and the costs of theoretical losses can be estimated, but doing so across an entire risk-control framework is tedious and uncertain because the probabilities of threat-event occurrence amount to little more than guesswork.

A key part of a privacy strategy might well be reducing risk (it could also be cost reduction or compliance improvement). When this is the case, the strategist will need to employ a method for determining reasonable, credible before-and-after risk levels. For the sake of consistency, a better approach would be to use a methodology—however specific or general—that aligns with other risk-related strategies and discussions.

Strategy Resources

A strategy describes the process by which goals and objectives are to be met. Before an organization can develop a privacy and security strategy, it must first understand what privacy and security measures are currently in place. Existing resources paint a picture of an organization's current capabilities, including behaviors, skills, practices, and posture. The gap between the current and future states can then be filled through technologies, skills, policies, or practices.

Two types of inputs must be considered: those that will influence the development of strategic objectives and those that define the current state of privacy and security programs and their protective controls. The following inputs must be considered before objectives are developed:

- Risk assessments
- Threat assessments

When suitable risk and threat assessments have been completed, a privacy or security strategist can develop strategic objectives, or, if objectives have already been created, determine whether they will satisfactorily address the risks and threats identified in those assessments.

Privacy and security strategists can examine additional inputs to better understand the workings of the current privacy and security program. Many of these activities are more security-centric than privacy-centric, because a successful privacy program requires an effective security program as a foundation. These activities include the following:

- **Program charter** The organization might have a privacy program charter that defines a strategy, roles and responsibilities, objectives, or other matters.
- **Risk assessments** A risk assessment can reveal privacy and security risks within the organization. This helps the strategist understand threat scenarios, their estimated impacts, and their frequency. Risk assessment results provide the strategist with valuable

information on the types of resources required to bring risks to acceptable levels. This is vital for developing and validating strategic objectives.

- **Threat assessments** A threat assessment provides the strategist with information on the types of threats most likely to affect the organization, regardless of the effectiveness of controls. A threat assessment provides an additional perspective on risk, because it focuses on external threats and threat scenarios, regardless of the presence or effectiveness of preventive or detective controls.

A threat assessment is an essential element of strategy development. Without a threat assessment, strategic objectives can fail to address important threats. This would result in a privacy or security strategy that would not adequately protect the organization.

- **Vulnerability assessments** A vulnerability assessment helps the strategist better understand the current privacy and security postures of the organization's processes and infrastructure. The vulnerability assessment can target personnel, business processes, network devices, appliances, operating systems, subsystems such as web servers and database management systems, and applications, or any suitable combination thereof.
- **Maturity assessments** A maturity assessment provides the strategist with valuable information about the maturity of business processes. A strategist will better understand whether processes are orderly, organized, consistent, measured, examined, and periodically improved.
- **Audits** Internal and external audits can tell the strategist quite a bit about the state of the organization's privacy and security programs. A careful examination of audit findings can potentially provide significant details on regulatory compliance, control effectiveness, vulnerabilities, disaster preparedness, or other aspects of the program—depending on the objectives of those audits.

The topic of audits is discussed in considerable detail in the book, *CISA Study Guide* (Wiley Publishing), by this author.

- **Policies** An organization's privacy and security policies, as well as its practices regarding them, can say a great deal about its desired current state. Privacy and security policies can be thought of as an organization's internal laws and regulations regarding the protection and proper use of personal information and other assets. Examining the current privacy and security policy can reveal a lot about the behaviors required within the organization. Assessments, discussed earlier in this list, help a strategist understand the organization's compliance with its policies.

Many organizations align their privacy and security policies with the privacy and security control frameworks they have adopted.

- **Standards** Privacy and security *standards* describe, in detail, the methods, techniques, technologies, specifications, brands, and configurations to be used throughout the organization. As with privacy and security policies, privacy and security managers must understand the breadth of coverage, strictness, compliance, and last review and update of the organization's standards. These all indicate the extent to which an organization's privacy and security standards are used, if at all.
- **Guidelines** The very presence of current, actionable *guidelines* can signal a higher-than-average maturity. Most organizations don't get beyond creating policies and standards, so the presence of proper guidelines means the organization might have (or had in the past) sufficient resources or prioritization to make documenting policy guidance important enough to do. By their very nature, guidelines are typically written for personnel who need assistance with policy and standard compliance.
- **Processes and procedures** An organization's *processes* and *procedures* might speak volumes about its level of discipline, consistency, risk tolerance, and the maturity of not only its privacy and security programs but also of IT and the business in general. Like other types of documents discussed in this section, the relevance, accuracy, and thoroughness of process and procedure documents are indicators of maturity and commitment to robust privacy and security programs. Strategists need to confirm whether processes and procedures are actually followed or merely written artifacts.
- **Architecture** An organization's documentation of systems, networks, data flows, and other aspects of its environment provides privacy and security strategists with valuable information about how the organization has implemented its information systems and the business processes it supports. Documentation in the form of architecture diagrams is as important as written policies, standards, guidelines, and other artifacts. The strategist needs to determine whether the organization's architecture supports the organization's goals, objectives, and operations.
- **Controls** The strategist should review artifacts and interview personnel to determine whether specific controls are in place. The presence of documentation alone might not indicate whether controls are being carried out or merely more shelfware. Interviewing personnel and observing controls in action are better ways to determine whether controls are in place. Internal and external audits, discussed earlier in the "Audits" item, are another way to understand control effectiveness. A strategist will also need to understand whether the controls in place are part of a control framework such as ISO/IEC 27701, ISO/IEC 27001, NIST 800-53, CIS CSC, GLBA, HIPAA, or PCI DSS.
- **Skills and knowledge** An inventory of skills provides the strategist with an idea of what staff members can accomplish. Understanding skills at all these levels helps the strategist identify the types of work the current staff can perform, where minor skills

gaps exist, and where the strategist might recommend additional staff through hiring, contracting, or professional services. A key consideration is the potential for a major shift in practices and technologies. A good example is when the organization has been "playing it loose" with personal information and has not yet adopted data governance and data management practices required in modern privacy programs. If the staff lacks knowledge of these practices, the organization will struggle to implement them to comply with applicable privacy regulations.

- **Metrics** Properly established metrics will serve as a guide for the long-term effectiveness of privacy and security controls and processes. Evaluating such metrics helps the strategist understand what works well and where there are opportunities for improvement. The strategist can then design end states with more certainty and confidence than if metrics didn't exist.
- **Assets** The strategist needs to determine whether the organization has formal asset management practices and records to track its hardware (including virtual machines and other virtual assets), software, and data. Asset management is a key activity for both privacy and security programs, as information security professionals often say, "You cannot protect what you cannot find."
- **Risk register** The presence of a risk register can give the strategist a great deal of insight into risk management and risk analysis activities within the organization. Depending on the detail available in the risk ledger, a strategist might be able to discern the scope, frequency, quality, and maturity of risk assessments; the presence of a risk management and risk treatment process; and whether there are records of incidents.
- **Risk treatment decision records** When available, risk treatment records reveal which issues warranted attention, discussion, and decision-making. Coupled with the risk ledger, this information can provide a record of issues addressed by the organization's risk management process.
- **Insurance** The privacy or security strategist might want to know whether the organization has cybersecurity insurance or any general insurance policy that covers some types of cyber events and incidents. As important as having cyber insurance is, equally important is the reason the organization purchased it: compliance requirements, customer requirements, prior incidents, or a risk treatment decision. It is vitally important to understand the terms of any cyber-insurance policy. While the amounts of benefits are important, the most important aspects of a cyber-insurance policy are its terms, conditions, and exclusions.
- **Data management practices** The strategist needs to understand whether the organization has formal data management practices, including but not limited to a data classification policy, an internal privacy policy, and whether any tooling exists (such as DLP in its many forms) to provide visibility and control over the movement and use of personal information and other sensitive data.
- **Critical data** Privacy and security strategists need to understand the nature and use of an organization's critical data. But first, it's important to understand the term *critical*.

There are at least three common uses of the term when associated with data: operational criticality, highly sensitive (including personal information), and market criticality (including intellectual property and other competitive data).

- **Business impact analysis** While a business impact analysis (BIA) identifies an organization's business processes, the interdependencies between processes, the resources required for process operation, and the impact on the organization if any business process is incapacitated for a time for any reason, the BIA is also useful for privacy and security professionals aside from business continuity purposes, by giving the security strategist a better idea of which business processes and systems warrant the greatest protection.

The presence of a recent BIA provides a strong indication of the organization's maturity, as it signals an intention to protect its most critical processes from disaster scenarios. Consequently, the absence of a BIA suggests that the organization does not consider BCDR to be of strategic importance.

- **Privacy and security incident logs** Privacy and security incident logs provide the strategist with a history of incidents that have occurred in the organization. Depending on the information captured in the incident log, the strategist might be able to discern the maturity of the organization's privacy and security programs, especially its incident response program. The absence of incident logs is a strong indicator of the absence of an incident response process.
- **Outsourced services** The degree to which any particular organization has outsourced its business applications to the cloud is not the concern. Instead, what's important is the level of due care exercised in the outsourcing process, namely, whether a formal third-party risk management (TPRM) program is in place.
- **Culture** The *culture* of an organization can tell the strategist a lot about the state of privacy and security. Many people mistakenly believe that privacy and information security are all about technology. While technology is part of privacy and security, people are the most important aspect of a privacy and security program. No amount of technology can adequately compensate for an incorrect attitude and understanding regarding the protection of an organization's information assets, or for the mishandling of personal information. People are absolutely key.

When considering an organization's culture, the strategist needs to rely more on the organization's *actual operations* than on its statements of culture and values. The actual organizational culture might not align with the organization's claims.

- *Maturity* The characteristics of privacy and security management programs discussed in this list all contribute to the overall maturity of the organization's program. By itself, the program's maturity level doesn't tell the strategist anything about its details. But the strategist's observations of the program will provide a visceral sense of its maturity.
- **Risk appetite** Undocumented in most organizations, risk appetite can be discerned from the record of risk treatment decisions and from observations of an organization's executive culture. Even then, however, the attitude and culture of risk appetite might differ from an organization's actual practices.

Privacy Program Strategy Development

After the strategist has performed risk and threat assessments and carefully reviewed the state of privacy and security *programs* by examining artifacts, the strategist can develop strategic objectives. Strategic objectives will fall into one or more of these categories:

- Improvements in data management processes
- Improvements in protective controls
- Improvements in incident visibility
- Improvements in incident response
- Reductions in risk, including compliance risk
- Reductions in cost
- Increased resiliency of key business systems

These categories all contribute to strategic improvements in an organization's privacy and security programs. Depending on the current and desired future state of privacy and security, objectives might represent large projects or groups of projects implemented over several years to develop broad new capabilities, or they might be smaller projects focused on improving existing capabilities.

Here are some examples of broad, sweeping objectives for developing new privacy and security capabilities:

- Define and implement a data loss prevention (DLP) system to provide visibility and control over the movement of personal information.
- Define and implement a SIEM system to provide visibility into privacy, security, and operational events.
- Define and implement a privacy incident response program.
- Define and implement a security awareness learning program.

Here are examples of objectives for improving existing capabilities:

- Integrate vulnerability management and GRC systems.
- Link privacy awareness and access management programs so that staff members must complete privacy awareness training to retain access to systems containing personal information.

Once one or more objectives have been identified, the strategist will undertake several activities required to meet them. These activities are explained in the remainder of this section.

The strategist must consider many inputs before developing objectives and strategies to achieve them. These inputs serve a critical purpose: to help the strategist understand the organization's current state. The process of developing and implementing a strategy is not possible without understanding the starting point. These are discussed in the previous section, "Strategy Resources."

Gap Analysis

When developing a privacy and security strategy and objectives, privacy and security professionals often spend too much time focusing on end goals and too little on the current state of the organization's privacy and security program. Without sufficient knowledge of the current state, however, the strategist will find that accomplishing objectives will be more difficult and achieving success less certain.

A gap analysis helps the strategist understand missing capabilities and augment existing capabilities to achieve the desired end state. When performing a gap analysis, the strategist examines the present condition of processes, technologies, and people.

A gap analysis focuses on several aspects of a privacy or security program, including items from the prior "Strategy Resources" section.

When examining all of this and other information about an organization's privacy and security programs, the strategist should bring the appropriate measure of skepticism. There is much to know about what information is found, but the absence of information can speak volumes as well. Here are some considerations:

- **Absence of evidence is not evidence of absence** This time-honored adage applies to artifacts in any program. For instance, a sparse or nonexistent incident log might be an indication of several things: the organization might not have the required visibility to know when an incident has taken place, the organization's staff might not be trained in the recognition of incidents, or the organization might be watching only for "black swan" events and might be missing routine incidents.
- **Freshness, usefulness, and window dressing** When it comes to policy, process, and procedure documentation, it is important to determine whether documents are created for appearances only (in which case they might be well-kept secrets except to their owners) or widely known and utilized. A look at these documents' revision histories tells part of the story, while interviewing the right personnel completes the picture by revealing how well the documents' existence is made known and whether they are really used.
- **Scope, turf, and politics** In larger organizations, privacy and security managers need to understand current and historical practices regarding roles and responsibilities for privacy, security, and related activities. For example, records for a global security

program might reflect only what is occurring in the Americas, even though there is no written record to the contrary.

- **Reading between the lines** Depending on the organization's culture and the ethics of current or prior privacy and security personnel, records might not accurately reflect goings-on in the program. In other words, there might be overemphasis, underemphasis, distortions, or simply "look-the-other-way" situations that might result in records being incomplete.
- **Off the books** For various reasons, certain activities and proceedings in a privacy or security program might not be documented. For example, certain incidents might conveniently be absent from the incident log—otherwise, external auditors might catch the scent and go on a foxhunt, causing all manner of unpleasantness.
- **Regulatory requirements** When examining each aspect of a privacy or security program, the program's manager needs to ask one important question: is that activity included because it is required by regulations (with hell and fury from regulators if absent) or because the organization is managing risk and attempting to reduce the probability and/or impact of potential threats?

A common approach to determining the future state in a gap analysis is to determine the current maturity of a process or technology and compare that to the desired maturity level. Continue reading in the next section for a discussion on maturity levels.

Strengths, Weaknesses, Opportunities, and Threats Analysis

A Strengths, Weaknesses, Opportunities, and Threats (SWOT) analysis is a tool used in support of strategic planning. SWOT involves introspective analysis, where the strategist asks questions about the four components of the object of study:

- **Strengths** What characteristics of the business give it an advantage over others?
- **Weaknesses** What characteristics of the business put it at a disadvantage?
- **Opportunities** What elements in the environment could the business use to its advantage?
- **Threats** What elements in the environment threaten to harm the business?

SWOT analysis involves using a matrix of the four elements, as shown in Figure 1.3.

Capability Maturity Models

The Software Engineering Institute (SEI) at Carnegie Mellon University accomplished a great deal in developing the Capability Maturity Model Integration for Development (CMMi-DEV). *Capability maturity models* in other technology disciplines have also been developed, such as the Systems Security Engineering *Capability Maturity Model Integration (SSE-CMMI)* developed by the International Systems Security Engineering Association (ISSEA).

The CMMI uses five levels of maturity to describe the formality of a process:

- **Level 1: Initial** This represents a process that is ad hoc, inconsistent, unmeasured, and unrepeatable.

FIGURE 1.3 A SWOT matrix with its four components.

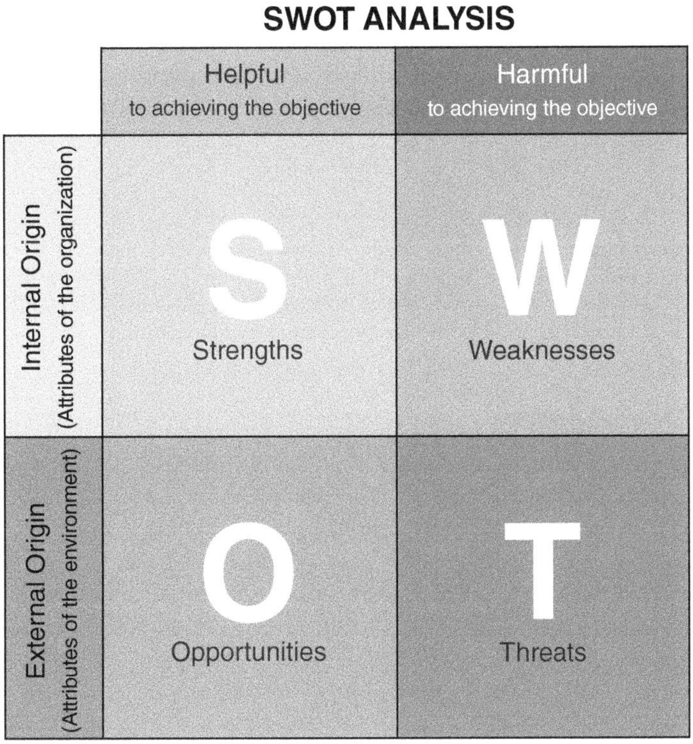

Source: Courtesy of Xhienne.

- **Level 2: Repeatable** This represents a process that is performed consistently and yields the same outcome. It might not be well-documented.
- **Level 3: Defined** This represents a process that is well-defined and documented.
- **Level 4: Managed** This represents a quantitatively measured process with one or more metrics.
- **Level 5: Optimizing** This represents a measured process that is under continuous improvement.

Not all strategists are familiar with maturity models. Strategists unaccustomed to capability maturity models need to understand two important characteristics of the models and how they are used:

- **Level 5 is not the ultimate objective** Most organizations' average maturity level targets range from 2.5 to 3.5. There are few organizations whose mission justifies level 5 maturity. The cost of developing a level 5 process or control is often prohibitive and misaligned with the associated risks.

- **Each control or process can have its own maturity level** It is neither common nor prudent to assign a single maturity-level target to all controls and processes. Instead, organizations with skilled strategists can determine the appropriate level of maturity for each control and process. They need not all be the same. Instead, it is more appropriate to use a threat-based or risk-based model to determine an appropriate level of maturity for each control and process. Some will be 2, some will be 3, some will be 4, and a few might even be 5.

A common use of capability maturity models is to determine the current maturity of a process, along with analysis, to identify the desired maturity level, process-by-process and technology-by-technology.

Roadmap Development

Once strategic objectives, risk and threat assessments, and gap analyses have been completed, the strategist can begin to develop roadmaps to accomplish each objective. A roadmap is a list of steps required to achieve a strategic objective. The term *roadmap* is an appropriate metaphor because it represents a journey whose details might not always appear to contribute to the objective, though not necessarily in a straight line. But in a well-designed roadmap, each task and each project gets the organization closer to the objective.

A roadmap is just a plan, but the term is often used to describe the steps an organization must take to achieve a long-term, complex, and strategic objective. Often, a roadmap is thought of as a series of projects—some running sequentially, others concurrently—that an organization uses to transform its processes and technology to achieve the objective.

Figure 1.4 depicts a roadmap for an 18-month identity and access management project.

A roadmap should be a top-down endeavor, following the usual hierarchy of control of an organization's operations. The roadmap can contain one or more of these:

- **Policy development** Sweeping changes in organizational practices around data protection and data management will likely require *policy* changes to codify expected behavior and system characteristics. While not generally required in most industries, it is common practice to structure the organization's security policy around one or more relevant standards or frameworks. Common standards and frameworks as a structure for security policy include NIST CSF, NIST SP 800-53, ISO/IEC 27001, HIPAA/HITECH, PCI DSS, and CIS CSC. Privacy controls can be adopted from ISO/IEC 27701 or the NIST Privacy Framework
- **Controls development** The strategist might need to enact one or more controls within specific business processes to ensure desired outcomes related to data management and data protection. Generally, controls are developed (and retired) as a result of a risk assessment, and this might be the case when developing a privacy program strategy.

FIGURE 1.4 Sample roadmap for identity and access management initiative.

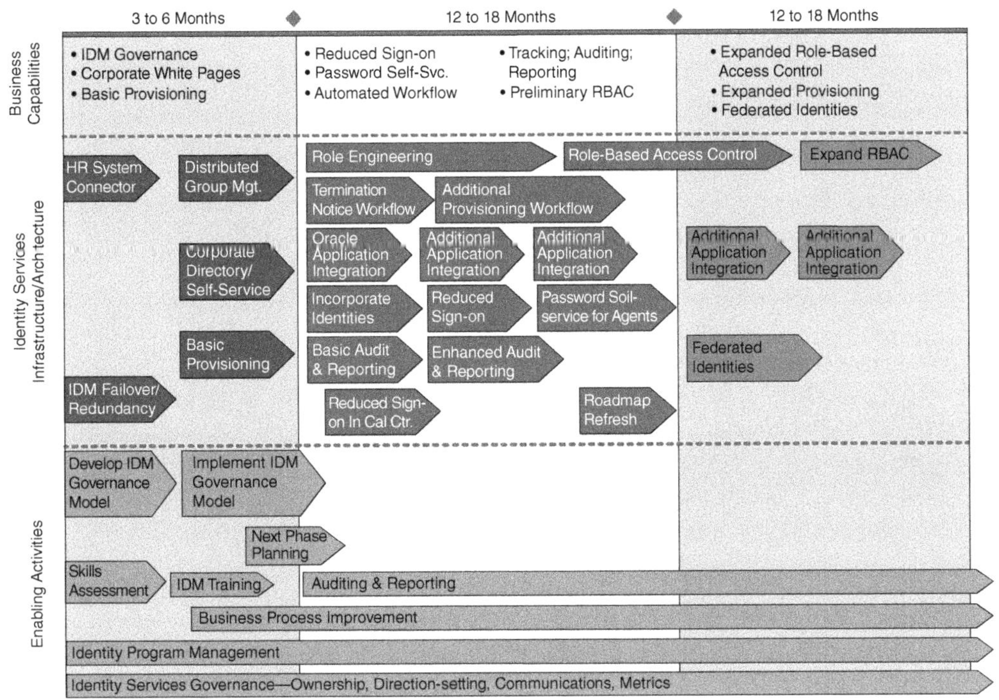

Source: Courtesy of *Hi-Tech Security Solutions* magazine.

> **Exam Tip**
>
> CDPSE candidates are not expected to memorize the contents of control frameworks for the exam, but are expected to understand their purpose and use.

- **Standards development** Changes in policies, controls, or underlying technologies might necessitate the development or updating of one or more standards. While standards are often thought of in terms of topics like passwords and encryption, privacy-related standards can also be developed for topics like aggregation and de-identification.
- **Processes and procedures** Often, the purpose of a new privacy or security strategy is to increase the maturity of privacy- or security-related technologies and activities within an organization. Because many organizations' privacy and security maturity levels are low, important tasks are poorly documented or not documented at all. The desired increase in maturity might compel an organization to identify undocumented processes and procedures and assign staff to document them.

Exam Tip

The CDPSE exam requires that candidates understand the structure and use of policies, standards, guidelines, and procedures.

- **Roles and responsibilities** When the strategy involves changes in technologies or processes (as it usually does), this can, in turn, affect the roles and responsibilities of privacy and security personnel, IT workers, and perhaps other staff. When business processes are added or changed, this often requires adjustments to personnel roles and responsibilities. There might also be new positions that require developing charter documents and job descriptions.
- **Training and awareness** Execution of a new privacy or security strategy often has a broad reach, impacting technology as well as policies, standards, processes, and procedures. The results of these are new information, in many forms and for several audiences, including general privacy and security awareness, updated policies and procedures, and new information systems.

Developing a Business Case

Many organizations require a business case before approving significant expenditures for privacy or security initiatives. A *business case* is a written statement that describes the initiative and its business benefits. The following are the typical elements included in a business case:

- **Problem statement** This is a description of the business condition or situation that the initiative is designed to solve. The condition might be a matter of compliance, a finding in a risk assessment, or a capability required by a customer, partner, supplier, or regulator.
- **Current state** This is a description of the existing conditions related to the initiative.
- **Desired state** This is a description of the future state of the relevant systems, processes, or staff.
- **Success criteria** These are the defined items that the program will be measured against.
- **Requirements** This is a list of required characteristics and components of the solution that will remedy the current state and bring about the desired future state.
- **Approach** This is a description of the proposed steps that will result in the desired future state. This section might include alternative approaches that were considered, along with the reasons they were not selected. If the initiative requires the purchase of products or professional services, business cases can include vendor proposals. Alternatively, the business case might include a request for proposal (RFP) or request for information (RFI) that will be sent to selected vendors for additional information.

- **Plan** This will include costs, timelines, milestones, vendors, and staff associated with the initiative.

Mature organizations use an executive *steering committee* to evaluate business cases for proposed initiatives and make go/no-go decisions. Business cases are often presented to a steering committee as an interactive discussion, allowing business leaders to ask questions and propose alternative approaches.

Characteristics of business cases should include the following:

- **Alignment with organization** The business case should align with the organization's goals and objectives, risk appetite, and culture.
- **Alignment with regulations** A business case should cite and align with applicable privacy and data protection regulations.
- **Statements in business terms** Problem statements, current state, and future state descriptions should all be expressed in business terms.

Establishing Communications and Reporting

Effective communications and reporting are critical elements of successful privacy and security programs. Because success depends mainly on people, in the absence of effective communication, they won't have the information required to make good privacy- and security-related decisions. Without regard for privacy or information security, decision outcomes can lead to unacceptable risks and even harmful incidents.

These are common forms of communication and reporting that are related to privacy and information security:

- **Board of directors meetings** Discussions of strategies, objectives, risks, incidents, and industry developments keep board members informed about privacy and security in the organization and elsewhere.
- **Governance and steering committee meetings** Discussions of privacy and security strategies, objectives, assessments, risks, incidents, and developments guide decision-makers as they discuss strategies, objectives, projects, and operations.
- **Privacy and security awareness** Periodic communications to all personnel help keep them informed about changes in privacy and security policies and standards, good privacy and security practices, and risks they can encounter, such as phishing and social engineering attacks.
- **Privacy and security advisories** Communications on potential threats help keep affected personnel aware of developments that might require them to take steps to protect the organization from harm.
- **Privacy and security incidents** Communications internally as well as with external parties during an incident keep incident responders and other parties informed. Organizations typically develop privacy and security incident plans and playbooks in advance that include business rules for internal communications and for interactions with outside parties, including customers, regulators, and law enforcement.

- **Metrics** Key metrics are reported upward within an organization, keeping management, executives, and board members informed as to the effectiveness and progress of the organization's privacy and security programs.

When building or expanding a privacy or security program, it's best to use existing communication channels and add relevant privacy and security content to them, rather than creating new parallel channels. Effective privacy and security programs make the best use of existing processes, channels, and methods in an organization.

Obtaining Management Commitment

The execution of a privacy or security strategy requires management commitment. Without that commitment, the strategist will be unable to obtain funding and other resources to implement the strategy.

Getting management commitment is not always straightforward. Often, executives and board members are unaware of their fiduciary responsibilities and the potency of modern threats. Many organizations mistakenly believe they are unlikely targets for hackers and cybercriminals because they are small or uninteresting. Further, the common perception of executives and senior managers is that privacy and security tactical problems are solved with "firewalls and antivirus software," and that privacy and information security are in no way related to business issues and business strategy.

A privacy or security strategist in a situation where top management lacks a strategic understanding of privacy and security will need to inform top management (in *their* language) about one or more aspects of modern privacy or information security management. When success is elusive, it might be necessary to bring in outside experts to convince executives that their privacy or security manager is not trying to build a kingdom but is simply trying to build a basic program to keep the organization out of trouble. As part of developing an effective communication approach, the strategist should not use fear, uncertainty, or doubt to move the leadership team toward adopting the strategy. The better approach, as noted in this section, is to relate it to the leadership team in business terms and opportunities to improve business functions.

Strategy Constraints

While the development of a new strategy can bring hope and optimism to the privacy or security team, there is no guarantee that organizational changes can be implemented without friction or even opposition. Instead, the privacy and security manager should anticipate and be prepared to maneuver around, over, or through many constraints and obstacles.

No privacy or security manager plans to fail. However, failing to anticipate obstacles and constraints might result in the inability to execute even the best strategy. The presence of an excellent strategy, even with executive support, does not mean obstacles and constraints will simply step aside. Instead, obstacles and constraints reflect the realities of human behavior, as well as structural and operational constraints that might pose challenges for the privacy and security manager and the organization as a whole. There is apt meaning to the phrase "the devil's in the details."

Typical constraints, obstacles, and other issues include:

- **Basic resistance to change** It is human nature to be suspicious of change, particularly when we as individuals have no control over it or say in it. Change is bad, or so we tend to think. "We've always done it this way," is a common refrain. Strategists need to consider methods for involving management and staff in anticipated changes, such as town hall meetings, surveys, and cross-functional committees.
- **Culture** Organizational culture can be thought of as the collective consciousness of all workers, regardless of rank. Privacy and security strategists should not expect to change the culture significantly; instead, they should work with the culture when developing and executing the privacy or security strategy.
- **Organizational structure** The strategist must understand the organization's command-and-control structure, often reflected in the organizational chart. However, there can be an undocumented aspect of the org chart that is more important: who is responsible for which activities, functions, and assets.
- **Staff capabilities** A strategy cannot be expected to succeed if the new or changed capabilities do not align with what staff members are able to do. A gap analysis to understand the present state of the organization's privacy or security program (discussed earlier in this chapter) needs to consider staff knowledge, skills, and capabilities. Where gaps are found, the strategy needs to include training or other activities to equip staff with the necessary skills and language. It is also important to understand who the true leaders and doers are in the organization so that the privacy leader can win their trust.

When an organization lacks staff with specific knowledge about privacy or security techniques or tools, it can look to external resources to augment its internal staff. The strategist needs to consider the costs and availability of these resources. Consultants and contracts in many skill areas are difficult to find; even larger firms can have backlogs of several months as a result.

- **Budget and cost** The strategist must determine, with a high degree of precision, all the hard and soft costs associated with each element of a strategy. Often, executive management will want to see alternative approaches; for example, if additional labor is required, the strategist might want to determine the costs of hiring additional personnel versus retaining consultants or contractors.
- **Time** Realistic project planning is needed so that everyone knows when project and strategy milestones will be completed. Project and strategy timelines must account for all business circumstances, including peak periods and holiday production freezes (when

IT systems are maintained in a more stable state), external events such as regulatory deadlines, audits, and other significant events that can impact schedules.

- **Legal and regulatory obligations** An organization might include items in its strategy that represent business capabilities required for legal or regulatory reasons. The enactment of new privacy laws might require considerable changes in practices in many organizations. The extraterritorial nature of some new privacy laws complicates this further.
- **Acceptable risk** Initiatives within the privacy or security strategy must align with executive management's risk appetite. However, increased pressure from privacy regulations might also be affecting risk appetite and forcing organizations to build more structure and defenses than they would otherwise.

The Obstacle of Organizational Inertia

Every organization has a finite capacity to undergo change. This is a fact that is often overlooked by overly ambitious strategists who want to accomplish a great deal in too short a time. I have coined the term *organizational inertia* to serve as an analogy to Newton's laws of motion: an object either remains at rest or continues to move at a constant velocity unless acted upon by a force. In an organization, this means that things will be done the same way until a force requires the organization to change what is done or how it is done. The greater the amount of change needed, the greater the outside force required to implement it.

The nature of organizational inertia, or its resistance to change, is threefold:

- Operational people changing their processes and procedures
- Learning curve
- Human resistance to change

Personal Information

Personal information is information about people, or as we like to say in the privacy business, *data subjects*. Because so many organizations use information technology to track, care for, service, or assist people, personal information often resides in information systems. As these systems became accessible from the Internet, cybercriminals realized they could *monetize* this information if they could obtain it.

Cybercriminals have been successfully stealing and monetizing personal information for at least 30 years, often through *identity theft*. The rate of identity theft rose dramatically in the 1990s, prompting numerous laws and regulations to protect personal information. This has led to the growth of the privacy profession, including professional certifications like the CDPSE, the subject of this book.

Ask ten business and technology professionals for a definition of *personal information*, and you'll get ten different definitions. This reflects privacy laws, each of which has its own bespoke definition. If we wind back the clock a few years, we find early definitions, such as:

- **European Privacy Directive (1995)** "'Personal data' means any information relating to an identified or identifiable natural person ('data subject'); an identifiable natural person is one who can be identified, directly or indirectly, in particular by reference to an identifier such as a name, an identification number, location data, an online identifier or to one or more factors specific to the physical, physiological, genetic, mental, economic, cultural or social identity of that natural person."
- **California Senate Bill 1386** "'Personal information' means an individual's first name or first initial and last name in combination with any one or more of the following data elements, when either the name or the data elements are not encrypted: (1) Social security number. (2) Driver's license number or California Identification Card number. (3) Account number, credit or debit card number, in combination with any required security code, access code, or password that would permit access to an individual's financial account."

Over many years, many U.S. states and numerous countries enacted privacy laws with their own definitions. Here are some more examples:

- **EU General Data Protection Regulation (GDPR)** "'Personal data' means any information relating to an identified or identifiable natural person ('data subject'); an identifiable natural person is one who can be identified, directly or indirectly, in particular by reference to an identifier such as a name, an identification number, location data, an online identifier or to one or more factors specific to the physical, physiological, genetic, mental, economic, cultural or social identity of that natural person." (Note that this definition is identical to the 1995 European privacy directive.)
- **California Consumer Privacy Act (CCPA)** "'Personal information' means information that identifies, relates to, describes, is reasonably capable of being associated with, or could reasonably be linked, directly or indirectly, with a particular consumer or household. Personal information includes, but is not limited to, the following if it identifies, relates to, describes, is reasonably capable of being associated with, or could be reasonably linked, directly or indirectly, with a particular consumer or household: (A) Identifiers such as a real name, alias, postal address, unique personal identifier, online identifier, Internet protocol address, email address, account name, Social Security number, driver's license number, passport number, or other similar identifiers. (B) Any categories of personal information described in subdivision (e) of Section 1798.80. (C) Characteristics of protected classifications under California or federal law. (D) Commercial information, including records of personal property, products or services purchased, obtained, or considered, or other purchasing or consuming histories

or tendencies. (E) Biometric information. (F) Internet or other electronic network activity information, including, but not limited to, browsing history, search history, and information regarding a consumer's interaction with an Internet website, application, or advertisement. (G) Geolocation data. (H) Audio, electronic, visual, thermal, olfactory, or similar information. (I) Professional or employment-related information. (J) Education information, defined as information that is not publicly available personally identifiable information as defined in the Family Educational Rights and Privacy Act (20 U.S.C. Sec. 1232g; 34 C.F.R. Part 99)." Note that the California Privacy Rights Act (CPRA) did not redefine "personal information," but retained and carried forward the existing definition from the CCPA. The CPRA added a new, narrower, higher-risk subcategory known as Sensitive Personal Information (SPI), which includes items such as Social Security numbers, driver's license numbers, passport numbers, and account login credentials.

- **Health Insurance Portability and Accountability Act (HIPAA)** "*Protected health information* means individually identifiable health information … that is: (i) Transmitted by electronic media; (ii) Maintained in electronic media; or (iii) Transmitted or maintained in any other form or medium."

These and many other laws have settled into a more-or-less consistent theme for what privacy professionals call *personally identifiable information (PII)*, which generally includes:

- Name
- Date of birth
- Contact information (any of: telephone number, email address, residence address, IP address, and so forth)
- Contextual information (any of: bank account number, Social Security number, medical record number, driver's license number, and so forth)
- Additional information (any of: religious preferences, sexual preferences, political preferences/membership)

For most organizations and government agencies, information about the following classes of people is generally included:

- Employees
- Customers
- Donors
- Constituents
- … and possibly others

If, upon reading this, you are a bit confused, don't worry: this is the privacy profession today. We are responsible for protecting information about people from misuse, abuse, and theft. With multiple laws, regulations, and standards that partly overlap, we are accountable for developing policies, processes, and safeguards to protect information about persons, including employees, customers, and others.

PII: Build Your Own Definition

Every organization is different from every other in terms of industry, business model, physical location, the locations of employees and customers, and the laws and regulations it is required to comply with. As such, many organizations develop a bespoke definition of PII that accounts for all these factors.

Some organizations take a somewhat different approach, separating employees from customers, each with their own PII definitions.

Privacy Principles

Privacy principles provide the conceptual foundation for how personal data is collected, used, and protected across systems and organizations. They translate legal obligations and ethical expectations into consistent, actionable guidance applicable throughout the data lifecycle. Frameworks such as the OECD principles and emerging models like FAIR (Factor Analysis of Information Risk, discussed in Chapter 3) help structure thinking about accountability, risk, and value. Core concepts, including transparency, consent, purpose limitation, and privacy by design, establish expectations for responsible data handling. Together, these principles enable organizations and privacy professionals to align governance, engineering, and operations, ensuring that privacy is not treated as an afterthought but as an integral design requirement.

Privacy by Design

Privacy and security by design is a concept that reinforces the need to have privacy and security considerations incorporated into systems and applications by default. In other words, the product is designed with privacy and security as priorities, along with any other functional purposes it serves.

Exam Tip

Implementing security and privacy by design involves not only development processes but a change in organizational culture.

Privacy by design is based on seven foundational principles:

- **Proactive not reactive; preventive not remedial** The privacy-by-design approach is characterized by proactive rather than reactive measures. It anticipates and prevents privacy-invasive events before they happen. Privacy by design does not wait for privacy risks to materialize, nor does it offer remedies for resolving privacy infractions once they have occurred; it aims to prevent them.
- **Privacy embedded into design** Privacy by design is embedded in the design and architecture of IT systems as well as business practices. It is not bolted on as an add-on, after the fact. The result is that privacy becomes an essential component of the core functionality being delivered. Privacy is integral to the system without diminishing its functionality.
- **Privacy as the default setting** Privacy by default seeks to deliver the maximum degree of privacy by ensuring that personal data is automatically protected in any given IT system or business practice. If an individual does nothing to protect their privacy, it should remain intact. No action should be required of the individual to protect their privacy.
- **Full functionality—positive-sum, not zero-sum** Privacy by design seeks to accommodate all legitimate interests and objectives in a positive-sum "win-win" manner, not through a dated, zero-sum approach, where unnecessary trade-offs are made. Privacy by design avoids the pretense of false dichotomies, such as privacy versus security, demonstrating that it is possible to have both.
- **End-to-end security—full lifecycle protection** Privacy by design, having been embedded into the system prior to the first element of information being collected, extends securely throughout the entire lifecycle of the data involved—strong security measures are essential to privacy, from start to finish. This ensures that all data is securely retained and then securely destroyed at the end of the process, in a timely fashion. Thus, privacy by design ensures end-to-end, cradle-to-grave secure lifecycle management of information.
- **Visibility and transparency—keep it open** Privacy by design seeks to assure all stakeholders that whatever the business practice or technology involved, it is, in fact, operating according to the stated promises and objectives, subject to independent verification. Its parts and operations remain visible and transparent to users and providers alike.
- **Respect for user privacy—keep it user-centric** Privacy by design requires architects and administrators to keep the interests of the individual uppermost by offering measures such as strong privacy defaults, appropriate notice, and user-friendly empowerment options.

Business application architectures, designs, data flows, and configurations all must contribute to and support privacy and security. The *systems development lifecycle* represents the business processes used to develop, maintain, and operate business applications. It must include steps to ensure that new and existing information systems do not impact security and privacy in unexpected ways. Policies and standards must also support security and privacy principles to ensure that personal information is adequately protected and properly used. Ongoing operations must likewise ensure that the security and privacy of systems are not compromised and that continuous monitoring is employed to detect security and privacy incidents early so that they might be contained.

Consent

In the context of data privacy, *consent* is a distinct action taken by a data subject to grant an organization permission to collect and/or process their personal information. Consent must be given freely, in a specific context, be revocable, and comply with applicable laws.

There are several ways in which consent is given and obtained, including the following:

- **At the time of data collection** When a data subject provides one or more items of personal information to an organization, the data subject also provides consent for the collection and processing of that information. In an online context, consent often takes the form of a checkbox with words citing agreement with a privacy policy that can be read in its entirety. On a paper form, consent often appears in the signature block.
- **Prior to data collection** When a data subject is establishing a relationship with an organization, a part of the agreement can include obtaining consent for future data collection.
- **Consent obtained through a third party** In some instances, it is not feasible for an organization to collect consent directly from a data subject. For example, in the case of advertising specifically chosen for and delivered to a data subject, the organization displaying the advertising will have collected consent "for other uses," including advertising. The advertiser will have been assured that consent has been obtained from all data subjects to whom the advertiser is displaying ad content.

Regardless of the method used to obtain consent, organizations must record the specific date, time, stipulations, and circumstances under which that consent was obtained. Organizations need to be quite specific regarding this collection. For instance, if an organization collects personal information for a specific context or event, and consent to use that information is limited to that context or event, the organization cannot later use that information for other contexts or events.

GDPR and CCPA/CPRA treat consent differently. Under the GDPR, consent is only one of several lawful bases for processing personal data. It is required only when no other lawful basis (such as contract, legal obligation, or legitimate interests) applies. When used, consent must be freely given, specific, informed, and unambiguous, and, in certain cases, explicit (e.g., for special categories of data).

In contrast, CCPA/CPRA does not rely on consent as the primary basis for processing. Instead, it generally permits the collection and use of personal information with required notice. It grants consumers the right to opt out of specific activities, particularly the sale or sharing of personal information, and to limit the use of sensitive personal information.

Transparency

In the context of privacy, *transparency* refers to the extent to which an organization discloses its practices regarding the collection, protection, and use of personal information. Transparency often begins with an organization publishing an external privacy policy, often called a *notice of privacy practices (NOPP)*, in which it fully discloses the collection, protection, use, distribution, and disposal of personal information. The NOPP will likely also contain guidance for data subjects who want to make inquiries, lodge complaints, and request corrections or the removal of their information.

Transparency requires trust. In terms of a posted privacy policy or NOPP, organizations need to "say what they do, and do what they say." Trust is hard to earn and easy to lose, so organizations must take transparency seriously. Privacy laws, described later in this chapter, require transparency and hold organizations accountable for their information collection and handling practices.

Minimization

In privacy, the concept of *minimization* stresses that the collection of personal information should include *only* the records and data fields that are required, and no more. These concepts include:

- **Collect only the personal information required for processing** Any personal items not used should not be collected. For instance, if an organization does not require a subject's date of birth to perform processing, then the date of birth should not be collected.
- **Retain personal information only as long as required** When an organization no longer needs personal information about a data subject, it should be discarded.

The reason for data minimization is this: data that is collected and needed provides value to the organization, but also poses a liability in the case of theft. However, data that is collected but *not* needed represents only liability for the organization, particularly if it is stolen.

Purpose Limitation

In privacy, the concept of *purpose limitation* states that personal information should be used only for explicitly stated purposes described in the NOPP. Any organization that collects personal information for one purpose must not subsequently use it for other purposes unless it obtains consent for the new purpose.

Legal Basis

In the context of data privacy and privacy regulations, organizations must identify the specific *legal basis* for collecting and/or processing personal information. Simply put, it must be lawful for the organization to collect and use data subjects' personal information, and the organization must be able to cite specifically how it is lawful.

In Article 6.1, the GDPR provides five possible avenues of legal basis (quoting directly from GDPR):

- *The data subject has given consent to the processing of their personal data for one or more specific purposes;*
- *Processing is necessary for the performance of a contract to which the data subject is party or in order to take steps at the request of the data subject prior to entering into a contract;*
- *Processing is necessary for compliance with a legal obligation to which the controller is subject;*
- *Processing is necessary in order to protect the vital interests of the data subject or of another natural person;*
- *Processing is necessary for the performance of a task carried out in the public interest or in the exercise of official authority vested in the controller;*
- *Processing is necessary for the purposes of the legitimate interests pursued by the controller or by a third party, except where such interests are overridden by the interests or fundamental rights and freedoms of the data subject which require protection. [This does not apply to public authorities in the performance of their duties.]*

EU member states might include additional provisions.

The CCPA/CPRA do not treat this in the same way as the GDPR. Instead, entities subject to the CCPA/CPRA must generally comply with the law. Certain use cases, such as healthcare and employment, with specific provisions, are cited.

Legitimate Interest

The term *legitimate interest* is defined in the GDPR as one of six bases for the lawful collection and processing of personal information. One might consider legitimate interest a loophole, but the author's opinion is that this provision was included so that the GDPR did not need to enumerate every possible use of personal information (which would soon be out of date, requiring frequent updates to the law).

Legitimate interest provides organizations with a basis for collecting and processing personal information when they benefit from doing so. But it doesn't end there: the real issue of legitimate interest is that organizations must balance their interests with those of the data subject.

Online advertising is an interesting case to consider. Advertisers have an interest in serving advertising content to readers and viewers. To stay in business and earn advertising revenue (which is the business model for a considerable number of websites), advertisers claim that readers and viewers benefit (their interest) in advertising that is aligned with topics of interest to them (the readers' and viewers' interest). Thus, there is an argument that online advertising benefits both the advertiser (and the website operator) and the viewer (the data subject).

Organizations are cautioned against relying on legitimate interest too readily. Some long-established industry and business practices might be forever altered because of GDPR, CCPA, CPRA, and other privacy laws.

ISACA Privacy Principles

ISACA has published a privacy-principles guide that includes the following topics:

- Management
- Notice
- Choice and consent
- Collection
- Use, retention, and disposal
- Access
- Disclosure to third parties
- Security
- Quality
- Monitoring and enforcement

ISACA's *Privacy Principles and Program Management Guide* is available from https://store.isaca.org.

Privacy Engineering Principles

Engineering is the disciplined application of scientific and mathematical principles to design, build, and operate systems that reliably meet defined objectives within real-world constraints. It begins with a clear problem definition and requirements, followed by a systematic decomposition of complex systems into manageable components. Engineers apply modeling, analysis, and empirical testing to evaluate alternatives, optimize performance, and manage trade-offs among cost, quality, safety, and time. Design decisions are guided by repeatability, scalability, and maintainability, ensuring that solutions perform consistently under expected conditions and degrade gracefully under stress. Risk management is integral, incorporating safety margins, failure analysis, and controls to reduce uncertainty and unintended consequences. Finally, engineering is inherently iterative: solutions are refined through continuous feedback, measurement, and improvement, grounded in evidence rather than assumption.

Privacy engineering is the application of these engineering principles with the twin objectives of privacy: identifying and protecting personal information, and ensuring that personal information is used only as directed by policy and approved by management.

Now, let us go into greater detail and speak to individual principles of privacy engineering, some of which were implied earlier in this discussion. NIST, in its publication NISTIR 8062, *Introduction to Privacy Engineering and Risk Management in Federal Systems*, describes privacy engineering principles as follows:

- **Predictability** Enabling reliable assumptions by individuals, owners, and operators about PII and its processing by an information system. The purpose of predictability is to establish trust and accountability through transparency.
- **Manageability** Providing the capability for granular administration of PII, including alteration, deletion, and selective disclosure.
- **Disassociability** Enabling the processing of PII or events without association with individuals or devices beyond the operational requirements of the system. This principle calls for data minimization: collecting *only* what personal information is truly needed, de-identifying when possible, and retaining it for the shortest possible time.

Privacy engineering is managed through *privacy governance*, including policies, roles and responsibilities, and processes such as the *systems development lifecycle (SDLC)*, in which key privacy-by-design activities are required and reviewed.

Privacy is wholly dependent upon sound data governance and data management, which are discussed in Chapters 5 and 6.

Privacy Laws, Regulations, and Standards

Laws passed by governments at the national, state, and provincial levels impose requirements on organizations that store or process personal information about natural persons. These laws have been enacted in response to citizens' outcry over the abuse of their personal information and violations of their right to privacy as technology and the Internet have become part of our daily lives. Activities such as telemarketing and tracking people's locations and habits have been the focus of growing concerns by citizens and privacy advocates. Advances in the capabilities of information systems and data mining of large databases containing personal information have enabled practices that many private citizens find inappropriate and even intrusive. Abuses of such capabilities would allow the creation of a new, highly invasive form of a surveillance police state, which is not difficult to imagine, as some governments around the world are already there. Legislators in many countries have sought to counterbalance these capabilities by defining the rights of natural persons concerning the data that is collected about them and used in various ways.

The most influential privacy laws include the EU GDPR, the U.S. Health Insurance Portability and Accountability Act (HIPAA), the U.S. Fair Credit Reporting Act (FCRA), the U.S. Electronic Communications Privacy Act (ECPA), the Canadian Personal Information Protection and Electronic Documents Act (PIPEDA), the CCPA, and the China Cybersecurity Law (CCSL). These and other laws are discussed in the remainder of this section. This is not intended to be an exhaustive or authoritative list, but instead a sampling of better-known privacy laws.

Privacy protection regulations fall into four categories:

- **Comprehensive** A single unified legal framework governing personal information across all sectors. Examples: GDPR, CCPA/CPRA.
- **Sectoral** Laws that are applied to specific industry sectors. Examples: HIPAA, GLBA.
- **Self-regulatory** Organizations define their own policies and practices, following industry standards. Examples: OECD privacy principles and Fair Information Practice Principles (FIPPs).
- **Co-regulatory** Government-industry partnerships in which laws set high-level requirements and industries develop detailed rules.

Because privacy and data amendment protection laws are being rapidly enacted and changed, organizations and privacy professionals must devise a way to remain fully aware of new and evolving laws.

EU General Data Protection Regulation

One of the most notable modern privacy laws, the *General Data Protection Regulation (GDPR)* enacts sweeping requirements upon organizations within and beyond the European Union that store, process, or transmit personal data about EU citizens and residents. The GDPR was passed in April 2016 and became effective in May 2018. The main privileges enacted by the GDPR include the following:

- **Rights of data subjects** Any organization collecting information about EU residents is required to operate transparently when collecting and using their personal information.

Chapter III of the GDPR defines eight data subject rights that have become foundational for other privacy regulations around the world:

- *Right to access personal data* Data subjects can access the data collected on them.
- *Right to rectification* Data subjects can request modifications to their data to correct errors and update incomplete information.
- *Right to erasure* Also referred to as *the right to be forgotten*, this right allows data subjects to request that their personal data be erased from an entity's processing activities.
- *Right to restrict processing* In certain circumstances, data subjects can request that processing of their personal data be stopped.
- *Right to be informed* Data subjects must be notified of what information is being collected at or before collection, and of its use.
- *Right to data portability* Data subjects can request that their personal data be provided in a commonly used, machine-readable format.
- *Right to object* Data subjects can object to the processing of their data when a controller attempts to argue that legitimate grounds for processing override the data subject's interests, rights, and freedoms, or that processing is for legal purposes.
- *Right to reject automated individual decision-making* Data subjects can refuse the automated processing of their personal data for decision-making.

- **Definitions of data controller and data processor** The GDPR defines a *data controller* as an organization that directs the use of personal data. A *data processor* is an organization that processes personal data as directed by a data controller. Controllers and processors are required to maintain records regarding the collection and processing of personal information.
- **Data protection and privacy by design and by default** Organizations are required to design, operate, and maintain their business processes and information systems with privacy and security as part of their default design.
- **Cybersecurity** Organizations that process personal information are required to implement cybersecurity measures to protect that data.
- **Breach notification** Organizations are required to notify supervisory authorities and affected data subjects in the event of a privacy or security breach of personal data.
- ***Data protection impact assessment (DPIA)*** The DPIA is a formal process to identify and minimize the data protection risks of a data processing activity. Organizations are required to perform DPIAs whenever they implement new systems or make significant changes to business processes or information systems.
- ***Data protection officer (DPO)*** Organizations are required to appoint a DPO if they process personal data on a large scale. The DPO is expected to have expert knowledge of data protection law and practices.

- **Certification** The GDPR permits the creation of certification authorities and the voluntary certification of organizations that process personal data.
- ***Cross-border data transfers*** The GDPR contains rules regarding the transfer of personal data out of the European Union.
- ***Binding corporate rules*** The GDPR accommodates the use of binding corporate rules that multinational organizations might enact to ensure the protection and appropriate use of personal data when transferred outside the European Union to their overseas systems.
- ***Supervisory authority*** Each member state in the EU establishes a supervisory authority responsible for monitoring GDPR compliance.
- **Penalties** The GDPR authorizes supervisory authorities to impose fines on organizations that violate its terms. Administrative fines can be as high as €20 million or 4% of global turnover, whichever is greater.

The GDPR claims to have *extraterritorial* jurisdiction over companies not based in the European Union that provide goods or services to EU citizens in EU member states. This claim of jurisdiction beyond its own borders has been seriously tested in courts, with numerous enforcement actions and cross-border rulings established. However, the enforcement of extraterritoriality has split into two types of situations. For U.S.-based organizations with operations in the EU, data protection authorities fined Marriott £99 million for a 2018 breach and Google €50 million for alleged abuses of privacy settings. For U.S.-based organizations with no EU establishment or assets, GDPR fines have been unenforceable. Subsequent fines and appeals against non-EU companies can result in additional types of cases.

U.S. Health Insurance Portability and Accountability Act

Enacted in 1996, the *Health Insurance Portability and Accountability Act (HIPAA)* includes two rules that address the protection of *protected health information (PHI)* and *electronic protected health information (ePHI)*. *Covered entities* are organizations that store or process medical information and are subject to one or both of these rules:

- **Security rule** This part of HIPAA requires that organizations implement several administrative, physical, and technical safeguards to protect ePHI. Many of these controls are compulsory, while others are "addressable" (an organization can rationalize their disuse).
- **Privacy rule** Effective in 2003, this part of HIPAA requires that organizations protect PHI, whether in electronic or hardcopy form.

Additional provisions of HIPAA are not related to security or privacy.

HIPAA defines various civil and criminal penalties for organizations that violate the law. Covered entities are required to enter into *business associate agreements (BAAs)* with all third parties that store or process ePHI on their behalf.

Health Information Technology for Economic and Clinical Health Act

Enacted in 2009, the *Health Information Technology for Economic and Clinical Health (HITECH)* law extends the Security Rule and Privacy Rule in HIPAA by expanding security breach notification requirements and expanding the disclosures of the use of a patient's PHI.

U.S. Fair Credit Reporting Act

Enacted in 1970, the *Fair Credit Reporting Act (FCRA)* provides visibility, remedies, and assurances, including civil liability, that the information in consumers' credit histories is accurate. Since credit reports are used by banks and other financial institutions (as well as employers in many states for making hire/no-hire decisions), the FCRA provides consumers with a means to obtain copies of their credit reports and procedures for correcting erroneous information in those reports.

FCRA is an early example of a privacy law that provides individuals with the ability to know what personal information is being stored, how it is used, and how to obtain copies and request corrections.

If consumers' rights are violated, they can recover damages, attorney fees, and court costs, and punitive damages can be awarded if actions against them were willful.

California Consumer Protection Act & California Privacy Rights Act

Effective January 1, 2020, the *California Consumer Privacy Act (CCPA)* is a state law designed to enhance California residents' privacy rights. Provisions of the CCPA give California residents certain rights, including the following:

- Knowledge of what personal information is being collected
- Notification of whether such personal information is subsequently transferred or disclosed to another party
- The ability to prohibit an organization from transferring or selling its personal information
- The ability to examine the personal information held by organizations, with the right to request that the information be corrected or removed
- The freedom from discrimination should they choose to exercise their privacy rights

Californians can sue for damages when nonencrypted and nonredacted personal information is subject to unauthorized access, exfiltration, theft, or disclosure due to a business's failure to implement and maintain reasonable security procedures.

Like the EU GDPR, the CCPA claims jurisdiction over companies not located in California if they collect personal information about California residents. And like the GDPR, this provision has yet to be tested in court.

Made effective on January 1, 2023, the *California Privacy Rights Act (CPRA)* extends the CCPA by:

- Introducing a new information category known as *Sensitive Personal Information (SPI)*
- Expanding consumer rights, including the right of information correction, limitations on sensitive data use, and rights to know how data is collected, shared, and retained
- Introducing data minimization, purpose limitation, and retention principles
- Expanding liability for contractors and service providers
- Increasing protection for minors
- Expanding risk and governance requirements
- Establishing the California Privacy Protection Agency that can issue regulations, investigate violations, and enforce the law

Further expansion of the CPRA, adopted by the California Privacy Protection Agency (CPPA) in June 2025 and effective in January 2026, includes enhancements concerning *automatic decision-making technology (ADMT)*, risk assessments, cybersecurity audits, and the lookback period for consumer data access requests.

Canadian Personal Information Protection and Electronic Documents Act

The *Personal Information Protection and Electronic Documents Act (PIPEDA)* took effect in 2000 and aims to protect consumer data privacy in the context of e-commerce. In part, PIPEDA was enacted to provide assurances to European countries and consumers that their personal information present in Canadian companies' information systems would be safe and free from abuse.

PIPEDA also gives Canadians the right to know why organizations collect, use, or disclose their personal information, and to be assured that their information will not be used for any other purpose. They can further know who within the organization is responsible for protecting their information. They can contact the organizations to ensure that their personal data is accurate and can lodge complaints if they believe their privacy rights have been violated. Canadian companies must obtain consent to collect personal information, and they cannot refuse to provide service to a Canadian citizen if the citizen refuses to provide such consent.

China's Cybersecurity and Personal Information Protection Laws

Enacted in 2016 and effective in 2017, the *China Cybersecurity Law (CSL)* consists of three main parts:

- **Data protection** Organizations holding personal information about Chinese citizens must take measures to protect that information.
- **Data localization** Organizations collecting information about Chinese citizens must keep such data within China. Organizations that want to transfer data out of China must undergo a data assessment by the Chinese government.
- **Cybersecurity** Organizations are required to implement controls to prevent malware, intrusions, and other attacks. The law includes mandatory standards, assessments, and certifications for network devices.

CSL's data protection principles resemble those of the GDPR. Both laws require that organizations inform citizens if they hold their personal data, explain how their personal data is used, identify collection methods, and obtain consent for continued use.

CSL was amended in 2025, effective January 1, 2026, to strengthen enforcement penalties and align it with other data governance laws.

In 2021, China enacted the *Personal Information Protection Law (PIPL)* that governs how organizations collect, process, and transfer personal information.

Brazilian General Data Protection Law (LGPD)

Enacted in 2019 and effective in August 2020, the LGPD is similar to the EU GDPR. The LGPD establishes a National Data Protection Authority, designated as the federal agency responsible for overseeing data protection regulation.

The LGPD establishes some individual rights over personal data, many of which are similar to those provided by the GDPR. However, the LGPD also provides additional rights, including access to information about entities with which an organization has shared the individual's personal data.

Like the GDPR and the CCPA, the LGPD claims jurisdiction over companies not located in Brazil if one of the following criteria is met:

- The processing operation is carried out in Brazil
- The purpose of the processing activity is to offer or provide goods or services to individuals located in Brazil
- The personal data was collected in Brazil

Privacy Laws Enforced by the FTC

In the United States, the Federal Trade Commission (FTC), the agency that monitors the rights of consumers, has brought legal action against scores of companies in alleged violation of consumer protection laws, including violations of posted privacy policies, breaches of personal information, improper collection of personal data without consent, and failures to protect personal information.

The FTC enforces more than 70 laws, including these:

- Federal Trade Commission Act, which protects consumers from unfair and deceptive practices
- Children's Online Privacy Protection Act (COPPA), which protects children's online privacy, particularly those under age 13
- Do-Not-Call Implementation Act, which provides for consumers to opt out of all telemarketing calls
- Controlling the Assault of Non-Solicited Pornography and Marketing Act (CAN-SPAM), which prevents misleading advertising and requires consumers to opt out
- Gramm-Leach-Bliley Act (GLBA), which protects and secures the privacy of consumer personal information by financial institutions
- HITECH, which extends the scope of HIPAA
- Identity Theft Assumption and Deterrence Act, which provides a central clearinghouse for identity theft complaints
- Fair Credit Reporting Act, which protects personal information collected by consumer credit bureaus, medical information companies, and tenant screening services
- The Clayton Act, which prevents illegal contracts, mergers, and acquisitions

Other Legal Obligations

In addition to abiding by applicable laws and regulations, organizations can negotiate additional terms and conditions regarding the protection of personal information. Such obligations might be related to specific services rendered by third-party service providers that store or process personal information on behalf of other organizations. For instance, a service provider might comply with all applicable laws, agree to specific protective measures, undergo periodic audits or examinations, or provide specific reporting regarding the storage or use of personal data.

Privacy Documentation and Records

Documentation is an inclusive term that describes many types of written artifacts, including but not limited to policies, standards, charters, processes, procedures, requirements, and others. Organizations that strive to operate with intentionality and consistency must document their principles and practices and make them available to personnel so they can conform to them.

Records are the written descriptions of business events such as meeting minutes, contracts, financial transactions, decisions, purchase orders, event logs, and reports.

Privacy programs are found to have many types of documentation and records, including these:

- **Policies** Statements defining required behavior and characteristics of processes and systems. A policy generally describes *what* must be (or not be) done. All personnel in an organization are required to comply with policy.
  - *Internal policies* An internal privacy policy, directed at an organization's workforce, defines required and prohibited behaviors regarding the collection, handling, distribution, and disposal of personal information. These internal policies must be consistent with public facing policies.
  - *External policies, aka notice of privacy practices (NOPP)* External-facing policies, often published on an organizational website, that describe the collection, use, distribution, and disposal of personal information, as well as guidelines for making inquiries and lodging complaints.
- **Standards** Statements that describe *how* (or *with what*) policies are to be carried out. All personnel in an organization are required to comply with standards. Some of the types of standards that an organization might have include:
  - *Methodology standards* Statements that specify methodologies to be used, such as systems development lifecycle methodologies like Agile.
  - *Technology standards* Statements that specify technologies to use, such as encryption algorithms.
  - *Protocol standards* Statements that specify protocols to use, such as network routing protocols or network encryption protocols.
  - *Vendor standards* Statements that specify which vendors are used for various products and services. For instance, an organization might establish Cisco Systems as a networking equipment vendor.
- **Guidelines** Optional guidance on how policies and standards can be carried out.
- ***Program charter*** A formal document describing a privacy (or any other) program, including mission and objectives, roles and responsibilities, principal processes and procedures, *program management*, and the location of documentation and records.
- **Risk register** A living business record containing all risks identified to date, along with detailed information about each.
- **Event logs** Usually found in information systems, event logs contain the individual events, such as login attempts, permission changes, changes to data, and configuration changes.
- ***Corrective action plan*** A plan of action that describes steps to be taken to correct a defect or anomaly.
- ***Preventive action plan*** A plan of action that describes steps to be taken to prevent an incident, defect, or anomaly.

- *Contracts* Binding legal agreements between organizations that are enforceable in a court of law.
- **Meeting minutes** A written record of the proceedings of official meetings.
- **Decision log** A written record of key decisions made, such as risk treatment decisions (these are also to be included in a risk register).
- **Issues log** A written record of program-level issues that must be dealt with at some point.

The annual review of documents is a recommended practice to ensure that policies, standards, procedures, and related materials are current. Auditors often consider any document not reviewed in over a year as ineffective.

Regulations and standards often include explicit and implicit requirements for the existence of documentation and records.

Summary

Privacy governance is the set of established governance activities that provide management with visibility and control over an organization's privacy program and operations. Governance begins with the development of strategic objectives that are translated into action plans, roles and responsibilities, policies, procedures, standards, and guidelines.

Privacy governance cannot succeed in the absence of data, security, and IT governance, all of which should be considered prerequisites. Factors influencing privacy governance include the nature of personal information, applicable laws, risk appetite, and societal expectations.

Activities required to protect personal information include risk management, process management, event management, incident response, metrics and reporting, resource management, and monitoring.

A privacy program must be business-aligned; that is, it supports the organization's mission, goals, objectives, culture, and practices. Further, a privacy program must operate within an organization's risk appetite, tolerance, and capacity.

A strategy is a plan to achieve an objective. Organizations building or improving their privacy programs develop a strategy to implement new and improved policies, practices, processes, records, tools, and more. To develop a strategy, it's necessary to define the desired future state of a privacy program, understand its current state, and perform a gap analysis to detail the improvements needed. Resources that describe the current state include risk assessments, threat assessments, vulnerability assessments, maturity assessments, risk register, audits, policies, standards, processes, architecture, controls, staff skills and knowledge, metrics and reports, business impact analysis, and culture.

A strengths, weaknesses, opportunities, and threats (SWOT) diagram can help a strategist visually understand a current privacy program. A maturity model can help a strategist better understand the maturity level of various components of privacy operations.

Armed with the foregoing, a strategist will develop a roadmap, which is a detailed plan of action to achieve the desired future state of the privacy program. Often, the privacy leader will need to develop a business case to sell the plan to executive management, who will need to provide resources for the strategy to be implemented.

Privacy leaders must recognize expected pockets of resistance to a strategic plan, including basic human resistance to change, as well as culture, organizational structure, staff capabilities, budget, time, and organizational priorities. Privacy is rarely a top priority in any organization.

Personal information is information about people, often including considerable detail, such as non-public information, such as addresses, phone numbers, health, financial, political, religious, sexual, and other details. There is no single universal definition of personal information, although definitions in various laws, regulations, and standards share recurring elements.

Several privacy operational practices have been developed over the years and are described in various standards. These practices include privacy by design, consent, transparency, legal basis, and legitimate interest. Privacy principles have been developed and published by ISACA, OECD, FAIR, and others.

As defined by NIST, privacy engineering principles are predictability, manageability, and disassociability. Privacy engineering is managed through privacy governance, including policies, roles and responsibilities, and processes such as the systems development lifecycle.

Numerous privacy laws and regulations exist today, including the European General Data Protection Regulation (GDPR), the California Privacy Rights Act (CPRA), the Health Insurance Portability and Accountability Act (HIPAA), the Health Information Technology for Economic and Clinical Health Act (HITECH), the U.S. Fair Credit Reporting Act, the Canadian Personal Information Protection and Electronic Documents Act (PIPEDA), the China Cyber Security and Personal Information Protection Laws, the Brazil General Data Protection Law (LGPD), and many others.

Privacy programs will have numerous documents and records, including policies, standards, guidelines, processes, procedures, a program charter, a risk register, event logs, corrective and preventive action plans, contracts, meeting minutes, a decision log, and an issues log.

Exam Essentials

Understand the purpose of privacy governance. Privacy governance provides structure, oversight, and accountability for how personal information is collected, used, protected, and managed. It ensures alignment with business objectives, regulatory requirements, and stakeholder expectations.

Know the components of a privacy program. A privacy program includes policies, standards, procedures, controls, metrics, and reporting mechanisms that collectively govern the collection, handling, and protection of personal information. These components must be applied consistently and reviewed regularly.

Understand the definition and scope of personal information. Personal information refers to data that identifies or can be linked to an individual, directly or indirectly. Definitions vary across laws, but generally include identifiers, sensitive attributes, and contextual data.

Understand the key privacy principles. Core principles such as privacy by design, transparency, consent, purpose limitation, and data minimization guide responsible data handling. These principles translate legal and ethical expectations into operational practices.

Understand lawful bases for processing personal data. Under regulations such as GDPR, processing must be justified by a lawful basis (e.g., consent, contract, legal obligation, legitimate interests). Consent is only one option and must meet strict requirements when used.

Recognize the role of governance structures and accountability. Effective privacy governance includes clearly defined roles such as data owners, privacy officers, and oversight bodies. Models such as the three lines of defense help ensure accountability and independent assurance.

Understand the role of privacy documentation and records. Documentation such as policies, notices, risk registers, and decision logs provides evidence of compliance and supports consistent operations. Records must be maintained, current, and aligned with regulatory expectations.

Review Questions

1. What is the primary purpose of privacy governance in an organization?
   - A. To implement security controls for IT systems
   - B. To ensure alignment of privacy practices with business objectives and legal requirements
   - C. To eliminate all privacy risks
   - D. To centralize all data processing activities
2. Which of the following best describes personal information?
   - A. Any data stored in a database
   - B. Data that is encrypted
   - C. Information that identifies or can be linked to an individual
   - D. Only financial and medical records
3. Under GDPR, which of the following is NOT a lawful basis for processing personal data?
   - A. Consent
   - B. Contractual necessity
   - C. Legitimate interests
   - D. Business convenience
4. Which privacy principle requires that personal data be collected only for specific, defined purposes?
   - A. Transparency
   - B. Purpose limitation
   - C. Data minimization
   - D. Accountability
5. What is the primary responsibility of the first line of defense in privacy governance?
   - A. Conduct independent audits
   - B. Define policies and standards
   - C. Implement and operate privacy controls
   - D. Report to regulators
6. Which of the following is a key characteristic of valid consent under GDPR?
   - A. Implied through inactivity
   - B. Freely given and specific
   - C. Permanent and irrevocable
   - D. Required for all processing activities

7. What is the primary role of the second line of defense?
   A. Execute business processes
   B. Provide independent assurance
   C. Establish policies and monitor compliance
   D. Perform system administration
8. Which document describes how an organization collects, uses, and shares personal information externally?
   A. Internal audit report
   B. Risk register
   C. Privacy notice
   D. Incident log
9. What is the main objective of privacy by design?
   A. Add privacy controls after deployment
   B. Minimize system costs
   C. Embed privacy into system from the start
   D. Eliminate the need for consent
10. Which of the following best describes data minimization?
    A. Encrypt all data
    B. Retain data indefinitely
    C. Collect only the data necessary for a specific purpose
    D. Share data across departments
11. What is the purpose of a risk register in a privacy program?
    A. Store personal data
    B. Track identified risks and treatment decisions
    C. Log system events
    D. Record employee training
12. Which of the following is the best example of transparency?
    A. Encrypting data
    B. Publishing a clear privacy notice
    C. Conducting internal audits
    D. Limiting data access

13. What is the primary function of internal audit in privacy governance?
    A. Implement controls
    B. Monitor daily operations
    C. Provide independent assurance
    D. Define policies

14. Which of the following best describes "legal basis" under GDPR?
    A. A justification for collecting personal data
    B. A contractual agreement with vendors
    C. A privacy policy requirement
    D. A security control framework

15. What is the primary purpose of a Data Protection Impact Assessment (DPIA)?
    A. Monitor employee performance
    B. Identify and mitigate privacy risks in processing activities
    C. Audit financial systems
    D. Classify data assets

16. Which of the following best describes accountability in privacy governance?
    A. Delegating all responsibility to IT
    B. Documenting and demonstrating compliance with privacy requirements
    C. Eliminating all risks
    D. Avoiding regulatory oversight

17. Which privacy law introduced the concept of Sensitive Personal Information (SPI) in California?
    A. HIPAA
    B. GDPR
    C. CPRA
    D. FCRA

18. What is the primary purpose of privacy documentation?
    A. Replace operational controls
    B. Provide evidence and guidance for consistent practices
    C. Eliminate audits
    D. Reduce system complexity

19. Which of the following best describes the difference between data and information?
    - A. Data is always structured; information is not
    - B. Data is raw; information is data with context and meaning
    - C. Information is always digital
    - D. There is no difference

20. Which lifecycle phase focuses on evaluating control effectiveness and identifying gaps?
    - A. Initiation
    - B. Design
    - C. Monitoring
    - D. Implementation

Answers to Review Questions

1. B. Privacy governance establishes the framework through which an organization manages personal information in alignment with its strategic objectives, regulatory obligations, and stakeholder expectations. It defines roles, policies, and oversight mechanisms to ensure that privacy is consistently addressed across the enterprise. It does not eliminate all risk; instead, it ensures that risks are identified, managed, and monitored appropriately.

2. C. Personal information encompasses any data that can directly or indirectly identify an individual, including names, identifiers, location data, and behavioral attributes. It is broader than just sensitive categories such as financial or medical records. It includes any information that can reasonably be associated with a person, either alone or in combination with other data.

3. D. GDPR specifies six lawful bases for processing personal data: consent, contract, legal obligation, vital interests, public task, and legitimate interests. Business convenience is not recognized as a lawful basis, emphasizing that organizations must justify processing with clearly defined legal grounds rather than operational preference or efficiency.

4. B. Purpose limitation requires organizations to define and document the specific purposes for which personal data is collected and to ensure that data is not used in ways incompatible with those purposes. This principle prevents function creep and helps maintain trust by ensuring that individuals' data is not repurposed without appropriate justification.

5. C. The first line of defense consists of business and operational teams that handle personal information in their daily activities. These teams are responsible for implementing privacy controls, adhering to policies, and managing risks across their processes. They are accountable for ensuring that personal data is handled appropriately at the point of use.

6. B. Valid consent under the GDPR must be freely given, specific, informed, and unambiguous, and, in some cases, explicit. It must also be revocable at any time. Consent cannot be assumed through silence or inactivity, and it is only one of several lawful bases for processing, not a universal requirement.

7. C. The second line of defense includes privacy, compliance, and risk management functions that define policies, provide guidance, and monitor adherence to requirements. They support the first line by interpreting regulations, advising on risks, and ensuring that controls are appropriately designed and functioning.

8. C. A privacy notice, also known as a notice of privacy practices (NOPP), informs individuals about how their personal information is collected, used, shared, and protected. It is a key mechanism for transparency and is often legally required. It differs from internal documents in that it focuses on external communication with data subjects.

9. C. Privacy by design requires that privacy considerations be incorporated into systems, processes, and products from the outset, rather than added later. This proactive approach reduces risk, improves compliance, and ensures that privacy protections are integral to how systems operate.

10. C. Data minimization limits the collection, use, and retention of personal data to what is strictly necessary to achieve a defined purpose. This reduces exposure, lowers risk, and supports compliance with regulatory requirements that discourage excessive data collection.

11. B. A risk register is a structured record of identified risks, their likelihood and impact, and the decisions made to mitigate or accept them. In a privacy context, it helps ensure that risks to individuals are systematically identified, evaluated, and managed over time.

12. B. Transparency involves clearly informing individuals about how their personal data is collected, used, and shared. A privacy notice is a primary tool for achieving transparency, enabling individuals to understand and exercise their rights.

13. C. Internal audit serves as the third line of defense and provides independent assurance that governance, risk management, and control processes are effective. It evaluates whether privacy controls are properly designed and operating as intended.

14. A. A legal basis under GDPR is the lawful justification for processing personal data. Organizations must identify and document a valid legal basis before processing, ensuring that the activity is permitted under the regulation.

15. B. A DPIA is a structured process used to identify, assess, and mitigate risks to individuals arising from data processing activities, particularly those that are high risk. It supports compliance and helps organizations proactively address privacy concerns.

16. B. Accountability requires organizations not only to comply with privacy requirements but also to demonstrate that compliance through documentation, controls, and evidence. This includes maintaining records, conducting assessments, and showing that appropriate governance is in place.

17. C. The California Privacy Rights Act (CPRA) expanded the CCPA by introducing the concept of Sensitive Personal Information (SPI), which includes categories such as precise geolocation data and financial data. It also provides additional rights to limit the use of such information.

18. B. Privacy documentation, including policies, procedures, and records, ensures consistent practices and provides evidence of compliance. It supports governance, facilitates audits, and helps organizations demonstrate accountability.

19. B. Data consists of raw values or observations, while information is created when data is processed and interpreted within a context. This distinction is important because privacy obligations typically apply to meaningful information about individuals.

20. C. The monitoring phase involves assessing the performance and effectiveness of privacy controls through metrics, audits, and reviews. It identifies gaps, weaknesses, and areas for improvement, enabling the organization to maintain compliance and strengthen its privacy program over time.

Privacy Operations

This chapter covers CDPSE Domain 1, "Privacy Governance," specifically the "Privacy Operations" subdomain.

This chapter covers these job practice elements:

✔ *B—PRIVACY OPERATIONS*

1. *Organizational Culture, Structure, and Responsibilities*
2. *Vendor and Supply Chain Management*
3. *Incident Management*
4. *Data Subject Rights, Requests, and Notification*

The other subdomain in Domain 1, Privacy Governance, is:

✔ *A—PRIVACY GOVERNANCE*—covered in Chapter 1.

The CDPSE Task Statements relevant to this domain are:

2. *Review organizational programs to align with privacy-related legal and regulatory requirements, industry best practices (e.g., privacy by design), and data subject's expectations.*
10. *Participate in the incident management process to address privacy impacts and support remediation.*

The topics in this chapter and in Chapter 1 account for 20% of the CDPSE examination.

This section addresses Privacy Operations within Domain 1, focusing on how organizations operationalize privacy governance through defined structures, processes, and controls. It examines the roles and responsibilities that support a privacy program, including coordination across business, legal, security, and compliance functions. The chapter also covers vendor and supply chain management, emphasizing due diligence, contractual safeguards, and ongoing oversight of third parties. Incident management is explored in the context of detecting, responding to, and reporting privacy events. Finally, the chapter addresses data subject rights, including mechanisms for intake, authentication, response, and notification. Together, these topics establish the operational capabilities needed to execute and sustain an effective, accountable privacy program.

While not explicitly part of the CDPSE job practice, this chapter begins with a narrative explaining steps to build a privacy operation. This can be helpful for privacy leaders who need to build a privacy operation from scratch.

Building a Privacy Operation

A privacy operation consists of activities to ensure that *data collection* and the use of personal information comply with privacy policies and applicable regulations. Privacy operations are often implemented in an oversight capacity or as an "overlay" in an organization. Often this is implemented through the formation of a *privacy office*, led by the organization's privacy leader (often, but not always, the CPO or DPO), and a team of one or more analysts. The privacy office serves as a catalyst to ensure that the intake, processing, and disposal of personal information throughout the organization are handled properly, in accordance with the organization's privacy policy, which should align with applicable privacy laws and other contractual and legal obligations.

It is said that, like information security, privacy is "everyone's job." This means that the procedures and practices followed by all persons involved in processing personal information include measures to ensure that personal information is used only in officially sanctioned ways. The main function of the privacy office is to ensure this ongoing outcome.

An organization establishing a privacy office needs to define the scope of its responsibilities. In smaller organizations, the scope typically includes all business operations across all locations. In larger organizations, particularly those with a presence in one or more countries with strict privacy laws (such as the GDPR), the organization can appoint local privacy personnel in each local country. This can help better align local business operations with local laws and requirements.

There is no single approach to implementing privacy operations in an organization. Some will designate separate staff, while others will appoint existing staff with various privacy-related responsibilities.

Identifying Privacy Requirements

Before the privacy office can begin enforcing privacy-related activities within an organization, it must first identify and document the requirements that define the specifics of the collection, protection, and use of personal information.

Culture and Values

At the risk of implying a "motherhood and apple pie" sentiment, it's necessary to consult with the organization's culture and stated values as a starting point. Culture and values define the personality and uniqueness of an organization; the way that the organization values its assets, including the personal information of its customers, constituents, and employees, should be reflected in its policies and requirements.

Applicable Regulations

All regulations that apply to the organization need to be identified. This includes industry-specific regulations such as GLBA and HIPAA, as well as geographically specific regulations such as the Personal Information Protection and Electronic Documents Act (PIPEDA), the California Consumer Privacy Act (CCPA), and the GDPR. These and other regulations are cited and described in Chapter 1.

Privacy regulations are evolving at a rapid pace. Organizations need an established system to keep them informed about new and changing regulations on information privacy and cybersecurity. Cybersecurity professionals and lawyers each have their industry news sources; at present, the best sources appear to be newsletters and paid subscriptions from legal sources that keep their subscribers up to date on new laws and related developments. It is recommended that organizations maintain an official inventory of applicable laws and regulations related to cybersecurity and privacy; depending on the organization's industry sector, this inventory can also include other industry-specific topics.

Legal Interpretation

It's advisable to engage internal or external legal counsel to provide an interpretation of privacy and cybersecurity laws. Legal counsel experienced in these fields should first provide guidance on the applicability of these laws. For those laws deemed applicable, legal counsel should then guide the organization on the meaning of the relevant provisions and how to implement them.

As the de facto risk officer, an organization's legal counsel is responsible for identifying legal and regulatory requirements and risks. In this capacity, legal counsel determines which laws apply and what the organization should do to comply with them. Like individuals in other professions, legal counsel will often confer with their industry peers and outside experts to gauge the consensus on the applicability and compliance approach to new and existing laws.

Legal interpretation of applicable regulations is a key function that organizations need to acquire with in-house or external legal counsel.

Cybersecurity Policies, Requirements, and Regulations

As is often cited in this book, it's impossible to implement privacy successfully without also implementing effective cybersecurity. For the protective aspect of information privacy, organizations also need to identify their cybersecurity practices, policies, requirements, and applicable regulations, and implement them through cyber-risk management and cybersecurity operations. If the protective side of privacy fails, the proper handling side will be at risk of failure due to unintended disclosures of personal information.

Organizations operating in the United States and the European Union might find it easier to apply their updated GDPR-compliant operations across the entire organization, rather than operating one way for EU-citizen data and another for non-EU-citizen data.

Developing Privacy Policies

Privacy policies are statements that describe the collection and use of personal information, as well as the actions that individuals can take to inquire about and request their personal information. If the organization collects personal information only from its internal workers, this policy might not be publicly available. If the organization collects information from external customers and constituents, its privacy policy will likely be published publicly, often on a website. Similarly, organizations that collect information from customers in person often post privacy notices prominently.

Organizations that collect personal information from persons outside the organization often also have internal, non-public privacy policies that affect their employees and other workers. Such policies, such as cybersecurity policies, will describe the required characteristics and expectations for staff members and for the organization's information systems.

If an organization that processes personal information employs any service providers that also store, process, or have access to the personal information used by the organization, the organization will also impose requirements upon those service providers. This aspect is discussed later in this chapter in the section, "Vendor and Supply Chain Management."

Internal Privacy Policy

Virtually all organizations possess information about their employees and other workers that is used in their role as employers. In many countries, those organizations are required to disclose to their employees that the organization has a confidentiality policy and that its workers' personal information is used only in its role as an employer.

Organizations lacking a formal privacy program often stop there and make no further attempts to define the meaning or enforcement of "for sanctioned business purposes only." This can, however, lead to improper use of personal information through tactical decisions made by nearly any staff members who might have some or no knowledge about applicable laws on this topic.

Organizations with more mature security and privacy programs will have detailed privacy policies that define expected behaviors of their workers and the required characteristics of their information systems. In many cases, their privacy policies will be part of their information security policies to protect that information. On the minimum side, security or privacy policies will include general statements that sensitive or personal information shall be used "for sanctioned business purposes only," without further detail.

Whether a part of an organization's information security policy or separate, an internal privacy policy should include content on the following topics:

- **Roles and responsibilities for the organization's privacy program** This should include:
  - Those who have data management responsibilities
  - Those who approve and review access to personal information
  - Those who review and approve of new uses for personal data
  - Those who receive and process subject data requests
  - Those who have responsibility for monitoring uses of personal data
  - Those who have responsibility for responding to incidents that represent the misuse of personal information
  - Those who review privacy business processes
  - Those who audit privacy business processes
- **Business processes governing the use of personal information** This should include periodic reviews of business processes to ensure that they remain compliant with applicable laws and regulations.

- **Protection of personal information** Generally, this will fall back to the organization's information security policy. However, this language can be included in its privacy policy (organizations are cautioned against duplicating it, as it will require care to keep both policies in sync).
- **Consequences for violations of privacy policy** Like an information security policy and other policies, this will describe the range of possible outcomes when persons are found to have violated the privacy policy. Typically, this ranges from verbal warnings to written warnings and even termination of employment.
- **Review and audit of privacy business processes** This will describe reviews and audits of privacy business processes. Process owners will typically conduct reviews to confirm that all necessary actions are taken. Audits of privacy business processes will be performed by persons outside of the organization's privacy office.
- **Measurements of privacy business processes** Any statistics, metrics, key performance indicators (KPIs), and key risk indicators (KRIs) required in the privacy program will be described here.
- **Citations of applicable regulations and other obligations** Privacy policy can be a place where applicable laws, regulations, and other obligations (such as terms and conditions in contracts with other organizations) are cited.

Some organizations will develop a privacy program charter. This high-level document describes the privacy program's goals, roles and responsibilities, authorities, key business processes, and other program-related matters. Other organizations will include these items in their internal privacy policies.

External Privacy Policy

Organizations that collect personal information about individuals outside the organization develop privacy policies that are accessible to those individuals. For organizations that sell products or services to the general public, the privacy policy is often available on a public website. It might also be posted on the premises where these products or services are sold.

Privacy laws enacted in many regions of the world have brought about the near-universality of public-facing privacy policies posted on websites or as visible notices at business locations. Driven by these privacy laws, public-facing privacy policies generally include the following:

- Descriptions of the methods used to collect personal information
- Descriptions of the methods used to protect personal information
- Descriptions of primary and secondary uses of personal information
- Descriptions of any international transfers of personal information
- Descriptions of any third parties that might store or process personal information on behalf of the organization

- Descriptions of any tracking or logging of activities performed by the organization, such as the use of web browser cookies
- Any procedures that might be available for persons to understand how their personal information has been used or is being used
- Statements describing the legal rights of data subjects concerning the organization's use of their personal data, often including several subsections for specific regions or localities
- Contact information or contact procedures for persons who want to initiate subject data requests, inquiries, or lodge complaints regarding the organization's use of their personal information
- Contact information or contact procedures for regulators or other authorities to whom persons can make inquiries or lodge complaints regarding the organization's collection or use of their personal information
- The date that the privacy policy was last updated

Some privacy laws require an organization to inform employees, customers, or constituents if it changes its privacy policy. For regulations that require organizations to collect an acknowledgment confirming that data subjects have received the privacy policy, those organizations must collect a new acknowledgment for the updated privacy policy. In business applications, this often appears as a brief statement that reads, "Continued use of this application constitutes consent to our updated privacy policy," with a link to the privacy policy. Alternatively, organizations can send email notices to system users about the updated privacy policy; the policy itself is often not included in the message, but links are provided to access it.

Like other aspects of service and service levels, organization privacy practices can soon become competitive differentiators.

Developing and Running Data Protection Operations

The protection of personal data is one of the primary responsibilities of an organization's information security function. In most organizations, this function is separate from the privacy office or privacy operations.

- Data protection operations are generally built on a framework of security controls. Security and privacy control frameworks are discussed in Chapter 4.
- The IT department typically manages data protection technologies, although in some organizations a separate security operations function manages them. The technology of data protection is discussed more fully in Chapters 5 and 6.
- Decisions regarding the ongoing development of security and privacy controls are a part of the larger risk management lifecycle, described in Chapter 3.

Information security management is discussed in greater detail in this author's textbooks on the CISM and CRISC certifications, the *CISM Certified Information Security Manager All-In-One Exam Guide* (McGraw-Hill), and *CRISC Certified in Risk and Information Systems Control Study Guide* (Wiley).

Developing and Running Data Monitoring Operations

Monitoring the use of personal data is at the core of many organizations' privacy programs. Since privacy concerns the protection and use of personal information, some privacy operations differ uniquely from operational security processes.

Data Discovery Scanning

To determine whether personnel are complying with privacy and data classification policies, organizations will conduct *data discovery* scans of their data storage. Typically performed by automated *data loss prevention (DLP)* scanning tools, these scans generally target file shares and other structured and unstructured repositories, employing rules to identify specific types of information.

Examples of scan targets include account numbers, credit card numbers, and government-issued identification numbers, to discover whether files containing personal information have been stored on file shares in violation of policy. Scans can also include nonpersonal information such as source code, financial information, and intellectual property.

Upon receiving the results of discovery scans, security or privacy analysts will investigate the presence of these files and attempt to determine why those files are there, who put them there, and why. Where such files are used as part of sanctioned business processes, security or privacy analysts will confirm that access rights comply with access policies, including the principles of least privilege and need-to-know. Where such files are not a part of legitimate business processes, corrective action is taken to prevent such security or privacy issues from recurring.

Data discovery often identifies undocumented procedures and improper behaviors. Over time, corrective actions will gradually improve the maturity of related business processes and inform staff of proper data-handling policies and procedures.

Privacy regulations are not always explicit about which data fields are considered personal information. Legal counsel might be needed to clarify this so that privacy operations can be sure they are monitoring effectively.

Data Movement Monitoring

Information systems can be supplemented with DLP tooling that will monitor the movement of sensitive and personal information in real time. Monitoring agents placed in key information systems can detect the creation, movement, and deletion of specific information and generate alerts that are sent to security or privacy personnel for investigation and follow-up.

The following are examples of data movement monitoring:

- **Email** Agents on endpoints can detect sensitive information in the contents of incoming or outgoing email.
- **Endpoint storage** Agents on endpoints can detect the local storage of information.
- **File servers** Agents on file servers and other storage systems can detect the creation and movement of information.
- **USB storage** Agents on endpoints can detect the movement of information to and from external USB storage devices.
- **Internet ingress/egress** Agents on endpoints and network ingress/egress points (including Internet connections) can monitor data movement.

In all these cases (and more that are not mentioned here), alerts can be sent to security or privacy analysts who would investigate these events to determine whether the data movement is legitimate (in which case, alerts can be adjusted to reduce the number of "false positives") or whether corrective action is warranted.

In addition to monitoring the movement of sensitive information, DLP monitoring agents can be configured to intervene and prevent attempts to move data. When implementing these DLP systems, organizations often configure them initially to operate in passive monitoring mode to help them understand and distinguish legitimate business processes from policy violations. Then, organizations can carefully configure DLP agents to intervene when data movement constitutes a policy violation.

In end-user systems, DLP agents often display a window to the end user requesting confirmation of the intended data movement. While the agents do not overtly block such data movement, asking for confirmation can remind users that some data movement can violate policy. Still, in some circumstances, users can be empowered to confirm that the intended data movement is legitimate. This action will still trigger an event or alert that can be investigated to determine whether the user is violating policy. If the movement is legitimate, privacy and security analysts can determine whether users should continue to confirm such data movement or whether the movement can be permitted without further intervention.

DLP systems, whether used to perform discovery scans or monitor data movement, require a good deal of "tuning" to ensure they do not interfere with legitimate business processes while properly alerting personnel to potential violations of data classification or privacy policies. Because business processes typically change slowly over time, the task of tuning DLP is never finished and is an ongoing activity.

Organizational Culture, Structure, and Responsibilities

Organization operations are defined by their culture, structures, and defined roles and responsibilities. Privacy leaders building, improving, and operating privacy programs must be acutely aware of these organizational aspects and able to drive change when needed.

Culture

Culture can be thought of as the behavioral norms within an organization—in other words, how people work and treat one another. Many books have been written about culture—what it is, how it works, and how to change it. Privacy leaders must understand the culture of the organization they work in to ensure that their efforts to build or improve a privacy program will succeed.

Culture is multifaceted and involves several aspects of behavior, including:

- **Empowerment** Whether management trusts their teams to make sound decisions.
- **Compliance** The degree to which the organization stresses the need to comply with organizational policy as well as applicable laws.
- **Collaboration** How much will staff members and managers help each other and work together on projects and tasks, including the degree of cooperation.
- **Accountability** The degree to which employees, including top executives, are held accountable for outcomes they contribute to. This is balanced by "blame-free" cultures in which employees need not fear taking risks.
- **Politics** How much "office politics" determines the degree of collaboration and empowerment, and how much management plays "favorites."

External factors influence an organization's culture, including:

- **Business health** Organizational culture reflects the health of the business. An organization in financial distress might have a culture laced with fear if budget cuts, hiring freezes, or layoffs are anticipated.
- **Industry sector** Culture in organizations in heavily regulated industries such as healthcare and financial services might suffer if they are experiencing regulatory fatigue. On the other hand, such organizations can have a positive culture if other factors, such as empowerment and collaboration, are positive.

Executives and owners set the tone and the culture in an organization, although I have observed organizations whose "stated culture" is far different from its "actual culture."

Some organizations publish a *corporate values statement* (also called a mission statement) that includes tactical statements, such as "We respect each other" and "Everyone will be heard."

A *code of ethics* (also known as a code of conduct) can influence corporate culture. A code of ethics is a formal statement that defines acceptable and unacceptable professional conduct. Many organizations include annual ethics training and require employees to acknowledge in writing their understanding of the code of ethics.

Structure

The structure of an organization often brings to mind the *organization chart*, which serves as a formal command-and-control structure. The "org chart" structure is used in many business processes, such as access control requests and approvals, employee performance reviews, expense report approvals, and more. Some larger organizations employ *matrix management*, in which staff members report to a manager, but work on a project team with its own leader. Figure 2.1 depicts a matrix organization. There might be other ways to organize a corporate structure, but such discussion goes beyond the purpose of this book.

In addition to the org chart, many organizations employ other types of groupings of personnel, including:

- **Steering committees** These are groups of stakeholders with advisory or decision-making authority, often serving in a governance function. Examples include a privacy steering committee and an IT steering committee.
- **Project teams** These are groups of staff members (and occasionally managers) contributing to a project. Project teams are temporary: they have a beginning and an end.

FIGURE 2.1 A matrix management organization.

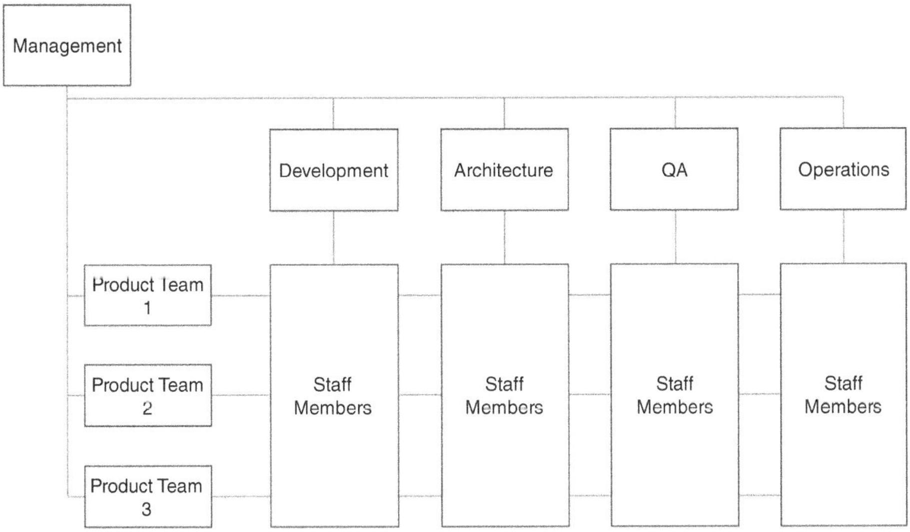

Source: Author.

- **Task groups** These are groups of staff members brought together to complete a task. These are smaller than projects and often lack a project manager, a project schedule, or other project artifacts.

Privacy Roles and Responsibilities

Privacy and information security governance are most effective when every person in the organization knows what is expected of them. More mature organizations develop formal roles and responsibilities that establish clear expectations for personnel regarding their part in all matters related to the protection and proper use of systems and personal information.

In the context of organizational structure and behavior, a *role* is a description of normal activities that employees are obliged to perform as part of their employment. Roles are typically associated with a *job* or *position title*, a label assigned to each person that designates their place in the organization. Organizations strive to adhere to more or less standard position titles so that other people in the organization, upon knowing someone's position title, will have at least a general idea of a person's role in the organization.

Typical roles include the following:

- IT auditor
- Systems engineer
- Privacy analyst
- Accounts receivable manager
- Individual contributor

Often, a position title also includes a person's *rank*, which denotes their seniority, placement within a command-and-control hierarchy, span of control, or any combination of these. Typical ranks include the following, in order of increasing seniority:

- Supervisor
- Manager
- Senior manager
- Director
- Senior director
- Executive director
- Vice president
- Senior vice president
- Executive vice president
- President
- Chief executive officer
- Member, board of directors
- Chairman, board of directors

This should not be considered a complete listing of ranks. Larger organizations also include the modifiers *assistant* (as in assistant director), *general* (general manager), *associate* (a junior position), and *first* (first vice president).

A *responsibility* is a statement of outcomes that a person is expected to support. As with roles, responsibilities are typically documented in position and *job descriptions*. Typical responsibilities include the following:

- Perform monthly corporate expense reconciliation
- Troubleshoot network faults and develop solutions
- Audit internal privacy controls and prepare exception reports

In addition to specific responsibilities associated with individual position titles, organizations typically also include general responsibilities in all position titles. Examples include the following:

- Understand and conform to information security policy, data protection policy, harassment policy, and other policies
- Understand and conform to a code of ethics and behavior

In the context of privacy and information security, an organization assigns roles and responsibilities to individuals and groups to meet the organization's privacy and security strategies and objectives.

RACI Charts

Many organizations use the *Responsible-Accountable-Consulted-Informed (RACI)* model to define key responsibilities across business processes, projects, tasks, and other activities. A RACI chart assigns levels of responsibility to individuals and groups. Developing a RACI chart helps personnel determine roles for various business activities. A typical RACI chart is shown in the following table:

Activity	Responsible	Accountable	Consulted	Informed
Request user account	End user	End user manager	IT service desk, end user manager	Asset owner, security team
Approve user account	Asset owner	Chief operating officer	End user manager, security team	End user, internal audit, IT service desk
Provision user account	IT service desk	IT service manager	Asset owner	End user, end user manager, security team, privacy team
Audit user account	Internal auditor	Internal audit manager	Asset owner, privacy manager	IT service desk, IT service manager, end user manager, privacy team

The same RACI chart can also be depicted as a second example in the next table. This RACI chart specifies the roles carried out by several parties in the user account access request process:

Activity	End User	Manager	IT Service Desk	IT Service Manager	Asset Owner	COO	Internal Audit	Audit Manager	Security Team	Privacy Team
Request user account	R	A	I		I				I	
Approve user account	I	C	I	I	R	A	I		C	
Provision user account	I	I	R	A	C				I	I
Audit user account		I	I	I	C		R	A	I	C

The meanings of the four roles in a RACI chart are as follows:

- **Responsible (R)** The person or group that performs the actual work or task.
- **Accountable (A)** The person who is ultimately answerable for complete, accurate, and timely execution of the work. This person often manages those in the Responsible role.
- **Consulted (C)** One or more people or groups who are consulted for their opinions, experience, or insight. People in the Consulted role can be subject-matter experts for the work or task, or owners, stewards, or custodians of an asset associated with it. Communication with the Consulted role is two-way.
- **Informed (I)** One or more people or groups who are informed by those in other roles. Depending on the process or task, the Informed role can be told of an activity before, during, or after completion. Communication with Informed is one-way.

Several considerations must be considered when assigning roles to individuals and groups in a RACI chart, including the following:

- **Skills** Some or all individuals in a team assignment, as well as specifically named individuals, need the skills, training, and competence to carry out required tasks.

- **Segregation of duties** Critical tasks, such as user account provisioning the RACI chart depicted earlier, must be free of segregation-of-duties conflicts. This means that two or more individuals or groups are required to carry out a critical task. In this example, the requestor, approver, and provisioner cannot be the same person or group.
- **Conflict of interest** Critical tasks must not be assigned to individuals or groups when such assignments will create conflicts of interest. For example, a user who is an approver cannot approve a request for their own access. In this case, a different person must approve the request—while also avoiding a segregation-of-duties conflict.

There are some variations of the RACI model, including PARIS (Participant, Accountable, Review Required, Input Required, Sign-off Required) and PACSI (Perform, Accountable, Control, Suggest, Informed).

Board of Directors

The board of directors in an organization is a body that oversees its activities. Depending on the type of organization, board members can be elected by shareholders or constituents or appointed. This role can be either paid or voluntary.

Activities performed by the board of directors, as well as directors' authority, are usually defined by a constitution, bylaws, or external regulation. The board of directors is typically accountable to the organization's owners or, in the case of a government body, to the electorate.

In many cases, board members have a *fiduciary duty*. This means they are accountable to shareholders or constituents for acting in the best interests of the organization, with no appearance of impropriety, conflict of interest, or ill-gotten profit.

In nongovernment organizations, the board of directors is responsible for appointing a chief executive officer (CEO) and possibly other executives. The CEO, then, is accountable to the board of directors and carries out the board's directives. Board members can also be selected for any of the following reasons:

- **Investor representation** One or more board members can be appointed by significant investors to give them control over the organization's strategy and direction.
- **Business experience** Board members bring outside business management experience, which helps them develop successful business strategies for the organization.
- **Access to resources** Board members bring business connections, including additional investors, business partners, suppliers, or customers.

Often, one or more board members will have business finance experience, bringing financial management oversight to the organization. For U.S. public companies, the Sarbanes-Oxley Act requires boards to form an audit committee, and one or more audit committee members must have financial management experience. External financial audits and internal audit activities are often accountable directly to the audit committee, which provides direct oversight of the organization's financial management. As issues of privacy and information security become more prevalent in executive-level discussions, some organizations have added a board member who is technically savvy or have formed an additional committee, often referred to as the technology risk committee.

The board of directors is generally expected to require that the CEO and other executives implement a corporate *governance* framework to ensure executive management has appropriate visibility and control over the organization's operations. Executives are accountable to the board of directors to demonstrate that they are effectively carrying out the board's strategies.

Many, if not most, organizations are highly dependent on information technology for their daily operations. Many also process personal information for their workforce and often for their customers or constituents. As a result, privacy and information security are important topics for boards of directors. Today's standard of due care for corporate boards requires that they incorporate privacy and information security considerations into the strategies they develop and the oversight they exercise over their organizations. In its publication, *Director's Handbook on Cyber-Risk Oversight*, the National Association of Corporate Directors (NACD, at nacdonline.org) has developed six principles about the importance of information security:

- **Principle 1** Directors need to understand and approach cybersecurity as a strategic, enterprise risk, not just an IT risk.
- **Principle 2** Directors should understand the legal implications of cyber risks as they relate to their company's specific circumstances.
- **Principle 3** Boards should have adequate access to cybersecurity expertise, and discussions about cyber-risk management should be given regular and adequate time on board meeting agendas.
- **Principle 4** Directors should set the expectation that management will establish an enterprise-wide, cyber-risk management framework and reporting structure with adequate staffing and budget.
- **Principle 5** Board management discussions about cyber risk should include identification and quantification of financial exposure to cyber risks and which risks to accept, mitigate, or transfer, such as through insurance, as well as specific plans associated with each approach.
- **Principle 6** Boards should encourage systemic resilience through collaboration with their industry and government peers and encourage the same from their management teams.

The wording of these information security principles makes them entirely relevant to the mission of protecting personal information and to its proper usage.

Executive Management

Executive management is responsible for carrying out directives issued by the board of directors. In the context of privacy and information security management, this includes ensuring that the organization has sufficient resources available to implement privacy and security programs and to develop and maintain controls to protect critical assets and personal information.

Executive management must ensure that priorities are balanced. In the case of IT, privacy, and security, these functions are usually tightly coupled, but are sometimes in conflict. IT's primary mission is the development and operation of business-enabling capabilities through the use of information systems. In contrast, the missions of privacy and information security include protection, compliance, and proper usage. Executive management must ensure that these sometimes-conflicting missions successfully coexist.

Typical IT, privacy, and security-related executive position titles include the following:

- Chief information officer (CIO)
- Chief technology officer (CTO)
- Chief privacy officer (CPO) or data protection officer (DPO)
- Chief information security officer (CISO)

To ensure the success of the organization's privacy and information security programs, executive management should be involved in three key areas.

- **Ratification and enforcement of corporate privacy and security policies** This can take different forms, such as formal ratification recorded in the meeting minutes of a governance meeting, a statement for the need for compliance along with a signature within the body of the privacy or security policy document, a separate memorandum to all personnel, or other visible communication to the organization's rank and file that stresses the importance of and need for compliance to the organization's privacy and information security policies.
- **Leadership by example** Executive management should lead by example and not exhibit behavior that suggests they are "above" policy. Executives should not have the appearance of enjoying special privileges of a nature that suggests that one or more policies do not apply to them. Instead, their behavior should visibly support privacy and security policies to which all personnel are expected to comply.
- **Ultimate responsibility** Executives are ultimately responsible for all actions carried out by the personnel who report to them. Executives are also ultimately responsible for all outcomes related to organizations to which operations have been outsourced.

Privacy and Security Steering Committees

Many organizations form a security and *privacy steering committee*—separate or combined—consisting of stakeholders from many (if not all) of the organization's business units, departments, functions, and key locations. Some organizations will separate privacy and security into separate committees, especially if there are differences in membership or focus.

A privacy or security steering committee can have a variety of responsibilities, including the following:

- **Risk treatment deliberation and recommendation** The steering committee can discuss relevant risks and potential avenues for risk treatment, and develop recommendations for said risk treatment for ratification by executive management.
- **Prioritization, discussion, and coordination of IT, privacy, and security projects** The steering committee members can discuss various IT, privacy, and security projects to resolve any resource or scheduling conflicts. They can also address potential conflicts among multiple projects and initiatives and develop solutions.
- **Review of recent risk assessments** The steering committee can discuss recent risk assessments to develop a shared understanding of their results and discuss remediation of findings.
- **Discussion of new laws, regulations, and requirements** The committee can discuss new laws, regulations, and requirements that might require changes in the organization's operations. Committee members can develop high-level strategies that their respective business units or departments can further build out.
- **Review of recent privacy and security incidents** Steering committee members can discuss recent privacy and security incidents and their root causes. This often results in changes to processes, procedures, or technologies to reduce the risk and impact of future incidents.

Reading between the lines, the primary mission of a steering committee is to identify and resolve conflicts and to maximize the effectiveness of privacy and security programs, balancing them with other business initiatives and priorities.

Business Process and Business System Owners

Business process and system *owners* are typically non-technical personnel in management positions within an organization. While they might not be technology or compliance experts, in many organizations, their business processes are enhanced by IT in business applications and other capabilities. In the context of information privacy, the term "business system" includes databases containing personal information.

Remembering that IT, privacy, and information security functions serve the organization, not the other way around, business process and business system owners are accountable for making business decisions that might impact the use of IT, the use of personal information, the organization's security posture, or any combination of these. A simple example is deciding whether an individual employee should have access to specific personal information. While IT or security might have direct control over which personnel have access to which information, the best decision is a policy-backed one by the manager responsible for the information.

The responsibilities of business process and business system owners include the following:

- **Access grants** Process owners decide whether individuals or groups should be given access to the system, as well as the level and type of access.

- **Access revocation** Process owners should decide when individuals or groups no longer require access to a system, signaling the need to revoke that access.
- **Access reviews** Process owners should periodically review access lists to determine whether each person and group should continue to have access.
- **Subject inquiries and requests** Process owners receive privacy-related inquiries from data subjects, including queries about personal data usage, corrections to personal data, opt-in and opt-out requests, requests to be removed, and complaints.
- **Configuration** Process owners determine the configuration required for systems and applications, ensuring their proper functioning and support for business processes.
- **Function definition** In the case of business applications and services, process owners determine which functions will be available, how they will work, and how they will support business processes. Typically, this definition is constrained by functional limitations within an application, service, or product.
- **Process definition** Process owners determine the sequence, steps, roles, and actions carried out in their business processes.
- **Physical location** Process owners determine the physical location of their systems. Factors influencing location choices include physical security, proximity to other systems and relevant personnel, and data protection and privacy laws.

Because business and system owners are non-technical personnel, it might be necessary to translate business needs and applicable laws and regulations into technical specifications.

Exam Tip

For the exam, do not confuse the terms *business owner* and *system owner* with those who hold a majority of the organization's shares. Instead, these terms connote responsibility for business operations.

Custodial Responsibilities

In many organizations, system owners are not involved in the day-to-day activities related to managing their systems, especially when those systems are applications and the data they use. Instead, someone (or several people) in the IT organization acts as a *custodian* for system owners and grants access and makes other decisions on their behalf. Although this is a common practice, it is often carried too far, leaving the system owner virtually unaware, uninvolved, and uninformed. Instead, system owners should be aware of, and periodically review, activities carried out by people, groups, and departments that make decisions on their behalf.

The most common arrangement is that IT personnel make access decisions on behalf of system owners, based on established policies and practices. Except in cases where there is a close partnership between these IT personnel and system owners, they often do not adequately understand the business nature of systems or the implications of granting certain people access to them. Often, far too many staff members have access to systems, usually with higher privileges than necessary.

Privacy by Design

Privacy by design involves proactively embedding privacy into the design and operation of IT systems, networked infrastructure, and business practices. The principle of privacy by design is explicitly stated in Article 25 of the General Data Protection Regulation (GDPR), "Data protection by design and by default." This principle should be included in every organization's privacy policy, whether or not it is subject to GDPR or other privacy regulations.

This is easier said for new information systems that benefit from a "clean sheet" design. It is more difficult and costly to retrofit existing information systems developed before modern privacy laws.

Exam Tip

For the exam, remember that privacy by design and by default are key tenets of the GDPR and are only implied by other privacy regulations.

Chief Privacy Officer

Some organizations, typically those that manage large volumes of personal information about employees, customers, or constituents, will employ a chief privacy officer (CPO). Some organizations have a CPO because applicable regulations, such as the Gramm–Leach–Bliley Act (GLBA), require it. Other regulations, such as the Health Insurance Portability and Accountability Act (HIPAA), the Fair Credit Reporting Act (FCRA), and the GLBA, impose a set of responsibilities on an organization that compel it to hire an executive responsible for overseeing compliance. Others have a CPO because they store large amounts of personal information and have chosen to appoint an executive-level individual to manage the privacy program.

The roles of a CPO typically include safeguarding personal information and ensuring that the organization does not misuse it. Because many organizations with a CPO also have a CISO, the CPO's duties primarily involve overseeing the organization's proper handling and use of personal information.

The CPO is sometimes seen as a customer advocate, and often this is the CPO's actual role, particularly when regulations require a privacy officer.

Another similar title with similar responsibilities is the *data protection officer (DPO)*. While responsibilities can be similar to those of the CPO, it is important to highlight that

DPOs are expected to operate in a strictly oversight role within governance. In some cases, a CPO might not be able to fulfill the role of a DPO, particularly in organizations where the CPO is responsible for implementing data processing activities or systems that enable them.

Many smaller organizations appoint an existing staff member as the acting privacy officer.

Does GDPR Require a DPO?

Much discussion and debate have ensued over GDPR's requirements for organizations to hire or retain a DPO. The GDPR is somewhat vague on the matter. Section 4, Article 37 reads:

> The controller and the processor shall designate a data protection officer in any case where:
>
> **a.** the processing is carried out by a public authority or body, except for courts acting in their judicial capacity;
>
> **b.** the core activities of the controller or the processor consist of processing operations which, by virtue of their nature, their scope and/or their purposes, require regular and systematic monitoring of data subjects on a large scale; or
>
> **c.** the core activities of the controller or the processor consist of processing on a large scale of special categories of data pursuant to Article 9 or personal data relating to criminal convictions and offences referred to in Article 10.

The key language is included in subsections (a) and (b), which have some subjectivity. Under the GDPR, most companies are required to appoint a DPO.

Chief Information Security Officer

The CISO is the highest-ranking information security title in an organization. A CISO will develop business-aligned security strategies that support present and future business initiatives and will be responsible for the development and operation of the organization's information risk program, the development and implementation of security policies, security incident response, and perhaps some operational security functions.

In some organizations, the CISO reports to the COO or the CEO. In other organizations, the CISO can report to the CIO, the chief legal counsel, or another executive.

Other similar titles with similar responsibilities include the following:

- **Chief security officer (CSO)** A CSO is often responsible for physical security and workplace safety in addition to cybersecurity.

- **Chief information risk officer (CIRO)** Generally, this represents a change in approach to the CISO position, from being protection-based to being risk-based.
- **Chief risk officer (CRO)** This position is responsible for all aspects of risk, including information risk, business risk, compliance risk, and market risk. This role is separate from IT.

Many organizations do not have a CISO but instead have a director or manager of information security who reports further down in the organization chart. There are several possible reasons for organizations not having a CISO, but generally, it can be said that they do not consider information security a strategic function. This will hamper the visibility and importance of information security and often results in it being treated as a tactical function focused on basic defenses such as firewalls, antivirus software, and other tools. In such situations, responsibility for strategy-level information security is implicitly assigned to another executive, such as the CIO. This situation often results in the absence of a security program and the organization's general lack of awareness of relevant risks, threats, and vulnerabilities.

For small to medium-sized organizations, a full-time strategic security leader might not be cost-effective. In these situations, it is advisable to contract with a *virtual CISO (vCISO)* to assist with strategy and planning. The benefit of this approach for organizations that might not require or cannot afford a full-time security professional is that it enables them to leverage a seasoned security professional's knowledge to help manage the information security program.

Software Development

Positions in software development are involved in the design, development, and testing of software applications and often include the following:

- **Systems architect** This position is usually responsible for the overall information systems architecture in the organization. This can include overall data architecture as well as interfaces to external organizations.
- **Systems analyst** A systems analyst is involved with the design of applications, including changes in any application's original design. This position might develop technical requirements, program design, and software test plans. If an organization licenses applications developed by other companies, the systems analyst designs interfaces to other applications.
- **Software engineer/developer** This position develops application software. Depending upon their level of experience, people in this position might also design programs or applications. In organizations that utilize purchased application software, developers often create custom interfaces, application customizations, and custom reports.
- **Software tester** This position tests changes to programs made by software engineers/developers.

While the trend toward outsourcing applications has led organizations to develop their own applications infrequently, software development roles persist. Developers are needed to create customized modules within software platforms, and integration tools to connect applications. Still, most organizations have fewer developers than they did decades ago.

Exam Tip

Remember that the regulatory requirements for privacy by design usually rest with the systems architect for organizations developing software that processes personal information.

Rank Sets Tone and Gives Power

A glance at the highest-ranking privacy and information security positions in an organization reveals much about executive management's opinion of privacy and information security in larger organizations. Executive attitudes about privacy and security are reflected in the privacy and security leaders' titles, which can resemble the following:

- **Privacy manager or security manager** Privacy and information security are tactical only and often viewed as consisting only of basic tactical controls. The privacy and security managers have no visibility into the development of business objectives. Executives consider privacy and security as unimportant and based on simple practices only.
- **Privacy director or security director** Privacy and information security are essential, and the director has moderate decision-making capability but little influence on the business. A director in a larger organization might have little involvement in overall business strategies and little or no access to executive management or the board of directors.
- **Vice president** Privacy and information security are strategic objectives but do not influence business strategy and objectives. The vice president will have some access to executive management and possibly the board of directors.
- **CISO/CIRO/CSO/vCISO/CPO/DPO** Privacy and information security are strategic objectives, and business objectives are developed with full consideration of risk. The C-level security and privacy personnel have free access to executive management and the board of directors.

Data Management

Positions related to data management are responsible for developing and implementing database designs and for maintaining databases. These personnel will be carrying out some of privacy's design principles. These positions are concerned with data within applications, as well as data flows between applications:

- **Data manager** This position is responsible for data architecture and management in larger organizations.
- **Database architect** This position develops logical and physical designs of data models for applications. With sufficient experience, this person can also design an organization's overall data architecture.
- **Big data architect** This position develops data models and analytics for large, complex datasets.
- **Database administrator (DBA)** This position builds and maintains databases designed by the database architect, as well as those included in purchased applications. The DBA monitors databases, tunes them for performance and efficiency, and troubleshoots problems.
- **Database analyst** This position performs tasks junior to the database administrator, carrying out routine data maintenance and monitoring.
- **Data scientist** This position applies scientific methods, builds processes, and implements systems to extract knowledge or insights from data.

The activities carried out by these data management roles is explored in detail in Chapter 5, "Data Collection and Processing" and Chapter 6, "Data Persistence and Destruction."

Exam Tip

CDPSE candidates need to understand that the roles of data manager, big data architect, database architect, database administrator, database analyst, and data scientist are distinct from those of data owners. The former are IT department roles for managing data models and data technology, whereas the latter role governs the business use of, and access to, data in information systems.

Network Management

Positions in network management are responsible for designing, building, monitoring, and maintaining voice and data communications networks, including connections to outside entities and the Internet:

- **Network architect** This position designs data and voice networks and implements changes and upgrades as needed to meet new organizational objectives.
- **Network engineer** This position implements, configures, and maintains network devices such as routers, switches, firewalls, and gateways.

- **Network administrator** This position performs routine network tasks, such as making configuration changes and monitoring event logs.
- **Telecom engineer** Positions in this role work with telecommunications technologies such as telecom services, data circuits, phone systems, and conferencing systems.

Systems Management

Positions in systems management are responsible for architecture, design, building, and maintenance of servers and operating systems. This can include desktop operating systems as well. Personnel in these positions also design and manage virtualized environments and microsegmentation.

- **Systems architect** This position is responsible for the overall architecture of systems (usually servers), including both internal architectures and relationships between systems.
- **Systems engineer** This position is responsible for designing, building, and maintaining servers and server operating systems.
- **Storage engineer** This position is responsible for designing, building, and maintaining storage subsystems.
- **Systems administrator** This position is responsible for performing maintenance and configuration operations on systems.

Operations

In larger organizations, positions in operations are responsible for day-to-day operational tasks that can include networks, servers, databases, and applications:

- **Operations manager** This position is responsible for overall operations carried out by others. Responsibilities will include establishing operations shift schedules.
- **Operations analyst** This position is responsible for developing operational procedures; examining the health of networks, systems, and databases; setting and monitoring the operations schedule; and maintaining operations records.
- **Controls analyst** This position is responsible for monitoring batch jobs, data entry, and other tasks to ensure they operate correctly.
- **Systems operator** This position is responsible for monitoring systems and networks, performing backup tasks, running batch jobs, printing reports, and performing other operational tasks.
- **Data entry** This position is responsible for keying batches of data from hardcopy or other sources.
- **Media manager** This position is responsible for maintaining and tracking the use and whereabouts of backup tapes and other media.

Privacy Operations

Though few organizations have personnel in a privacy operations function, staff in many business departments have access to the personal information of the organization's workforce, customers, or constituents. These business functions include:

- Human resources
- Sales and marketing
- Customer support
- Warranty or assurance services
- Business operations

Workers in these and other business functions need to be aware of the implications of having access to personal information and the organization's privacy policy, so that their day-to-day work does not run afoul of privacy policy or applicable laws.

For the most part, it's more important to know that an organization has assigned various privacy responsibilities to designated personnel. The structure of the organization (or "org chart") is less important.

Security Operations

Positions in security operations are responsible for designing, building, and monitoring security systems and security controls to ensure the confidentiality, integrity, and availability of information systems:

- **Security architect** This position is responsible for the design of security controls and systems such as authentication, audit logging, intrusion detection systems (IDSs), intrusion prevention systems (IPSs), and firewalls.
- **Security engineer** This position is responsible for designing, building, and maintaining security services and systems as specified by the security architect. Such systems include firewalls, IDSs and IPSs, WAFs, web content filters, cloud access security brokers (CASBs), and others.
- **Security analyst** This position is responsible for examining firewall, IDS, and system and application audit logs. A security analyst could also have other responsibilities, such as performing security reviews, performing risk analyses, and maintaining security-related business records. This position might also be responsible for issuing security advisories to other IT teams.
- **Access administrator** This position is responsible for accepting approved requests for user access management changes and performing the necessary changes at the network, system, database, or application level. Often, this function is carried out by personnel in network and systems management; in larger organizations, user account management is handled by information security or in a separate user access department.

Privacy Audit

Positions in privacy audit are responsible for examining process design and for verifying the effectiveness of privacy policies and controls:

- **Privacy audit manager** This position is responsible for audit operations, scheduling, and audit management.
- **Privacy auditor** This position is responsible for performing internal audits of privacy controls to ensure they are operating properly.

The topic of auditing privacy programs and operations is discussed in Chapter 4.

Security Audit

Positions in security audit are responsible for examining process design and for verifying the effectiveness of security controls:

- **Security audit manager** This position is responsible for audit operations, scheduling, and audit management.
- **Security auditor** This position is responsible for performing internal audits of IT controls to ensure they are operating properly.

While a privacy and security audit might not be a formal internal audit function, those performing security audits need to be able to exercise independence from the functions they audit.

Service Desk

Positions at the service desk are responsible for providing frontline support services to IT and IT customers:

- **Service desk manager** This position serves as a liaison between end users and the IT service desk.
- **Service desk analyst** This position is responsible for providing frontline user support services to personnel within the organization. This is sometimes known as a help-desk analyst.
- **Technical support analyst** This position is responsible for providing technical support services to other IT personnel and, perhaps, to IT customers.

Quality Assurance

In larger organizations, positions in quality assurance (QA) are responsible for evaluating IT systems and processes to confirm their accuracy and effectiveness:

- **QA manager** This position is responsible for facilitating quality improvement activities throughout the IT organization.
- **QC manager** This position is responsible for testing IT systems and applications to confirm they are free of defects.

Other Roles

Other roles in IT organizations include the following:

- **Third-party risk management manager** This position is responsible for assessing third-party service providers to ensure that their practices do not pose unacceptable risks to the protection of sensitive information, particularly the personal information of customers, constituents, or employees.
- **Vendor manager** This position is responsible for maintaining business relationships with external vendors, measuring their performance, and handling business issues.
- **Program manager** This position is responsible for managing teams of project managers and overseeing larger, more complex projects.
- **Project manager** This position is responsible for creating project plans and managing IT projects.

General Staff

The rank-and-file in an organization might not have explicit privacy or information security responsibilities. This is determined in part by executive management's understanding of the broad capabilities of information systems and the personnel who use them. It also determines executives' understanding of the human role in privacy and information security.

Typically, general staff privacy- and security-related responsibilities include the following:

- Understanding and compliance with the organization's privacy and security policy
- Acceptable use of organization assets, including information systems and personal information
- Proper judgment, including proper responses to people who request access to personal information or request that staff members perform specific functions (the primary impetus for this is the phenomenon of social engineering and its use as an attack vector)
- Reporting of privacy and security-related matters and incidents to management

Organizations with a more mature privacy and security culture include standard language in job descriptions that specify general responsibilities for protecting assets, systems, and personal information.

Vendor and Supply Chain Management

Third-party risk management (TPRM) refers to activities used to identify and manage risks associated with external organizations that perform operational functions for an organization. Many organizations outsource some of their information processing to third-party organizations, often in the form of cloud-based software-as-a-service (SaaS) and platform-as-a-service (PaaS), and often for economic reasons: it is less expensive to pay for software in a leasing arrangement than to develop, implement, integrate, and maintain software internally. Similarly, many organizations prefer to lease server operating systems rather than purchase their own hardware.

TPRM involves extending techniques used to identify and treat privacy and security risks within the organization. The same risks present in third parties' services are present within an organization's processing environment. The discipline of third-party risk exists because of the complexities of identifying risks in third-party organizations, as well as the risks inherent in doing business with specific third parties. At its core, third-party risk is like other risk management; the difference lies in acquiring relevant information to identify risks outside of the organization's direct control.

Organizations lacking a mature TPRM program should implement a process that incorporates both security and privacy requirements for relevant service providers.

Cloud Service Providers

Organizations moving to cloud-based environments often assume that cloud service providers have handled many or all information security functions, but this is often not the case. This often results in security and privacy breaches, due to each party believing the other was performing key data protection tasks. Many organizations are unfamiliar with the shared responsibility model that delineates which party is responsible for which operations and security functions. Tables 2.1 and 2.2 depict shared responsibility models for operations and security, respectively.

The specific responsibilities for operations and security between an organization and a particular service provider might differ from those in these tables. It is vital that an organization clearly understand its precise responsibilities for each third-party relationship, so that no responsibilities that might introduce risks to the organization are overlooked or neglected.

TABLE 2.1 Operational Shared Responsibility Model

Operation	On-premise	IaaS	PaaS	SaaS
Applications	Org	Org	Org	Provider
Data	Org	Org	Org	Provider
Runtime	Org	Org	Provider	Provider
Middleware	Org	Org	Provider	Provider
Operating system	Org	Org	Provider	Provider
Virtualization	Org	Provider	Provider	Provider
Servers	Org	Provider	Provider	Provider
Storage	Org	Provider	Provider	Provider
Networking	Org	Provider	Provider	Provider
Data center	Org	Provider	Provider	Provider

TABLE 2.2 Security and Privacy Shared Responsibility Model

Activity	On-premise	IaaS	PaaS	SaaS
Human resources	Org	Shared	Shared	Provider
Privacy	Org	Org	Org	Shared
Application security	Org	Org	Shared	Provider
Identity and access management	Org	Org	Shared	Shared
Log management	Org	Org	Shared	Provider
System monitoring	Org	Org	Shared	Provider
Incident response	Org	Org	Shared	Shared
Data governance	Org	Org	Shared	Shared
Data encryption	Org	Org	Shared	Provider

Activity	On-premise	IaaS	PaaS	SaaS
Host intrusion detection	Org	Org	Shared	Provider
Host hardening	Org	Org	Shared	Provider
Asset management	Org	Org	Shared	Provider
Network intrusion detection	Org	Org	Provider	Provider
Network security	Org	Org	Provider	Provider
Security policy	Org	Shared	Shared	Provider
Physical security	Org	Provider	Provider	Provider

The privacy officer should recognize that third-party service providers generally play little or no role in data handling. These functions are fully the responsibility of the organization using third-party services, not the third party itself.

TPRM has been the subject of numerous standards and regulations that compel organizations to proactively identify security risks in their critical third-party providers. Historically, many organizations were not voluntarily assessing these third parties. Statistical data on breaches over several years have revealed that more than half of all breaches have a nexus to third parties. This statistic has illuminated the magnitude of the third-party risk problem. It has led to the enactment of laws and regulations across many industries, now requiring organizations to build and operate effective third-party risk programs.

Privacy Regulation Requirements

In privacy regulation parlance, organizations that use third-party service providers are often, but not always, considered *data controllers*, which are entities that determine the purposes and means of the processing of personal data, which can include directing third parties to process personal data on their behalf. The third parties that process data for data controllers are known as *data processors*.

When outsourcing IT operations to third parties that process personal information, organizations often develop a *data processing agreement (DPA)* that defines data processing specifics, including processing instructions, security requirements, breach notifications, and restrictions on the use of the organization's data. Sometimes these terms are in the contract between the parties, and sometimes they exist as a separate exhibit.

Some privacy laws address the matter of personal data being transmitted from one legal jurisdiction (a *cross-border data transfer*) to another in one of two ways:

- **From one organization to another** *Standard contractual clauses (SCCs)* define the business rules for such transfers to outside organizations in other jurisdictions, ensuring compliance with applicable regulations.
- **Within one organization** *Binding corporate rules (BCRs)* define business rules for transfers within an organization with a presence in multiple jurisdictions.

HIPAA requires that covered entities (organizations subject to HIPAA regulations) establish *business associate agreements (BAAs)* with every service provider that has access to the covered entity's information or information systems. Gramm-Leach Bliley Act (GLBA) requires that financial institutions oversee service providers and periodically assess their safeguards.

TPRM Lifecycle

The management of business relationships with third parties is a lifecycle process. The lifecycle begins when an organization considers using a third party to augment or support its operations. The lifecycle continues during the ongoing relationship with the third party and concludes when the organization no longer uses the third party's services: all connections are severed, and all data stored at the third party is removed or destroyed.

Initial Assessment

Before establishing a business relationship with a third party, an organization will assess the third party's suitability. Often, this evaluation is competitive, where two or more third parties are vying for the formal relationship. During the evaluation, the organization will require that each third party provide information describing its services, generally in a structured manner through a *request for information (RFI)* or a *request for proposal (RFP)* process.

In their RFIs and RFPs, organizations often include sections on privacy and security so they can better understand how each third party protects the organization's information. This, together with information about the services themselves, pricing, and other details, reveals the criteria the organization uses to select the third party that will provide services.

Organizations with a large number of vendors often establish a *vendor standard* document that lists approved vendors. This practice helps avoid costly assessments of new vendors when existing vendors can provide additional products or services.

Contract

Before services can begin, the organization and the third party will negotiate a *contract* that describes the services provided, including service levels, quality, pricing, and other terms typical of legal agreements. Based on the details uncovered during the assessment phase, the organization can develop tailored language for the legal agreement that addresses privacy and security concerns. This part of the legal agreement will typically cover these subjects:

- **Privacy and/or security program** Require the third party to have a formal privacy and/or security program, including but not limited to governance, policy, risk management, annual risk assessment, internal audit, vulnerability management, incident management, secure development, privacy and security awareness training, data protection, and third-party risk.
- **Security and/or privacy controls** Require the third party to have a controls framework, including linkages to risk management and internal audit.
- **Vulnerability assessments** Require the third party to undergo penetration tests or vulnerability assessments of its service infrastructure and applications, performed by a competent security professional services firm, with reports made available to the organization upon request.
- **External audits and certifications** Require the third party to undergo annual SOC 1 and/or SOC 2 Type 2 audits (SOC stands for System and Organization Controls), TrustArc audits, ISO/IEC 27001 certifications, HITRUST certifications, Payment Card Industry Reports on Compliance (PCI ROCs), or other industry-recognized and applicable external audits, with reports made available to the organization upon request.
- **Privacy and security incident response** Require the third party to have a formal privacy and security incident response capability that includes testing and training.
- **Privacy and security incident notification** Require the third party to notify the organization in the event of a suspected or confirmed breach, within a specific timeframe, typically 24–48 hours. The language around "suspected" and "confirmed" needs to be carefully crafted so that the third party cannot sidestep this responsibility.
- ***Right to audit*** Require the third party to permit the organization to conduct an audit of the third-party organization without cause. If the third party does not want to permit this, one fallback position is to insist on the right to audit in the event of a suspected or confirmed breach or other circumstances. Further, include the right to have a competent security professional services firm audit the third-party privacy and security environment on behalf of the organization (useful for several reasons, including geographic location; the external audit firm will be more objective).
- **Periodic review** Require the third party to permit an annual review of its operations, privacy, and security. This can improve confidence in the third party's privacy and security.
- **Third-party disclosures** Require the third party to list any contracted parties it uses to perform services and to include a suitable third-party due diligence process.
- **Annual due diligence** Require the third party to respond to annual questionnaires and evidence requests as a part of the organization's third-party risk program.
- **Cyber-insurance** Require the third party to carry a cyber-insurance policy with minimum coverage levels. Require the third party to comply with all policy requirements so the policy will pay out in the event of a privacy or security incident. A great option is to have the customer organization named as a beneficiary on the policy, in the event of a widespread breach that could result in a large payout to many customers being diluted.

Organizations with many third parties might consider developing standard privacy and security clauses that include all of these provisions. Then, when a new third-party service is being considered, the organization's privacy and security teams can conduct an upfront examination of the third party's privacy and security environment and adjust the privacy and security clauses as needed.

During the vetting process, organizations often find one or more shortcomings in the third party's privacy or security program that the third party is unwilling or unable to remediate immediately. There are still options, however: the organization can compel the third party to implement improvements within a reasonable period after the business relationship begins. For example, a third-party service provider might not have an external audit, such as a SOC 1 or SOC 2 audit, but might agree to undergo one year later. Or a third-party service provider that has never had external penetration testing could be compelled to begin testing at regular intervals. Alternatively, the third party could be required to undergo a penetration test and remediate all critical- and high-level issues before the organization begins using the third party's services.

Classifying Third Parties

Organizations utilizing third parties often discover a wide range of risks: Some third parties might have access to large volumes of operationally critical or personal information. In contrast, others might have access to small volumes of personal information, and still others do not access data associated with critical operations at all. Because of this wide range of risk levels, many organizations choose to develop a scheme with risk levels based on criteria important to the organization. Typically, this risk scheme will have two to four risk levels, with each third party assigned to a risk level.

Organizations need to periodically assess their third parties to ensure they remain at the correct classification level. Third parties that provide a variety of services might initially be classified as low risk, but if retained to provide additional services, they could be reclassified to a higher risk level.

The purpose of this classification is explained in the following sections on questionnaires and assessing third parties.

Questionnaires and Evidence

Organizations that use third parties need to assess them periodically. Generally, this involves creating a privacy and/or security questionnaire that is sent to the third party, requesting that they answer all questions and return it to the organization within a reasonable time. The organization might choose not to rely simply on the answers provided by the third party. In that case, the organization can also request that the third party furnish specific artifacts that serve as evidence to support the responses in the questionnaire. Here are some typical artifacts that an organization will request of its third party:

- Privacy and security policies
- Privacy and security controls
- Privacy and security awareness training records

- New-hire checklists
- Details on employee background checks (not necessarily actual records, but a description of the checks performed)
- Non-disclosure and other agreements signed by employees (not necessarily signed copies, but blank copies)
- Vulnerability management process
- Secure development process
- Copy of general insurance and cyber-insurance policies
- Incident response plan and evidence of testing

An organization that uses many third parties might find that it utilizes various types of services: some store or process large volumes of personal or critical data, others are operationally critical but do not access personal information, and other categories. Often, it makes sense for an organization to utilize different versions of questionnaires, one or more for each category of third party, so that most questions asked of each third party are relevant. Organizations that don't do this risk having large portions of their questionnaires be irrelevant, which could be frustrating to third parties who would rightfully complain about wasted time and effort.

As described earlier regarding the classification of third parties, organizations often use different questionnaires for different risk levels. For example, third parties in high-risk categories would be asked to complete very extensive questionnaires that request many pieces of evidence. In contrast, medium-risk third parties would receive shorter questionnaires, and low-risk third parties would receive very short questionnaires. While it is courteous to send questionnaires of appropriate length to various third parties (mainly to avoid overburdening low-risk third parties with huge questionnaires), remember that this practice also increases the burden on the organization, since someone must review the questionnaires and attached evidence. An organization with hundreds of third parties does not want to overburden itself by analyzing hundreds of questionnaires, each with hundreds of questions, when most of the third parties are lower risk and warrant shorter questionnaires.

Assessing Third Parties

To discover risks, organizations need to assess their third parties not only at the onset of the business relationship (before the legal agreement is signed, as explained earlier) but also periodically thereafter. Business conditions and operations often change over time, necessitating that third parties be assessed throughout the relationship.

Organizations assessing third parties often recognize that IT, privacy, and security controls are not the only risks that require examination. Instead, organizations generally will seek other forms of information about their more important third parties, including:

- Financial risk
- Geopolitical risk
- Inherent risk

- Recent security breaches
- Lawsuits

These and other factors can influence the overall risk to the organization and manifest in various ways, including degradation of privacy and security, failure to meet production or quality targets, and even business failure.

Because of the effort required to collect information on these other risk areas, organizations often rely on external service organizations that gather data on companies and make it available on a subscription basis. Of course, these are also third-party organizations that require an appropriate measure of due diligence.

Risk Mitigation

When assessing third parties, organizations that carefully examine the information provided by the parties often discover some unacceptable aspects. In these cases, the organization will analyze the issues and decide on a course of action.

For instance, a highly critical third party indicates that it does not perform annual privacy and security awareness training for its employees, and the organization finds this unacceptable. To remedy this, the organization needs to analyze the risk (in a manner similar to any internal risk) and decide on a course of action. In this example, the organization contacts the third party and attempts to compel the third party to institute annual privacy and security awareness training for its employees.

Sometimes, a deficiency problem in a third party is not so easily solved. For example, a third party that has been providing services for many years indicates in its annual questionnaire that it does not encrypt stored personal information. At the outset of the third-party business relationship, this was not common practice, but over time, it has become standard in the organization's industry. The service provider, when confronted with this, explains that it is not operationally feasible to implement encryption of personal information in a manner acceptable to the organization, primarily due to financial considerations. Because of the significant impact of costs on its operations, the third party would have to increase its prices to cover them. In this example, the organization and the third party would need to determine the most pragmatic course of action so that the organization can be satisfied with the level of risk and control its costs.

Incident Management

A *privacy incident* is an event in which one or more data subjects' personal information has been inappropriately used or disclosed in a manner contrary to applicable laws or regulations. A privacy incident can also be thought of as an event that represents a violation of an organization's privacy and/or security policy. For instance, if an organization's privacy policy states that copying personal information to an external data storage device is not permitted, then such use would be considered a privacy incident.

The management of a privacy incident follows the same overall methodology as for a *security incident*.

Organizations seeking to align their incident management program to well-known standards might want to obtain a copy of *ISO/IEC 27035*, an international standard for security incident response.

This section focuses primarily on privacy breaches. For a more detailed explanation of security breach response, refer to this author's study guide on the Certified Information Security Manager (CISM) certification.

Phases of Incident Response

An effective response to a privacy incident is organized, documented, and rehearsed. The phases of a formal *incident response* plan are explained in this section.

For incident response to be effective, organizations must anticipate that incidents will occur and, accordingly, develop incident response plans, test them, and train personnel so that incident response is effective and timely.

Briefly, the phases of incident response, in order, are:

- Planning
- Detection
- Initiation
- Analysis
- Containment
- Eradication
- Recovery
- Remediation
- Closure
- Post-incident review
- Retention of evidence

Organizations should consider modeling their privacy incident response after their *security incident response* procedures to ensure consistency.

Planning

The planning step involves developing written response procedures to follow when an incident occurs. These procedures are created once the organization's practices, processes, and technologies are well understood. This helps ensure that incident response procedures align with the privacy policy, security policy, business operations, the technologies in use, and the practices in place for its architecture, development, management, and operations.

Detection

Detection is the point in time when an organization becomes aware that a privacy incident is occurring or has occurred. Because of the variety of events that characterize a privacy incident, an organization can become aware of an incident in several ways, including:

- Application or network slowdown or malfunction
- Alerts from IDS, IPS, DLP system, web filter, CASB, and other detective and preventive security systems
- Alerts from a security incident and event management system (SIEM)
- Alerts from media outlets, their investigators, and reports
- Notification from an employee or business partner
- Notification, complaint, or inquiry from a data subject
- Anonymous tips
- Notification from a regulator

Initiation

This is the phase where a response to the incident begins. Typically, this will include a declaration of the incident, followed by notifications to response team members so that response operations can begin. Notifications are typically also sent to business executives so they can be informed.

While each organization's privacy incident response plan will vary, an incident is typically confirmed during either the initiation or analysis phase. At that time, organizations might be required to notify regulators, supervisory authorities, and/or affected parties.

Analysis

In this phase, response team members analyze available data to understand the cause, scope, and impact of the incident. This can involve using forensic analysis tools to understand activities on individual systems.

Containment

Here, incident responders perform or direct actions that halt the progression of an incident. The steps required to contain an incident will vary according to the means used by the attacker.

Eradication

In this phase of incident response, responders take steps to remove the source of the incident. This could involve removing malware, blocking incoming attack messages, or removing an intruder.

Recovery

When the incident has been evaluated and eradicated, there is often a need to recover systems or components to their pre-incident state. This can include restoring data or configurations, or replacing damaged or stolen equipment.

Remediation

This activity involves any necessary changes to reduce or eliminate the possibility of a similar incident in the future. This can take the form of process or technology changes.

Closure

Closure occurs when eradication, recovery, and remediation are completed. Incident response operations are officially closed.

Post-incident Review

Shortly after the incident closes, incident responders and other personnel will meet to discuss the incident: its cause, its impact, and the organization's response. The discussion will range from lessons learned to possible improvements in technologies and processes to improve defense and response.

Retention of Evidence

Incident responders and other personnel will direct the retention of evidence and other materials used or collected during the incident. This can include information that is used in legal proceedings, including prosecution, civil lawsuits, and internal investigations. A *chain of custody* might be required to ensure the integrity of evidence.

Several standards are available to guide organizations toward structured incident response, including NIST SP 800-61 Rev. 3, *Incident Response Recommendations and Considerations for Cybersecurity Risk Management.*

Privacy Incident Response Plan Development

Effective incident response plans take time to develop. A privacy manager developing an incident response plan must first thoroughly understand business processes, privacy policy, data flows, and underlying information systems, and then identify resource requirements, dependencies, and failure points. A privacy manager might first develop a high-level incident response plan, which is usually followed by the development of several incident response playbooks, which are step-by-step instructions to follow when specific incidents occur.

Because many privacy incidents are also security incidents, developing a privacy incident response plan should be conducted in close cooperation with the security manager to avoid duplication of effort and leverage existing response plan resources and practices.

Resources

Before developing privacy incident response procedures, a privacy manager needs to identify required and available resources for incident detection and response. Perhaps the most important resource is the organization's security incident response plan. A correctly designed security incident response plan will recognize and respond to incidents, including information theft and destruction. When this is in place, two elements are needed to develop a privacy incident response plan:

- Callouts to privacy incident responders, so that they can orchestrate notifications to regulators and affected parties
- Detection and response to incidents of misuse of personal information that are not themselves security incidents

Besides these, other resources that privacy managers need to identify include:

- Privacy incident response personnel, beyond those workers identified as security incident responders. Privacy incident response personnel will be responsible for examining information systems to understand the nature of a "misuse of personal information" incident.
- Forensics capabilities, including chain of custody procedures. Since a privacy incident can involve notifications to external parties, a chain of custody will ensure robust evidence retention.
- *Attorney-client privilege*, to ensure that certain aspects of incident response are protected.
- Contact information and methods for regulators and supervisory authorities.
- Prewritten notifications to regulators, supervisory authorities, affected parties, and the public.

Incident Response Playbooks

More mature organizations have developed numerous playbooks (as many as a dozen or more), detailed procedures to follow when specific types of security incidents occur. Typical playbook scenarios include ransomware, denial-of-service attacks, loss or theft of a laptop or mobile device, destructive malware, compromise of a user account, and more.

Privacy incident response plans need their playbooks as well, since many privacy incidents are not security incidents per se, but instead represent the misuse of personal information. Thus, privacy managers developing privacy incident response plans need to develop their own response playbooks so that incident responders can quickly work through investigation, containment, and recovery steps. A privacy incident is not a good time to begin learning how a specific system works, where its logs reside (and how to read them), or how to run reports to understand the steps that led to the incident. Better organizations develop these playbooks in advance so incident responders can quickly determine what happened and why.

Response Plan Tabletop Testing

When privacy incident response plans (and playbooks) have been developed, they need to be tested in one or more *tabletop* exercises. These are facilitated discussions led by an experienced incident responder, who walks personnel through a typical privacy incident scenario, step by step. At the same time, participants read their privacy incident response plans and discuss the steps they'd take if a real incident were occurring.

Privacy Incident Response Metrics

Privacy incident response is a critical function, so much so that it warrants being measured. These measurements help management understand the effectiveness of incident response within a typical feedback loop that identifies improvement opportunities. Some of the ways that incident response can be measured include:

- **Preparation** The creation and review of playbooks and incident responder training help management better understand the level of preparedness to respond to an incident.
- **Responsiveness** Key metrics include *mean time to detect* (*MTTD*, defined as the time between the onset of an incident and the time an organization realizes it), *mean time to respond* (*MTTR*, a measure of the elapsed time between the time of incident realization until response proceedings commence), and *mean time to restore service* (*MTTRS*, formerly known as *mean time to resolve*) the measure of time from incident realization to closure).

Privacy Continuous Improvement

The philosophy of continuous improvement is a mainstay of quality-oriented organizations. Rather than assuming that all of an organization's processes, procedures, controls, and other operations are operating at an optimum level, a more realistic approach is to recognize that there is always room for meaningful improvement.

Continuous improvement is primarily concerned with the fact of process and control improvement rather than the appearance of improvement. Still, an organization should consider all operations of its privacy and security programs as "works in progress," meaning that management and staff recognize that their processes and controls have not achieved perfection and likely never will.

An organization can improve processes and controls in the following ways:

- **Accuracy** Organization strives to improve its controls and processes to reduce exceptions and errors.
- **Efficiency** Organization will seek opportunities to make controls and processes more efficient, meaning they will require less effort or fewer resources while still maintaining quality objectives.
- **Timeliness** Organization will seek ways to make controls and processes more responsive so that routine and nonroutine tasks take less time to complete.
- **Risk** Organization will look for ways to reduce risks in controls and processes, thereby creating fewer opportunities for incidents.

Continuous improvement is so important that it is officially a requirement in ISO/IEC 27001:2022. Requirement 10.1 of the standard reads, "The organization shall continually improve the suitability, adequacy, and effectiveness of the information security management system." Similarly, ISO/IEC 27701 (*Information security, cybersecurity and privacy protection—Privacy information management systems—Requirements and guidance*) Clause 10 (Improvement) extends this to include the privacy information management system.

Data Subject Rights, Requests, and Notification

Privacy programs have operational components, some of which concern communications between the organization and data subjects, whether customers, employees, constituents, or combinations thereof. Other components are concerned with communications with authorities. Both aspects are discussed here.

Working with Data Subjects

Modern data privacy laws require transparency not only regarding the collection and use of personal data, but also to provide one or more means for data subjects to make inquiries and requests regarding the use of their personal information. The procedures for making such subject data requests are typically spelled out in an organization's privacy policy (laws such as the GDPR require a privacy policy to describe these procedures). Occasionally, such procedures might be located elsewhere, such as in a user guide or in system documentation.

The primary vehicle for data subjects to contact an organization regarding their personal data is known as a *data subject request (DSR)*, also known as a *data subject access request (DSAR)*. The remainder of this section describes the various types of DSRs.

When receiving a DSR from a data subject, organizations follow a defined *request fulfillment workflow*, which outlines the steps to process the DSR.

Inquiries for Data Usage

Data subjects can submit an inquiry regarding the collection and use of their personal information. Their request might be general or quite specific. For instance, a data subject can ask whether any of their personal information is present in the organization's systems. Or a data subject can ask about specific personal information, such as a home address.

Smaller organizations might provide only an inquiry form, an email address, a telephone number, or a surface mail address where such inquiries can be sent. These organizations must train personnel to manage these inquiries properly and respond to data subjects within specific timeframes (which are sometimes spelled out in regulations). Personnel who handle these requests will need access to systems and applications containing personal information to respond accurately.

Larger organizations automate inquiries in some cases. For instance, a data subject with an existing account on an organization's systems can log in and click a link to learn how and where personal information is used. Often, such tools provide data subjects with the means to modify some of their information. This is discussed more fully in the next section.

Organizations typically maintain a log of inquiries, including the subject's name (or other identifying information), so that management can better understand the frequency of requests and the workload incurred. Privacy personnel will recognize that these logs themselves might also contain protected personal information.

Requests for Corrections

In some circumstances, a data subject can request changes to their personal information used by an organization. For instance, a data subject might change their residence and need to update their mailing or shipping address. Or they can change a payment method, family status, or service provider, such as insurance. Finally, sometimes personal information is mistyped, and spelling and other corrections are needed.

Organizations are required to provide one or more means through which data subjects can request these corrections. Data subjects can often make these changes through self-service programs, but sometimes they must request that organization personnel make the changes on their behalf.

Privacy policies often provide one or more methods that data subjects can use to make these requests. Whether the means are automated or manual, organizations typically log these events as part of routine systems and activity measurements. Like other mature business processes, this logging will sometimes compel management to make changes or improvements to systems and processes. For example, if the organization receives numerous requests that personnel must handle manually, it might provide more self-service tools for data subjects to make some changes themselves.

Requests for Removal

GDPR made famous the notion of "the right to be forgotten," meaning the outright removal of a data subject from an organization's records. Not a new concept, data subjects often want to opt out of an activity a particular organization might be conducting that involves them. As with other subject data requests, the privacy policy will provide specific means for making such requests.

Organizations accepting opt-out or data-removal requests must understand the nature of the data and other laws that require the retention of records. For example, a former employee can request that their employment records be removed; however, employment law might require that employment records be retained for many years after the end of employment. Similarly, a similar request made to a bank or credit union might conflict with laws requiring the retention of banking transaction records. However, marketing organizations that facilitate mail or telephone marketing campaigns might have few or no retention requirements and are compelled to remove a subject's data on request. The same can be said of social networking organizations with few statutory requirements to retain subject data. Finally, privacy laws cite specific exclusions to data removal requests: GDPR, for instance, does not require courts or prison systems to expunge a person's criminal history. Nice try, though!

Complaints

To improve customer service or comply with regulations, organizations might include a mechanism for data subjects to lodge complaints about the organization's use of their personal information. A data subject might be venting in the complaint, or the complaint might be an implicit request to change the person's relationship with the organization.

Personnel in the organization will need to carefully consider complaints, including whether a complaint describes an activity that could violate the organization's privacy policy. For this reason alone, organizations should pay close attention to data subject complaints, as they might be the only way organizations can become aware of privacy or security incidents.

Working with Authorities

Many privacy laws provide for the creation of government authorities that act in a supervisory capacity as a part of the enforcement of these laws. For instance, Articles 51 through 54 of the GDPR define supervisory authorities and their responsibilities. (Although this book does focus on organizations that will, from time to time, work with supervisory authorities, details on work performed by supervisory authorities are beyond its scope.)

In my experience as a privacy and security professional for more than 25 years, I have learned that the most important ingredient to successful relationships and encounters with external parties, including auditors, regulators, and supervisory authorities, is this: completeness of business records. This includes the following:

- Up-to-date process information
- Data flow diagrams (or detailed descriptions of data flows)

- Effective processes
- Complete business records

Nothing frustrates these external parties more than an organization that is disorganized and out of control. When such organizations do produce information, it will be regarded with skepticism, as external parties will wonder whether the data was conjured up at the last minute or "cooked" (altered to avoid accountability). This could even be regarded as a lack of cooperation with a supervisory authority. (GDPR Article 31 reads, "The controller and the processor and, where applicable, their representatives, shall cooperate, on request, with the supervisory authority in the performance of its tasks.")

Privacy and cybersecurity laws often require organizations that store or process personal information to have procedures for handling privacy and security breaches. Further, organizations should identify, in advance of any incident or breach, all applicable laws, regulations, and other obligations, and all instances where notification to regulators, supervisory authorities, and affected parties is required should a breach occur. Then, at the onset of an incident or breach, the organization simply carries out its procedures, which are known and practiced in advance.

Summary

Building a privacy operation requires an understanding of organizational culture and applicable regulations. Privacy leaders need to understand that cybersecurity and data governance are key prerequisites, without which any privacy program will struggle to succeed.

Building a privacy operation requires detailed knowledge of privacy requirements—that is, the activities and outcomes the organization is required to undertake at present and in the foreseeable future. Those requirements generally stem from applicable regulations; implicit and explicit expectations from employees, customers, and constituents; and other legal obligations.

External privacy policies, often referred to as notices of privacy practices (NOPPs), are the official statements describing the organization's practices for the collection, use, and ultimate disposal of personal information. Privacy policies also describe how data subjects can make inquiries and requests regarding their personal information. Internal privacy policies describe the roles, responsibilities, practices, standards, and expectations of all staff members.

The management of a privacy program in an organization begins with understanding all IT, security, and privacy-related roles and responsibilities. A role is a description of expected activities that each employee is obliged to perform as part of their employment. A responsibility is a statement of outcomes that a person is expected to support.

Active data monitoring is an essential activity in a privacy operation. Data discovery scanning helps organizations identify the presence of personal information. Data loss prevention (DLP) tools help organizations control the movement of sensitive data.

Organizational culture is described as the behavioral norms regarding empowerment, compliance, collaboration, accountability, and politics. Culture is influenced by executive and upper management behavior, as well as by established value statements, codes of conduct, and ethical standards.

Privacy and information security governance are most effective when every person in the organization knows what is expected of them. Privacy program roles and responsibilities need to be formally established and documented.

The formation of a privacy steering committee helps ensure that an organization's privacy plan aligns with its core business operations, fulfills business objectives, and meets compliance requirements.

Models such as RACI charts are used to determine and illustrate levels and types of responsibilities in selected business processes. RACI charts show who performs tasks, who helps, and who is to be told of them. Alternatives to RACI include PARIS (Participant, Accountable, Review Required, Input Required, Sign-off Required) and PACSI (Perform, Accountable, Control, Suggest, Informed).

Through the concepts of privacy by design and by default, privacy affects the processes, procedures, and activities of many (if not all) IT and IT security personnel.

Third-party risk management (TPRM) refers to activities used to identify and manage risks associated with external organizations that perform operational functions for an organization. TPRM industry practices are well-developed and can be adopted in various ways by each organization.

The best practice in TPRM is to establish risk tiers for an organization's service provider population and apply varying levels of rigor to each tier. This ensures a risk-based allocation of resources in upfront and ongoing due diligence of service providers.

A privacy incident is an event in which one or more data subjects' personal information has been inappropriately used or disclosed, contrary to applicable laws or regulations. A privacy incident can also be thought of as an event that violates an organization's privacy and/or security policy.

The overall techniques used for privacy incident response are similar to those used for security incident response. Incidents are detected, analyzed, contained, and eradicated. Systems are recovered, and remediation steps are carried out to prevent recurrence. Incidents are closed, and post-incident reviews are performed.

Privacy incident response plans need to be tested periodically, and all incident responders need to be trained periodically. Key metrics, including mean time to detect (MTTD), mean time to respond (MTTR), and mean time to restore service (MTTRS), help management measure the effectiveness of incident response.

It is vital that an organization's culture not be satisfied with its current state of policies, practices, and operations. Instead, a spirit of continuous improvement instills a culture of "we can and should do better."

Modern privacy laws require organizations to establish mechanisms for accepting inquiries and requests from internal and external data subjects. Effective procedures and controls are required to ensure an accurate and timely response to these incoming communications.

Subject requests for data correction and removal require that an organization understand whether applicable laws require retention of such data and whether anonymization or pseudonymization can effectively be used to fulfill some of these requests.

Supervisory authorities are government or quasi-government agencies that investigate potential wrongdoing by organizations and their management of personal information. Organizations need to be prepared to respond to their requests and inquiries, not unlike those of subject data requests.

Exam Essentials

Understand organizational roles and responsibilities. Privacy operations require clearly defined roles across functions, including privacy, legal, security, IT, and business units, with documented accountability and reporting structures.

Recognize the importance of vendor and supply chain oversight. Organizations must perform up-front due diligence, establish contractual protections, and implement ongoing monitoring to manage third-party privacy risks.

Identify key components of privacy incident management. Effective incident management includes detection, escalation, investigation, containment, notification, and post-incident review aligned with legal and regulatory requirements. Metrics help measure performance and identify opportunities for improvement.

Understand data subject rights handling processes. Organizations must implement procedures for receiving, authenticating, tracking, and responding to data subject requests (DSRs) within required timeframes.

Apply data minimization and purpose limitation principles. Personal data collection, use, and retention should be limited to what is necessary for defined, legitimate purposes to reduce risk and support compliance.

Ensure integration of privacy operations into business processes. Privacy controls and procedures must be embedded into daily operations, systems, and workflows to ensure consistent and scalable program execution.

Review Questions

1. What is the primary purpose of defining roles and responsibilities in a privacy program?
   - **A.** To reduce operational costs
   - **B.** To ensure accountability and clear ownership of privacy activities
   - **C.** To eliminate regulatory requirements
   - **D.** To centralize all decision-making authority
2. Which function is typically responsible for overseeing privacy compliance across an organization?
   - **A.** Chief Financial Officer
   - **B.** Data Owner
   - **C.** Data Protection Officer or Privacy Officer
   - **D.** Internal Audit
3. Which organizational structure most effectively embeds privacy into daily operations?
   - **A.** Fully centralized privacy team
   - **B.** Fully decentralized approach with no coordination
   - **C.** Federated model with central governance and distributed execution
   - **D.** Outsourced privacy function
4. What is the primary objective of vendor risk assessments in privacy operations?
   - **A.** To evaluate vendor profitability
   - **B.** To ensure vendors comply with privacy and data protection requirements
   - **C.** To reduce procurement timelines
   - **D.** To eliminate all third-party relationships
5. Which document most directly governs a vendor's handling of personal data?
   - **A.** Service Level Agreement (SLA)
   - **B.** Data Processing Agreement (DPA)
   - **C.** Statement of Work (SOW)
   - **D.** Non-disclosure Agreement (NDA)
6. What is the key purpose of incident management in privacy operations?
   - **A.** To eliminate all system vulnerabilities
   - **B.** To ensure timely detection, response, and mitigation of privacy incidents
   - **C.** To assign blame for data breaches
   - **D.** To automate compliance reporting

7. Which of the following is a required component of most breach notification laws?
   A. Notification only if financial loss occurs
   B. Notification only to internal stakeholders
   C. Notification only if encryption was not used
   D. Notification within a defined timeframe after discovery
8. Which role is typically responsible for approving vendor onboarding from a privacy perspective?
   A. Procurement
   B. Privacy or compliance function
   C. IT operations
   D. Marketing
9. What is the primary purpose of a data subject access request (DSAR)?
   A. To allow individuals to access their personal data held by an organization
   B. To request deletion of all company data
   C. To audit internal systems
   D. To monitor employee behavior
10. Which process ensures that data subject requests are handled consistently and within legal timeframes?
   A. Change management
   B. Request fulfillment workflow
   C. Vendor onboarding
   D. Data classification
11. Which metric is most useful for evaluating the effectiveness of privacy incident response?
   A. Number of employees trained
   B. Number of vendors onboarded
   C. Mean time to detect and respond to incidents
   D. Total IT budget
12. Which of the following best describes "privacy by design" in operations?
   A. Applying privacy controls only after deployment
   B. Embedding privacy considerations into processes and systems from the start of their development
   C. Delegating privacy solely to legal teams
   D. Limiting privacy to regulatory compliance

13. What is the primary risk of inadequate vendor oversight?
    A. Increased employee turnover
    B. Unauthorized or non-compliant processing of personal data
    C. Reduced system performance
    D. Higher marketing costs

14. Which activity is essential when managing cross-border data transfers by vendors?
    A. Reducing vendor costs
    B. Ensuring appropriate transfer mechanisms (e.g., SCCs) are in place
    C. Limiting vendor access to financial data only
    D. Eliminating all international vendors

15. Which team typically coordinates communication during a privacy incident?
    A. Human resources
    B. Incident response or crisis management team
    C. Procurement
    D. Sales

16. Which of the following best describes the primary purpose of data minimization in a privacy program?
    A. To ensure that all available data is collected to maximize analytical value
    B. To encrypt all personal data at rest and in transit
    C. To centralize all personal data into a single repository for easier governance
    D. To limit the collection, use, and retention of personal data to what is necessary for a defined purpose

17. Which factor determines whether a data subject request can be denied?
    A. Organizational preference
    B. Legal exemptions or limitations defined by applicable laws
    C. Request complexity
    D. Cost of processing the request

18. Which of the following best aligns with the principle of accountability in vendor management?
    A. Transferring all liability to the vendor through contracts
    B. Relying solely on vendor certifications
    C. Continuously monitoring vendor compliance and performance
    D. Limiting vendor access to non-sensitive data only

19. An organization experiences a data breach involving encrypted personal data. Under most regulations, when is notification typically required?

    A. Always required regardless of risk

    B. Only if encryption keys were compromised or the risk to individuals exists

    C. Never required if encryption was used

    D. Only if regulators request it

20. Which operational control best supports the timely fulfillment of data subject deletion requests?

    A. Data retention schedules aligned with deletion workflows

    B. Increased storage capacity

    C. Manual approval processes only

    D. Vendor audits

Answers to Review Questions

1. B. Clearly defined roles and responsibilities ensure that specific individuals or functions are accountable for privacy-related tasks such as data handling, incident response, and compliance monitoring. Without clear ownership, gaps and overlaps can occur, increasing the risk of non-compliance. This structure also supports governance by enabling effective oversight and escalation.

2. C. The Data Protection Officer (DPO) or Privacy Officer is tasked with monitoring compliance with privacy laws and internal policies, advising leadership, and serving as a point of contact for regulators. While other roles contribute, the DPO provides centralized oversight and ensures alignment with regulatory obligations.

3. C. A federated model balances centralized governance with decentralized execution, allowing business units to manage privacy risks within their operations while adhering to enterprise standards. This approach improves scalability, accountability, and integration of privacy into business processes compared to purely centralized or decentralized models.

4. B. Vendor risk assessments evaluate whether third parties have adequate controls to protect personal data and comply with applicable regulations. This includes reviewing security measures, data handling practices, and legal commitments. The goal is to reduce the organization's exposure to regulatory, operational, and reputational risks stemming from vendor relationships.

5. B. A Data Processing Agreement (DPA) specifies how a vendor processes personal data, including instructions, security requirements, breach-notification obligations, and restrictions on data use. While other documents can include related provisions, the DPA is the primary legal instrument for ensuring compliant data processing.

6. B. Incident management focuses on identifying and responding to privacy incidents quickly to limit harm to individuals and the organization. This includes detection, containment, investigation, and recovery. Effective incident management also supports compliance with breach-notification requirements and helps prevent recurrence by capturing lessons learned.

7. D. Many privacy regulations mandate that organizations notify regulators and/or affected individuals within a specified timeframe after becoming aware of a breach. This requirement ensures timely awareness and enables affected parties to take protective actions. The exact timeframe and conditions vary by jurisdiction.

8. B. While procurement manages vendor selection and contracting, the privacy or compliance function evaluates whether the vendor meets data protection requirements. This includes reviewing contractual terms, security controls, and regulatory alignment before approving onboarding.

9. A. A DSAR enables individuals to obtain information about the personal data an organization holds about them, including how it is used and shared. This supports transparency and is a core right under many privacy laws, including the GDPR and the CCPA/CPRA.

10. B. A defined request fulfillment workflow standardizes how requests are received, validated, processed, and completed. This ensures consistency, reduces errors, and helps organizations meet statutory deadlines for responding to data subject requests.

11. C. Metrics such as mean time to detect (MTTD) and mean time to respond (MTTR) provide direct insight into how quickly an organization can identify and address incidents. Faster response times typically reduce impact and demonstrate operational maturity.

12. B. Privacy by design requires integrating privacy principles into system and process development from the beginning, rather than retrofitting controls later. This approach reduces risk, improves compliance, and enhances trust by proactively addressing privacy concerns.

13. B. Without proper oversight, vendors might mishandle personal data, fail to meet regulatory requirements, or introduce security vulnerabilities. Since organizations remain accountable for their vendors' actions, inadequate oversight can result in legal penalties and reputational damage.

14. B. Cross-border data transfers are subject to legal restrictions in many jurisdictions. Mechanisms such as standard contractual clauses (SCCs) or adequacy decisions ensure that transferred data receives appropriate protection consistent with regulatory requirements.

15. B. The incident response or crisis management team is responsible for coordinating communications with internal stakeholders, regulators, customers, and the public. Effective communication is critical to managing reputational impact and ensuring regulatory compliance.

16. D. Data minimization is a foundational privacy principle requiring organizations to collect, use, and retain only the personal data strictly necessary to achieve a specified legitimate purpose. This reduces exposure, limits the impact of potential breaches, and supports compliance with regulations such as GDPR.

17. B. Privacy laws often include specific exemptions that allow organizations to deny or limit requests, such as those protecting trade secrets or those that require compliance with legal obligations. Decisions must be based on these legal criteria, not operational convenience.

18. C. Accountability requires organizations to actively oversee vendors' activities rather than merely rely on contractual terms or certifications. Continuous monitoring, audits, and performance reviews ensure that vendors maintain compliance over time, reflecting the organization's ongoing responsibility for outsourced processing.

19. B. Many regulations adopt a risk-based approach to breach notification. If strong encryption renders the data unintelligible and keys remain secure, the risk to individuals can be minimal, and notification might not be required. However, if keys are compromised or risk remains, notification obligations are triggered.

20. A. Well-defined data retention schedules, combined with automated or standardized deletion workflows, ensure that personal data is removed in accordance with both regulatory requirements and data subject requests. This reduces delays, minimizes errors, and supports compliance with legal obligations.

Risk Management

This chapter covers CDPSE Domain 2, "Privacy Risk Management and Compliance," specifically the "Risk Management" subdomain.

This chapter covers these job practice elements:

✔ *A—RISK MANAGEMENT*

1. *Risk Management Process and Policies*
2. *Privacy-focused Assessment (e.g., Privacy Impact Assessment (PIA))*
3. *Privacy Training and Awareness*
4. *Threats and Vulnerabilities*
5. *Risk Response*

The other subdomain in Domain 2, Privacy Risk Management and Compliance, is:

✔ *B—COMPLIANCE*—covered in Chapter 4.

The CDPSE Task Statements relevant to this domain are:

5. *Perform privacy impact assessments (PIAs) and other privacy-focused assessments.*
8. *Identify and assess privacy-related threats and vulnerabilities.*
15. *Advise on data classification for personal information to enable risk assessment and implementation of controls.*
18. *Contribute to the development of educational content and conduct privacy training to promote a privacy aware culture.*

The topics in this chapter and in Chapter 4 account for 18% of the CDPSE examination.

Because so much of privacy management has its roots in information security (remember that privacy is the lawful processing, purpose limitation, and protection of personal information), privacy risk cannot be separated from information risk any more than data protection can be removed from privacy.

This chapter describes risk management through three lenses:

- **Risk management lifecycle** This is the "big picture" process of risk management—the cyclical, iterative process used by any organization that stores or processes personal information in information systems. Organizations need to create and implement an overall privacy and cybersecurity risk management process that might not be a part of an existing enterprise risk management (ERM) process.
- **Privacy impact assessments** PIAs assist in the development of risk assessments focused on changes in business processes or information systems. A PIA is an analysis of how personally identifiable information (PII) is collected, used, shared, and maintained, and is intended to identify privacy risks associated with a project or proposed change to systems or business processes.
- **Threats, vulnerabilities, and attacks** To perform a proper PIA, privacy specialists need to understand the threats, vulnerabilities, and attacks associated with privacy risk. Knowledge of these will result in a PIA that is less likely to overlook any factors.

Privacy programs can succeed if they include regular risk assessments within a formal risk management program. Indeed, risk management is a core tenet of cybersecurity programs, often referred to as *information security management systems (ISMSs)*. Within a privacy program, organizations will undergo PIAs as a part of their standard *business change management* and *IT change management* processes. PIAs are not much different from cybersecurity risk assessments for these change management processes: they focus on identifying privacy risks that could arise as part of these planned changes. Training management and staff on the organization's privacy policy and practices is essential to ensure they understand what is expected of them.

Risk Management Processes and Policies

Like other lifecycle processes, *risk management* is a cyclical, iterative activity used to identify, analyze, and manage risks. This book focuses on privacy risk, but overall, the privacy risk lifecycle is functionally similar to that for information risk or even business risk: a new risk is introduced into the process, the risk is studied, and a decision is made about its outcome.

Like other lifecycle processes, risk management is formally defined in policy and process documents that define the scope, roles and responsibilities, workflow, business rules, and business records. Several frameworks and standards from U.S. and international sources define the full lifecycle risk process. Privacy and security managers are generally free to adopt any of these standards, use a blend of different standards, or develop a custom framework.

Both privacy and information risk management rely on risk assessments that account for valid threats to the organization's information assets and current vulnerabilities. Several standards and models for risk assessments can be used. The results of risk assessments are recorded in a risk register, the official business record that contains current and historical information on risks.

Risk treatment is the process of making decisions about risks after weighing various risk treatment options. Risk treatment decisions are typically made by a business owner associated with the affected business activity and ratified by an executive steering group.

The Risk Management Process

The risk management process consists of a set of structured activities that enable an organization to manage risks systematically. Like other business processes, risk management processes vary somewhat from one organization to the next, but generally they consist of the following activities and concepts:

- **Scope definition** The organization defines the scope of the risk management process itself. Typically, scope definitions include geographic or business-unit parameters. The scope definition is not part of the iterative phase of the risk management process, although it might be redefined from time to time. In an organization's privacy program, the scope should include:
  - Business processes related to the collection, use, and transfer (or sale) of personal information
  - Information systems that support these processes
  - The work centers and processing centers supporting the information systems

  - Information security in support of these systems and processes
  - All of the aforementioned items that are outsourced to third parties
- **Asset identification and valuation** The organization uses various means to discover and track its information (including personal information) and information system assets. A classification scheme might be present that identifies risk and criticality levels. Asset valuation is a key part of asset management processes, and the value of assets is appropriated for use in risk management.
- **Risk appetite** Developed outside of the risk management lifecycle process, *risk appetite* is an expression of the level of risk that an organization is willing to accept. A risk appetite related to information and privacy risks is typically expressed qualitatively.
- **Risk tolerance** Also developed outside the risk management lifecycle, *risk tolerance* is an organization's level of acceptable variation from its risk appetite.
- ***Risk capacity*** The amount of potential loss an organization can tolerate without its continued existence being called into question.
- ***Inherent risk*** The amount of risk that exists in the absence of any controls or mitigation measures. It represents the exposure that naturally exists in a process or system before any safeguards are implemented.
- **Risk identification** This is the first step in the iterative portion of the risk management process, when the organization identifies a risk that comes from one of several sources, including the following:
  - *Risk assessment* This includes an overall risk assessment or a focused risk assessment.
  - *Privacy impact assessment (PIA)* This is an analysis of how PII is collected, used, shared, and maintained as part of planned changes to a business process or information system to identify any changes in privacy risk.
  - *Data protection impact assessment (DPIA)* This is an analysis of how planned changes to a business process or information system will affect an organization's ability to protect specific types of data (such as PII).
  - *Vulnerability assessment* This might be one of several activities, including a security scan, a penetration test, or a source code scan.
  - *Threat advisory* This is an advisory from a product vendor, threat intelligence feed, or news story.
  - *Internal audit* A routine internal audit might reveal a weakness in a business process that warrants attention in the risk management process.
  - *Control self-assessment (CSA)* The self-assessment of an internal control might identify a weakness that needs to be managed in the risk management process.
  - *Change in regulations* A new privacy regulation, a change in an existing regulation, or a precedent set in enforcement or legal proceedings might compel organizations to

see their processes in a new light. Occasionally, this means that a process or control once thought to be compliant (or secure) might need to be revised.

- *Risk analysis* This analysis focuses on information that might uncover additional risks requiring attention.
- *Incident* A security or privacy incident might reveal risks, whether associated with the incident or not. While this is sometimes a matter of risk identification in hindsight, such risks cannot be overlooked.

Threat events encompass various aspects of *compliance risk*, such as audits or examinations (with their findings), fines, penalties, sanctions, or notifications to affected parties (employees, customers, or constituents).

- ***Risk analysis*** This is the second step in a typical risk management process, including a PIA or DPIA. After the risk has been identified, it is then analyzed to determine several characteristics, including the following:
  - *Probability of event occurrence* The risk analyst studies event scenarios and calculates the likelihood that an event associated with the risk will occur. This is typically expressed in the number of likely events per year.
  - *Impact of event occurrence* The risk analyst studies different event scenarios and determines the impact of each. This might be expressed in quantitative terms (dollars or other currency) or qualitative terms (high–medium–low or a numeric scale of 1–5 or 1–10).
  - *Mitigation* The risk analyst studies available methods for mitigating the risk. Depending upon the type of risk, there are many techniques to choose from, including changing a process or procedure, training staff, changing architecture or configuration, or applying a security patch.
  - *Recommendation* After studying a risk, the risk analyst can develop a recommended course of action to address it. This reflects the fact that the individual performing risk analysis is often not the risk decision-maker.
- ***Risk treatment*** Also known as *risk response*, this is the last step in a typical risk management process. Here, the privacy steering committee (or appropriate authoritative group) makes or approves a decision about a specific risk. The basic options for risk treatment are as follows:
  - *Risk acceptance* The organization elects to take no action related to the risk.
  - *Risk mitigation* The organization chooses to mitigate the risk by taking actions that reduce the probability or impact of a risk event. The actual steps taken can include business process changes, system configuration changes, the enactment of a new control, or staff training.

   - *Risk transfer* The practice of transferring risk is typically achieved through an insurance policy, although other forms are available, including contract assignment.
   - *Risk avoidance* The organization chooses to discontinue the activity associated with the risk. This choice is typically selected for an outdated business activity that is no longer profitable, or for one that was not formally approved in the first place.
- **Risk communication** This takes many forms, including formal communications within risk management processes and procedures, as well as information communications among risk managers and decision-makers.

In addition to business processes, a risk management process has associated business records. The *risk register*, sometimes known as a *risk ledger*, is the primary business record in most risk management programs. A risk register is a list of identified risks. Typically, a risk register contains many items, including a description of each risk, its level and type, and information about risk treatment decisions.

Figure 3.1 shows the elements of a typical risk management lifecycle.

Risk Management Methodologies

Several established methodologies are available for organizations that want to manage risk using a formal standard. Organizations select one of these standards for a variety of reasons;

FIGURE 3.1 The risk management lifecycle.

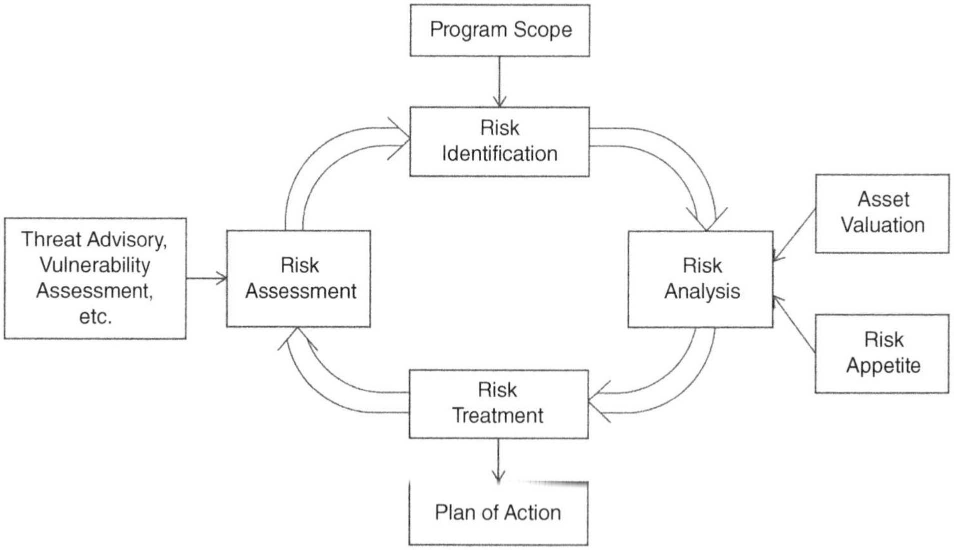

Source: Author.

they might be required to use a specific standard to address regulatory or contractual terms, they might believe that a specific standard better aligns with their overall information risk program or the business as a whole, or they might want to start with a known standard process as opposed to creating one from scratch.

NIST Standards

The National Institute of Standards and Technology (NIST) develops standards for information security and related areas. NIST Special Publication (SP) 800-39, *Managing Information Security Risk: Organization, Mission, and Information, System View*, describes the overall risk management process. NIST SP 800-37, *Risk Management Framework for Information Systems and Organizations*, is a lifecycle risk management process. NIST SP 800-30, *Guide for Conducting Risk Assessments*, is a detailed, high-quality standard that describes the steps for conducting risk assessments.

NIST SP 800-39

NIST SP 800-39 defines how risk management fits within overall organizational governance and enterprise risk management. The methodology described in NIST SP 800-39 consists of multilevel risk management at the information systems level, the mission/business process level, and the overall organization level. Communications up and down these levels ensure that risks are communicated upward for overall awareness, while risk awareness and risk decisions are communicated downward for overall awareness. Figure 3.2 depicts this approach.

FIGURE 3.2 Multitier risk management in NIST SP 800-39.

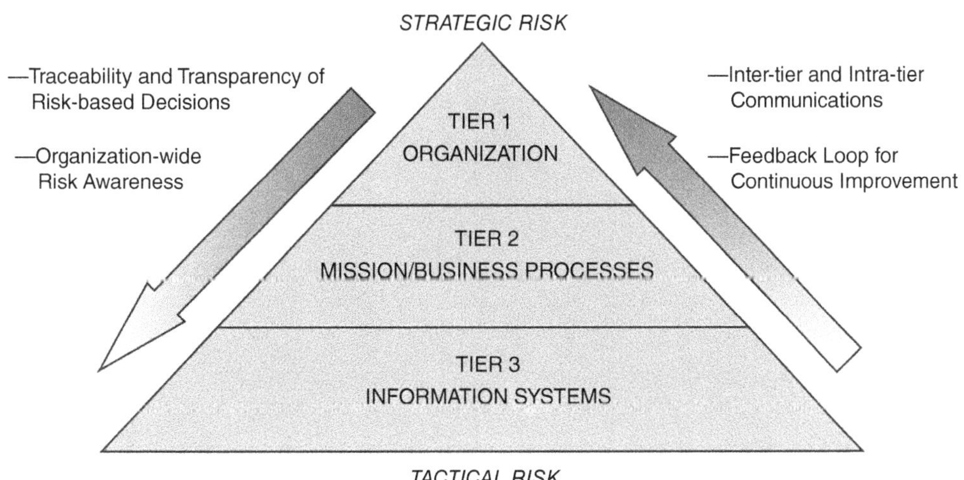

Source: Adapted from National Institute of Standards and Technology.

At first glance, this might appear to be a discussion of cybersecurity risk, but you should know that risk management and risk assessment methodology have wide application. Organizations practicing risk management can do so in the context of operationally critical information systems, manufacturing assembly lines, biomedical laboratory operations, or the protection and use of personal information. For all these, and more, the methodologies of identifying, analyzing, and treating risk are the same.

The tiers of risk management are described in NIST SP 800-39 in this way:

- **Tier 1: Organization view** This level focuses on the role of governance, the activities performed by the risk executive, and the development of risk management and investment strategies.
- **Tier 2: Mission/business process view** This level is all about enterprise architecture and enterprise security architecture, and ensuring that business processes are risk-aware.
- **Tier 3: Information systems view** This level focuses on more tactical aspects, such as system configuration and hardening specifications, vulnerability management, and the detailed steps in the systems development lifecycle.

Other concepts discussed in NIST SP 800-39 include trust, system trustworthiness, and organizational culture.

The overall risk management process defined by NIST SP 800-39 consists of several steps:

- **Step 1: Risk framing** This consists of the assumptions, scope, tolerances, constraints, and priorities—in other words, the business context considered before later steps take place.
- **Step 2: Risk assessment** This is the actual risk assessment, where threats and vulnerabilities are identified and assessed to determine the levels and types of risk.
- **Step 3: Risk response** This is the process of analyzing each risk and developing strategies to reduce it through appropriate risk treatment. Risk treatment options are *accept, mitigate, avoid*, and *transfer*. This step is described in more detail in NIST SP 800-30, which is described next.
- **Step 4: Risk monitoring** This is the process of performing periodic and ongoing evaluation of identified risks to determine whether conditions and risks are changing.

NIST SP 800-37

NIST SP 800-37 describes the risk management framework as an iterative lifecycle process applied to individual systems. The standard provides detailed activities, tasks, and roles for practitioners.

The risk management process includes these steps:

- **Step 1: Prepare** Carry out essential activities at the organization, process, and system levels to prepare to manage security and privacy risks. Seven distinct tasks are defined at this level, including defining roles and responsibilities, the risk management strategy, performing risk assessments, and identifying common controls.

- **Step 2: Categorize the system** Document the characteristics of the system, and categorize it according to the impact on the organization should the system be compromised.
- **Step 3: Select controls** Using the system categorization from Step 2 and the risk framing from Step 1, protective controls are selected, tailored, and documented. Note that controls are selected prior to any risk assessment taking place, which might sound counterintuitive. This is a "chicken and egg" scenario that starts with control selection, followed later by risk assessments that inform control modifications.
- **Step 4: Implement controls** The controls selected in Step 3 are implemented and documented. Updates to controls are also documented.
- **Step 5: Assess controls** Controls are assessed to determine whether they have been implemented properly. Findings are documented and remediation plans are developed.
- **Step 6: Authorize the system** Risks identified in Step 5 are analyzed and rated. A member of senior management determines whether these security and privacy risks (including third-party risk) are at an acceptable level. If not, senior management will stipulate the acceptable level of risk, thereby identifying which risks must be treated. When the level of risk is acceptable, senior management will authorize the use of the system.
- **Step 7: Monitor controls continuously** Ongoing assessments of control effectiveness are performed, risks are analyzed, remediation is implemented, and continued authorizations are issued as required.

NIST SP 800-37 is an iterative process that cements the relationship between control selection and risk assessment. As risk assessments are performed, organizations adjust controls, which are examined in subsequent risk assessments, and so on.

This lifecycle process is depicted in Figure 3.3.

NIST SP 800-30

NIST SP 800-30 describes in greater detail a standard methodology for conducting an individual risk assessment. The techniques in this document are quite structured and essentially involve setting up several worksheets in which threats and vulnerabilities are recorded, along with the probability of their occurrence and the impact if they occur.

In this standard, these are the steps for conducting a risk assessment:

- **Step 1: Prepare for assessment** The organization determines the purpose of the risk assessment. Primarily, it is important to understand the purpose of the risk assessment results and the decisions that will be made as a result. Next, the scope of the assessment must be determined and made known. This can take many forms, including geographic and business-unit boundaries, specific business processes, and the range of threat scenarios to be included. Also, any assumptions and constraints about the assessment

FIGURE 3.3 The NIST SP 800-37 risk management framework.

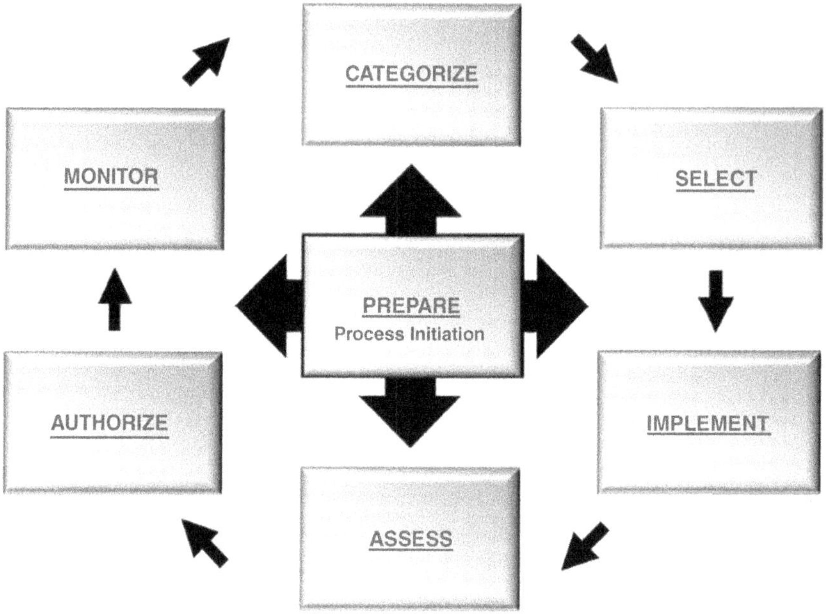

CATEGORIZE
SELECT
IMPLEMENT
ASSESS
AUTHORIZE
MONITOR
PREPARE
Process Initiation

Source: Adapted from National Institute of Standards and Technology.

should be identified. Further, the sources of threat, vulnerability, and impact information must be identified. (NIST SP 800-30 includes exemplary lists of threats, vulnerabilities, and impact in its appendices.)

- **Step 2: Conduct assessment** The organization performs the actual risk assessment. This consists of several tasks.

  a. *Identify threat sources and events* The organization identifies a list of threat sources and events that will be considered in the assessment. The following sources of threat information are included in the standard and can be used. Organizations are advised to supplement these sources with other information as needed.

  - Table D-1: Threat source inputs
  - Table D-2: Threat sources
  - Table D-3: Adversary capabilities
  - Table D-4: Adversary intent
  - Table D-5: Adversary targeting
  - Table D-6: Nonadversarial threat effects
  - Table E-1: Threat events

- Table E-2: Adversarial threat events
- Table E-3: Nonadversarial threat events
- Table E-4: Relevance of threat events

b. *Identify vulnerabilities and predisposing conditions* The organization examines its environment (people, processes, and technology) to identify vulnerabilities that could increase the likelihood of threat events. The following sources of information on vulnerability and predisposing conditions are included in the standard and can be used in a risk assessment. Like the catalog of threats, organizations are advised to supplement these lists with additional vulnerabilities as needed.

- Table F-1: Input—vulnerability and predisposing conditions
- Table F-2: Vulnerability severity assessment scale
- Table F-4: Predisposing conditions
- Table F-5: Pervasiveness of predisposing conditions

c. *Determine the likelihood of occurrence* The organization determines the probability that each threat scenario identified will occur. The following tables guide the risk manager in scoring each threat:

- Table G-1: Inputs—determination of likelihood
- Table G-2: Assessment scale—likelihood of threat event initiation
- Table G-3: Assessment scale—likelihood of threat event occurrence
- Table G-4: Assessment scale—likelihood of threat event resulting in adverse impact
- Table G-5: Assessment scale—overall likelihood

d. *Determine the magnitude of impact* In this phase, the risk manager determines the impact of each type of threat event on the organization. These tables guide the risk manager in this effort:

- Table H-1: Input—determination of impact
- Table H-2: Examples of adverse impacts
- Table H-3: Assessment scale—impact of threat events
- Table H-4: Identification of adverse impacts

e. *Determine the risk level* The organization determines the level of risk for each threat event. These tables aid the risk manager in this effort:

- Table I-1: Inputs—risk
- Table I-2: Assessment scale—level of risk (combination of likelihood and impact)
- Table I-3: Assessment scale—level of risk
- Table I-4: Column descriptions for adversarial risk table

    - Table I-5: Template for adversarial risk table to be completed by risk manager
    - Table I-6: Column descriptions for nonadversarial risk table
    - Table I-7: Template for nonadversarial risk table to be completed by risk manager
- **Step 3: Communicate results** When the risk assessment has been completed, the results are communicated to decision-makers and stakeholders in the organization. The purpose of communicating risk assessment results is to ensure that the organization's decision-makers make decisions that include considerations for known risks. Risk assessment results can be communicated in several ways, including the following:
    - Publishing to a central location
    - Briefings
    - Distributing via email
    - Distributing hard copies
- **Step 4: Maintain assessment** After a risk assessment has been completed, the organization will maintain the assessment by monitoring the risk factors identified in it. This enables the organization to maintain a view of relevant risks that incorporates changes in the business environment since the risk assessment was completed. NIST SP 800-137, *Information Security Continuous Monitoring (ISCM) for Federal Information Systems and Organizations*, provides guidance on the ongoing monitoring of information systems, operations, and risks.

NIST SP 800-30, 37, and 39 are available at `https://csrc.nist.gov/publications/sp`.

ISO/IEC 27005

ISO/IEC 27005, Information security, cybersecurity, and privacy protection—Guidance on managing information security risks, is an international standard that defines a structured approach to risk assessments and risk management. The methodology outlined in this standard is summarized here.

Step 1: Establish Context

Before a risk assessment can be performed, several parameters need to be established, including the following:

- **Scope of the risk assessment** This includes which portions of an organization are to be included, based on business unit, service, line, geography, organizational structure, or other criteria.

- **Purpose of the risk assessment** Reasons include legal, due diligence, or support of an ISMS, business continuity plan, vulnerability management plan, or incident response plan.
- **Risk evaluation criteria** Determine how risks will be examined and scored.
- **Impact criteria** Determine how the impact of identified risks will be described and scored.
- **Risk acceptance criteria** Specify the method the organization will use to determine risk acceptance.
- **Logistical plan** This includes which personnel will perform the risk assessment, which personnel in the organization need to provide information, such as control evidence, and what supporting facilities are required, such as office space.

Step 2: Risk Assessment

The risk assessment is performed with the following tasks:

- **Asset identification** Risk analysts identify assets, along with their value and criticality.
- **Threat identification** Risk analysts identify relevant and credible threats that have the potential to harm assets, along with their likelihood of occurrence. There are many types of threats, both naturally occurring and human-caused, and accidental or deliberate. Note that some threats can affect more than one asset. ISO/IEC 27005 contains a list of threat types, as does NIST SP 800-30 (in Table D-2), described earlier.

A risk analyst is encouraged to consider additional threats specific to the organization that are not contained in ISO/IEC 27005 or NIST SP 800-30.

- **Control identification** Risk analysts identify existing and planned controls. Those controls that already exist should be examined to see whether they are effective. The criteria for examining a control include whether it adequately reduces the likelihood or impact of a threat event. The results of this examination will conclude whether the control is effective, ineffective, or unnecessary. Finally, when identifying threats, the risk analyst might determine that a new control is warranted.
- **Vulnerability identification** Vulnerabilities that can be exploited by threat events causing harm to an asset are identified. Remember that a vulnerability does not cause harm, but its presence might permit a threat event to harm an asset. ISO/IEC 27005 contains a list of vulnerabilities. Note that a risk analyst might need to identify additional vulnerabilities.
- **Consequences identification** The risk analyst will identify the consequences that would occur for each identified threat against each asset. Consequences can include the loss of confidentiality, integrity, or availability of any asset, as well as a loss of human safety. Depending on the nature of the asset, consequences can take many forms, including

service interruption or degradation, reduced service quality, loss of business, reputational damage, or monetary penalties such as fines. Note that consequences can be a primary result or a secondary result of the realization of a specific threat. For example, the theft of sensitive financial information might have little or no operational impact in the short term. Still, legal proceedings over the long term could result in financial penalties, unexpected costs, and loss of business.

Step 3: Risk Evaluation

Levels of risk are determined according to the risk evaluation and risk acceptance criteria established in Step 1. The output of risk evaluation is a list of risks, with their associated threats, vulnerabilities, and consequences.

Step 4: Risk Treatment

Decision-makers in the organization will select one of four *risk treatment* options for each risk identified in Step 3:

- **Risk modification (aka risk mitigation, risk reduction)** The organization alters something in information technology (such as security configuration, application source code, or data), business processes and procedures, or personnel (such as training). In many cases, an organization will choose to update an existing control or enact a new one so that the risk reduction can be monitored more effectively over time. The cost of updating or creating a control—as well as the impact on ongoing operational costs of the control—will need to be weighed against the value of the asset being protected and the consequences associated with the risk being treated. A risk manager remembers that a control can reduce many risks, and potentially for several assets, so the risk manager will need to consider the benefit of risk reduction in more complex terms. Chapter 8 covers a comprehensive discussion of the types of controls.[1]
- **Risk retention (aka risk acceptance)** The organization chooses to accept the risk and decides not to change anything.
- **Risk avoidance** The organization decides to discontinue the activity associated with the risk. For example, an organization assesses the risks associated with accepting credit card data for payments and decides to change the system so that credit card data is sent directly to a payment processor, after which the organization will no longer accept credit card data.
- **Risk sharing (aka risk transfer)** The organization transfers risk to another party. The common forms of risk transfer are insurance and outsourcing security monitoring to a third party. When an organization transfers risk to another party, there will usually be residual risk that is more difficult to treat. For example, while an organization might have incurred lower costs due to a breach because of cyber insurance, it can still suffer reputational damage in the form of reduced goodwill.

[1] My book, *CRISC Certified in Risk and Information Systems Control* (Wiley Publishing), has a more complete discussion on controls.

Decision-makers weigh the costs and benefits of each of these four options and determine the best course of action for the organization. These four risk treatment options are not mutually exclusive; sometimes a combination is the best choice for a specific situation. For instance, a business application was found to accept weak passwords; the chosen risk treatment was a combination of security awareness training (mitigation) and acceptance (the organization elected not to modify the application, as this would have been too expensive).

Further, some treatments can address more than one risk. For example, security awareness training might reduce several risks associated with end-user computing and behavior.

Often, after risk treatment, some risk—known as *residual risk*—remains. When analyzing residual risk, the organization might elect to undertake additional risk treatment to reduce it further, or accept the residual risk as is. Note that residual risk cannot be reduced to zero—there will always be some level of risk.

Because some forms of risk treatment (mainly risk reduction and risk transfer) might require an extended period to complete, risk managers usually track ongoing risk treatment activities to completion.

Step 5: Risk Communication

All parties involved in information risk—the chief information security officer (CISO) or another top-ranking information security official, risk managers, business decision-makers, and other stakeholders—need channels of communication throughout the entire risk management and risk treatment lifecycle. Examples of risk communication include the following:

- Announcements and discussions of upcoming risk assessments
- Collection of risk information during risk assessments (and at other times)
- Proceedings and results from completed risk assessments
- Discussions of risk tolerance
- Proceedings from risk treatment discussions, risk treatment decisions, and plans
- Educational information about security and risk
- Updates on the organization's mission and strategic objectives
- Communication about security incidents to affected parties and stakeholders

Step 6: Risk Monitoring and Review

Organizations are not static, and neither is risk. The value of assets, impacts, threats, and vulnerabilities, and the likelihood of risk occurrence should be periodically monitored and reviewed so that the organization's view of risk remains relevant and accurate. Monitoring should include:

- Discovery of new, changed, and retired assets
- Change in business processes and practices
- Changes in technology architecture

- New threats that have not been assessed
- New vulnerabilities that were previously unknown
- Changes in threat event probability and consequences
- Security incidents that might alter the organization's understanding of threats, vulnerabilities, and risks
- Changes in market and other business conditions
- Changes in applicable laws and regulations

ISO/IEC 27005 is available at `www.iso.org/home.html`.

Factor Analysis of Information Risk

Factor Analysis of Information Risk (FAIR) is an analysis method that helps a risk manager understand the factors that contribute to risk, the probability of threat occurrence, and the potential losses. In the FAIR methodology, there are six types of loss:

- **Productivity** Lost productivity caused by the incident
- **Response** The cost expended in incident response
- **Replacement** The expense required to rebuild or replace an asset
- **Fines and judgments** All forms of legal costs resulting from the incident
- **Competitive advantage** Loss of business to other organizations
- **Reputation** Loss of goodwill and future business

FAIR also focuses on the concept of asset value and liability. For example, a customer list is an asset because the organization can reach its customers to solicit new business; however, it is also a liability because the organization's reputation could be damaged if the list is obtained by an unauthorized person.

Exam Tip

CDPSE candidates are not expected to memorize risk assessment methodologies, but they should be familiar with the overall concepts of risk assessment.

FAIR guides a risk manager through an analysis of threat agents and the different ways in which a threat agent acts upon an asset:

- **Access** Threat agent reads data without authorization
- **Misuse** Threat agent uses an asset differently from its intended usage

- **Disclose** Threat agent shares data with other unauthorized parties
- **Modify** Threat agent modifies asset
- **Deny use** Threat agent prevents legitimate subjects from accessing assets

FAIR is often cited as complementary to risk management methodologies such as NIST SP 800-30 and ISO/IEC 27005.

You can obtain information about FAIR at `www.fairinstitute.org`.

Asset Identification

After the scope of a risk assessment has been determined, the initial step is identifying assets and determining each asset's value. In a typical information risk assessment, assets will consist of various types of information (including intellectual property, internal operations, and personal information), the information systems that support and protect these assets, and the business processes supported by these systems.

Chapter 8 contains a detailed discussion on the types, valuation, and classification of assets.

Risk Identification

Risk identification is the activity during a risk assessment in which various scenarios are studied for each asset. Several considerations are applied in the analysis of each risk, including:

- **Threats** A *threat* is an event that, if realized, would bring harm to an asset. All realistic threat scenarios are examined for each asset to determine which are reasonably likely to occur.
- **Threat actors** A *threat actor* is a person who is able to carry out a threat. It is important to understand the variety of threat actors and which ones are more motivated to target the organization, and why. This further illuminates the likelihood that a given threat scenario will occur.
- **Threat agents** A *threat agent* is a human or non-human capable of carrying out a threat. A threat agent can be a *hacker*, cybercriminal, a disgruntled employee, or a hurricane.
- **Vulnerabilities** For each asset (both information and information systems), business process, and staff member being examined, vulnerabilities need to be identified. Then, various threat scenarios are considered to determine which are made more likely because of corresponding vulnerabilities.
- **Asset value** The value of each asset is an important factor to include in risk analysis. As described in the earlier section on asset value, assets can be valued in several ways.

For instance, a customer database might have a modest recovery cost if it is damaged or destroyed; however, if that same customer database is stolen and sold on the black market, the value of the data can be much higher to cybercriminals, and the resulting costs to the organization to mitigate the harm done to customers can be higher still. Another way to examine asset value is through the revenue derived from its existence or use. The financial consequences of a ruined reputation are not included here but are a part of the impact, discussed in the next item.

Qualitative and quantitative risk analysis techniques help to distinguish higher risks from lower risks. These techniques are discussed later in this section.

Risks above a certain level are recorded in a risk register, where they will be processed through risk analysis and risk treatment.

Risk, Likelihood, and Impact

During risk analysis in a risk assessment, the risk manager will perform simple calculations on all identified risks. The standard calculation for risk is as follows:

Risk = probability × impact

ISO/IEC Guide 73, *Risk management—Vocabulary*, defines *risk* as "the combination of the probability of an event and its consequence." This is an excellent way to understand risk in simple, qualitative terms.

Likelihood

In risk assessments, *likelihood* is an important dimension that helps a risk manager understand several aspects related to the unfolding of a threat event. The likelihood of a serious security incident has less to do with technical details and more with an adversary's thought process.

Considerations related to likelihood include the following:

- **Hygiene** This is related to an organization's security operations practices. Organizations that do a poor job of vulnerability management, patch management, and system hardening, for example, are more likely to suffer incidents simply because they make it easier for adversaries to gain access to their systems.
- **Data management** Relevant to a privacy program, the quality and effectiveness of an organization's data management program will bear on the probability of a privacy breach. If an organization has mature data management capabilities, it will likely be aware of anomalous behavior indicating a potential breach. On the other hand, an organization that pays little attention to its data is more likely to have its data compromised without the organization being aware.
- **Visibility** This factor is related to the organization's standing: how broad and visible the organization is and how much the attacker's prestige will increase as a result of a successfully compromised target.

- **Velocity** The timing of various threat scenarios and whether there is any warning or foreknowledge are factors. For example, an adversary determined to exfiltrate a large volume of data undetected is likely to proceed very slowly; on the other hand, ransomware can destroy an organization's data in minutes.
- **Motivation** It is essential to consider various types of adversaries to understand the factors that would motivate them to attack the organization. It could be about money, reputation, or rivalry.
- **Skill** For various threat scenarios, what skill level is required to attack the organization successfully? A higher skill level does not always mean an attack is less likely; other considerations, such as motivation, also come into play.

Impact

During risk assessments, impact is a key attribute of any threat scenario that a risk manager needs to understand fully. In the context of privacy, the definition of *impact* is the actual or expected result from some action, such as a breach.

Impact is perhaps the most critical attribute to understand for a threat scenario. A risk assessment can describe all types of threat scenarios, the reasons behind them, and how to minimize them. Still, without understanding the impact of threat scenarios, a risk manager cannot determine how important one threat is relative to another in terms of the urgency to mitigate the risk.

A wide range of impact scenarios is possible:

- Direct cash losses
- Reputation damage
- Loss of business—decrease in sales
- Drop in share price—less access to capital
- Reduction in market share
- Diminished operational efficiency (higher internal costs)
- Civil liability
- Legal liability
- Compliance liability (fines, censures, and so on)
- Interruption of business operations

Some of these impact scenarios are easier to analyze qualitatively than others, and the magnitude of most is difficult to quantify except in specific threat scenarios.

One of the main tools in the business continuity and disaster planning world, the *business impact analysis (BIA)* is highly useful for privacy and information security managers. A BIA can be conducted as part of a risk assessment or separately from it.

A BIA differs from a risk assessment. Although a risk assessment is used to identify risks and, perhaps, suggest remedies, a BIA is used to identify the most critical business processes, together with their supporting IT systems and dependencies on other processes or systems.

FIGURE 3.4 Qualitative risk matrix.

Probability				
	Likely	Medium Risk	High Risk	Extreme Risk
	Unlikely	Low Risk	Medium Risk	High Risk
	Highly Unlikely	Insignificant Risk	Low Risk	Medium Risk
		Slightly Harmful	**Harmful**	**Extremely Harmful**
		Consequences		

Source: Author.

The value that a BIA brings to a risk assessment is the understanding of which business processes and IT systems are the most important to the organization. The BIA helps the security manager better understand which processes are the most critical and, therefore, warrant the most protection, all other considerations being equal.

In qualitative risk analysis, where probability and impact are rated on simple Low-Medium-High scales, a *risk matrix* is sometimes used to depict risk levels based on probability and impact. Figure 3.4 shows a typical risk matrix.

Risk Analysis Techniques and Considerations

As part of a risk assessment, the risk manager examines assets, associated vulnerabilities, and likely threat scenarios. The *risk analysis* is the detailed examination conducted here.

Risk analysis considers many dimensions of an asset, including these:

- Asset value
- Threat scenarios
- Threat probabilities
- Relevant vulnerabilities
- Existing controls and their effectiveness
- Operational criticality (according to a BIA, if available)
- Impact

Various risk analysis techniques are discussed in the remainder of this section.

Information Gathering

A risk manager needs to gather a considerable amount of information so that the risk analysis and the risk assessment are valuable and complete. Several sources are available, including:

- Interviews with process owners
- Interviews with application developers
- Interviews with privacy and security personnel
- Interviews with external privacy and security experts, including legal counsel
- Privacy and security incident records
- Analysis of incidents that occur in other organizations
- Prior risk assessments (however, caution is advised to stop the propagation of risk calculation errors from one assessment to the next)

Qualitative Risk Analysis

Most risk analysis begins with *qualitative risk analysis*. This technique does not seek to identify the exact (or even approximate) asset value, impact, or the exact probability of occurrence. Instead, these items are expressed on a scale such as high, medium, or low. The purpose of qualitative risk analysis is to understand how risks relate to one another so that higher risks can be distinguished from lower ones. This is a valuable pursuit because it enables an organization to focus on more critical risks based on qualitative impact.

Semi-quantitative Risk Analysis

In *semi-quantitative risk analysis*, the probability of occurrence can be expressed as a numeric value, such as 1 to 5 (where 5 is the highest probability). Impact can also be expressed as a numeric value, also in the range 1 to 5. Then, for each asset and each threat, risk is calculated as *probability × impact*.

For example, suppose an organization has identified two risk scenarios. The first is a risk of data theft from a customer database; the impact is scored 5 (highest), and the probability is scored 4 (highly likely). The risk is scored as $5 \times 4 = 20$. The second is the risk of theft of application source code; the impact is scored as 2 (low), and the probability is scored as 2 (less likely). This risk is scored as $2 \times 2 = 4$.

The risk manager understands that the data theft risk is more significant (scored 20) than the source code theft risk (scored 4). These risk scores do not indicate that the larger risk is five times as likely to occur; neither do they mean that the larger risk is five times as expensive. They indicate that one risk is rated higher than the other. The scores also do not directly indicate whether the probability or the impact alone is high or low: analysis of the detailed scores is necessary to know that.

Note that some risk managers consider this a qualitative risk analysis because the results are no more accurate regarding costs and probabilities than the qualitative technique.

Quantitative Risk Analysis

In *quantitative risk analysis*, risk managers attempt to determine the actual costs and probabilities of events. This technique provides executives with more specific information about the costs they can expect to incur in various security event scenarios.

Two aspects of quantitative risk analysis prove to be a continuing challenge:

- **Event probability** It is difficult to come up with even an order-of-magnitude estimate of the probability for nearly every event scenario. Even with better information coming from industry sources, the probability of high-impact incidents depends on many factors, some of which are difficult to identify or even quantify.
- **Event cost** It is difficult to put an exact cost on any given privacy or security incident scenario. Privacy and security incidents are complex events that involve many parties and have unpredictable short- and long-term outcomes. Despite ever-improving information from research organizations on breach costs, these remain rough estimates and might not account for all aspects of cost.

Because of these challenges, quantitative risk analysis should be regarded as an effort to develop estimates rather than exact figures. Partly, this is because risk analysis measures events that *might* occur, not those that *do* occur.

Standard quantitative risk analysis involves the development of several figures:

- ***Asset value (AV)*** This is the value of the asset, which is usually (but not necessarily) the asset's replacement value. Depending on the type of asset, different values might need to be considered.
- ***Exposure factor (EF)*** This is the financial loss that results from the realization of a threat, expressed as a percentage of the asset's total value. Most threats do not eliminate the asset's value; instead, they reduce its value. For example, if an organization's $120,000 server is rendered unbootable by malware, it will still have salvage value, even if only 10% of the asset's total value. In this case, the EF would be 90%. Note that different threats will have varying impacts on EF, as the realization of different threats will cause different amounts of damage to assets.
- ***Single loss expectancy (SLE)*** This value represents the financial loss when a threat scenario occurs once. SLE is defined as $AV \times EF$. Note that different threats have varying impacts on EF, so they will have the same multiplicative effect on SLE.
- ***Annualized rate of occurrence (ARO)*** This is an estimate of the number of times a threat will occur per year. If the probability of the threat is 1 in 50 (one occurrence every 50 years), then ARO is expressed as 0.02. However, if the threat is estimated to occur four times per year, then ARO is 4.0. Like EF and SLE, ARO will vary by threat.
- ***Annualized loss expectancy (ALE)*** This is the expected annualized loss of asset value due to threat realization. ALE is defined as $SLE \times ARO$.

ALE is based upon the verifiable values AV, EF, and SLE, but because ARO is only an estimate, ALE is only as good as the ARO. Depending on the asset's value, the risk manager might need to take extra care to develop the best possible estimate of ARO based on the available data. Sources for estimates include the following:

- History of event losses in the organization
- History of similar losses in other organizations
- History of dissimilar losses
- Best estimates based on available data

When performing a quantitative risk analysis for a given asset, the ALEs for all threats can be summed. The sum of all ALEs is the annualized loss expectancy for the complete array of threats. An unusually high number of ALEs would mean that a given asset is facing many significant threats that are more likely to occur. But in terms of risk treatment, ALEs are better off left as separate and associated with their respective threats.

OCTAVE

Operationally Critical Threat, Asset, and Vulnerability Evaluation (OCTAVE) is a risk analysis approach developed by Carnegie Mellon University. The latest version, OCTAVE Allegro, is used to assess privacy and security risks so an organization can obtain meaningful results from a risk assessment.

The OCTAVE Allegro methodology uses eight steps:

- **Step 1: Establish risk measurement criteria** The organization identifies the most critical impact areas, which, in the model, include *reputation/customer confidence, financial, productivity, safety and health, fines/legal penalties,* and *other*. For example, reputation can be the most critical impact area for one organization, while privacy or safety can be most important for others.
- **Step 2: Develop an information asset profile** The organization identifies its in-scope information assets and develops a profile for each that describes their features, qualities, characteristics, and value. Noting whether regulated personal information is included is of particular use for an organization's privacy program.
- **Step 3: Identify information asset containers** The organization identifies all internal and external information systems that store, process, and transmit in-scope assets, especially personal information. Note that many of these systems can be operated by third-party organizations.
- **Step 4: Identify areas of concern** This is the start of identifying threats that, if realized, could cause harm to information assets. Typically, this is identified in a brainstorming activity.

- **Step 5: Identify threat scenarios** This is a continuation of Step 4, where threat scenarios are expanded upon (and unlikely ones are eliminated). A threat tree can be developed that first identifies actors and basic scenarios, then expands to include more details.
- **Step 6: Identify risks** A continuation of Step 5, the consequences of each threat scenario are identified.
- **Step 7: Analyze risks** This simple quantitative measure is used to score each threat scenario based on risk criteria developed in Step 1. The output is a ranked list of risks.
- **Step 8: Select mitigation approach** A continuation of Step 7, the risks with higher scores are analyzed to determine methods available for risk reduction.

The OCTAVE Allegro methodology includes worksheets for each step described here, making it easy for an individual or team to perform a risk analysis using this technique.

Further information about OCTAVE Allegro is available at `www.cert.org/resilience/products-services/octave/`.

Other Risk Analysis Methodologies

Additional risk analysis methodologies provide more complex approaches that can be useful for certain organizations or in selected risk situations.

- **Delphi method** In this method, questionnaires are distributed to a panel of experts in two or more rounds. A facilitator will anonymize the responses and distribute them to the experts. The objective is for the experts to converge on the most critical risks and mitigation strategies.
- **Event tree analysis (ETA)** A logic modeling technique for analyzing the potential consequences given a specific starting event scenario—in this case, a threat scenario.
- **Fault tree analysis (FTA)** A logical modeling technique used to identify how an undesired event occurs. FTA begins with a specific top-level event and works backwards to identify root cause that led to the event. A large "tree" diagram can result, which depicts many different chains of events.
- **Monte Carlo analysis** Derived from Monte Carlo computational algorithms, this analysis begins with a given system and inputs, with the inputs constrained to minimum, likely, and maximum values. Running the simulation provides some insight into actual likely scenarios.

> **Exam Tip**
>
> CDPSE candidates are not expected to memorize risk analysis techniques, but you should be familiar with general risk analysis concepts.

Privacy-focused Assessments

A *privacy impact assessment (PIA)*, sometimes confused with a *data protection impact assessment (DPIA*, as coined in the General Data Protection Regulation [GDPR]), is a targeted risk assessment undertaken to identify impacts to individual privacy and impacts to an organization's ability to protect information resulting from a proposed change to a business process or information system. PIAs are not a new concept. They have been required since 2002 for U.S. government electronic services and processes under the E-Government Act of 2002, and the European Union Article 29 Working Party endorsed the requirement to conduct PIAs for radiofrequency identification applications in 2011. However, Article 35 of the GDPR increased the visibility of this process because it applies to all businesses that process personal data.

While a DPIA generally focuses on an organization's ability to protect personal data, Article 35 of the GDPR goes a step further to include risks to the rights and freedoms of individual data subjects.

Generally, a PIA is conducted for new processes or systems that collect, store, or transmit PII, or for significant modifications to existing processes or systems that might create a new privacy risk. The purpose of a PIA is to ensure that personal information collected is used only for the intended purpose, and it identifies the impact(s) that any process or system change has on the organization's compliance with its privacy policy and applicable privacy laws and regulations.

One could also say that the purpose of a PIA is to validate the proposed change from a privacy perspective. By "validate," I mean that the proposed change has been well-designed (presumably with privacy and security by design) and that its impact on privacy is neutral or better.

> **Exam Tip**
>
> CDPSE candidates are not expected to memorize PIA procedures. You should, however, be familiar with the concepts, purposes, and approaches for performing PIAs.

Two excellent resources for PIAs and how PIAs achieve these objectives are:

- `www.gsa.gov/reference/gsa-privacy-program/privacy-impact-assessments-pia`
- `www.ftc.gov/site-information/privacy-policy/privacy-impact-assessments`

Privacy Impact Assessment (PIA) Procedure

The following is a procedure for conducting a PIA:

1. Obtain a description of the project or proposed change, including the purpose of PII data collection and relevant details on business processes or information systems.
2. Identify all changes to data collection, data flows, and storage of personal information.
3. Determine whether the proposed change violates any terms of the organization's external privacy policy, internal privacy policy, or security policy. Identify and describe all such violations. Identify any compensating controls or changes that would reduce or eliminate the violations. This determination must include identifying the original purpose of the collection and/or use of personal information, and whether the proposed change violates or exceeds the purpose.
4. Determine whether the proposed change violates any terms of privacy or security laws, regulations, or related guidelines or codes of conduct.
5. Determine whether the proposed change introduces any new security risks and, if so, what potential alterations to the proposed change might reduce or eliminate those risks.
6. Determine whether the proposed change alters any previously known security risks and, if so, what potential alterations to the proposed change might reduce or eliminate those risks.
7. Develop a list of all such impacts (and possible countermeasures) identified in the preceding steps.
8. Write a formal report describing all of the above.

A PIA is nothing more than a risk assessment that focuses on the privacy and security of subject data in a specific context.

Several organizations, including the governments of Canada, Singapore, Europe, the Philippines, and the United States, have published established methodologies for conducting PIAs.

Engaging Data Subjects in a PIA

The GDPR, in Article 35, Paragraph 9, suggests that the organization consult with *data subjects* or their representatives to obtain their opinion of proposed changes to a PIA. Such engagement could take the form of:

- Surveys
- Focus groups
- Announcement of the proposed change with a request for comments

The EU GDPR outlines its PIA requirements in Articles 35 and 36.

The Necessity of a PIA

Not all regulations explicitly require an analysis of proposed changes to stated or implied data subject rights or the security of their personal information. The absence of a specific requirement for a risk assessment does not, however, absolve an organization of the obligation to perform one. It is a standard business practice to analyze the various impacts of a proposed change to a business process or supporting information system. A failure to assess the impact of a proposed change could even be seen as negligence: a reasonable person would find such an organization at fault for not seeking to understand the potential impacts of a proposed change upon the security, privacy, or proper use of personal information.

Integrating a PIA into Existing Processes

Organizations building their privacy programs need to place "hooks" into three types of existing business processes:

- **Product development** The PIA is a tool designed to promote "privacy by design" by ensuring that privacy is considered in technical, organizational, and security measures at the beginning of product development and throughout the product lifecycle.
- **IT change control** This process needs to include a security risk assessment and a privacy impact assessment. The data privacy officer must be informed of all changes and counted among the approvers for changes that potentially impact privacy.
- **Business process change control** This process must include a PIA. The data privacy officer needs to be informed of all changes and counted among the approvers for changes that potentially impact privacy.

Organizations lacking IT change control or business process change control need to implement these processes and ensure that all relevant personnel are aware of and will comply with their terms.

PIA Recordkeeping and Reporting

All PIAs that are performed must be preserved as a part of the organization's recordkeeping. The DPO is typically assigned this responsibility. The DPO can elect to include statistics about PIAs as a part of regular privacy metrics reported to executive management and the board of directors. Aspects of this reporting can include:

- The number of PIAs performed and the level of effort expended
- The projects associated with PIAs that were performed
- The number of exceptions noted where processes or systems required remediation
- The regulations in scope for PIAs (applicable for organizations subject to multiple privacy laws)
- If findings for PIAs are placed in a risk register, statistics on the risk register's contents, including the number of items, aging, time to remediation, and context

Risks Specific to Privacy

To perform an effective PIA, the privacy specialist needs to be aware of privacy-specific threats, vulnerabilities, and attacks. A typical risk assessment considers threats and vulnerabilities in the context of some particular asset. Being familiar with specific threats and vulnerabilities will result in a better PIA.

Privacy Vulnerabilities

During a PIA, the privacy specialist must identify vulnerabilities in an information system, business process, or whatever the PIA focuses on. A good definition of the term *vulnerability* is "a weakness present in a system that makes the probability of one or more threats more likely."

Weaknesses in processes or systems create opportunities for business processes to deviate from expectations. The nature of the deviation can be a skipped step in a manual procedure, a software program that behaves unexpectedly when presented with unexpected input, or a worker deliberately performing something incorrectly without being detected.

Identifying Vulnerabilities

When examining business processes, the following can indicate the presence of vulnerabilities:

- Manual steps that rely upon human decision-making

- Steps that require workers to be proactive (such as checking a mailbox for incoming requests)
- Steps that involve data entry (the possibility of mis-keying data)
- Steps performed that do not include recordkeeping
- The absence of reconciliation procedures (such as matching the number of incoming requests to the number of outgoing replies)
- Lack of written documentation describing the steps in processes and procedures
- Lack of training for personnel who perform processes and procedures
- Lack of oversight for personnel who perform processes and procedures
- Lack of a human-in-the-loop for AI-driven and AI-enabled decisions and outputs

When examining information systems, the techniques performed in typical system vulnerability assessments apply and include the following:

- Misconfiguration
- Missing security patches
- Software vulnerabilities that permit an attacker to cause software to behave in unintended ways (such as script injection, SQL injection, denial-of-service)
- Poor user access management controls (including easily guessed passwords, failure to remove user accounts for terminated users, and password settings that invite brute-force attacks)

Automated tools such as port scanners, vulnerability scanners, and code scanning tools are often used to perform these activities.

In the context of system and data protection, a security vulnerability is a privacy vulnerability.

Vulnerability Severity

When identifying vulnerabilities, you should also rate the severity of each one. Severity can be expressed on a high–medium–low scale or a numeric scale such as 1–5 or 1–10. A severity rating is generally based on the ease of exploiting the vulnerability, the skill level required, and the consequences of exploitation.

A standard vulnerability rating scale, the *Common Vulnerability Scoring System (CVSS)*, is used in the information security world. The current version of CVSS (CVSSv4.0) was released in 2023. The severity of vulnerabilities identified in information systems is measured using CVSS, which ranges from 0 to 10, with 10 being the highest severity. A CVSS score is calculated using several inputs grouped into metric categories, including attack vector (whether exploitation requires network access, adjacent network access, local access, or physical access to the target), attack complexity, privileges required by the attacker, whether user interaction is required, and the impact of an exploit on the confidentiality, integrity, and availability of information in the system. Additional metric categories enable organizations to refine the base score, providing a more accurate risk view of their environment. Additional metrics include environmental (reflecting an organization's specific context and exploit maturity (is there an exploit actively in use in the wild).

Data Storage and Data Flow Vulnerabilities

It's also necessary to understand the flow of personal information in the context of the PIA. The examiner needs to identify all instances of data storage, and then examine access control processes and the security of systems associated with stored data.

In addition, the examiner needs to identify all instances of data movement within the organization, as well as data entering and leaving the organization. For each case, the measures taken to protect the confidentiality and integrity of personal information in transit must be identified.

Application Security Vulnerabilities

If an application is new or undergoing significant changes, it should be subjected to a variety of tests to ensure it is free of vulnerabilities that attackers could exploit to obtain personal information or cause it to malfunction illicitly. Testing includes penetration tests, Static Application Security Testing (SAST) code reviews, Dynamic Application Security Testing (DAST) code reviews, and Software Composition Analysis (SCA).

The lists of vulnerabilities in Appendix F of NIST SP 800-30 and in Table A.11 of ISO/IEC 27005 are good starting points for vulnerability analysis.

Privacy Threats

The performance of a PIA should consider reasonable and likely threats that can occur within the business process or system being examined. As mentioned, a PIA is a risk assessment focused on the potential impact on privacy compliance and security, targeted to a process or system that will be changing. A good definition of the term *threat* is "an event that, if realized, would bring harm to an asset."

In this case, the asset is, of course, personal information. Still, a threat can include the business process being examined, the underlying information systems that facilitate its operation, the persons who perform the process, and those who operate and manage the systems. All of these are a part of the *attack surface* that must be considered.

When analyzing a variety of threats, the privacy specialist considers each threat and determines:

- Whether the threat is relevant
- How the threat might be carried out (including consideration for any corresponding vulnerabilities that have been identified)

- The likelihood that the threat will be carried out
- The impact on the organization (and the data subject) if the threat were carried out

In a typical PIA, the analyst will create a chart listing all reasonable threats. Each threat is scored for relevance, likelihood, and impact. The scoring can be in the form of qualitative values, such as high, medium, or low, or on a numeric scale, such as 1–5 or 1–10 (where the highest number in the scale represents the highest probability and impact).

The lists of threats in Appendix E of NIST SP 800 30 serves as a good starting point for threat analysis.

Privacy Countermeasures

After the privacy analyst has completed the vulnerability and threat analysis of the process or system under examination, they might conclude that one or more threats or vulnerabilities constitute unacceptable conditions. They might then suggest that one or more *countermeasures* be implemented to reduce unacceptable risks.

Here are some example countermeasures:

- In a data subject request (DSR) process, have a second employee check the contents of the response to be sent back to the data subject.
- Implement a web application firewall (WAF) to offer further protection for a web application that collects and manages personal information.
- Implement automated search tools to ensure more accurate (and timely) results in a DSR.

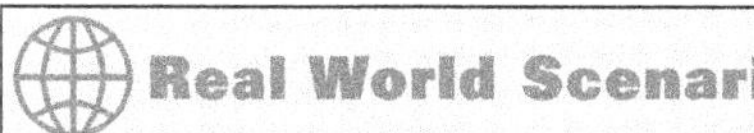

PIA Case Study

Let's look at a case study that represents a likely scenario. An organization in the retail industry has conducted most of its business through a web application. The organization has developed a mobile app for iOS and Android to make it easier for its customers to place orders and check their order status. The privacy officer was informed of the mobile app late in its development.

As is typical in the organization, a security firm was commissioned to perform a vulnerability analysis of the mobile app. Several vulnerabilities were identified and later remediated by the organization's developers. A retest confirmed that the vulnerabilities were remediated.

The privacy officer also determined that the mobile app uses simple user ID and password authentication with no other options. As a result, the privacy officer's PIA made the following recommendations:

- Make multifactor authentication available to mobile app users who prefer to use it.
- Change the systems development lifecycle so that a PIA can be completed during the design of a new application or system, rather than an analysis of a nearly finished product.
- Include privacy requirements in future system development projects.

Privacy Training and Awareness

Personnel are the primary weak point in an organization's privacy and cybersecurity status. Such breaches are mainly caused by lapses in judgment, inattentiveness, fatigue, work pressures, a shortage of skills, and a lack of awareness of corporate policies. Personnel are generally considered the largest and most vulnerable portion of an organization's *attack surface*, and for good reason: most breaches start with a social engineering attack, often in email.

Many organizations conduct security awareness training to help personnel recognize common attacks and other topics that fall under the category of *Internet hygiene*, the safe use of computers and mobile devices while accessing the Internet. Fewer organizations provide privacy awareness training that enables personnel to understand the expectations regarding the proper use of customer, constituent, and employee personal information.

Training Objectives

The primary objective of privacy and security awareness programs is to ensure that all personnel have a clear understanding of the proper protection and handling of personal information, the reality of the different types of attacks they might be subject to, and what they are expected to do in various situations. Further, personnel must understand and comply with an organization's acceptable use policy, privacy policy, security policy, code of ethics or code of conduct, and other applicable policies.

Better *privacy awareness* and *security awareness* training programs include opportunities to practice skills, with testing at the end of training sessions. In computer-based training, users must pass the test with a minimum score of 70%, which is the typical minimum required to complete the course.

The best privacy and security awareness training courses, whether in-person or online, are engaging and relevant. While some organizations conduct privacy and security awareness training for compliance purposes, many genuinely want their personnel to get the most value from the training. The point of privacy and security awareness training is, after all, to reduce risk.

Business records should be created to record when each employee receives training. Many organizations are subject to privacy and security regulations that require personnel to complete awareness training; business records provide ample evidence of users' completion of their training.

Creating or Selecting Training Content

Privacy and security managers need to develop or acquire awareness training content for the organization's personnel. The content that is selected or developed should be as follows:

- **Understandable** The content should make sense to all personnel. A common mistake security and privacy managers make is creating or selecting content that is overly technical and difficult for many non-technical personnel to understand.
- **Relevant** The content should apply to the organization and its users. For example, training on cryptography would be irrelevant to most personnel in most organizations. Irrelevant content can cause personnel to disengage from further training.
- **Actionable** The content should ensure that personnel know what to do (and not do) in common scenarios.
- **Memorable** The best content will give personnel opportunities to practice their skills on some of the basic tasks important to privacy and security, including selecting and using passwords, reading and responding to email, making good decisions about the use of personal information, and interacting with persons inside and outside the organization.

Audiences

When planning an awareness training program, privacy and security managers need to understand the entire workforce and their various roles within the organization. This helps managers understand what training subject matter is relevant to which groups of workers. Managers need to ensure that all workers receive the training they need and not overburden them with training that is not relevant to their jobs.

For example, workers in a large retail organization fall into four categories:

- **Corporate workers** These persons all use computers, and most use mobile devices. Most have access to sensitive information, including personal information about customers and/or employees.
- **Retail floor managers** These persons work in retail stores and use computers daily in their jobs.
- **Retail floor cashiers** These persons work in retail store locations. They do not use computers, but they do accept cash, checks, and credit cards.
- **Retail floor workers** These persons work in retail stores and warehouses and do not use computers.

Privacy and security managers should package awareness training so that each audience receives relevant training. In this example, retail floor workers probably need little Internet- or computer-related security awareness training; instead, they would receive training on physical security and workplace safety topics. Cashiers need training on fraud techniques, including counterfeit currency, currency-counting fraud, and credit card payment fraud (such as skimming). Corporate workers and retail floor managers should probably receive full-spectrum privacy and security training, since they all use computers and many have access to personal and sensitive information. Retail floor managers should also receive all training delivered to retail floor workers and cashiers, as they work in retail locations and supervise these personnel.

Privacy training ensures that all personnel understand the organization's privacy policies, practices, and expectations.

Information Workers

Workers in an organization who have contact with the personal information of employees, customers, or constituents should receive privacy awareness training. Information workers need to be aware of the organization's policies on the protection and proper use of personal information, so that the organization is less likely to suffer a privacy breach caused by poor judgment.

Technical Workers

Technical workers in an organization, typically IT personnel, should be trained in security techniques relevant to their positions. Technical workers are responsible for system architecture, system and network design, implementation, and administration. Without security training, these workers might unknowingly make lapses in judgment that could result in significant vulnerabilities and compromises.

Technical workers also need privacy awareness training to understand proper handling of personal information. This is especially important for the organization, so that information systems are designed and configured to provide the greatest possible protection and sound handling of personal information.

Software Developers

Software developers typically receive little or no education on privacy by design or secure software development in colleges, universities, and tech schools. The art and science of privacy by design and of secure coding, then, is new to many software developers. Training for software developers helps them to be more aware of the common mistakes made by software developers, including:

- Broken access control
- Security misconfiguration
- Software supply chain failures
- Cryptographic failures
- Injection

- Insecure design
- Authentication failures
- Software or data integrity failures
- Security logging and alerting failures
- Mishandling of exceptional conditions

This list, which changes from time to time, is published by the *Open Web Application Security Project (OWASP*, at `www.owasp.org`). This organization helps software developers better understand the techniques needed for secure application development and deployment.

Privacy and security training for software developers should also include protection of the software development process itself. Topics in secure software development generally include the following:

- Protection of source code
- Source code reviews
- Care when using open-source code
- Testing of source code for vulnerabilities and defects
- Archival of changes to source code
- Protection of systems used to store source code, edit and test source code, build applications, test applications, and deploy applications

Note that some of these aspects relate to the architecture of development and test environments and might not be necessary for all software developers.

Third Parties

Privacy and security awareness training needs to be provided to all personnel who have access to personal information, whether through any means. Because this can include personnel from other organizations, those workers need to participate in the organization's privacy and security awareness training. In larger organizations, the curriculum for third-party personnel might be adjusted slightly, since some portions of the privacy and security awareness training content might not apply to outsiders.

New Hires

New employees, consultants, and contractors should be required to attend privacy and security training as soon as possible. There is a risk that new employees could make mistakes early in their employment, before training, since they would not be familiar with all the organization's practices.

Better organizations link access control with privacy and security training: new employees are not given access to systems until after they have completed their privacy and security training. This gives new workers an added incentive to complete their training quickly, since they want to gain access to corporate applications and get to work.

Training Frequency

Most privacy and security awareness programs include annual refresher training for all workers. Required by some regulations, annual training is highly recommended, as it helps keep privacy, security, and Internet safety part of every worker's day-to-day thinking and helps them avoid common mistakes. Further, because handling procedures, protective techniques, and attack techniques change quickly, annual refresher training helps workers be aware of these developments.

Training takes time, and people tend to put it off for as long as possible. Workers can be offered incentives to complete their training through various types of rewards. For example, all workers who complete their training in the first week can win gift cards or other prizes.

Organizations generally choose one of two options for annual training:

- The entire organization all at once
- One-twelfth of the organization on workers' hire month anniversaries

Many organizations recognize that training workers annually on privacy and security might not be sufficient, as they might forget the policies, principles, and tools they're expected to use. As a result, many organizations conduct shorter training sessions more often (sometimes cycling through a variety of subtopics), to keep security and privacy "top of mind" with their workers.

Communication Techniques

Privacy and security awareness training programs often use a variety of methods to impart information on handling procedures, Internet hygiene, and safe computing to their workers. Communication techniques often include:

- **Email** Privacy and security managers might occasionally send advisories to affected personnel about recent developments, such as a new phishing attack. Occasionally, a senior executive will send a message to all personnel emphasizing that security is every worker's job and must be taken seriously.
- **Internal websites** Organizations with internal websites or web portals might, from time to time, include privacy and security content.
- **Video monitors, posters, and bulletins** Sometimes a privacy or security message can be delivered on monitors, posters, or bulletins on various topics, keeping people thinking about privacy and security.

Threats and Vulnerabilities

The terms threat and vulnerability are foundational in all of risk management, including cyber-risk management and privacy risk management. Privacy leaders directing or conducting risk assessments must be familiar with the concepts of threats and vulnerabilities and have the knowledge and experience to identify and analyze them.

Threat Identification

The identification of threats is a key step in a risk assessment. A *threat* is defined as an event that, if realized, would bring harm to an asset and, thus, to the organization.

In the privacy and cybersecurity industries, key terms in risk assessments are often misunderstood and misused. These terms are distinguished from one another as follows: a threat is an actual action that would cause harm, not the person or group (generically called an *actor* or *threat actor*) associated with it. A threat is *not* the same as a weakness that might permit it; this is known as a *vulnerability*. Work undertaken to reduce the likelihood or impact of a threat is known as *remediation*.

Threats are typically classified as external or internal, as intentional or unintentional, and as human-caused or natural. The origin of many threats is outside the organization's control, but not necessarily outside its awareness. A good privacy or security manager can develop a list of privacy- and security-related threats that are likely (more or less) to occur to any given asset.

When performing a risk assessment, the risk manager needs to develop a complete list of threats for use in the risk assessment. Because it's not always possible for a risk manager to memorize all possible threats, the security manager can turn to one or more well-known sources of threats, including the following:

- NIST SP 800-30's Appendix E, "Threat Events"
- Earlier versions of ISO/IEC 27005 in Appendix C, "Examples of Typical Threats"

Upon capturing threat events from one or both of these sources, the risk manager might well identify a few additional threats not found in these lists. These additional threats can be specific to the organization's location, business model, or other factors. A risk manager will typically remove a few of the threats from the list that do not apply to the organization. For instance, an organization located far inland is not going to be directly affected by tsunamis or hurricanes, so this threat source can be eliminated.

Internal Threats

Internal threats originate within the organization and are most often associated with employees. Internal employees can be the intentional actors behind these threats.

Privacy managers need to understand the nature of internal threats and the interaction between personnel and information systems. A wide range of events can take place that constitute threats, including the following:

- Well-meaning personnel making errors in judgment
- Well-meaning personnel making errors in haste
- Well-meaning personnel making errors because of insufficient knowledge or training
- Well-meaning personnel being tricked into doing something harmful
- Disgruntled personnel being purposefully negligent or reckless
- Disgruntled personnel deliberately bringing harm to an asset
- A trusted individual in a trusted third-party organization doing any of these

After understanding all the ways that something can go wrong, privacy and security managers might sometimes wonder if things can ever proceed as planned!

A privacy manager must understand this important concept: While employees are at the top of a short list of potential threat actors, they are also the people who need broad access to sensitive data to do their jobs and for the organization to function. Although there have been marginal improvements in technologies such as data loss prevention (DLP), employers must trust employees by giving them access to large sets of the organization's information, hoping that they will not accidentally or deliberately abuse those privileges and cause the organization great harm.

Here are some examples of employees gone rogue:

- A disgruntled internal auditor discloses salary and other personal information relating to 100,000 staff members at a supermarket chain to frame a colleague.
- A consulting firm for a large insurer finds that one of its consultants, who was discovered to be involved in identity theft, has emailed a file with more than 18,000 Medicare member details to a personal email account.
- An engineer at a cloud services company breaks into and exposes millions of customer records at a large bank.
- A systems administrator at an intelligence agency acquires and leaks thousands of classified documents to the media.

A significant factor in employees going rogue is access control policy and access management practices, which result in individual employees having access to more information than is prudent. That said, increasing the granularity of access controls is time-consuming and costly, and it increases the friction of doing business; few organizations tolerate this despite the identified risks.

Table 3.1 includes internal and external human-caused threats that can be included in an organization's risk assessment.

It might be useful to build a short list of threat actors (the people or groups that would initiate a threat event), but remember that these are not the threats themselves. However, building such a list can help the security manager identify additional threat events not on it.

Table 3.2 shows some natural threats.

External Threats

External threats originate outside of the organization. Like internal threats, they can include both deliberate and accidental actions and can be human-caused or associated with naturally occurring events.

The security or privacy manager performing a risk assessment or PIA needs to understand the full range of threat actors and their motivations. This is particularly important for organizations where specific types of threat actors or motivations are more common. For example, certain industries, such as aerospace and weapons manufacturers, attract industrial espionage and intelligence agencies, and certain industries attract hacktivists.

TABLE 3.1 Internal and External Human-caused Threats

Internal and External Human-caused Threats
Leak data via email
Leak data via upload to unauthorized system
Leak data via external USB storage device or medium
Leak information face to face to unauthorized person
Perform programming error
Misconfigure system or device
Shut down application, system, or device
Perpetrate error created by any internal staff
Respond to phishing attack
Respond to social engineering attack
Share login credentials with another person
Install or run unauthorized software program
Copy sensitive data to unauthorized device or system
Destroy or remove sensitive or critical information
Retrieve discarded, recycled, or shredded information
Conduct security scan
Conduct denial-of-service attack
Conduct physical attack on systems or facilities
Conduct credential-guessing attack
Eavesdrop on sensitive communication
Impersonate another individual

(*Continued*)

TABLE 3.1 (Continued)

Internal and External Human-caused Threats
Obtain sensitive information through illicit means
Cause data integrity loss through any action
Intercept network traffic
Obtain sensitive information through programmatic data leakage
Perform reconnaissance as part of an attack campaign
Attack via social engineering
Failure or anomaly in power
Failure in communications
Failure in heating, venting, or air conditioning
Degradation of electronic media
Damage via fire
Damage via smoke
Damage via fire retardant
Flood from water main break or drainage failure
Damage via vandalism
Damage from demonstrations/protests/picketing
Attack by terrorist
Damage via electromagnetic pulse
Damage via explosion
Damage via bombing

TABLE 3.2 Natural Threats

Natural Threats
Forest fire or range fire
Smoke damage from a forest fire or range fire
River flood
Landslide
Avalanche
Tornado
Hurricane
Windstorm
Hailstorm
Earthquake
Tsunami
Lightning
Epidemic/pandemic
Explosion of naturally occurring substances
Solar storm

Tables 3.3 and 3.4 present external threat actors and their motivations, respectively.

In a risk assessment, the assessor must identify all threats that have a reasonable likelihood of occurrence. Threats that are unlikely due to geographic and other conditions are usually excluded. For example, hurricanes can be excluded from locations far from oceans, and earthquakes and volcanoes can be excluded from locations where these are not known to occur. Threats such as falling meteorites and space debris are rarely included in risk assessments because of the minute chance of occurrence.

TABLE 3.3 External Threat Actors

External Threat Actors
Former employees
Current and former consultants
Current and former contractors
Competitors
Hacktivists
Personnel in current and former third-party service organizations, vendors, and suppliers
Government intelligence agencies (foreign and domestic)
Criminal organizations (including individuals)
Terrorist groups (including individuals)
Activist groups (including individuals)
Armed forces (including individuals)

TABLE 3.4 Threat Actor Motivations

Threat Actor Motivations
Competitive advantage
Economic espionage
Monetary gain
Political gain
Intelligence
Revenge
Ego
Curiosity
Unintentional errors

Exam Tip

CDPSE candidates are not expected to memorize lists of threats, but they should be familiar with the concepts behind them.

Advanced Persistent Threats

An *advanced persistent threat (APT)* is a particular type of threat actor, so named in the early 2000s to describe a new kind of adversary that worked slowly but effectively to compromise a target organization. Whether perpetrated by an individual or a cybercrime organization, an APT involves techniques that indicate resourcefulness, patience, and resolve. Rather than employing a "hit-and-run" or "smash-and-grab" operation, an APT actor will patiently conduct reconnaissance on a target, use tools to infiltrate it, and build a long-term presence there.

APT is defined by NIST SP 800-39 as follows:

> An APT is an adversary that possesses sophisticated levels of expertise and significant resources that allow it to create opportunities to achieve its objectives using multiple attack vectors (e.g., cyber, physical, and deception). These objectives typically include establishing and extending footholds within the IT infrastructure of the targeted organizations for purposes of exfiltrating information, undermining or impeding critical aspects of a mission, program, or organization; or positioning itself to carry out these objectives in the future. The advanced persistent threat: (i) pursues its objectives repeatedly over an extended period of time; (ii) adapts to defenders' efforts to resist it; (iii) is determined to maintain the level of interaction needed to execute its objectives.

Before APTs, threat actors were less sophisticated and conducted operations that ran for shorter periods of time—a few days at most. But as more organizations put more valuable information assets online, threat actors became craftier and more resourceful; they resorted to longer-term campaigns to study targets for extended periods before attacking them. Once an attack began, it would carry on for months or longer. APTs would compromise multiple systems within the target organization and employ a variety of stealthy techniques to establish and maintain a presence across as many compromised targets as possible. Once an APT was discovered (if it is *ever* discovered), the security manager would clean up the compromised target, often unaware that the APT had compromised many other targets, using different techniques.

This cat-and-mouse game could continue for months or even years, with the adversary compromising targets and studying the organization's systems—all the while searching for specific targets—while the security manager and others would continually chase the adversary around like the carnival game of "whack a mole."

TABLE 3.5 The Cascade of Emerging Threats

Phenomenon	Response
Emerging technologies, including AI systems and agents, bring-your-own-device (BYOD), cloud computing, virtualization, and Internet of Things (IoT)	New targets of opportunity, many of which are poorly guarded when first implemented
End user behavior analytics (EUBA) that detect anomalous end user behavior	Slower exfiltration of sensitive data to stay "under the radar"
Improved technologies (faster processing time)	More rapid compromise of cryptosystems
Improved technologies (faster network speeds)	More rapid exfiltration of larger datasets; easier transport of rainbow tables used to crack hash tables
Improved antimalware controls	Attack innovation—techniques evaded antimalware controls

Emerging Threats

The world in which cyberwarfare takes place today is constantly changing. Several forces (see Table 3.5) are at work and continually "push the envelope" in both attack and defense techniques.

The subject of emerging threats should be seen as a continuing phenomenon of new techniques, rather than a fixed set. Often, the latest techniques are difficult to detect because they fall outside the range of attack techniques one expects to encounter from time to time. Emerging threats represent the cutting edge of attack techniques that are difficult to detect and/or remediate when they are discovered. But these threats will eventually become routine, and even newer threat techniques will emerge. Privacy and security managers need to understand that, even as defensive technologies improve to help prevent and/or detect increasingly sophisticated attacks, attackers will continually improve their ability to evade detection by even the most sophisticated defenses.

Vulnerability Identification

The identification of vulnerabilities is an essential part of any risk assessment. A *vulnerability* is any weakness in a process or system that allows an attacker to successfully compromise a target process or system. In the privacy and security industries, key terms in risk assessments are often misunderstood and misused. These terms are distinguished from one another as follows: a vulnerability is a weakness in a system that could permit an attack. A vulnerability is not the attack vector or technique—this is known as a *threat*.

Vulnerabilities usually take one of these forms:

- **Configuration fault** A system, program, or component with configuration settings has one or more settings set incorrectly, which could provide an attacker with additional opportunities to compromise a system. For example, the authentication settings on a system might permit an attacker to employ a brute-force password-guessing attack that will not be blunted by target user accounts being automatically locked out.
- **Design fault** The relationship between components of a system might be arranged in a way that makes it easier for an attacker to compromise a target system. For instance, an organization might have placed a database server in its DMZ instead of its internal network, making it easier for an attacker to identify and target it.
- **Business process weakness** A business process related to the processing of personal information might fail to prevent or detect unwanted activities in certain circumstances. For instance, an end user who extracts a large volume of personal information from a customer application and saves it directly to a personal cloud drive might bypass controls that would detect or prevent this if the file were saved locally.
- **Known unpatched weakness** A system might have one or more vulnerabilities for which security patches are available but not yet installed. For example, a secure communications protocol might have a flaw in how an encrypted session is established, which could allow an attacker to take over an established session. A security patch might be available for the flaw, but until it is installed, the flaw remains and can be exploited by anyone who understands the vulnerability and has the techniques to do so. Sometimes, known weaknesses are made public through a disclosure by the system's manufacturer or a responsible third party. Although a patch might not yet be available, other avenues to mitigate the vulnerability might be available, such as a configuration change on the target system.
- **Undisclosed unpatched weakness** A system might have vulnerabilities known only to the system's manufacturer and not publicized. Until an organization using one of these systems learns of the vulnerability through a security bulletin or news article, it can do little to defend itself, short of employing essential security techniques such as system and network hardening and secure coding.
- **Undiscovered weakness** Security managers have long accepted the fact that all kinds of information systems have security vulnerabilities, known as *zero-days*, that are yet to be discovered, disclosed, and mitigated. New techniques for attacking systems are constantly being developed, and some exploit weaknesses no one knew to look for. As newly discovered techniques involve examining active memory for snippets of sensitive information, system and tool designers continue to develop defenses to detect and even block attacks. For example, techniques were developed that enabled an attacker to harvest credit card numbers from PCI-compliant point-of-sale software. Soon, effective attacks were developed, enabling cybercriminal organizations to steal tens of millions of credit card numbers from global retail companies.

TABLE 3.6 Vulnerabilities and Detection Techniques

Vulnerability Context	Detection Technique
Network device	Vulnerability scanning Penetration testing Code analysis Network architecture review
Operating system	Vulnerability scanning Penetration testing System architecture review
Database management system	Vulnerability scanning Penetration testing
Software application	Vulnerability scanning Penetration testing Dynamic application scanning Static code scanning Application architecture review
Physical security	Physical security controls review Social engineering assessments Physical penetration testing
Business process	Process reviews Internal audits Control self-assessments
Personnel	Social engineering assessments Competency assessments Phishing assessments (continual)

Vulnerabilities exist everywhere—in software programs, database management systems, operating systems, virtualization platforms, business processes, encryption algorithms, and personnel. As a rule, privacy and security managers should consider that every component of every type in every system has both known and unknown vulnerabilities, some of which, if exploited, could result in painful and expensive consequences for the organization. Table 3.6 contains the places where vulnerabilities can exist, together with techniques that can be used to discover at least some of them.

Third-party Vulnerability Identification

Most organizations outsource at least a portion of their software development and IT operations to third parties. Mainly, this occurs through the use of cloud-based applications and services, such as software-as-a-service (SaaS), platform-as-a-service (PaaS), and infrastructure-as-a-service (IaaS) environments. Many organizations have the misconception that third parties handle all security concerns for their services. Instead, organizations should thoroughly understand the security responsibility model for each outsourced service to determine which security responsibilities are their own and which are managed by the outsourced service.

Regardless of whether the organization or the outsourcing organization bears security responsibilities for any given aspect of operations, vulnerabilities need to be identified and managed. For aspects of privacy and security that are the organization's responsibility, it needs to employ standard means to identify and manage them. For aspects of privacy and security that are the service provider's responsibility, the provider needs to identify and manage vulnerabilities. In many cases, it will make these activities available to its customers upon request.

Exam Tip

CDPSE candidates are expected to be familiar with the concepts of, and differences among, threat, vulnerability, probability, impact, asset value, and risk.

Risk Response

After they have been identified, analyzed, and rated, risks are assigned to owners, and decisions are made on how to address each risk. This section describes the next steps.

Risk Evaluation and Ranking

Upon completion of a risk assessment, once all risks have been identified and scored, the risk manager, together with others in the organization, will analyze the results and begin developing a strategy for moving forward. Risks can be evaluated individually, but the organization will benefit more from analyzing all the risks together. This is because many risks are interrelated, and the right combination of mitigation strategies can adequately address them.

The results of a risk assessment should be analyzed in several ways, including the following:

- Looking at all risks by business unit or service line
- Looking at all risks by asset type (in particular, personal information)
- Looking at all risks by activity type
- Looking at all risks by type of consequence

Because no two organizations (or their risk assessment results) are alike, this type of analysis is likely to identify risk treatment *themes* with broad implications across many risks. For example, an organization might identify several tactical risks, all of which are associated with access and vulnerability management. Rather than treating individual tactical risks, a better approach might be to improve or reorganize access and vulnerability management programs from the top down, thereby mitigating many identified risks programmatically. Organizations need to consider not just the details of a risk assessment but also the big picture.

Another type of risk to look for is one with a low probability of occurrence and high impact, which is typically the type of risk treated by transfer. *Risk transfer* most often comes in the form of cyber insurance, but it is also relevant to privacy and security monitoring when it includes indemnification.

Risk Ownership

When considering the results of a risk assessment, the organization needs to assign individual risk management tasks to *owners:* individual people, typically middle- to upper-management leaders. These leaders, who should also have ownership of controls that operate within their span of oversight, use a budget, staff, and other resources in daily business operations. These are the risk owners, and, to the extent there is a formal policy or statement on risk tolerance or appetite, they should be the ones making risk-treatment decisions for risks within their domain. To the extent that these individuals are accountable for operations in their part of the organization, they should also be responsible for risk decisions, including risk treatment, in their operational areas. A simple concept to approach risk ownership is that if nobody owns the risk, then nobody is accountable for managing the risk, which will lead to a higher probability of the risk becoming an ongoing, unresolved issue with negative impacts on the business, along with the possible identification of a scapegoat who will be blamed if an event occurs.

Risk Treatment

To determine the best *risk treatment* plan, management can review reports and other information that list risks identified, assessed, and analyzed. At this stage, the organization has completed identifying risks and is beginning to determine what should be done about them. Risk treatment comprises the decisions and the activities that follow. A key element in determining the appropriate risk treatment is ensuring that the right people at the right level of the organization are actively involved in the decision. This is achieved by having a formalized risk management program that includes all the key elements of an effective program outlined in this chapter.

In a general sense, risk treatment refers to the actions an organization undertakes to reduce risk to an acceptable level. More specifically, for each risk identified in a risk assessment, an organization can consider four responses, or actions:

- Risk acceptance
- Risk mitigation
- Risk avoidance
- Risk transfer

These four actions are explained in more detail in the following sections.

There is a fifth potential action—or, rather, *inaction*—related to risk treatment, known colloquially as *ignoring the risk*. A potentially dangerous undertaking, ignoring a risk amounts to an organization pretending that the risk does not exist. In this case, the organization has unofficially accepted the risk and is responsible if it becomes an issue later. By unofficially accepting the risk and not assigning a risk owner, the organization might increase the likelihood and impact of the risk evolving into an incident.

Ignoring a *known risk* is different from an organization's ignoring an *unknown risk*. This is usually a result of a risk assessment or risk analysis that is not sufficiently thorough in identifying all relevant risks. The best solution for these "unknown unknowns" is to have an external, competent firm perform an organization's risk assessment every few years or for an organization to examine its risk assessment thoroughly to discover opportunities for improvement, including expanding the span of threats, threat actors, and vulnerabilities so that there are fewer or no unknown risks.

Risk Acceptance

In deciding to accept a risk, the organization determines that the risk requires no reduction or mitigation.

If only *risk acceptance* were this simple! Further analysis of risk acceptance shows that there are conditions under which an organization will elect to accept risk:

- The cost of risk mitigation exceeds the value of the asset being protected.
- The impact of compromise is low, or the asset's value or classification is low.

Organizations can elect to establish a framework for risk acceptance, like the example shown in Table 3.7.

TABLE 3.7 Framework for Risk Acceptance

Risk Level	Level Required to Accept
Low	Business department leader, plus chief information officer (CIO) or manager of information security
Medium	Business unit leader, plus CISO or director of information security
High	Chief executive officer (CEO), chief operating officer (COO), or organization president
Severe	Board of directors

When an organization accepts a risk, instead of closing the matter for perpetuity, the organization should review it at least annually for the following reasons:

- The value of the asset might have changed since the prior risk review.
- The way that the asset is used might have changed since the prior risk review.
- The value of the business activity related to the asset might have changed since the prior risk review.
- The potency of threats might have changed since the prior risk review, potentially leading to a higher risk rating.
- The cost of mitigation might have changed since the prior risk review, potentially increasing the feasibility of risk mitigation or transfer.

As with other risk treatment activities, detailed recordkeeping helps the risk manager better track matters such as risk assessment review.

Risk acceptance should consider not only an asset's value, but also the organization's reputation should the asset be compromised.

Risk Mitigation

In *risk mitigation*, the organization decides to reduce risk through means such as changing a process or procedure, improving a privacy or security control, or adding a privacy or security control.

Risk mitigation is generally chosen when management understands that the cost of mitigation is less than the value of the asset being protected. Sometimes, however, an asset's value is difficult to measure, or there might be a high degree of goodwill associated with the asset. For example, the value of a customer database that contains personal information, including bank account or credit card information, might itself be low; however, the impact of a breach of this database might be higher than its book value because of the fines, loss of business, or adverse publicity that could result.

Risk mitigation can result in a task that can be carried out in a relatively short time. However, risk mitigation can also involve one or more major projects that begin in the future, perhaps in the next budget year or in many months or quarters. Further, such a project might be delayed, its scope might change, or it might be canceled altogether. Thus, the risk manager needs to monitor risk mitigation activities carefully to ensure that they are completed as originally agreed so that the risk mitigation is not forgotten or set aside.

Risk Avoidance

In *risk avoidance*, the organization decides to discontinue an activity that precipitates the risk. Often, risk avoidance is selected in response to an activity that was not formally approved in the first place. For example, a risk assessment might have identified a department's use of an external service provider that represented a measurable risk to the organization. The service provider might not have been formally vetted in the first place. Regardless, once a risk is identified in a risk assessment (or by other means), the organization might choose to cease activities with that service provider to mitigate it.

Risk Transfer

After deciding to transfer a risk, the organization will engage an external entity to assume it. In this case, the organization lacks the operational or financial capacity to accept the risk, and risk mitigation is not the best choice. In *risk transfer*, an organization might have identified a significant financial risk related to a breach of its stores of personal information, for example. The risk transfer decision, in this case, might involve purchasing cyber insurance to offset the costs associated with such a breach. A risk transfer decision might also include purchasing an incident response retainer, which is essentially a pre-purchase of incident response services in the event of a breach.

A risk assessment might reveal the absence of security monitoring of a critical system. Another form of risk transfer involves using an external security services provider to monitor the critical system.

Residual Risk

When an organization undergoes risk treatment for identified risks, in most cases, the treatment does not eliminate the risk but reduces it to some degree. *Residual risk* is the risk that remains after risk treatment is applied.

Some organizations approach risk treatment and residual risk improperly. They identify a risk, employ some risk treatment, and then fail to understand the residual risk and close the risk matter. A better way to approach residual risk is to analyze it as a new risk and apply risk treatment to it. This iterative process provides organizations with an opportunity to revisit residual risk and make new risk treatment decisions. Ultimately, after one or more iterations, the residual risk will be accepted, and then the matter can be closed.

For instance, suppose a privacy manager identifies a risk in the organization's access management system where multifactor authentication is not used. This is considered high risk, and the IT department implements a multifactor authentication solution. When the privacy manager reassesses the access management system, they find that multifactor authentication is required in some circumstances but not in others. A new risk is identified, perhaps at a lower level than the original risk. But the organization once again has an opportunity to assess the risk and decide on it. It might further improve the access management system by requiring multifactor authentication in more cases than before, thereby reducing risk, which should be examined again for additional risk treatment opportunities. Finally, the risk will be accepted as is when the organization is satisfied that it has been sufficiently reduced.

In addition to the risk treatment lifecycle, subsequent risk assessments and other activities will identify residual risks from earlier risk treatment activities. And over time, the nature of residual risk might change due to evolving threats, vulnerabilities, or business practices, resulting in an initially acceptable residual risk that is no longer acceptable.

Controls

A common outcome of risk treatment, when mitigation is chosen, is the enactment of *controls*. Put another way, when an organization identifies a risk in a risk assessment, the organization might decide to develop (or improve) a control that will mitigate the risk that was found.

Suppose an organization determined that its procedures for terminating access for departing employees were resulting in many user accounts *not* being deactivated. The existing control was a simple, open-loop procedure, in which analysts were instructed to deactivate user accounts. Often, they were deactivating user accounts late or not at all. To reduce this risk, the organization modified the procedure (updated the control) by adding a step in which a second person would verify all account terminations daily.

Controls are measures put in place to ensure desired outcomes. Controls can take the form of procedures or be implemented directly in a system. There are many categories and types of controls, as well as standard control frameworks.

You can find a thorough discussion of controls in this author's certification guides on the CISM and CRISC certifications.

Costs and Benefits

As organizations ponder options for risk treatment (and in particular, risk mitigation), they generally will consider the costs of the mitigating steps and the expected benefits they receive. When an organization understands the costs and benefits of risk mitigation, it can develop strategies that are more cost-effective or result in greater cost avoidance.

When weighing mitigation options, an organization needs to understand several cost and benefit-related considerations, including these:

- **Change in threat probability** Organizations need to understand how a mitigating control changes the probability of threat occurrence and what that means in terms of cost reduction and avoidance.
- **Change in threat impact** Organizations need to understand the change in the impact of a mitigated threat in terms of an incident's reduced costs and avoided costs versus the cost of the mitigation.
- **Change in operational efficiency** Aside from the direct cost of the mitigating control, organizations need to understand its impact on other operations. For instance, adding code review steps to a software development process might mean the development organization completes fewer fixes and enhancements in a given time period.
- **Total cost of ownership (TCO)** When an organization considers a mitigation plan, the best approach is to understand its TCO, including the following costs:

  - Acquisition
  - Deployment and implementation
  - Recurring maintenance
  - Testing and assessment
  - Compliance monitoring and enforcement
  - Reduced throughput of controlled processes
  - Training
  - End-of-life decommissioning
- **Compliance-related fines and penalties** The matter of compliance with privacy and security laws and regulations often involves fines and penalties when there are findings of non-compliance. The risk of fines and penalties should be considered a consequence of failing to mitigate certain risks.

While weighing costs and benefits, organizations need to keep in mind several things:

- Estimating the probability of a specific threat or event is difficult, particularly for infrequent, high-impact events such as large-scale data thefts.
- Estimating the impact of any particular threat is difficult, especially for those rare, high-impact events.

Thus, the precision of cost-benefit analysis is no better than estimates of event probability and impact.

An adage in information security states that an organization would not spend $20,000 to protect a $10,000 asset. Although that might be true in some cases, there is more to consider than just the asset's replacement (or depreciated) value. For example, loss of the asset could result in an embarrassing and costly public relations debacle, or the asset might play a key role in the organization's earning hundreds of thousands of dollars in revenue each month.

Still, the principle of proportionality is valid and is often a good starting point for making cost-conscious decisions on risk mitigation. The principle of proportionality is described in NIST 800-30 Security and Privacy Engineering Principles in control number SA-8(25) Economic Security.

Summary

Privacy programs can succeed if they include regular risk assessments as part of a formal risk management program. Risk management is a core tenet of cybersecurity programs, often referred to as information security management systems (ISMSs).

Risk management is an iterative process used to identify, analyze, and manage risks. This book focuses on privacy risk, but overall, the privacy risk lifecycle is functionally similar to that for information risk or even business risk: a new risk is introduced into the process, the risk is studied, and a decision is made about how to address it.

The risk management lifecycle consists of risk assessment, risk identification, risk analysis, and risk treatment. The lifecycle is bounded by the scope of the risk management program and the organization's risk appetite.

After the scope of a risk assessment has been determined, the initial step is to identify assets and determine each asset's value. In a typical information risk assessment, assets will consist of various types of information (including intellectual property, internal operations, and personal information) and the information systems that support and protect those information assets.

In asset classification, an organization assigns an asset to a category that represents its usage or risk. The purpose of asset classification is to determine each asset's level of criticality to the organization. In an organization with a formal privacy program, asset classification will include one or more classifications for assets related to personal information.

The identification of threats is a key step in a risk assessment. A threat is defined as an event that, if realized, would bring harm to an asset and, thus, to the organization. The identification of vulnerabilities is another essential part of any risk assessment. A vulnerability is any weakness in a process or system that allows an attacker to compromise a target successfully. Risk identification is performed during a risk assessment, and various scenarios are studied for each asset. Considerations include threats, threat actors, vulnerabilities, asset value, and the impact of a threat event.

In a risk assessment, the risk manager examines assets, associated vulnerabilities, and likely threat scenarios. The risk analysis is the detailed examination of each risk.

Qualitative risk analysis uses rankings such as high, medium, or low. Semi-quantitative risk analysis uses simple numeric scales. In contrast, quantitative risk analysis expresses risks in financial terms, including asset value (AV), exposure factor (EF), single loss expectancy (SLE), annualized rate of occurrence (ARO), and annualized loss expectancy (ALE).

Operationally Critical Threat Asset and Vulnerability Evaluation (OCTAVE) is a risk analysis approach developed by Carnegie Mellon University. The latest version, OCTAVE Allegro, is used to assess privacy and security risks, enabling an organization to obtain meaningful results from a risk assessment.

A privacy impact assessment (PIA), sometimes known as a data protection impact assessment (DPIA, as coined in the GDPR), is a targeted risk assessment undertaken to identify impacts to individual privacy and impacts to an organization's ability to protect information resulting from a proposed change to a business process or information system. The purpose of a PIA is to ensure that personal information collected is used only for the intended purpose, and it identifies the impact(s) that any process or system change has on the organization's compliance with its privacy policy and applicable privacy laws and regulations.

A PIA considers vulnerabilities, threats, data storage, and data flows to identify potential impacts on proposed changes in business processes and information systems.

After a privacy analyst has completed the vulnerability and threat analysis of the process or system being examined in a PIA, they might conclude that one or more threats or vulnerabilities represent unacceptable conditions and suggest countermeasures be enacted to reduce the risk.

Like security awareness training, which informs the workforce of expectations for behavior and safe Internet use, privacy awareness training informs the workforce of expectations for accessing and managing personal information.

A threat is an event that, if realized, would bring harm to an asset. A vulnerability is a weakness that could enable a threat to materialize. Risk is the combination of threat and vulnerability considered together.

In general, risk treatment refers to the actions an organization takes to reduce risk to an acceptable level. The four possible actions are risk acceptance, risk mitigation, risk avoidance, and risk transfer. Risk treatment is the formal decision and the action taken in response to that decision.

Exam Essentials

Understand the privacy risk management lifecycle. Risk management is a continuous, iterative process that includes identifying, analyzing, evaluating, treating, and monitoring risks associated with personal data.

Distinguish key risk concepts. Risk is the combination of likelihood and impact; threats are potential harmful events; vulnerabilities are weaknesses that can be exploited.

Know the primary risk treatment options. Organizations respond to risk through acceptance, mitigation, transfer, or avoidance, based on cost, impact, and alignment with risk appetite.

Understand the purpose of PIAs and DPIAs. These assessments evaluate how systems or process changes affect personal data and identify risks to individuals' rights and freedoms.

Recognize the importance of asset, threat, and vulnerability analysis. Effective risk assessments depend on identifying valuable data assets, realistic threat scenarios, and relevant vulnerabilities.

Understand governance, ownership, and monitoring. Risks must be assigned to accountable owners, decisions must align with the organization's risk appetite, and risks must be continuously monitored for changes.

Review Questions

1. What is the primary purpose of a privacy risk management program?
   - A. To eliminate all risks associated with personal data
   - B. To ensure compliance with all security standards
   - C. To identify and manage risks to individuals' privacy
   - D. To maximize data collection for business value
2. Which of the following best defines a vulnerability?
   - A. A potential event that could cause harm
   - B. A weakness that can be exploited by a threat
   - C. The financial impact of a security incident
   - D. A control designed to reduce risk
3. Which step in the risk management lifecycle involves estimating the likelihood and impact of identified risks?
   - A. Risk identification
   - B. Risk analysis
   - C. Risk treatment
   - D. Risk monitoring
4. What is the primary objective of a Privacy Impact Assessment (PIA)?
   - A. To certify compliance with ISO standards
   - B. To evaluate system performance
   - C. To assess risks to personal data and individuals
   - D. To identify all system vulnerabilities
5. Which of the following best describes risk appetite?
   - A. The amount of risk an organization is willing to accept
   - B. The level of risk that must be eliminated
   - C. The maximum financial loss an organization can sustain
   - D. The number of risks identified in an assessment
6. Which of the following is an example of risk transfer?
   - A. Encrypting sensitive data
   - B. Discontinuing a high-risk process
   - C. Purchasing cyber insurance
   - D. Accepting residual risk

7. What distinguishes a Data Protection Impact Assessment (DPIA) from a general PIA?
   - A. DPIAs are only used for financial data
   - B. DPIAs are optional, while PIAs are mandatory
   - C. DPIAs focus only on technical vulnerabilities
   - D. DPIAs assess risks to individuals' rights and freedoms under GDPR
8. Which activity is most important during risk identification?
   - A. Estimating financial loss
   - B. Assigning risk ownership
   - C. Identifying assets, threats, and vulnerabilities
   - D. Selecting risk treatment strategies
9. Which of the following best describes residual risk?
   - A. Risk remaining after controls are applied
   - B. Risk that has not yet been identified
   - C. Risk transferred to a third party
   - D. Risk that has been fully eliminated
10. What is the primary goal of privacy training and awareness programs?
    - A. To eliminate insider threats
    - B. To ensure employees understand and follow privacy practices
    - C. To replace formal policies
    - D. To certify employees in privacy frameworks
11. Which of the following best describes a threat?
    - A. A weakness in a system
    - B. A control failure
    - C. A potential event that could cause harm
    - D. A quantified risk value
12. Which risk analysis method uses descriptive categories such as high, medium, and low?
    - A. Quantitative analysis
    - B. Qualitative analysis
    - C. Statistical modeling
    - D. Semi-quantitative analysis

13. Why is asset valuation important in risk management?
    A. It helps determine potential impact and prioritization
    B. It determines the number of threats
    C. It defines compliance requirements
    D. It eliminates vulnerabilities

14. Which of the following best represents risk avoidance?
    A. Implementing encryption controls
    B. Accepting low-level risk
    C. Eliminating the activity that creates the risk
    D. Purchasing insurance

15. Which factor is most important when determining appropriate risk treatment?
    A. Employee preferences
    B. Cost-benefit considerations
    C. Number of vulnerabilities
    D. Vendor capabilities

16. Which of the following is the best example of a privacy-specific risk?
    A. Server hardware failure
    B. Network latency issues
    C. Software performance degradation
    D. Unauthorized profiling of individuals

17. What is the role of risk ownership?
    A. To eliminate all risks
    B. To assign accountability for managing specific risks
    C. To perform all risk assessments
    D. To approve all security controls

18. Why is continuous monitoring important in risk management?
    A. It reduces compliance requirements
    B. It eliminates the need for assessments
    C. It ensures risks are updated as conditions change
    D. It guarantees zero incidents

19. Which of the following best explains why privacy risk cannot be assessed solely using traditional information security methods?
    A. Privacy risk includes impacts to individuals beyond organizational harm
    B. Privacy risk is always financial in nature
    C. Privacy risk focuses on systems rather than data
    D. Privacy risk does not involve threats or vulnerabilities
20. During a DPIA, which factor is most critical when evaluating risk severity?
    A. System uptime requirements
    B. Volume of data storage
    C. Potential impact on individuals' rights and freedoms
    D. Number of security controls implemented

Answers to Review Questions

1. C. Privacy risk management focuses on identifying, analyzing, and addressing risks arising from the processing of personal data, particularly those affecting individuals' rights and freedoms. While compliance and security are important components, the central objective is to protect individuals from harm, such as misuse, unauthorized disclosure, or unfair processing.
2. B. A vulnerability is a weakness in a system, process, or control environment that a threat can exploit. For example, poor access controls or unencrypted data storage can be vulnerabilities. Threats exploit vulnerabilities to create risk, while controls are implemented to reduce or eliminate those weaknesses.
3. B. Risk analysis is the stage in which identified risks are evaluated based on their likelihood of occurrence and potential impact. This step provides the basis for prioritizing risks and determining appropriate treatment strategies. Identification simply catalogs risks, while treatment and monitoring occur later in the lifecycle.
4. C. A PIA is designed to evaluate how a project, system, or process affects personal data and to identify risks to individuals. It focuses on data flows, processing activities, and potential harms, rather than purely technical vulnerabilities or system performance metrics.
5. A. Risk appetite refers to the level and type of risk an organization is willing to accept in pursuit of its objectives. It guides decision-making during risk treatment and helps ensure consistency in how risks are evaluated and managed across the organization.

6. C. Risk transfer involves shifting some or all of the financial or operational impact of a risk to another party, typically through insurance or contractual agreements. Encryption is risk mitigation, discontinuation is avoidance, and acceptance involves taking no further action.

7. D. A DPIA, as defined under the GDPR, specifically evaluates risks to individuals' rights and freedoms arising from the processing of personal data. While similar to PIAs, DPIAs have a stronger regulatory basis and focus on broader impacts beyond technical risks, including fairness and proportionality.

8. C. Risk identification involves determining which assets exist, which threats could affect them, and which vulnerabilities could be exploited. This foundational step ensures that subsequent analysis and treatment are based on a comprehensive understanding of potential risk scenarios.

9. A. Residual risk is the level of risk that remains after risk treatment measures have been implemented. Since it is rarely possible to eliminate risk entirely, organizations must decide whether the remaining risk is acceptable based on their risk appetite.

10. B. Privacy training and awareness programs aim to ensure that personnel understand their responsibilities for handling personal data and can recognize and respond to privacy risks. While training can reduce insider threats, it does not eliminate them and does not replace formal policies.

11. C. A threat is any potential event or action that could cause harm to an asset, such as unauthorized access or data leakage. It differs from a vulnerability, which is the weakness that enables the threat to materialize.

12. B. Qualitative risk analysis uses descriptive scales to assess likelihood and impact, making it easier to apply when precise numerical data is unavailable. Quantitative methods use numerical values and statistical techniques.

13. A. Asset valuation helps organizations understand the importance of data and systems, which in turn informs the potential impact of a risk event. This enables prioritization of risk treatment efforts based on business significance.

14. C. Risk avoidance involves eliminating the source of risk entirely, such as discontinuing a high-risk data processing activity. This differs from mitigation, which reduces risk, and transfer, which shifts it.

15. B. Risk treatment decisions are guided by cost-benefit analysis, balancing the cost of implementing controls against the risk's potential impact. This ensures that resources are used efficiently while maintaining acceptable risk levels.

16. D. Unauthorized profiling directly impacts individuals' rights and freedoms, making it a privacy-specific risk. The other options are operational or technical risks that might not directly affect personal privacy.

17. B. Risk ownership ensures that specific individuals are accountable for monitoring, evaluating, and treating risks. This accountability supports effective governance and ensures that risks are actively managed rather than ignored.

18. C. Risks evolve due to changes in technology, threats, and business processes. Continuous monitoring ensures that risk assessments remain current and that new risks are identified and addressed promptly.

19. A. Traditional information security risk focuses primarily on organizational impact (e.g., financial loss, operational disruption). Privacy risk extends beyond this to include harm to individuals, such as loss of autonomy, discrimination, or reputational damage. Therefore, additional considerations are required.

20. C. Under GDPR, DPIAs focus on assessing risks to individuals' rights and freedoms. While technical factors such as data volume and controls are relevant, the most critical determinant of severity is the potential harm to individuals, including legal, social, and ethical impacts.

Chapter 4 Compliance

This chapter covers CDPSE Domain 2, "Privacy Risk Management and Compliance," specifically the "Compliance" subdomain.

This chapter covers these job practice elements:

✔ *B—COMPLIANCE*

1. *Privacy Frameworks*
2. *Evidence and Artifacts*
3. *Program Monitoring and Metrics*

The other subdomain in Domain 2, Privacy Risk Management and Compliance, is:

✔ *A—RISK MANAGEMENT*—covered in Chapter 3.

The CDPSE Task Statements relevant to this domain are:

2. *Review organizational programs to align with privacy-related legal and regulatory requirements, industry best practices (e.g., privacy by design), and data subject's expectations.*
11. *Collaborate with relevant stakeholders to address privacy compliance and risk response.*
14. *Design, implement, and monitor processes and procedures to keep personal information inventory and data flow records current and accurate.*
16. *Develop and monitor metrics to report on privacy program performance to relevant stakeholders.*

The topics in this chapter and in Chapter 3 account for 18% of the CDPSE examination.

This chapter addresses privacy compliance by examining frameworks, documentation, monitoring, metrics, and audit practices that support accountable privacy governance. It introduces widely used privacy frameworks to provide structure for compliance programs and alignment with regulatory expectations. Next, the chapter explains evidence and artifacts that demonstrate operational effectiveness, including documentation, records, and audit-relevant materials. Program monitoring and metrics are discussed as mechanisms for measuring performance, risk, control effectiveness, and strategic outcomes through KPIs, KRIs, KGIs, and KCIs. The chapter also outlines layered metrics for different stakeholder audiences and emphasizes trend analysis and SMART measurement criteria. Finally, the chapter examines privacy audits, including scope, objectives, planning, evidence collection, sampling, reporting, and follow-up. Together, these elements enable organizations to monitor compliance, demonstrate accountability, and continuously improve the effectiveness of their privacy programs.

Privacy Frameworks

While every organization likely has unique missions, objectives, business models, tolerance for risk, and so on, organizations need not invent privacy frameworks from scratch to manage their privacy programs.

Several privacy and a few security frameworks are discussed in the remainder of this section:

- ISO/IEC 27701
- NIST Privacy Framework
- NIST Cybersecurity Framework (CSF)
- ISO/IEC 27001
- NIST SP 800-122
- APEC Privacy Framework
- GDPR Principles
- OECD Privacy Principles

- Fair Information Practice Principles (FIPP)
- Privacy Management Framework (PMF)
- COBIT

This chapter discusses privacy frameworks and other topics. For detailed information on privacy-related security controls, go to Chapter 8. For detailed information on privacy controls, go to Chapter 9.

Exam Tip

CDPSE candidates are not expected to memorize the contents of any privacy frameworks for the exam, but you should be generally aware of them and their purposes.

ISO/IEC 27701

ISO/IEC 27701:2025, *Information security, cybersecurity and privacy protection—Privacy information management systems—Requirements and guidance*, is an international standard that directs the formation and management of a *Privacy Information Management System (PIMS)*, including the controls and processes to ensure privacy by design and proper ongoing monitoring and management of personal information. First published in August 2019, the standard was revised in 2025.

ISO/IEC 27701 follows a similar structure to ISO/IEC 27001 and is divided into three main sections: requirements, guidance, and controls.

Requirements

The requirements section describes the required activities included for an effective PIMS. The structure of the requirements section uses the same seven sections as ISO/IEC 27001.

Guidance

The guidance section outlines how privacy programs can use ISO/IEC 27002 within the PIMS and offers specific considerations for controllers and processors. The guidance section is broken into three groups: PIMS-specific guidance related to ISO/IEC 27002, additional ISO/IEC 27002 guidance for personally identifiable information (PII) controllers, and additional ISO/IEC 27002 guidance for processors.

PIMS-specific guidance related to ISO/IEC 27002 expands on the four control categories, enabling an organization to evaluate control objectives and controls in the context of information security and privacy risks.

The sections on additional ISO/IEC 27002 guidance for PII controllers and for processors provide specific guidance on privacy management for controllers and processors.

Controls

The controls section contains a baseline set of controls for controllers and processors that can be used in context with ISO/IEC 27001.

The controls for controllers and processors in ISO/IEC 27701 are described in these four categories:

- Conditions for collection and processing
- Obligations to PII principals
- Privacy by design and privacy by default
- PII sharing, transfer, and disclosure

ISO/IEC 27701 is available from `www.iso.org/standard/27701`.

NIST Privacy Framework

The *NIST Privacy Framework (NIST PF)* is a guide for organizations that need to protect and handle personal information properly. The Privacy Framework is deliberately organized similarly to the NIST CSF to facilitate the parallel use of both tools. The framework consists of three parts:

- **Core** A set of privacy protection activities that facilitate the communication of protection activities. There are five core activities: Identify-P, Govern-P, Control-P, Communicate-P, Protect-P.
- **Profile** An organization's current set of activities used to protect personal information. You can think of the profile as a baseline that can be referenced in the future to gauge progress, as well as a foundation for defining the desired future state of a privacy program.
- **Implementation tiers** These are similar to maturity levels, from least to most mature: Partial, Risk-Informed, Repeatable, and Adaptive.

Similar to the extension of ISO/IEC 27001 with ISO/IEC 27701, the integration with the NIST CSF is highlighted in the Privacy Framework Core, with a key that indicates whether control objectives are identical to the CSF or align with the CSF, with descriptions adapted for privacy programs. This approach reinforces the idea that an effective privacy program requires the integration with information security and risk management programs.

Organizations seeking to adopt the framework will find a wealth of information, including crosswalks (mappings to other standards), profiles, guidance, and tools to build and improve their privacy practices.

All of this information is available at `www.nist.gov/privacy-framework`.

NIST Cybersecurity Framework

The *National Institute of Standards and Technology Cybersecurity Framework (NIST CSF)* is a risk-based lifecycle methodology for assessing risk, enacting controls, and measuring control effectiveness, unlike ISO/IEC 27001. The components of the NIST CSF are as follows:

- **Framework Core** This set of functions—*identify*, *protect*, *detect*, *respond*, and *recover*—makes up the lifecycle of high-level operational functions in an information security program. CSF 2.0 introduces a new function, *govern*, that serves as a governance foundation for the other functions. The Framework Core includes a complete set of controls (known as *informative references*) within the five functions.
- **Framework implementation tiers** These are similar to maturity levels, from least mature to most mature: Partial, Risk-Informed, Repeatable, and Adaptive.
- **Framework profile** This is an alignment of elements of the Framework Core (the functions, categories, subcategories, and references) with an organization's business requirements, risk tolerance, and available resources.

Organizations implementing the NIST CSF would first assess maturity (Implementation Tiers) for each activity in the Framework Core. Next, the organization would determine the desired maturity levels for each activity within the Framework Core. The differences found would be gaps that need to be filled through several means, which could include the following:

- Hiring additional resources
- Training resources
- Adding or changing business processes or procedures
- Changing system or device configuration
- Acquiring new systems or devices

The NIST CSF is available from `www.nist.gov/cyberframework`.

The NIST CSF and the NIST PF (Privacy Framework) are in an update cycle and, as of the time of this writing, are out of sync. The next iteration of the PF (v1.1) will align with CSF 2.0.

Big picture—standards like these, as well as ISO, PCI DSS, and so many others, strive to stay in sync, but since they all have their unique update cycles, they often are in a constant state of catching up.

ISO/IEC 27001

ISO/IEC 27001, Information security, cybersecurity and privacy protection—Information security management systems—Requirements, is an international standard for *information security management*. This standard contains a requirements section that outlines a properly functioning information security management system (ISMS) and a comprehensive control framework.

ISO/IEC 27001 is divided into two sections: requirements and controls. The requirements section describes required activities found in effective ISMSs. The controls section contains a baseline set of controls that serve as a starting point for the organization. The standard is updated periodically; the latest version, ISO/IEC 27001:2022, was released in 2022.

The requirements in ISO/IEC 27001 are described in these seven sections: Context of the organization, Leadership, Planning, Support, Operation, Performance Evaluation, and Improvement.

While ISO/IEC 27001 is a highly respected control framework, its adoption has been modest, partly because a single copy of the standard costs more than U.S. $100. Unlike NIST standards, which are free of charge, it is unlikely that students or professionals will pay this much for a standard to learn more about it. Despite this, ISO/IEC 27001 is growing in popularity among organizations worldwide.

ISO/IEC 27001 is available from `www.iso.org/standard/27001` (registration and payment required).

NIST SP 800-122

NIST SP 800-122, Guide to Protecting the Confidentiality of Personally Identifiable Information (PII), provides guidance on protecting personal information. While the guidelines are required of U.S. government agencies, many other organizations employ them, as they are considered good practices.

The sections in this standard include:

- PII Confidentiality Impact Levels
- PII Confidentiality Safeguards
- Incident Response for Breaches Involving PII

NIST SP 800-122 is available from `csrc.nist.gov/publications/PubsSPs.html`.

APEC Privacy Framework

The APEC Privacy Framework is a standard developed by the Asia-Pacific Economic Cooperation (APEC) to promote consistent privacy protections while enabling the free flow of personal information across its 21 member economies. The framework was developed in 2005 and updated in 2015 to align with evolving digital trade needs and the OECD *Guidelines on Privacy and Trans-Border Data Flows.*

Core principles of the APEC privacy framework are as follows:

- Accountability
- Preventing harm
- Notice
- Choice
- Collection limitation
- Use of personal information
- Integrity of personal information
- Security safeguards
- Access and correction

These principles guide organizations in managing personal data responsibly and support cross-border data transfers within the APEC region. The framework is available from `www.apec.org`.

GDPR Privacy Principles

The EU General Data Protection Regulation (GDPR) is built on a foundation of core principles governing the lawful processing of personal information. These core principles are as follows:

- Lawfulness, fairness, and transparency
- Purpose limitation
- Data minimization
- Accuracy
- Storage limitation
- Integrity and confidentiality
- Accountability

GDPR is discussed in more detail in Chapter 1.

OECD Privacy Principles

The *Organisation for Economic Co-operation and Development (OECD) Privacy Principles* are a foundational set of eight internationally recognized guidelines, established in 1980, to protect personal data and ensure the free flow of information across borders. Updated in 2013 to reflect evolving digital environments, they remain a global benchmark for privacy and data protection.

The principles are as follows:

- **Collection Limitation Principle** Personal data should be collected only through fair and lawful means, with the knowledge or consent of the data subject where appropriate.

- **Data Quality Principle** Personal data should be accurate, complete, and kept up to date to ensure relevance and reliability.
- **Purpose Specification Principle** The purposes for which data is collected must be clearly specified at the time of collection and not used for incompatible purposes.
- **Use Limitation Principle** Data should not be used for purposes other than those specified, unless consent is obtained or permitted by law.
- **Security Safeguards Principle** Reasonable security measures must be implemented to protect data against risks such as loss, unauthorized access, disclosure, or modification.
- **Openness Principle** Organizations must be transparent about their data practices, including the existence of data, its nature, intended use, and the identity of the data controller.
- **Individual Participation Principle** Individuals have the right to access their personal data, correct inaccuracies, and challenge its use.
- **Accountability Principle** Data controllers are responsible for complying with these principles and must demonstrate adherence through appropriate policies and procedures.

The OECD principles are available from `www.oecd.org/en/topics/sub-issues/privacy-principles.html`.

Fair Information Practice Principles (FIPP)

Fair Information Practice Principles (FIPPs) are a set of internationally recognized guidelines that form the foundation of modern privacy regulation. First introduced in 1973 by the U.S. Department of Health, Education, and Welfare in the report *Records, Computers and the Rights of Citizens*, these principles were developed to address growing concerns about privacy in automated data systems. The principles were later expanded and formalized by the Organisation for Economic Co-operation and Development (OECD) in 1980, resulting in eight widely adopted principles that continue to influence privacy laws globally. While historically related, FIPPs and OECD remain separate today.

The core principles are as follows:

- **Transparency** about PII policies and practices, including providing clear and accessible notice about the collection and handling of PII.
- **Individual Participation** Individuals should be involved in the process of collection and use of PII with consent.
- **Authority** Only handle PII that is directly relevant to the purpose for collection.
- **Purpose Specification and Use Limitation** The purposes for collecting data must be clearly defined at the time of collection, and subsequent use must be limited to those purposes or compatible ones.
- **Minimization** Only handle PII that is necessary for authorized purpose.
- **Quality and Integrity** Personal data must be accurate, complete, and kept up to date to ensure fairness and reliability.

- **Access and Amendment** Provide individuals with appropriate access to PII and opportunity to correct or amend their PII.
- **Security** Reasonable measures must be taken to protect personal data from loss, unauthorized access, destruction, use, modification, or disclosure.
- **Accountability** Data controllers must be accountable for complying with these principles and demonstrate adherence through policies, training, and audits.

The FAIR information practice principles are available from `www.councils.gov/resources/?council=FPC`.

Privacy Management Framework

The *Privacy Management Framework (PMF)* is a foundational element for privacy programs and addresses privacy obligations and risks. The PMF is an update to the former Generally Accepted Privacy Principles (GAPP).

The components of the PMF are as follows:

- Management
- Agreement, notice, and communication
- Collection and creation
- Use, retention, and disposal
- Access
- Disclosure to third parties
- Security for privacy
- Data integrity and quality
- Monitoring and enforcement

The PMF can be obtained from `www.aicpa-cima.com/` (registration required).

COBIT

The COBIT framework from ISACA is primarily an IT governance framework. As stated elsewhere in this book, privacy governance depends on sound data, security, and IT governance. Many privacy considerations are built into the core model and contribute to privacy programs.

COBIT is available from `www.isaca.org/resources/cobit`.

Evidence and Artifacts

In Chapter 1, I describe the role and importance of documentation and records in support of a sound privacy program. In this chapter, I go into more detail on the topic of evidence. Later in this chapter, a discussion of privacy audits explains how evidence is used to determine the effectiveness of a privacy program.

In the context of privacy and information security, *artifacts* are information that represents ongoing activities and the directives driving them. While practitioners often use the term artifacts, auditors often use the term *evidence* to describe the same thing.

This section describes the types of evidence and artifacts typically found in privacy and security programs.

The types of evidence include:

- Data management
  - *Data classification policy* The organization's data classification scheme, together with handling policies and guidelines for data across various contexts and classification levels
  - *Data inventory* The results of periodic or continuous data inventory
  - *Data discovery* The results of data discovery scans that are used to identify the presence of personal information (and information of other types, such as trade secrets)
  - *Data access* Records of individuals and systems that access data records, whether located in databases or file shares
  - *Data modification* Records of modifications to the contents of data, as well as to access permissions
  - *Data movement* Records of the movement of sensitive data, such as email, saving a report to a hard drive or file share, or uploading data to an Internet website
- Privacy management
  - *Privacy policy and notices of privacy practices (NOPPs)* Internal and customer/employee-facing privacy policies and notices of privacy practices
  - *Privacy impact assessments (PIAs)* The output from PIAs
  - *Data protection impact assessments (DPIAs)* The output from DPIAs
  - *Data subject requests (DSRs)* Incoming inquiries, requests, and complaints from data subjects
  - *DSR responses* Responses sent to data subjects who submit DSRs
  - *Consent records* The details of the consent to process personal information
  - *Privacy incident reports* A report summarizing the response to a privacy incident
  - *Privacy regulation analysis* Reports or correspondence from privacy attorneys on the applicability and interpretation of privacy laws
  - *Regulator correspondence* Formal and informal correspondence with privacy-related regulators
  - *Privacy awareness training records*
  - *Approved changes to business processes*
  - *Reviews and modifications to charters, policies, standards, and guidelines*

  - *Minutes from privacy governance and privacy management meetings*
  - *Decision logs*
- Security management
  - *Security policy, standards, and guidelines* The organization's *information security policies*, and various standards and guidelines
  - *Identity and access management* The creation and modification of user and system accounts
  - *Privileged access management* The creation and modification of privileged user and system accounts
  - *System access* Records of successful and unsuccessful logins
  - *System modifications* Records of changes to information system configurations and configuration files
  - *Security events* Records that indicate system abuse or attack
  - *Forensic data* Data obtained from computer and network forensics in support of a security event or incident
  - *Security incident response* Records describing the steps taken during a security incident, including post-incident review
  - *Risk assessments* The output from risk assessments
  - *Third-party risk assessments* The output from risk assessments of third parties (including questionnaires)
  - *Risk register* Risks that have been identified
  - *Threat intelligence* Records of incoming threat intelligence data
  - *Security awareness training records*
  - *Approved changes to business processes*
  - *Reviews and modifications to charters, policies, standards, and guidelines*
  - *Minutes from security governance and security management meetings*
  - *Decision logs*
- IT management
  - *Acceptable use policy (AUP)* Policy defining accepted and prohibited uses of organizational information and information systems
  - *System health, performance, and resources* Events related to the health of information systems, their performance, and available resources
  - *Change requests and approvals* Formal requests for change to information systems, with approvals and related artifacts
  - *Approved changes to business processes*

  - *Reviews and modifications to charters, policies, standards, and guidelines*
  - *Minutes from IT governance and IT management meetings*
  - *Decision logs*
- **Audit**
  - *Audit plans* The plans for audits to take place in a calendar or fiscal year
  - *Audit reports* Reports from audits that have been performed
- **Public sentiment**
  - *Social media monitoring* Output from monitoring social media to see how customers and the public feel about the organization
  - *Customer surveys* Output from customer surveys
  - *Focus groups* Output from customer focus groups

The program charters for data governance, privacy governance, security governance, and IT governance should define these and other types of documents and records in their respective programs.

Program Monitoring and Metrics

Program monitoring involves the periodic, continuous observation of key program activities to ensure compliance with policy and to identify actionable events and incidents.

Metrics are the ongoing and continuous measurements of system and process activities. Some metrics are automatically generated, such as the number of database accesses or DSRs, while others are manually generated, such as the number of privacy incidents.

Privacy and security professionals recognize that metrics are contextual and that their relevance is tied to the recipients to whom they are sent. For instance, board members will have no interest in the number of packets dropped by a firewall; instead, they would want to know how many privacy incidents occurred. When establishing metrics, privacy and security leaders must identify the audience for each metric, so that each recipient of metric data receives only those relevant to their roles and responsibilities.

Regardless of the audience or type of measurements, metrics should be SMART:

- Specific
- Measurable
- Attainable
- Relevant
- Timely

An important aspect of metrics is identifying trends over time. These help management understand whether processes and systems are improving or declining.

Privacy Governance Metrics

Metrics are the means through which management can measure key processes and determine whether its strategies are working. Metrics are used in many operational processes, but in this discussion, metrics in the privacy governance context are the focus. In other words, there is a distinction between tactical privacy metrics and those that reveal the state of the overall privacy program.

Privacy metrics are often used to observe technical privacy controls and processes to determine whether they are operating correctly. This helps management better understand the impact of past decisions and can help drive future decisions. Examples of technical metrics include the following:

- Number of personal information records received
- Number of personal information records purged
- Number of personal information records anonymized
- Number of personal information records accessed
- Number of subject data requests received

While useful, these metrics do not address the bigger picture of an organization's overall privacy program's effectiveness or alignment. They do not answer key questions that boards of directors and executive management often ask, such as the following:

- How should privacy resources be invested and applied?
- What is the potential impact of a threat event?
- Is our privacy policy aligned with applicable privacy laws?
- Are our privacy practices aligned with customer or constituent expectations?
- How much security is enough?

These and other business-related questions can be addressed using the appropriate metrics, which are discussed in the remainder of this section.

Risk Management Metrics

Effective risk management is the culmination of the highest-order activities in information privacy and security programs; these include risk analysis, the use of a risk ledger, formal risk treatment, and adjustments to the suite of privacy and security controls.

While it is difficult to measure the success of a risk management program effectively and objectively, it is possible to take indirect measures—much like measuring a tree's shadow to gauge its height. Thus, the best indicators of a successful risk management program would be improving trends in metrics involved with the following:

- Reduction in the number of privacy and security incidents
- Reduction in the impact of privacy and security incidents

- Reduction in the time to remediate privacy and security incidents
- Reduction in the time to remediate vulnerabilities
- Reduction in the number of new unmitigated risks

Regarding the reduction in the number of privacy and security incidents, a privacy and security program improving its maturity from low levels should first expect the number of incidents to increase. This would not be due to lapses in privacy or security controls, but rather to the development—and improvement—of mechanisms used to detect and report privacy and security incidents. If a tree falls in the forest, it will be heard if microphones are installed in key locations. Similarly, as a privacy and security program improves and matures over time, the number of new risks will first increase and then decrease.

Performance Measurement Metrics

Metrics on the performance of privacy information security provide measures of timeliness and effectiveness. Generally speaking, performance measurement metrics provide a view of tactical privacy and security processes and activities. As discussed earlier in this section, performance measurements are often the operational metrics that need to be transformed into executive-level metrics for those audiences.

Performance measurement metrics can include any of the following:

- Time to detect privacy and security incidents
- Time to remediate privacy and security incidents
- Time to provision user accounts
- Time to deprovision user accounts
- Time to respond to subject access requests
- Time to discover vulnerabilities
- Time to remediate vulnerabilities

Nearly every operational activity that is privacy- or security-related and measurable is a candidate for performance metrics. Few of these, however, will be of interest to senior executives.

Convergence Metrics

Larger organizations with multiple business units, geographic locations, privacy functions, or security functions (often due to mergers and acquisitions) might be experiencing issues with overlapping or underlapping coverage or activities. For instance, an organization that recently acquired another company might have some duplication of effort in its privacy and risk management functions. In another example, local privacy personnel in a large, distributed organization might be performing privacy functions that are also being performed on their behalf by other personnel at headquarters.

Metrics in the convergence category will be highly individualized, based on specific circumstances within an organization. Some of the categories of metrics include the following:

- Gaps and overlaps in asset coverage
- Gaps and overlaps in data management tools coverage
- Consolidation of licenses for privacy and security tools
- Gaps or overlaps in skills, responsibilities, or coverage

Resource Management Metrics

Resource management metrics are like value delivery metrics; both convey an efficient use of resources in an organization's privacy program. But because the emphasis here is on program efficiency, these are areas where resource management metrics can be developed:

- Standardization of privacy-related processes—because consistency drives costs down
- Privacy and security involvement in every procurement and acquisition project
- Percentage of personal information records protected by privacy and security controls

Developing Metrics in Layers for Audience Relevance

When embarking on the quest to develop privacy and security metrics, a common pitfall is creating a one-dimensional metrics framework that publishes one set of metrics to all audiences. For instance, a metrics program might publish figures on vulnerabilities discovered, vulnerabilities remediated, privacy incidents, security incidents, and internal audits and their exceptions. Publishing this or a similar set of metrics to various stakeholders will add little value to some audiences and no value to others.

A better approach is to develop operational metrics, which are usually easy to identify and measure. The next step is to transform those operational metrics into business terms for business audiences. In a given organization, a privacy program might employ two, three, or more layers of metrics, usually related to one another, and expressed in relevant technical or business terms for each audience.

While it can be a good starting point to ask business leaders what metrics they want to see, in many cases, privacy and security leaders will be asked the same question. This can be a challenge at times, but by understanding the business, culture, compliance climate, and individuals involved at the stakeholder level, the privacy and security leader can start with a set of metrics that show success in investments made, or use them as a call to action for the leadership team.

Key Indicators

Key indicators provide measurable insight into privacy program performance and effectiveness.

Key Performance Indicators (KPIs)

A *key performance indicator (KPI)* is a measure of how well a process or system is performing. A KPI can indicate whether processes and systems are operating within expected workloads, and whether they are sufficiently responsive (e.g., that data subjects don't wait unnecessarily for responses from websites). A KPI can serve as a measure of quality when it indicates the rate of errors, for instance.

Examples of KPIs include:

- System performance, such as response time
- Process performance, such as the time to respond to DSRs
- The percentage of staff attending relevant training

Key Risk Indicators (KRIs)

A *key risk indicator (KRI)* is a measure of risk levels that informs management of key business risks related to privacy, indicating whether unacceptable outcomes, such as privacy breaches, are becoming more or less likely. KRIs should serve as *leading indicators*, predicting the likelihood of future events.

Example KRIs include:

- The time taken to apply critical security patches
- Whether DSR responses fall within regulatory requirements and policy
- Mean time to detect (MTTD), mean time to restore service (MTTRS), and mean time to recover (MTTR) related to privacy and security incidents (see Chapter 2)
- Percentage of key vendors meeting privacy and security requirements

Key Goal Indicators (KGIs)

A *key goal indicator (KGI)* is a measure of an organization's progress toward its strategic goals. Examples include:

- Improvements in customer Net Promoter Score results
- Reduction in the number of privacy-related complaints
- Attainment of privacy approvals in new jurisdictions

Key Control Indicators (KCIs)

A *key control indicator (KCI)* is a measure of selected controls to determine their effectiveness. When organizations implement privacy or security controls, some controls warrant measurement so that management can determine whether they are meeting their objectives.

Examples of KCIs include:

- Number of privacy exceptions identified
- Number of unauthorized data elements collected that are not needed
- Percentage of systems that collect only defined minimum data elements

Organizations can have several dozen to hundreds of controls. It's likely infeasible to measure and develop KCIs for all of them. Instead, organizations generally develop KCIs for new controls, for controls updated as a result of historical problems, and for controls that represent significant risk if and when they fail.

Auditing a Privacy Program

The purpose of any audit is to confirm, using objective means, the effectiveness of controls and processes. An audit can be performed by a customer, regulator, audit firm, or internal audit staff. An audit of an organization's privacy processes and underlying information system will be performed using established audit practices.

This section summarizes audit practices in the context of information privacy. For more detailed information about audit planning and audits, refer to the *CISA Certified Information Systems Auditor Study Guide* (Wiley Publishing), Chapter 2, "The Audit Process" by this author.

Strictly speaking, the topic of auditing a privacy program is not formally a part of the CDPSE job practice. However, any privacy professional who is aware of audit techniques is likely to be better informed of privacy program practices and expectations, whether their privacy program will be audited or not. This section is included for this reason.

Audit Knowledge Also Helps Auditees

Because privacy is increasingly regulated, more organizations are being subjected to audits. While useful to privacy auditors, the information in this section is equally valuable to auditees (organizations being audited), as auditees will be better prepared for audits when they understand how audits are conducted. It's also useful to be familiar with key audit terms, so that auditors and auditees are on the same page.

Privacy Audit Scope

An audit is planned for good reason. Because audits are disruptive and often expensive, one or more compelling business drivers should be identified to help management determine whether an audit is needed and what the desired outcome is likely to be.

For privacy, the *scope* of a privacy audit is likely to be the controls, processes, and systems used to protect personal information, or to collect, process, and use personal information. Just as privacy itself has two perspectives (the protection of personal information and the use of personal information), a privacy audit is likely to focus on one or both perspectives.

Privacy Audit Objectives

The term *audit objectives* refers to the specific goals of a privacy audit. The objectives of a privacy audit are to determine whether privacy controls exist and are effective in a specific aspect of an organization's business operations. Generally, a privacy audit is performed to comply with applicable privacy regulations or related legal obligations. An audit can also be conducted in response to a recent privacy incident or event.

Depending on the subject and nature of the audit, the auditor might examine privacy controls and related evidence or focus instead on the business content processed by the controls. For example, if the focus of a privacy audit is an organization's data subject request process, the auditor might review requests in the system to determine whether they comply with the organization's privacy policy or applicable regulations. Or the auditor could focus on the information systems processes that support the processing of personal information. Formal audit objectives should make such a distinction so that the auditor has a sound understanding of the objectives. Objectives tell the auditor what to examine during the audit. Of course, knowing the type of audit to be undertaken helps too; this is covered in the next section.

Types of Privacy Audits

The scope, purpose, and objectives of a privacy audit will determine the type of audit that will be performed. Auditors need to understand each type of audit, including the procedures that are used for each:

- ***Operational audit*** This type of audit involves an examination of privacy, security, or business controls to determine their existence and effectiveness. The focus of an operational audit is usually the operation of one or more controls, and it could concentrate on the management of a business process or on the business process itself.
- ***Information systems audit*** This type of audit involves a detailed examination of an IT department's operations related to the storage and processing of personal information. An IS audit assesses IT governance to determine whether the IT department is aligned with the organization's overall goals and objectives, privacy and security policies, and applicable regulations. The audit might also look closely at all the major IT processes, including service delivery, change and configuration management, security management, systems development lifecycle, business relationship and supplier management, and incident and problem management. The integrity of a privacy process ultimately depends upon the integrity of the underlying IT systems and processes. This audit will determine whether each control objective and control is effective and operating properly.
- ***Integrated audit*** This type of audit combines an operational audit and an information systems audit to help the auditor fully understand the integrity of the

entire environment. Such an audit will closely examine privacy operations processes, procedures, and records, as well as the IT applications used to store and process personal information.

- *Administrative audit* This type of audit involves an examination of the operational efficiency of privacy-related business processes.
- *Compliance audit* This type of audit is performed to determine the level and degree of compliance with one or more applicable privacy regulations, other legal requirements, or internal policies and standards. If a particular privacy law requires an external audit, the compliance audit might have to be performed by approved or licensed external auditors and/or follow specific audit standards. If, however, the law does not explicitly require audits, the organization might still decide to conduct one-time or regular audits to assess compliance with the law. Internal or external auditors might perform this type of audit, typically to give management a better understanding of the level of compliance risk.
- *Forensic audit* This type of audit is usually performed by an IS auditor or a forensic specialist in support of an anticipated or active legal proceeding. This is typically part of the investigation of a privacy breach. To withstand cross-examination and avoid having evidence ruled inadmissible, strict procedures must be followed in a forensic audit, including the preservation of evidence and a *chain of custody*.
- *Service provider audit* Because many organizations outsource parts of their operations, third-party service organizations will undergo one or more external audits to increase customer confidence in the integrity of their services. In the United States, a *System and Organization Controls (SOC) 2 audit* can be performed on a service provider's operations, and the audit report can be transmitted to customers of the service provider. The auditing guidelines for how auditors examine and report on controls at a service organization are established in the *Statement on Standards for Attestation Engagements No. 18, Reporting on Controls at a Service Organization (SSAE 18)*.

Privacy Audit Planning

The auditor must obtain information about the privacy audit to establish the audit plan. Information needed includes the following:

- Location or locations that need to be visited
- A list of the business processes and supporting applications to be examined
- The personnel to be interviewed
- The technologies supporting each application
- Privacy policies, security policies, standards, and data flow diagrams that describe the environment and the personal data stored and processed there

This and other information will enable the auditor to determine the resources and skills required to examine and evaluate privacy-related business processes and information systems. The auditor will be able to establish an audit schedule and a good idea of the types of evidence needed. The auditor might make advance requests for certain other types of evidence even before the on-site phase of the audit begins.

For an audit with a risk-based approach, the auditor has a couple of options:

- Precede the audit itself with a risk assessment to determine which privacy processes or controls warrant additional audit scrutiny.
- Gather information about the organization and its historical events to identify risks warranting additional audit scrutiny.

Audit Statement of Work

For an external audit, the auditor might need to prepare a statement of work or an engagement letter outlining the audit purpose, scope, duration, and costs. The auditor might require written approval from the client before audit work can officially begin.

Establish Audit Procedures

Using information obtained regarding audit objectives and scope, the auditor can develop *audit procedures*. For each privacy process, control, and objective to be tested, the auditor can specify the following:

- A list of people to interview
- Inquiries to make during each interview
- Documentation (policies, procedures, and other documents) to request during each interview
- Audit tools to use
- Sampling rates and methodologies
- How and where evidence will be archived
- How evidence will be evaluated
- How findings will be reported

Communication Plan

The auditor will develop a communication plan to keep the auditor's management and the auditee's management informed throughout the audit project. The communication plan can contain one or more of the following:

- A list of evidence requested, usually in the form of a *provided-by-client (PBC) list*, which is typically a worksheet that lists specific documents or records and the names of personnel who can provide them (or who provided them in a prior audit).
- Regular written status reports that include activities performed since the last status report, upcoming activities, and any significant findings that require immediate attention.

- Regular status meetings are held to discuss audit progress, issues, and other matters, in person or via conference call.
- Contact information for the auditor and the auditee so both parties can contact each other quickly if needed.

Report Preparation

The auditor needs to develop a plan that describes how the *audit report* will be prepared. This will include the report's format and content, as well as how findings will be established and documented.

The auditor will need to ensure that the audit report complies with all applicable audit standards, including applicable regulations and ISACA IS audit standards.

Wrap-up

The auditor must perform some tasks at the conclusion of the audit, including the following:

- Deliver the report to the auditee.
- Schedule a closing meeting to discuss the audit results with the auditee and collect feedback.
- For external audits, send an invoice to the auditee.
- Collect and archive all work papers. Enter their existence into a document management system so they can be retrieved later if needed and destroyed when they have reached the end of their retention life.
- Update PBC documents if the auditor anticipates the audit will be performed again.
- Collect feedback from the auditee and convey to audit staff as needed.

Post-audit Follow-up

After a specified period (which could range from days to months), the auditor should contact the auditee to assess the progress made in remedying any audit findings. This establishes a tone of concern for the auditee organization and helps establish a dialogue in which the auditor can help auditee management work through any necessary process or technology changes resulting from the audit.

Privacy Audit Evidence

Evidence is the information collected by the auditor during the audit project. The auditor uses the contents and reliability of the evidence obtained to reach conclusions on the effectiveness of privacy controls and control objectives. The auditor needs to understand how to evaluate various types of evidence and how (and if) it can be used to support audit findings.

The auditor will collect many kinds of evidence during an audit, including observations, written notes, correspondence, independent confirmations from other auditors, process and procedure documentation, and business records.

When the auditor examines evidence, they need to consider several characteristics that will contribute to its weight and reliability, including the following:

- ***Independence* of the evidence provider** Evidence provided by the process owner might be tainted (to influence audit results); an independent evidence provider might be preferred.
- **Qualifications of the evidence provider** The evidence provider should be a person qualified to represent the process or system being audited.
- ***Objectivity*** The evidence should be objective. Digital evidence is more objective than a process owner's opinion, for instance.
- **Timing** The evidence should be timely and appropriate to the issue at hand. Some evidence, such as system logs, might be available only for a short period.

Evidence collected in a privacy audit is likely to contain personal information. The auditor and auditee will need to understand the protective measures required to protect this evidence, whether it can be anonymized, and how long it must be retained.

Gathering Evidence

The privacy auditor must understand and be familiar with the methods and techniques used to gather evidence during an audit. The methods and techniques used most often in audits include reviews of the *organization chart*, department and project charters, third-party contracts and service level agreements (SLAs), policies and procedures, risk register, incident log, *audit log*, standards, system documentation, interviews of personnel, *walkthroughs* (where control owners describe procedures to auditors), *reperformance* (where auditors will confirm that the organization's processes and systems calculate results properly), and passive observation.

Privacy auditors should pay attention to what department charters, policies, and procedure documents do say, as well as what they don't say. They should conduct corroborative interviews to determine whether these documents reflect the organization's behavior or are just window dressing. This will help the auditors understand the organization's maturity, a valuable insight for writing the audit report.

Sampling

Sampling is a technique used when it is not feasible to test the entire *population* of privacy events or transactions. The objective of sampling is to select a portion (called a *sample*) of a population so that the characteristics observed will reflect the characteristics of the entire population. There are several methods for sampling, including the following:

- *Statistical sampling*
- *Judgmental sampling* (also known as nonstatistical sampling)
- *Attribute sampling*
- *Variable sampling*
- *Stop-or-go sampling*
- *Discovery sampling*
- *Stratified sampling*

Exam Tip

CDPSE candidates are not expected to memorize specific sampling techniques or their purposes, although you should understand these concepts.

Relying on the Work of Other Auditors

Audit departments and external auditors, like other IT service organizations, are challenged to find qualified audit professionals who understand all aspects of organizations' technologies in use. Increased specialization in IT is resulting in auditors with greater technical knowledge in certain areas and fewer auditors with the full knowledge required to perform an audit. Third-party service providers usually do not permit customers to audit them; instead, they rely on external auditors to perform audits and then make those audit reports available to the customer. These and other factors are putting increasing pressure on organizations to outsource some auditing tasks (or entire audits) to third parties and to rely on audit reports from other sources.

For example, it's unlikely that Amazon Web Services or Microsoft Azure will permit any customer to audit them. Amazon and Microsoft will instead commission a range of external audits, such as *SOC 1*, *SOC 2*, ISO/IEC 27001, or PCI DSS, and make those audit reports (or summaries) available to their customers upon request. The auditors in customer organizations often have little choice but to rely on them.

Reporting Privacy Audit Results

The work product of a privacy audit project is the *audit report*. This written report describes the entire audit project, including the audit objectives, scope, evaluated controls, opinions on the effectiveness and integrity of those controls, and recommendations for improvement.

While an auditor or audit firm will generally use a standard format for an audit report, some privacy laws and standards require that an audit report regarding those laws or standards contain specific information or be presented in a particular format. Still, there will be some variance in the structure and appearance of audit reports created by different audit organizations.

The auditor is typically asked to present findings at a closing meeting, explain the audit and its results, and be available to answer questions about it. The auditor might include an electronic presentation to guide audit discussions.

Auditing Specific Privacy Practices

An audit of an organization's privacy likely focuses on one or more key aspects of its privacy policy and operations. Several are discussed here.

Auditing Privacy Policy

An audit of an organization's privacy policy will focus on one or more of these:

- **Compliance with applicable privacy regulations** Does the organization's privacy policy align with the privacy regulations the organization is required to comply with?
- **Compliance with privacy policies** Does the organization's practices align with its internal and external privacy policies? For example, if the organization's external privacy policy states that it does not sell personal information, the auditor will determine whether this is true.
- **Alignment with security policy and practices** Is the organization's security policy content adequate for protecting personal information? Do the organization's practices align with its policies?

Auditing Data Management

An organization's data management audit, which should include the protection and management of personal information, is likely to focus on one or more of these:

- **Data inventory** The auditor will examine the organization's data inventory, along with the procedures and tools used to establish and maintain it. Of particular interest is whether the organization attempts to inventory unstructured data found on *file servers* and *file shares*.
- **Data classification** The auditor will examine the organization's data classification policy and handling procedures. Since most organizations lack automation, auditors will want to interview workers to assess whether there is widespread awareness of the classification policy and how often it is applied in practice. If automation is present in the form of DLP or other solutions, the auditor will examine those systems to understand their capabilities and how they are managed.
- **Data protection** The auditor will examine one or more facets of information security to assess how effectively the organization protects personal information. This potentially covers a large variety of topics, from system hardening to identity and access management.
- **Data flows** The auditor will examine data flow diagrams and supporting documentation to determine whether the organization truly knows where personal information flows and resides in its environment.

- **Data loss prevention** The auditor will examine any DLP systems to determine whether they effectively identify the presence and flows of personal information.

Auditing Data Collection

Auditors looking at an organization's practice of collecting personal information will examine several aspects of data collection:

- **Security** The auditor will look for secure protocols to ensure the protection of personal information in transit and upon arrival within the organization's systems.
- **Alignment with privacy policy** The auditor will compare data collection practices with the privacy policy to determine whether they align. For instance, if the privacy policy states that only name, address, and phone number are collected, the auditor will compare that policy with systems that collect data to confirm whether these are the only items collected from data subjects.
- **Alignment with applicable regulations** The auditor will confirm whether data collection practices comply with specific privacy regulations.
- **Consent** The auditor will examine the privacy policy and data collection practices to understand how the organization obtains consent from the data subject at the time of collection. Note that an absence of consent is not necessarily a violation of policy or regulations, as there are circumstances in which it is infeasible or unnecessary for an organization to obtain consent.
- **Data aggregation** The auditor will seek to understand the organization's practices for aggregating personal information collected from data subjects with data obtained from other sources.

Auditing Data Subject Requests

The auditor will examine business processes and supporting information systems to understand how the organization receives data subject requests and responds to them. Aspects of an audit will include the following:

- **Data subject authentication** The auditor will examine the procedures used by the organization to authenticate the user. The authentication process itself might include the collection of data used to authenticate the user; the auditor will need to understand how that information is used, whether it is retained, and if it is disclosed in subsequent requests.
- **Effectiveness of response** The auditor assesses the organization's procedures to determine whether they identify all areas where a subject's data resides and whether all instances are disclosed to the data subject.
- **Accuracy of response** Here, the auditor examines procedures to determine whether the organization correctly processes the request, including any changes or corrections.
- **Completeness of response** The auditor checks whether the organization's response to a data subject includes all instances of the storage and use of personal information.

- **Timeliness of response** The auditor examines records to determine how long the organization takes to respond to requests.
- **Recordkeeping** The auditor examines business records to determine what information about the data subject request is retained.
- **Compliance with policy and applicable regulations** Finally, the auditor will confirm whether the organization's processing of data subject requests aligns with its privacy policy and applicable regulations.

Auditing Data Minimization

The auditor will examine data collection and aggregation practices and compare them with the organization's services to determine whether the organization appears to be collecting more items of personal information than necessary to provide its services. This will include a comparison of the language in the organization's privacy policy to see whether it, too, is aligned.

Auditing Anonymization and Pseudonymization

The auditor will examine the organization's anonymization and pseudonymization practices to determine whether they are effective. Here, the auditor will need to "think outside the box" to determine whether anonymized and pseudonymized data can be re-identified and associated with specific natural persons. Whether through ineptness, simple system misconfiguration, or outright deception, some organizations tend to provide only the *appearance* of anonymization and pseudonymization, not the reality. For instance, merely removing the name of a person otherwise identified as a "46-year-old male electrical engineer with a family of four living on Main Street" is probably insufficient anonymization.

Auditing Privacy Incident Management

Auditing privacy-related incident management and investigative procedures requires attention to several key activities, including these:

- **Investigation policies and procedures** The auditor should determine whether there are any policies or procedures regarding privacy and security investigations. This would include who is responsible for performing investigations, where information about investigations is stored, and to whom the results of investigations are reported. When subject data is examined in an investigation, the auditor will seek to understand how it is protected and used, and whether this aligns with the organization's privacy policy and applicable regulations.
- **Computer crime investigations** The auditor should determine whether there are policies, processes, procedures, and records regarding computer crime investigations. The auditor should understand how internal investigations are transitioned to supervisory authorities, regulators, or law enforcement.
- **Security incident response** Because security incident response is relevant to privacy in instances involving personal data, the auditor should examine security incident response

policies, procedures, and plans to determine whether they are up to date. Interviewing incident responders to gauge their familiarity with incident response procedures can indicate the effectiveness of training and tabletop exercises. The auditor should examine records of actual security incidents to determine whether the responses were effective and whether the organization conducted post-incident reviews to identify process improvements.

- **Privacy incident response** For incidents involving the misuse of personal information, the auditor will examine incident response plans and records to assess how the organization responds to such incidents. If any personal information becomes part of the incident response record, the auditor will assess whether the organization complies with its privacy policy and applicable regulations governing the storage and use of those records.
- **Computer forensics** The auditor should determine whether there are procedures for conducting computer forensics. The auditor should also identify tools and techniques available to the organization for the acquisition and custody of forensic data. The auditor should identify whether any employees in the organization have received computer forensics training and are qualified to perform forensic investigations. Because some organizations employ outside firms for forensic assistance, the auditor should examine any existing contract to determine whether this prearranged capability was properly established.

Audit Standards

ISACA has published its *IT Assurance Framework* in the *ITAF: A Professional Practices Framework for IS Audit/Assurance* (currently in its third edition and available free of charge at `www.isaca.org/ITAF`). ITAF consists of the ISACA Code of Professional Ethics, *IS audit standards*, *IS audit guidelines*, *IS audit procedures*, and IS audit and assurance tools and techniques. The relationship between these is illustrated in Figure 4.1.

FIGURE 4.1 Relationship between ISACA audit standards, audit guidelines, and the ISACA Code of Professional Ethics.

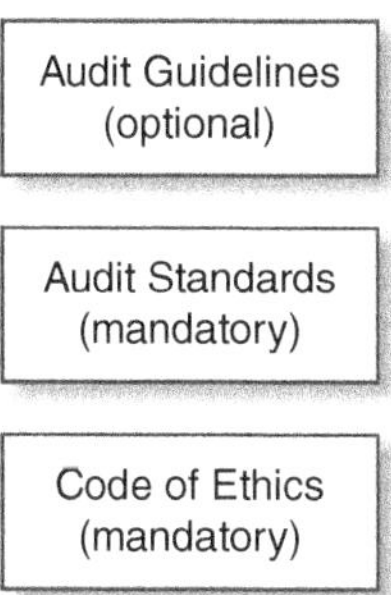

Source: Author.

Monitoring Privacy Responsibilities

The practice of monitoring privacy responsibilities helps an organization confirm that personal information is properly collected, used, protected, and discarded when no longer needed, and that subject requests are handled in a timely and proper manner. There is no single approach, but several activities provide information to management, including the following:

- **Controls and internal audit** Developing one or more controls around specific responsibilities increases management's ability to direct key activities. An internal audit of privacy and security controls provides an objective analysis of the controls' effectiveness.
- **Metrics and reporting** Developing metrics for routine activities helps management better understand work output and quality.
- **Work measurement** This structured activity is used to carefully measure routine tasks and help management better understand the volume of work performed.
- **Performance evaluation** This traditional qualitative method is used by management to evaluate employee performance.
- **360 feedback** Soliciting structured feedback from peers, subordinates, and management helps subjects and management better understand characteristics related to specific responsibilities.
- **Position benchmarking** This technique is used by organizations that want to compare job titles and the people holding them with equivalent roles in other organizations. Benchmarking does not involve direct monitoring of responsibilities. Still, it helps an organization determine whether the appropriate positions are in place and ensure that they are staffed by competent and qualified personnel. This can be useful for organizations that are troubleshooting employee performance.

Summary

This chapter examined the compliance dimension of a privacy program, emphasizing frameworks, evidence, metrics, and auditing as foundational components for demonstrating accountability and effectiveness.

Privacy frameworks provide structure for privacy programs and help organizations align with legal, regulatory, and operational expectations. Widely used frameworks such as ISO/IEC 27701, the NIST Privacy Framework, and OECD Privacy Principles establish governance models, control objectives, and program management approaches. Security-oriented frameworks such as ISO/IEC 27001 and the NIST Cybersecurity Framework also support privacy programs by strengthening information protection capabilities. Organizations typically adapt one or more frameworks to fit their business model, risk tolerance, and regulatory environment.

Evidence and artifacts are essential for demonstrating that privacy controls and processes exist and operate effectively. These materials include policies, data inventories, PIAs, DSR records, consent documentation, incident reports, governance meeting minutes, and system logs. Auditors and management rely on these artifacts to evaluate compliance, assess control effectiveness, and validate that privacy responsibilities are being fulfilled. Maintaining accurate and current documentation is critical for transparency and accountability.

Program monitoring and metrics provide visibility into privacy program performance. Metrics should be tailored to specific audiences and should follow SMART principles. Operational metrics measure technical and process activities, while executive-level metrics communicate business impact and program effectiveness. Trend analysis over time helps management determine whether privacy practices are improving or deteriorating.

Several categories of metrics support privacy governance. Risk management metrics focus on reductions in incidents, vulnerabilities, and unmitigated risks. Performance metrics measure operational timeliness and efficiency, such as incident response times and data subject request turnaround times. Convergence metrics help identify overlaps or gaps in responsibilities and tool coverage. Resource management metrics evaluate efficiency and the effective use of organizational resources.

Key indicators provide structured measurement approaches. Key performance indicators (KPIs) measure operational effectiveness. Key risk indicators (KRIs) provide insight into emerging risk levels. Key goal indicators (KGIs) measure progress toward strategic objectives. Key control indicators (KCIs) evaluate the effectiveness of selected controls. Together, these indicators provide layered visibility into privacy program performance.

Auditing is a formal mechanism for evaluating privacy controls and compliance. Privacy audits can be operational, information systems, integrated, administrative, compliance, forensic, or service-provider focused. Audit planning includes defining scope, objectives, procedures, and communication plans. Auditors gather evidence through documentation review, walkthroughs, observation, and sampling. The audit report communicates findings, recommendations, and opportunities for improvement.

Monitoring privacy responsibilities involves ongoing oversight of data handling, controls, and operational activities. Techniques such as internal audits, metrics reporting, performance evaluation, and benchmarking help organizations confirm that privacy responsibilities are being fulfilled. Together, frameworks, documentation, metrics, and audits form a comprehensive compliance capability that enables organizations to demonstrate accountability and to continuously improve the effectiveness of their privacy programs.

Exam Essentials

Understand the purpose of privacy frameworks. Privacy frameworks provide structure for privacy governance, controls, and operational processes. Organizations typically adapt one or more frameworks to align with regulatory requirements, business objectives, and risk tolerance rather than creating a program and controls from scratch.

Recognize the role of evidence and artifacts. Evidence and artifacts demonstrate that privacy controls and processes exist and operate effectively. Examples include policies, data inventories, PIAs, consent records, DSR logs, incident reports, and governance meeting documentation used during audits and compliance assessments.

Understand the characteristics of effective metrics. Privacy metrics should follow SMART principles: specific, measurable, attainable, relevant, and timely. Metrics should also be tailored to the intended audience and evaluated over time to identify meaningful trends in program performance.

Differentiate between KPIs, KRIs, KGIs, and KCIs. KPIs measure operational performance, KRIs indicate risk exposure, KGIs measure progress toward strategic objectives, and KCIs evaluate the effectiveness of controls. Together, these indicators provide layered visibility into the effectiveness of privacy programs.

Understand categories of privacy program metrics. Common metric categories include risk management, performance, convergence, and resource management. Each category provides insight into different aspects of privacy governance and operational effectiveness.

Recognize the purpose and types of privacy audits. Privacy audits evaluate controls, processes, and compliance with policies or regulations. Types include operational, information systems, integrated, administrative, compliance, forensic, and service provider audits.

Understand the role of monitoring privacy responsibilities. Ongoing monitoring activities, such as metrics reporting, internal audits, performance evaluation, and benchmarking, help organizations confirm that personal information is properly collected, used, protected, and disposed of in accordance with policy and regulations.

Review Questions

1. A privacy leader adopts a recognized privacy framework instead of creating a new one internally. What is the primary benefit of this decision?
   - **A.** Eliminates need for privacy metrics
   - **B.** Provides structured governance aligned with accepted practices
   - **C.** Guarantees regulatory compliance
   - **D.** Reduces documentation requirements
2. Which of the following would most likely be considered audit evidence in a privacy program?
   - **A.** Data subject request processing logs
   - **B.** IT hardware inventory
   - **C.** Software procurement budget
   - **D.** Marketing analytics dashboard
3. Which metric is the best example of a key risk indicator (KRI)?
   - **A.** Percentage of employees completing privacy training
   - **B.** Mean time to detect privacy incidents
   - **C.** Number of privacy policies approved
   - **D.** Number of privacy audits completed
4. What is the primary purpose of maintaining privacy artifacts such as PIAs and consent records?
   - **A.** Reduce operational overhead
   - **B.** Replace risk assessments
   - **C.** Eliminate the need for audits
   - **D.** Demonstrate control effectiveness and compliance
5. Which statement best describes a KCI?
   - **A.** Measures strategic business outcomes
   - **B.** Measures operational efficiency
   - **C.** Measures effectiveness of controls
   - **D.** Measures regulatory changes

6. Executive leadership requests metrics that demonstrate progress toward privacy-related strategic goals. Which metric type should be used?
   A. KPI
   B. KRI
   C. KCI
   D. KGI
7. Which of the following is most appropriate for a key performance indicator (KPI)?
   A. Percentage of systems using encryption controls
   B. Time required to respond to data subject requests
   C. Reduction in regulatory fines
   D. Number of new privacy regulations
8. Which item best represents privacy program evidence?
   A. Data inventory documentation
   B. Employee productivity reports
   C. Office space utilization data
   D. Hardware depreciation schedules
9. Why should privacy metrics be tailored to specific audiences?
   A. To reduce reporting frequency
   B. To ensure technical metrics are hidden
   C. To ensure relevance to stakeholder decision-making
   D. To simplify metric calculations
10. Which of the following is an example of a key goal indicator (KGI)?
    A. Reduction in privacy-related customer complaints
    B. Number of PIAs completed
    C. Time to detect privacy incidents
    D. Percentage of systems reviewed quarterly
11. What is the primary purpose of trend analysis in privacy metrics?
    A. Track regulatory changes
    B. Compare frameworks
    C. Determine improvement or decline over time
    D. Replace audits

12. Which document would most likely support compliance during a privacy audit?
    A. Product roadmap
    B. Marketing segmentation plan
    C. IT equipment warranty
    D. Privacy incident response report
13. Which metric category focuses on operational efficiency and timeliness?
    A. KGI
    B. KCI
    C. KPI
    D. KRI
14. An organization tracks the percentage of vendors meeting privacy requirements. This is best classified as which of the following?
    A. KPI
    B. KRI
    C. KCI
    D. KGI
15. Which of the following best demonstrates layered metrics?
    A. Reporting the same metrics to all stakeholders
    B. Eliminating operational metrics
    C. Using only KRIs
    D. Providing operational metrics to technical staff and strategic metrics to executives
16. Which artifact would best support evidence of data minimization controls?
    A. HR organizational chart
    B. Data collection form reviews
    C. Employee training attendance logs
    D. Procurement contracts
17. Why are SMART criteria important for privacy metrics?
    A. They reduce audit scope
    B. They ensure metrics are actionable and meaningful
    C. They eliminate risk
    D. They standardize frameworks

18. Which indicator measures operational performance?
    A. KPI
    B. KRI
    C. KGI
    D. KCI
19. An organization reports: increased privacy incidents, improved detection capabilities, reduced impact severity, and faster remediation. What is the most appropriate interpretation?
    A. Privacy controls are failing
    B. Risk exposure is increasing significantly
    C. Program maturity is improving despite higher incident counts
    D. Compliance requirements are not being met
20. Which combination best demonstrates comprehensive privacy program measurement?
    A. KPIs only
    B. KRIs and KPIs only
    C. KGIs only
    D. KPIs, KRIs, KGIs, and KCIs used together

Answers to Review Questions

1. B. Established privacy frameworks provide structured governance models, terminology, and control guidance that align with recognized industry practices. This helps organizations design consistent privacy programs and demonstrate alignment with regulatory expectations. Frameworks do not eliminate metrics, documentation, or compliance activities, but they provide a foundation that improves program maturity and defensibility.
2. A. Data subject request logs document how the organization receives, authenticates, and responds to requests. These records demonstrate compliance with regulatory timelines and operational procedures, making them valuable audit evidence. While other items might be useful for broader governance, they do not directly demonstrate the operation of privacy control.
3. B. KRIs serve as leading indicators that signal changes in risk exposure. Mean time to detect privacy incidents reflects how long personal data might remain exposed during an event. Longer detection times increase risk, making this metric useful for predicting potential negative outcomes.

4. D. Privacy artifacts provide objective evidence that controls and processes exist and are operating. Auditors and management rely on documentation and records, such as PIAs, consent records, and incident reports, to confirm compliance and evaluate the effectiveness of privacy governance activities.

5. C. Key control indicators (KCIs) evaluate whether specific controls are functioning properly. For example, measuring the percentage of systems enforcing data minimization directly assesses control effectiveness. KCIs focus on operational control performance rather than strategy or risk prediction.

6. D. Key goal indicators (KGIs) measure achievement of strategic objectives. Examples include reductions in privacy complaints or improved customer trust metrics. These indicators are designed for executive audiences and demonstrate whether the privacy program supports organizational goals.

7. B. KPIs measure operational performance and efficiency. Response time for data subject requests reflects how effectively the organization performs a routine privacy process. Strategic outcomes and risk measures fall under other indicator categories.

8. A. A data inventory demonstrates knowledge of the locations and flows of personal information. It supports compliance with accountability requirements and provides auditors with insight into data management practices.

9. C. Different stakeholders require different information. Executives need strategic indicators, while operational teams need process-level metrics. Tailoring metrics ensures that recipients receive actionable information relevant to their responsibilities.

10. A. KGIs measure achievement of strategic outcomes. Reducing customer complaints reflects improved trust and program effectiveness, aligning with organizational objectives.

11. C. Trend analysis shows whether controls, processes, and risks are improving or deteriorating. A single data point provides limited insight, while trends enable management to make informed decisions.

12. D. Incident response reports document detection, containment, and resolution of privacy events. These demonstrate operational capability and regulatory compliance, making them valuable audit evidence.

13. C. Key performance indicators (KPIs) measure process performance, such as response times or training completion rates. These indicators focus on operational efficiency rather than strategic outcomes or risk levels.

14. B. Vendor compliance rates indicate risk exposure related to third parties. If fewer vendors meet requirements, risk increases, making this a key risk indicator (KRI).

15. D. Layered metrics translate operational data into business-relevant indicators for different audiences. This improves decision-making and ensures stakeholders receive meaningful information.

16. B. Reviews of data collection forms demonstrate whether only necessary personal data is collected. These directly support data minimization principles and control effectiveness.

17. B. SMART metrics are specific, measurable, attainable, relevant, and timely. These characteristics ensure metrics can guide decisions and accurately reflect performance.

18. A. Key performance indicators (KPIs) measure how well processes perform. They typically track timeliness, quality, and efficiency of privacy-related activities.

19. C. Improved detection often increases reported incident counts. Simultaneous reductions in severity and remediation time indicate better controls and maturity. The increased volume reflects improved visibility, not necessarily increased risk.

20. D. Using all four indicator types provides layered insight. KPIs measure operations, KRIs measure risk exposure, KCIs measure control effectiveness, and KGIs measure strategic outcomes. Together, they provide complete program visibility.

Data Collection and Processing

This chapter covers CDPSE Domain 3, "Data Life Cycle Management," specifically the "Data Collection and Processing" subdomain.

This chapter covers these job practice elements:

✔ A—DATA COLLECTION AND PROCESSING

1. *Data Inventory, Data flow Diagram, and Classification*
2. *Data Quality (e.g., Accuracy)*
3. *Data Use Limitation*
4. *Data Analytics (e.g., Aggregation, AI, Data Warehouse)*

The other subdomain in Domain 3, Data Life Cycle Management, is:

✔ B—DATA PERSISTENCE AND DESTRUCTION—covered in Chapter 6.

The CDPSE Task Statements relevant to this domain are:

3. *Advise on data life cycle policies and practices to ensure privacy considerations for data governance.*
4. *Design and evaluate the implementation of technical and operational controls for data classifications and data life cycle requirements.*
15. *Advise on data classification for personal information to enable risk assessment and implementation of controls.*
19. *Promote accountability, fairness, and transparency throughout the data life cycle.*

The topics in this chapter and in Chapter 6 account for 23% of the CDPSE examination.

Privacy programs require an effective data governance program to provide management visibility and control of personal information. Data governance is discussed in this chapter, including data collection, data inventory, data classification and handling, supplemented by data loss prevention (DLP) tools and techniques, measures to ensure data quality and accuracy, and measures to ensure data use limitation. The chapter concludes with a discussion on data analytics techniques and benefits.

Data Governance

Put simply, *data governance* is management's visibility and control over the use of information in an organization. By defining strict, tangible consequences for failing to protect and use personal information transparently, privacy laws have spurred policies and practices that shine a light on data collection, use, and protection. Organizations are now accountable for confronting data sprawl and indiscriminate use of personal information.

A typical data governance structure contains the following:

- High-level policy and related standards defining data management practices
- A defined data lifecycle
- Defined roles and responsibilities for data management
- Key controls
- Assessments of key controls to ensure they are effective
- Reporting to management, describing incidents, activities, and assessments

A key prerequisite to effective data governance is organizational change management—that is, management must have visibility into and control over changes made to business processes. Organizations lacking organizational change management will find that processes change—including new or altered uses of personal information that might be contrary to policy—without management's awareness.

Policies and Standards

In the context of data governance, *policies* and *standards* define required behavior for personnel involved in data architecture, data management, and data usage. Data governance policies and standards will address topics including these:

- Approvals required for the acquisition of new data sources
- Approvals required for new or changed uses of existing data sources
- Safeguards to protect data from unauthorized access and use

Policies and standards will also define roles and responsibilities and imply the development of controls.

Roles and Responsibilities

A data governance *program charter* or policy should define roles and responsibilities for data management, including those listed in Table 5.1.

Readers versed in information security will recognize these roles and responsibilities as similar to those in a comprehensive information security program.

Control Objectives and Controls

Following the development of policies, standards, roles, and responsibilities, control objectives and controls can be developed. Control objectives and individual controls specify key desired outcomes to ensure that data governance policies will be carried out.

TABLE 5.1 Data Governance Roles and Responsibilities

Role	Activity
Data protection officer (DPO)	▪ Data classification policy ▪ Data governance program ▪ Investigations into misuse and unauthorized access to data
Data owner	▪ Approval for access to data ▪ Approval for uses of data ▪ Reviews of access rights to data
Data custodian	▪ Storage and protection of personal information
Data steward	▪ Data quality
Control owner	▪ Ownership and operation of individual controls
Other personnel	▪ Comply with data classification policy and all other policy

The functional areas where controls will be developed include:

- Approvals for the acquisition of new data sources
- Approvals for new uses of data
- Monitoring of data usage
- Approvals for requests to access data
- Reviews of access to data

Organizations will develop processes and procedures that include these controls.

Data Lifecycle

Data in an organization follows a lifecycle that starts with the creation, collection, or acquisition of data, then moves through processing, storage, and finally disposal. The phases of the data lifecycle are shown in Figure 5.1.

This chapter explores data collection, inventory, and processing, while Chapter 6 discusses retention and disposal.

Assessments

The effectiveness of policies and controls cannot be fully known unless they are assessed or audited. The criticality of controls and the applicability of specific regulations will determine the approach and rigor needed to assess controls, whether they are reviewed, assessed, or audited.

Before the enactment of privacy laws, many organizations paid little attention to the risks associated with the protection and use of personal information. Overall and focused risk assessments concerning the use of personal information are warranted, however.

FIGURE 5.1 The data lifecycle.

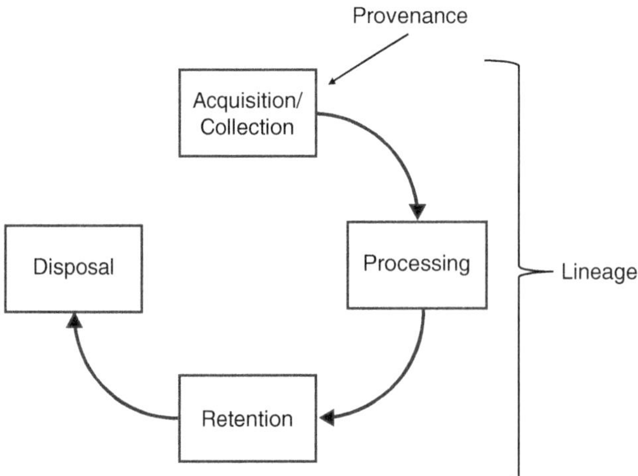

Source: Author.

Assessing controls alone addresses their effectiveness but might overlook aspects of privacy and security where no controls exist. Control assessments and risk assessments should be included in the organization's overall risk management lifecycle, as discussed in Chapter 3.

Reporting

Governance is incomplete if management is unaware of routine business activities and incidents within a program. Management needs to be periodically informed of the number of incidents, how effective they have been at circumventing controls, and the effectiveness of incident response, corrective actions, and improvements.

Data Collection

Data collection, sometimes known as data acquisition, represents any activity in which data is introduced into an organization's environment. In the context of privacy, *data collection* is the gathering of personal information from individuals or systems, for some defined purpose. Methods of data collection include:

- **User input** A user enters information about themselves into a computer or in written form.
- **User directed** A user directs that information about themselves be acquired by some means.
- **Acquired from an external source** An organization acquires or purchases data about one or more data subjects, with or without their knowledge or consent.

GDPR and other regulations have moved the entire online industry to the point where virtually every website that collects personal data displays a link to a privacy policy, requiring the data subject to agree to the site's privacy policy and possibly other terms and conditions. Figure 5.2 depicts such a website.

When receiving information from any outside source, input validation should be performed as early as possible. *Input validation* is the process of examining data in each input field to ensure that all data received has the correct data types and values within reasonable ranges

Enriching Customer Data

A retail organization with a customer loyalty program wants to learn more about its customers. Rather than solicit additional details about its customers, the organization purchases data from a data broker to add more data fields to its customer records. In this case, the retailer knows its customers' mailing addresses, but knows little about their income or interests. The retailer purchases these additional items from data brokers through *data aggregation*.

FIGURE 5.2 User prompted to read and understand a privacy notice.

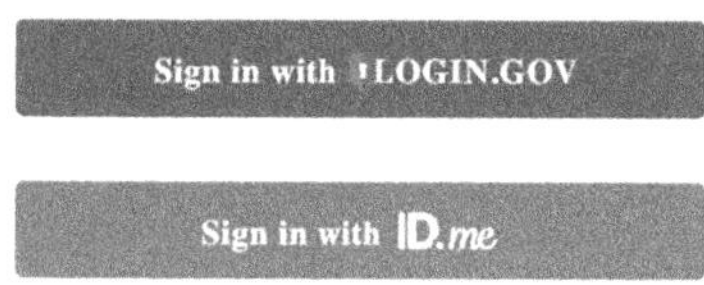

Source: U.S. Government.

Data Inventory

A nearly worn-out but still highly relevant cliché in data security is this: *you cannot protect what you don't know you have*. This statement underscores the need for effective asset management at all levels, because only specifically identified data can be managed and protected.

For a privacy program to be effective, organizations must have a complete and accurate inventory of all personal information. Although an inventory of structured information (data residing in application database management systems) will remain fairly static, the transient nature of unstructured data creates additional challenges. Somehow, organizations must identify ways to know about all structured and unstructured data, particularly when it contains personal information that is within the scope of relevant privacy laws. Proactive *data discovery* can be implemented to provide visibility into the existence, creation, and use of unstructured data.

In my experience, few IT departments track their data until regulation forces them to. They then employ data discovery tools to identify datasets they should have been tracking all along.

For an organization's data inventory to remain current, three activities need to become a part of business-as-usual processes:

- Change management processes must call out an update to the data inventory whenever an addition or change to an information system affects it.
- Business processes that interact with personal information must be documented.
- Periodic reviews of the data inventory should be performed to confirm its accuracy.

Periodic data inventory reviews should not only catalog existing instances of sensitive and personal information, but also determine, for each instance, whether the data *should* exist where it is found. By understanding the business processes that handle personal information, we can better identify where it is collected, processed, and stored. Thus, a data inventory should be thought of less as a census and more as a gap analysis. Every instance of sensitive information should be examined through the lens of the business processes and data management policy to determine whether each instance should exist and whether current protective controls are adequate.

Organizations with lower process maturity are more likely to use unstructured methods to perform procedures and complete tasks. Often, this will result in greater use of email for process workflows and of unstructured data stores for data storage. Email, file servers, and cloud storage services represent the majority of unstructured data in many organizations.

When inventorying data, you should include the following information in each catalog entry:

- Unique identifier
- Name of the file(s) or directory/directories
- Physical location, critical for identifying *data sovereignty* issues
- Description of the contents, including personally identifiable information (PII) data fields
- Provenance
- Purpose
- Date of last update (this will aid in the removal of old data)
- Access permissions
- Data owner/custodian
- Retention period

This information will be useful for developing data flow diagrams, which are discussed in the next section.

Automation in larger organizations will ease the burden of manual, time-consuming processes for identifying datasets and keeping data inventories up to date.

Data Lineage and Provenance

When building information systems that process personal information, organizations need to understand where data comes from, how it moves, and how it changes. The concepts of data lineage and data provenance form the backbone of this understanding. Although most organizations do not follow these practices, documenting lineage and provenance is crucial for accountability and regulatory compliance.

Figure 5.3 depicts data provenance and data lineage.

Lineage and provenance tracking might feel like behind-the-scenes work (and so they are), but they are essential to building systems that comply with privacy laws. Organizations that neglect this domain expose themselves to failure, while those who prioritize it create systems worthy of trust, creating a competitive advantage in the private sector.

While important for information systems that process personal information, data provenance and data lineage are critical for AI systems. Organizations that cannot trace their AI systems' training data back to its sources will struggle to understand their AI systems' predictions and outputs.

Defining Data Lineage and Data Provenance

It is essential to clearly distinguish data lineage and data provenance, as they are often used interchangeably but refer to distinct (though related) concepts.

Data lineage refers to the lifecycle of data *within* a system. *Data lineage* documents how data flows through pipelines, from ingestion, storage, transformation, consumption, maintenance, and disposal. Lineage tracks the "how and where" of data, including:

FIGURE 5.3 Data provenance and data lineage.

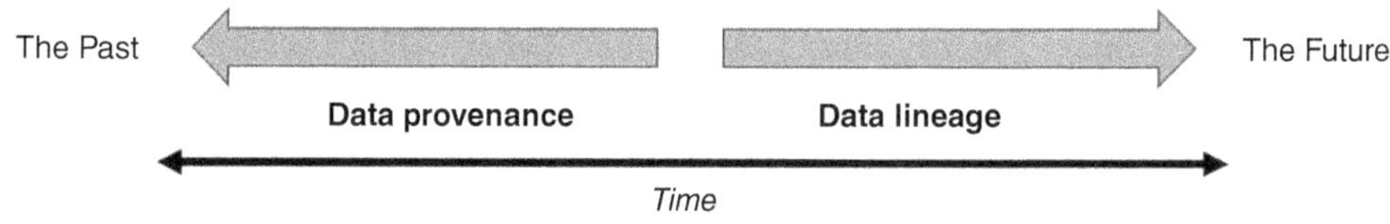

Source: Author.

- How it was generated (or from where it was obtained—this is where data lineage and data provenance meet)
- Where it was stored
- What processes transformed it
- Which models or systems consumed it
- What processes carried out modifications, corrections, and removals
- What processes carried out data retention operations
- How and when the data was disposed of when no longer needed

Data provenance refers to the origin and original characteristics of a dataset, including:

- From where the data was obtained
- Who created or collected the data
- Under what conditions was it collected
- What was its intended purpose

For example, an organization's customer behavior dataset used in an AI recommendation engine might have a clear lineage within the company's data lake. Still, its provenance might be unknown if it was initially acquired from a third party with insufficient documentation. Lineage ≠ provenance.

When viewed together, data lineage and provenance support a complete picture of data trustworthiness. They help organizations identify the source(s) of errors and demonstrate compliance with applicable regulations and other legal obligations.

Data Lineage for Datasets Used in Multiple Systems

Over time, organizations are apt to use a dataset, including those containing personal information, in multiple information systems. In some cases, an organization might make a copy of a dataset for use in a new system in what's called a *data migration*. But how does the organization handle data lineage records?

Organizations that duplicate data across multiple systems should create separate data lineage records for each system to document transformations and other operations. This helps the organization understand each separate dataset's history.

Capturing Data Provenance

Effective provenance tracking begins with *metadata* collection and documentation. Such metadata should include:

- Source entity (owner, organization, system)
- Collection method and date

- Version information
- Data licensing (terms of use)
- Access rights
- Intended use or original context
- Lineage
- Jurisdictional considerations (where collected, applicable regulations)
- Context (intended use, assumptions, limitations)

Metadata should be a required element of a system's overall documentation package. AI governance and data governance can enforce this through policy.

Data obtained from third parties, including vendors, brokers, partners, or public repositories, can include additional risks. Data governance policies should require the organization to obtain data provenance declarations from data sources, proof of lawful collection and consent, and documentation of any modifications or aggregations performed by the source.

For example, a system developer in an organization acquires data about potential customers for use in future marketing campaigns. After deployment, the organization learns that the dataset contained personal information obtained without consent. As a result, the organization now faces legal exposure and potential damage to its brand.

Standards, including *W3C PROV* or *ISO/IEC 5181 (Information security, cybersecurity and privacy protection—Data provenance)*, define formal models for provenance tracking. Adoption is limited, and ISO/IEC 5181 is still in development. Still, these standards can provide direction for organizations that want to adopt a standard approach for collecting and documenting data provenance.

Tracking Data Lineage

While provenance looks backward to origin, lineage tracks the path forward in time. Lineage records should include:

- Data source and format
- Storage location
- Version history
- Transformation scripts or *extract, transform, load (ETL)* processes
- Data pipeline paths
- Systems and models using datasets
- Data retention and disposal processes

Backward lineage, sometimes confused with data provenance, traces each data point back to its origin. *Forward lineage* tracks how data elements flow through systems to influence downstream processes.

Modern data observability platforms, such as Monte Carlo, Collibra, or OpenLineage, offer visualization tools to represent lineage graphically. These tools are especially valuable when multiple teams interact with shared datasets.

Several privacy laws implicitly or explicitly require organizations to maintain a *record of processing activities (ROPA)* for datasets containing personal information. The GDPR and the UK GDPR explicitly require an ROPA. However, other privacy laws, such as CCPA/CPRA and Brazil's data protection law, strongly imply the need. While data lineage describes technical activities (e.g., CRM > ETL > data lake > reporting dashboard), an ROPA describes business activities (e.g., purpose, legal basis, data subjects, and so forth).

Common Failure Modes

Many organizations fail to implement effective lineage and provenance tracking due to structural and cultural barriers. Organizations either decide that lineage is unimportant or are unaware of the practice altogether. Some of the failure nodes include:

- **Data and organizational silos** Data silos and organizational silos inhibit effective lineage and provenance. When datasets are transferred between departments without clear ownership or established standards, lineage and provenance can both become unclear. Governance frameworks should require consistent documentation across silos.
- **Informal data use** When IT developers implement IT systems and manipulate datasets outside sanctioned pipelines, this creates potential blind spots. Without governance, these ad hoc projects can feed unreliable data into unapproved systems, leading to inaccurate results.
- **Manual and fragmented processes** If documentation is manual or scattered across multiple tools, tasks, and procedures, it is often overlooked. Automation can help provide consistent lineage and provenance capture.

As an example, a large retailer manually documents transformations in spreadsheets. An intern renames a feature column and forgets to update the spreadsheet. Months later, the error causes errors in inventory reports during the holiday season.

Building a Provenance and Lineage Framework

Traceability doesn't occur in a vacuum; organizations need to be intentional about provenance and lineage by establishing policies, tools, and processes to operationalize it.

Establishing provenance and lineage begins with policy, which should define:

- Mandatory metadata fields for new datasets
- When and how provenance must be verified and approved
- Ownership responsibilities for provenance and lineage documentation
- Requirements for automated capture and audit trails
- Required granularity of tracking (e.g., dataset-level, record-level, or feature-level lineage)

In the tech stack, a provenance and lineage framework can include:

- Metadata repositories (e.g., data catalogs)
- Data lineage visualizers
- ETL tools with integrated tracking and logging
- Version control systems for datasets and transformation scripts
- Security controls (e.g., encryption and access management) to protect lineage and provenance records themselves

Provenance and lineage data can be integrated with MLOps tools, such as MLflow, DVC (Data Version Control), or Amazon SageMaker, enabling traceability from raw data through training to deployment.

System documentation must include references to lineage and provenance data, thereby increasing transparency for stakeholders and regulators, and linking applications and AI models to their corresponding datasets.

Use Cases

Traceability practices can vary by industry, but the principles of traceability are broadly applicable. Some examples include:

- **Financial services** Regulators might require a clear lineage for all data used in credit scoring, fraud detection, and algorithmic trading. Documentation should indicate how decisions are made and what data influenced them.
- **Healthcare** HIPAA compliance and patient data safety concerns require that all health-related systems can trace data back to validated sources. The provenance of clinical trial or electronic health record data is often scrutinized.
- **Public sector** Transparency is critical in government projects. The auditability of data sources ensures democratic accountability, particularly in criminal justice or welfare automation.

Benefits of Strong Traceability

Organizations that invest in lineage and provenance capabilities reap benefits across technical, legal, and business domains, including:

- Reduced debugging time and faster issue resolution for issues related to input data
- Greater confidence in system outputs for stakeholders
- Improved audit response and regulatory posture
- Higher data quality results in fewer data-related issues and more rapid issue resolution

Traceability Challenges and Trade-offs

Building a comprehensive provenance and lineage program presents technical and organizational hurdles. The trade-off comes down to the overhead of additional processes and tooling that provide vital data, or foregoing traceability to improve agility.

Automated lineage tracking can add latency to data pipelines and increase storage requirements. Governance teams must work with engineering to find the right balance between traceability and performance.

Organizations using third-party or open-source models might not be able to obtain full provenance or lineage data, as such data might be considered *intellectual property*. Organizations should evaluate traceability when selecting external tools to ensure optimal performance and reliability.

Organizations need to determine the level of investment required to build infrastructure for metadata management, auditing, and visualization. As with other initiatives, traceability itself might warrant developing a business case. Like similar initiatives, many organizations will under-resource these functions until forced to do so by an incident or investigation.

Data Flow and Usage Diagrams

The efforts undertaken to build and maintain data inventories do not end when it is known where all data comes from, where it is stored, who the owners are, and what access permissions are granted. An essential aspect of data inventory is the knowledge of two additional data characteristics: data flow and data usage.

Understanding data flow requires a deeper study of information systems where data resides, to understand how data arrives in the system and where data is sent from the system. Interviews with business users regarding the business process, as well as with IT personnel at the application layer and in the system and network layers, are needed to build a complete picture. The term *picture* is used deliberately: it's often useful to build a visual schematic of data flows, which can help privacy and security professionals, as well as business leaders, better understand the use of personal information within an organization. A *data flow diagram (DFD)*, like the one shown in Figure 5.4, is a visual depiction of the flow of information between systems.

In this effort, privacy professionals need to understand that data flow implies usage, and data usage implies flow. One is often perceived with the other.

Privacy professionals mapping data flow and usage will discover both sanctioned and unsanctioned uses of data.

FIGURE 5.4 A simple, high-level DFD depicting the general data flow among IT applications.

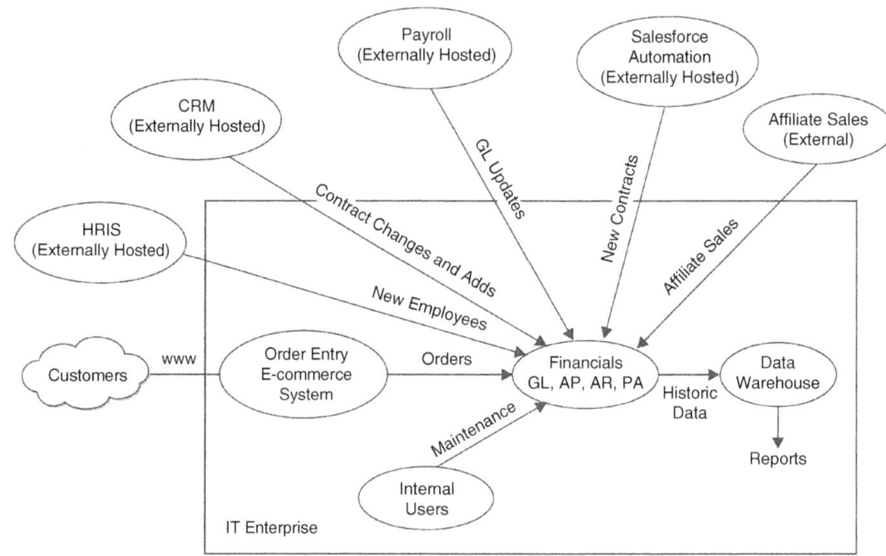

Source: Author.

Discovering Data Flow and Usage

Before the passage of privacy laws, including GDPR, the California Consumer Privacy Act (CCPA), and the California Privacy Rights Act (CPRA), many organizations had no idea of the extent of their data's existence and movement. In many organizations, a common first step toward compliance was developing a data inventory, creating data flow diagrams, and identifying data usage. Amazing as it sounds, in many organizations, nobody was responsible for knowing these things.

The next step in most organizations is developing data governance, providing management with visibility and control over the storage and use of personal information. It's as though there were no real rules for the management of personal information before GDPR and other privacy regulations.

Data Classification

Many types of information reside in an organization's information systems. Some of this information is highly sensitive because it contains personal information, intellectual property, and internal financial information; some is important but not sensitive; and some is not very important. Because limited resources are required to protect information, it doesn't make much sense to apply the same rigor to protecting unimportant data as to protecting highly secretive or sensitive information. To this point, former U.S. National Security Advisor McGeorge Bundy is attributed with saying, "If we guard our toothbrushes and diamonds with equal zeal, we will lose fewer toothbrushes and more diamonds." Organizations employ *data classification* to distinguish highly sensitive information from less sensitive information.

Data Classification Levels

A *data classification policy* is a formal, intentional way for an organization to define levels of importance or sensitivity for information. The criteria used to classify data include:

- **Monetary value** Some information might be easily monetized by intruders who steal it, such as credit card numbers, bank account numbers, gift certificates or cards, and discount or promotion codes. Loss of this type of information might cause direct financial losses.
- **Operational criticality** This information must always be available, or it might relate to factors of business resilience. Examples include virtual server images, incident response procedures, and business continuity procedures. Corruption or loss of this type of information can significantly impact ongoing business operations.
- **Accuracy or integrity** Information in this category must be highly accurate. If altered, the organization could suffer significant financial or reputational harm. Examples include exchange rate tables, product or service inventory data, machine calibration data, and price lists. Corruption or loss of this type of information impacts business operations by causing incomplete or erroneous transactions.
- **Regulation** Information in the scope of regulations and other legal obligations might have protection or usage requirements that organizations must comply with. Data classification policy must incorporate these and other external requirements.
- **Sensitivity** Information of a sensitive nature is commonly associated with individual citizens, including personal contact information, personal financial data such as credit card and bank account numbers, and medical records.
- **Reputational value** Another dimension of classification, denoting the potential loss of reputation should certain sensitive or critical information be lost or compromised. Information such as customers' personal information fits here.

A typical data classification policy will define two or more (but rarely more than five) data classification levels, such as the following:

- Secret
- Restricted
- Confidential
- Public

TABLE 5.2 Examples of Information at Varying Data Classification Levels

Classification Level	Examples of Information at this Level
Secret	Merger and acquisition proceedings, pre-announcement
Restricted	Customer PII Employee PII Program source code Unpublished financial records
Confidential	Internal email messages Marketing plans Policies
Public	Website content Released marketing brochures Social media postings Published financial reports

Along with defining classification levels, a data classification policy will include examples showing which levels should be assigned to various datasets. Table 5.2 provides an example of this concept.

Data classification policies need to be reasonably simple so that workers can easily understand the classification of data and handle it accordingly.

The data classification policy can go further still and explicitly state the classification levels assigned to specific datasets. This is shown in Table 5.3.

These levels of information, examples of the types of levels within each category, and instructions for handling information at each level form the heart of a typical information classification program.

The next step in information classification is the development of handling procedures that instruct users in the proper acquisition, storage, transmission, and destruction of information at every classification level. Table 5.4 shows a sample information-handling procedure matrix.

The classification and handling guidelines shown here illustrate the differences in information handling across classification levels. Table 5.4 can serve as a starting point for a data classification and handling procedure.

Organizations that develop and implement information classification programs find that personnel will often misclassify information, either because they do not understand the nature of the sensitivity of a particular set of data or because they know that at a higher level of classification, they might believe that they cannot store or transmit the information in a way they think is needed. This is a classic case of people taking shortcuts in the name of expediency, especially when they are unaware of the potential harm that might befall the organization.

TABLE 5.3 Examples of Official Data Classification Levels

Classification Level	Datasets at this Level
Secret	Merger and acquisition proceedings, pre-announcement Service account passwords
Restricted	Customer Relationship Management system database Human Capital Management system database Program source code repositories Unpublished Enterprise Resource Management system records Unpublished annual report, 10-K, 10-Q IT network diagrams IT data flow diagrams Contents of internal HR and legal investigations All legal contracts
Confidential	Internal email messages Internal memos Contents of an internal intranet site, including policy and benefit information Marketing plans
Public	www.company.com website content Released marketing brochures Official @Company social media postings on LinkedIn, Facebook, and X Public 10-K and 10-Q filings, when published Annual report, when published

TABLE 5.4 Example Information-handling Requirements

	Secret	Restricted	Confidential	Public
Example information types	Passwords, merger and acquisition plans and terms	Credit card numbers, bank account numbers, Social Security numbers, detailed financial records, detailed system configuration, vulnerability scan reports	System documentation, end-user documentation, internal memos, network diagrams	Brochures, press releases
Storage on server	Must be encrypted; store only on servers labeled sensitive	Must be encrypted	Access controls required	Access controls required for update

(Continued)

TABLE 5.4 (Continued)

	Secret	Restricted	Confidential	Public
Storage on mobile device	Must never be stored on a mobile device	Must be encrypted	Access controls required	No restrictions
Storage in the cloud	Must never be stored in the cloud	Must be encrypted	Access controls required	Access controls required for update
Email	Must never be emailed	Must be encrypted	Authorized recipients only	No restrictions
Website	Must never be stored on any web server	Must be encrypted	Access controls required	No restrictions
Fax	Encrypted; attended fax only	Attended fax only; no email–based fax	Attended fax only	No restrictions
Courier and shipment	Double wrapped; signature and secure storage required	Signature and secure storage required	Signature required	No restrictions
Hardcopy storage	Double locked in authorized locations only	Double locked	Locked	No restrictions
Hardcopy distribution	Only with owner permission; must be registered	To authorized parties only, only with owner permission	To authorized parties only	No restrictions
Hardcopy destruction	Cross-cut shred; make specific record of destruction	Cross-cut shred	Cross-cut shred or secure waste bin	No restrictions
Soft-copy destruction	Erase following NIST SP 800-22r2 guidelines and/or IEEE 2883-2022 certified tool	Erase following NIST SP 800-22r2 guidelines and/ or IEEE 2883-2022 certified tool	Delete and empty recycle bin	No restriction

The Ideal Number of Classification Levels

Would it be easier if we handled all information the same way, treating it as the organization's most sensitive information? While this would make it easier to remember how to handle and dispose of all information, it might also be onerous, particularly if all information is handled at the level warranted for the organization's most sensitive or critical information. Encrypting everything and shredding everything would be a wasteful use of resources.

That said, it is incumbent on an organization to build a simple information classification program that is easy to understand and follow. Too many levels of classification would be as burdensome as a single level. With too many classification levels, there is a greater chance that information will be misclassified and then put at risk when handled at too low a level. With too few levels, the organization will either have excessive resources protecting all information at a higher level or insufficient resources to protect information adequately.

Data-handling Standards

Because so much information is handled daily by personnel, the data classification policy goes further to define acceptable handling procedures for data at various levels of classification and in numerous situations. Often called *data-handling standards*, these procedures provide real-world guidance that workers can easily follow and apply. Because information can be used and moved in many ways, data-handling standards should clearly specify what is expected of personnel when handling sensitive data.

Data-handling standards usually take the form of a matrix, with various levels of classification as the columns and different data-handling situations as rows. Each cell defines the standard for handling data at a given classification level. Table 5.4 shows a part of such a matrix.

To help the workforce better understand handling standards, organizations should develop training content or tutorials that explain their meanings in detail and introduce appropriate procedures.

Exam Tip

CDPSE candidates need to understand the typical structure of roles and responsibilities for data protection. While a data protection officer, general counsel, or CISO is responsible for establishing the organization's data classification policy, it is usually the responsibility of a document owner to classify and mark a document correctly. It is then the responsibility of any party that uses a document to handle it in accordance with its classification level.

The Culture Shift

Privacy professionals in organizations introducing data classification, handling standards, training, and automation must understand that this undertaking can represent a significant cultural shift. It's potentially a tall order to expect a workforce that formerly took data handling for granted to become data aware and to understand and follow new policies and procedures. Such a change does not happen overnight. Even when executives lead by example, and an internal marketing plan is in place, many workers' responses will range from confusion to resistance to outright evasion. It is therefore important for the workforce to understand the purpose of data classification. Monitoring for compliance is essential.

Data Loss Prevention Automation

Along with defining classification levels, a data classification policy will outline procedures for handling information across these levels in various settings. For instance, a data-handling standard will specify the conditions at each level under which sensitive information might be emailed, faxed, stored, transmitted, or shipped. Note that some handling methods might be prohibited, such as emailing a secret document over the Internet.

Relying on an organization's workers to apply data-handling standards consistently is risky at best—not because of a lack of good intentions, but because workers will not have safe data handling on their minds all the time. This situation is not unlike workers who click on the occasional phishing message despite having attended effective security awareness training. People are not "on their guard" all of the time.

Data loss prevention (DLP) systems can greatly aid efforts to provide visibility and even control over the use of personal and other sensitive information. Approaches to implementing DLP capabilities fill the remainder of this section.

Static DLP

Static DLP tools scan static data stores to identify files containing data matching specific patterns. Most often, static DLP scanning is performed on file servers—both on-premises and cloud-based. DLP scanning can also be performed on database management systems, either using dedicated tools or by scanning flat-file exports of databases.

Organizations undertaking static DLP scanning for the first time might find an abundance of files containing PII and other sensitive data. Privacy managers need to keep in mind that such data might have accumulated over a long period and might also reflect current practices or former activities that are no longer performed.

A careful analysis of the results of an initial DLP scan should be undertaken to determine the following:

- The age of files containing PII found in file stores
- The extent to which files containing PII are still being deposited in file stores

- The access rights of files containing PII
- Which users actively access the files (available in some DLP static scanning tools)
- Whether current use follows sanctioned policies, procedures, or practices

Privacy managers should not be overly hasty in the quest to "solve" any or all the discovered instances of PII in static data stores. Some uses might be part of key business processes, with adequately restricted access controls. Often, privacy managers find that files containing PII in file stores result from one-time or ad hoc activities. For instance, a business analyst might be asked to perform research on customer demographics; the business analyst would run a query or report in the customer relationship management (CRM) system, export the report to a spreadsheet, and save it to a file server. After completing the task, the business analyst will keep the file there in case questions are asked about it later. Soon, the existence of the spreadsheet containing PII is forgotten, and it will reside there in perpetuity unless a purge, cleanup, or DLP scan discovers it.

Exam Tip

CDPSE candidates need to understand the detective nature of Static DLP tools. As they merely scan file stores to determine whether sensitive data is present, Static DLP is an indicator of behavior but does nothing on its own to alter it.

Data Tagging

Although the process is similar to static DLP analysis, organizations can employ *data tagging* on their datasets if they are found to contain PII or other sensitive information. Such tagging can take on several forms, including these:

- **Metadata tagging** The metadata of a data file can be updated to include a specially coded tag that will be recognized by DLP tooling.
- ***Watermarking*** Visible or invisible watermarks can be added to data files.
- ***Data marking*** According to the data file–marking policy, a human-readable word or phrase can be added to the header, footer, or another location in a data file (such as "XYZ Company restricted to internal use only").

Including human-readable watermarks or other markings on documents provides a visual reminder to workers using a data file about the sensitivity of the files they are working with. The main purpose of including machine-readable marks or tags in a data file is to facilitate appropriate action by dynamic DLP tools, discussed next.

Dynamic DLP

Dynamic data loss prevention (DLP) represents a variety of technologies used to detect and even intervene in the transfer of PII and other sensitive information. Dynamic DLP tools can take the form of network devices or software running on operating systems, with the ability to observe data in motion across many circumstances. These tools can be configured to identify the sensitivity of data files in motion by reading their contents to determine whether they contain PII or other sensitive information, or to look for previously applied tags.

Dynamic DLP Types

There are several common forms of dynamic DLP:

- **Email DLP** DLP tools can examine the contents of an outgoing email message to determine whether it contains specific sensitive information. Email-based DLP will consider whether the information is being sent to internal or external recipients.
- **USB storage control** Host-based DLP tools restrict USB usage to company-approved (and usually encrypted) USB drives only, or they block USB storage entirely.
- **Local file storage control** Host-based agents observe and optionally block actions that violate policy, such as local storage of highly classified documents.
- **File server storage control** Host- or server-based agents observe and optionally block actions violating policy, such as storage of highly classified documents on shares with broad access.
- **Cloud server storage controls** DLP capabilities in cloud storage services are configured to mimic local or file server DLP controls, monitoring and optionally blocking actions that violate policy.
- **Network DLP** Network devices, or DLP modules in next-generation firewalls, observe the content of data in motion.

Dynamic DLP Actions

Most of these forms of dynamic DLP, when operating in the context of an interactive user, can present the following to the user:

- Silently note the occurrence
- Block the action and inform the user
- Warn the user that the intended action is forbidden by policy and give the user the ability to permit the action anyway after providing a user-entered business justification to complete the action

Other tools can be used to assist in dynamic DLP efforts:

- **Firewalls** Blocking access to/from specific networks or systems
- **IDS/IPS** Blocking access to/from networks and systems thought to be hazardous
- ***Web content filter*** Blocking browser access to sites based on policy

- *Cloud access security broker (CASB)* Monitors and controls access to cloud-based service providers based on organization policy
- *NetFlow* A network protocol that collects metadata about traffic flows, which analytics tools can then analyze to detect and alert on anomalous activity

Exam Tip

CDPSE candidates need to understand the role of dynamic DLP as a detective control, a preventive control, or both.

Implementing Dynamic DLP

Dynamic DLP controls, in any of the forms discussed, can be highly valuable for preventing the mishandling of sensitive information. Unfortunately, dynamic DLP is also adept at interfering with legitimate business processes by blocking activities approved by management (including the privacy or security manager). Legitimate activities are blocked either because the DLP system is misconfigured or due to a *false positive*, where the DLP system misidentifies data. Examples of such false positives include strings of numerals that are mistaken for social insurance numbers, bank account numbers, phone numbers, or credit card numbers. Similarly, a *false negative* occurs when a DLP system fails to identify sensitive data.

Run in Learn Mode First

Despite what readers might be told by experienced users of DLP systems or DLP vendors themselves, readers are *highly* recommended to run any dynamic DLP system in "learn" mode first for an extended period. The best way to do this is to configure the DLP system to silently log occurrences that are considered file-handling policy violations. This enables privacy and security personnel to see whether the DLP system properly identifies the actual motion of private and other sensitive information.

Another highly useful benefit of running DLP in learn mode is similar to that of running static DLP scans: learning what data movement currently occurs in the organization to help personnel better understand existing business processes, as well as those occasional (hopefully not frequent) actions that represent actual policy violations.

When privacy and security personnel are confident in their dynamic DLP system's ability to correctly identify sensitive data movement without false positives, they can proceed to activate preventive actions to be performed by the DLP system. It is suggested that organizations proceed slowly as they build confidence in the system's proper operation.

Enlist Friendly Users

Privacy and security personnel should identify "friendly" departments or groups when first implementing the preventive features of a DLP system to increase confidence in the system and resolve any remaining configuration issues.

Develop Response and Exception Procedures

Before activating any rules in a dynamic DLP system that will block file-handling actions, privacy and security personnel—preferably in cooperation with the IT service desk—should develop a playbook of response procedures for when end users encounter DLP systems blocking their intended actions. Rather than be caught by surprise, IT service desk personnel (or others designated to work with end users) must have clear procedures in place for handling users who insist that the DLP system is blocking legitimate actions. Often, IT service desk personnel need to contact privacy or security personnel to investigate these matters and determine the best course of action. The response will often require that a privacy or security manager approve exceptions and direct the configuration of the DLP system to permit specific activities that are contrary to policy. Recordkeeping of all such exceptions is important, whether as a part of an existing change control, incident management, or policy exception, or as part of another process.

System and Site Classification

Once an organization has established its data classification policy and completed its data inventory, it can proceed to classify its systems and sites. These additional classification activities can help the organization improve its security and privacy controls and use its resources more effectively. This is discussed in detail in Chapter 8.

The principle of system classification is this: a system can be classified by the highest level of data it stores, processes, or transmits. An organization can develop a system classification scheme that directs the levels and types of controls and monitoring commensurate with the classification level. In other words, a system that stores or processes information at the highest classification level can be protected and monitored with more controls than a system at a lower classification level.

Done properly, system classification should involve more than just classifying the data that systems store, process, or transmit. Other system classification criteria should include operational criticality, which can be derived from the results of a business impact analysis (BIA) as part of an organization's business continuity program. Business continuity planning is discussed in detail in this author's book on the CISM (Certified Information Security Manager) certification.

Site classification is a further extension of the same concept. Organizations with multiple work locations can implement a site classification scheme based on the sensitivity of data stored or accessed there, as well as operational criticality. Sites with higher classification levels might be equipped with more advanced physical security controls and other security controls, whereas sites with lower classification levels would have fewer controls. For instance, a call center with workers who routinely access PII would be equipped with keycard access controls and extensive video surveillance. At the same time, a sales office would have fewer of these controls and features. Workplace safety is an important consideration in physical security controls, alongside operational criticality and information sensitivity. Workers' lives matter.

Data Quality and Accuracy

In the context of data privacy, *data quality* or data accuracy is a gauge of the care an organization places on the fidelity of its personal data stores. Since the reality of data use involves the transfer of personal information from organization to organization, maintaining the accuracy of PII is important.

Article 5(1)(d) of the EU General Data Protection Regulation (GDPR) reads, "Personal data shall be accurate and, where necessary, kept up to date; every reasonable step must be taken to ensure that personal data that are inaccurate, having regard to the purposes for which they are processed, are erased or rectified without delay ('accuracy')." What was once just a good idea is now required by law.

Data quality and accuracy are more than just the completeness and accuracy of data fields for data subjects; they also include whether records for specific data subjects should even reside in an organization's database at all. Data subjects' information sometimes ends up in an organization's database by accident, often due to a matching error. Here are some examples:

- **Matches by name** Some organization databases key off a subject's name only, resulting in snafus of every sort. In a real-life instance, this book's author and another person of the same name were in the Seattle job market at the same time, applying for some of the same jobs. Communications between companies and the two applicants were frequently crossed up.
- **Matches by characteristic** Some organizations use ancillary information to associate people. In a real-life instance decades ago, parking tickets in Reno, Nevada, were entered into a computer system; if there was no license plate on the offending vehicle, the word "none" was entered. Then a citizen ordered a vanity plate that read "NONE" and was soon arrested and charged with tens of thousands of dollars in unpaid parking tickets over many years (all predating the issuance of the vanity plate).
- **Data entry errors** These are certainly the most common reason that things get fouled up. With literally billions of people using email today, countless errors occur when email addresses are mis-keyed, resulting in messages being sent to the wrong people. This book's author regularly receives emails intended for a physician in the U.S. Northeast, as well as for the owner of a private jet aircraft maintenance company in Southeast Asia. This problem goes way beyond email addresses: mis-keying dates of birth and other personal characteristics results in communications and records being crossed up, as well as many intended actions not being carried out because some of the information is incomplete or incorrect.

Before the introduction of modern privacy laws such as the GDPR, many private-sector organizations had little reason to care about the accuracy of personal information unless it had a monetary impact on them. For instance, an automobile manufacturer's database of vehicle owners is likely to contain incorrect mailing addresses for customers who move without informing the manufacturer. The result is twofold: marketing materials sent by mail are no longer reaching the customer, and neither are safety recall notices that represent cost-per-vehicle repairs.

Data Use Limitation

Purpose limitation is a key tenet of the GDPR and other privacy laws, which is the concept of limiting the use of personal information. Following numerous abuses of PII by private organizations, privacy laws now restrict how organizations can use the personal information they collect.

Article 5(1)(b) of GDPR reads:

> Personal data shall be collected for specified, explicit and legitimate purposes and not further processed in a manner that is incompatible with those purposes; further processing for archiving purposes in the public interest, scientific or historical research purposes or statistical purposes shall, in accordance with Article 89(1), not be considered to be incompatible with the initial purposes ("purpose limitation").

Title 1.81.5 of the CCPA states:

> A business that collects a consumer's personal information shall, at or before the point of collection, inform consumers as to the categories of personal information to be collected and the purposes for which the categories of personal information shall be used. A business shall not collect additional categories of personal information or use personal information collected for additional purposes without providing the consumer with notice consistent with this section.

Data Use Governance

One could say that these and other privacy laws are "sunshine laws" governing organizations' use of personal information. They have sparked lively debate in organizations accustomed to doing "whatever they wished" with personal information they collected from customers and others.

Organizations need to include governance structures to provide visibility and control over data usage. Such a structure would include the following:

- Internal policies stating permitted use of personal information
- External privacy policy accessible by relevant parties that describes all such uses
- Establishment of controls to ensure these outcomes
- Monitoring of these controls to verify their effectiveness

- Corrective action to remedy all deviations
- Metrics that measure all the above

In the absence of effective data use governance, organizations are at risk of *function creep*, where datasets are used for purposes beyond those approved by management and consented to by data subjects.

External Privacy Policy

A privacy policy (sometimes known as the *notice of privacy practices (NOPP)* published for consumption by affected parties must include descriptions of all primary and secondary uses of parties' personal information. Because a privacy policy functions as a legal contract, the organization's legal counsel should review it to ensure it meets the requirements of applicable privacy laws.

> **Market Forces and Personal Choice**
>
> As modern privacy laws shape new norms for the collection and use of personal information, we might soon enter an era in which consumers make conscious choices regarding their perception of an organization's use of their personal information. Consumers will choose to patronize organizations whose privacy practices best meet their preferences and align with their risk appetite.

Data Analytics

Mainstream organizations have access to advanced data management and analytics capabilities that provide additional insights into their businesses. Indeed, monetization is a primary impetus for an organization to mine its own data to better exploit its customers' buying preferences and increase revenue. Data analytics techniques have other purposes as well, including the discovery of new potential customers and improved insight into the use of an organization's products and services.

Some of the methods used in support of these objectives are discussed in this section.

Data Aggregation

Marketing departments in organizations frequently engage in targeted marketing and advertising, whether via email, postal mail, online ads, or other channels. To reach their target markets with the right message at the right time, organizations often purchase lists of targeted individuals from data brokers and merge that data into their marketing databases.

Data aggregation is the practice of combining databases to enrich available data. For instance, suppose a marketing department wants to send flyers about a new line of luxury vehicles to wealthier people (who are more likely to buy than those with lower incomes), and it purchases data from a data broker that includes household income and other details. The organization merges this information into its database and then selects those wealthy persons as targets for its campaign.

This sort of activity occurs far more frequently than most people realize. There exists an entire industry of organizations with vast dossiers on virtually all adults in the United States and many other countries. This data is traded, bought, sold, merged, sorted, culled, updated, and recirculated in an endless cycle. Most of this occurs in companies most people have never heard of until a breach occurs—and, even then, personal notices are rarely sent to affected parties.

Returning to the main point of data aggregation and embellishment, another activity that frequently takes place is this: organizations seeking to aggregate customer data purchase additional data from data brokers to add specific data to their databases. Sometimes they receive additional data fields that are also retained, resulting in the organization having more details about its customers and prospects than it really wants or needs. This phenomenon is an example of *data sprawl*.

Aggregation works in other ways. Organizations with large customer and prospect databases can purchase data from data brokers to keep their customer data up to date. For instance, a motor vehicle manufacturer can purchase data from data brokers to obtain up-to-date mailing addresses for its customers so that its safety recalls will actually reach these people.

Citizens are most concerned about the potential for data aggregation among various government agencies. One can only imagine the abuses that could occur if data from one agency were accessible by malevolent persons in other agencies. To this end, citizens need to be aware of whether privacy laws apply to government agencies as well as private businesses. For example, while GDPR applies to both private businesses and government agencies (with some exceptions for purposes of the prevention, investigation, detection or prosecution of criminal offences), CCPA applies only to private businesses, with government agencies exempt.

Data Lakes and Big Data

Advances in *big data* analysis techniques are driving organizations to develop *data warehouses* (structured data copied from production systems and used for reporting, research, or archival purposes), data lakes, and other large datasets to further analyze and monetize their data. While a data warehouse is used to store structured/processed data in defined database schemas, a *data lake* is an aggregation of structured and unstructured data into a single data store, enabling various analytics or the discovery of previously unknown relationships within the datasets. The value of a data lake is that the structure of storage and data does not need to be defined, which means you can store all types of unrelated data without needing to design relational structures carefully, or without even knowing what questions the data might help answer. *Data science* techniques can enable valuable insights and analytics into company operations and customer data, with results becoming more accurate as more data is included. Indeed, there are many legitimate business reasons for building data lakes for big data analysis, including quality assurance and control, and real-time analytics to understand customers' uses of their products and services. A data lake can also enable powerful analytics and business intelligence insight, which can require close oversight for privacy, especially if data enrichment feeds are included from third parties or some level of automated profiling or decision-making affects individuals.

Machine Learning and AI

Machine learning (ML) and artificial intelligence (AI) are mainstream and appearing in enterprise business applications to improve customer service and product and service quality, and to help organizations better understand their current and future customers and their preferences. When properly used, ML and AI can improve product and service quality, help the organization find new and better customers, and enhance how the organization serves existing customers.

The value of ML and AI depends on the quality and quantity of data available for analysis. More data makes analysis more powerful and more detailed. However, this power can enable unanticipated inferences or unintended decisions if it's not properly understood and controlled. For instance, if AI or ML is tasked with making inferences about people, an organization might end up making misinformed marketing or operational decisions. For example, an e-commerce organization might use ML to determine individual customers' preferences based on past purchase choices and then market to them accordingly. Or, analysis can enable intrusion into sensitive areas—for example, an organization might send advertisements for baby products to the family of an individual who has not yet revealed that they are pregnant.

AI systems consume data in new ways that complicate data operations and privacy. The author's book on the AI Governance Professional certification expands on many aspects of data management.

Discussions on ML and AI continue in Chapter 9.

While organizations might not be prohibited from undertaking activities, including building data lakes and applying ML and AI, they do need to determine whether to include these activities in their privacy policies as declared uses of personal information.

Summary

Data governance is management's visibility and control over the use of information in an organization. Data governance takes on new meaning and relevance for organizations seeking to comply with recent privacy laws.

The governance structure concerning the use of personal information will include policies, defined roles and responsibilities, controls, processes, procedures, assessments of these, and reporting.

Data collection represents the start of the data lifecycle for a given data record or dataset. Data collection occurs in several ways, primarily through data provided by the data subject or obtained from another organization.

For a privacy program to be effective, organizations must have a complete and accurate inventory of all personal information. This inventory must include structured and unstructured data. Periodic data inventory reviews should not only catalog existing instances of sensitive and personal information but also determine, for each instance, whether the data should exist where it is found.

Data provenance, data lineage, and records of processing activities (ROPA) help track an organization's acquisition and use of personal information.

Data flow diagrams (DFDs) and descriptions of data usage serve to complete a data inventory effort. The visual aspect of DFDs helps organizations better understand the flow and use of personal information and guide privacy and security personnel to focus on systems and processes where personal information is used.

A data classification policy is a formal, intentional way for an organization to define levels of importance or sensitivity for information. A typical data classification policy will define two or more (but rarely more than five) data classification levels. Derived from data classification policy, data-handling standards define required storage and use of data.

Static DLP tools scan static data stores to identify files containing data matching specific patterns. Generally, static DLP scanning is performed on file servers, both on-premises and in the cloud.

Dynamic DLP can greatly improve compliance with a data classification policy; however, organizations need to proceed slowly to avoid interfering with sanctioned business processes.

Data tagging can provide needed assistance to DLP automation by enabling DLP to act based on the tag, without having to examine an entire data file in real time.

Data quality or data accuracy is a measure of the care an organization places on the fidelity of its personal data stores.

Data use limitation is a key tenet of privacy laws, including GDPR and CCPA/CPRA. Data use limitation should be a part of overall data governance.

Data analytics is a powerful tool for improving the understanding of business operations, customer behaviors, and service quality.

Data aggregation is the practice of combining databases to enrich available data.

Advances in big data analysis techniques, including machine learning and artificial intelligence, are driving organizations to build data lakes and other large-scale data stores to further analyze and monetize their data.

Artificial intelligence (AI) and machine learning (ML) represent significant business improvement opportunities but also pose unique challenges when these systems are trained on personal information.

Exam Essentials

Understand the role of data inventory in privacy management. A data inventory catalogs personal data assets, including their sources, locations, owners, purposes, and retention requirements. It enables organizations to understand what data exists and supports compliance, risk assessments, and data lifecycle controls.

Recognize how data flow diagrams support transparency and risk identification. Data flow diagrams visually depict how data moves between systems, users, and third parties. They help identify collection points, processing activities, transfers, and storage locations, which are essential for assessing privacy risks and implementing controls.

Distinguish data provenance, data lineage, and records of processing activities (ROPA). Data provenance documents the origin of data and how it was created or obtained. Data lineage traces the movement and transformation of data across systems throughout its lifecycle. ROPA provides a regulatory-focused record detailing processing purposes, data categories, recipients, retention, and safeguards. Together, these artifacts provide complementary visibility: provenance establishes source integrity, lineage shows operational flow and transformations, and ROPA documents compliance with privacy processing requirements.

Apply data classification to align protection with data sensitivity. Data classification categorizes data based on sensitivity, regulatory requirements, and business impact. Classification informs handling requirements such as access controls, encryption, retention, and monitoring.

Ensure data quality as a foundational privacy requirement. Data quality principles, such as accuracy, completeness, and timeliness, reduce risk and support fair processing. Poor data quality can lead to incorrect decisions, regulatory violations, and adverse impacts on data subjects.

Implement data use limitations consistent with stated purposes. Data should only be used for purposes defined at the time of collection or otherwise permitted by law. Use limitations enforce purpose specification and prevent function creep, secondary misuse, and excessive processing.

Understand privacy implications of data analytics and aggregation. Analytics techniques, including aggregation and modeling, can reduce identifiability but can also create re-identification risks. Privacy professionals must evaluate anonymization strength, aggregation thresholds, and residual risk.

Recognize governance risks associated with advanced processing environments. Data warehouses, AI systems, and large-scale analytics platforms often centralize and repurpose data. These environments require strong controls for access, purpose limitation, monitoring, and data minimization to prevent unauthorized or unintended use.

Review Questions

1. Which artifact provides a structured listing of personal data assets within an organization?
   A. Risk register
   B. Control matrix
   C. Data inventory
   D. Incident log
2. What is the primary purpose of a data flow diagram in privacy management?
   A. To classify data sensitivity levels
   B. To visualize how data moves between entities
   C. To define retention schedules
   D. To document data lineage
3. Data classification is primarily used to do which of the following?
   A. Assign handling requirements based on sensitivity
   B. Eliminate unnecessary data collection
   C. Document legal bases for processing
   D. Define data quality metrics
4. Which of the following best describes data quality in a privacy context?
   A. The ability to encrypt data at rest
   B. The completeness and accuracy of stored data
   C. The classification of sensitive data types
   D. The retention period of collected data
5. Data use limitation requires that personal data:
   A. Be used only for specified and authorized purposes
   B. Be stored in a centralized repository
   C. Be retained indefinitely for analytics
   D. Be anonymized before storage
6. Which document is most helpful for identifying third-party data transfers?
   A. Data retention schedule
   B. Data flow diagram
   C. Access control list
   D. Training record

7. An organization aggregates customer data to produce statistical reports. What is the primary privacy consideration?
   - A. Encryption key rotation
   - B. Data retention enforcement
   - C. Re-identification risk
   - D. Network segmentation
8. Which activity most directly supports maintaining data accuracy?
   - A. Periodic data validation procedures
   - B. Increasing storage capacity
   - C. Expanding analytics capabilities
   - D. Implementing multi-factor authentication
9. A data inventory should include which of the following elements?
   - A. Encryption algorithms used
   - B. System patch levels
   - C. Encryption keys
   - D. Data owner and processing purpose
10. Which scenario represents a violation of data use limitation?
    - A. Using customer email addresses for unrelated marketing
    - B. Using collected data to fulfill a customer order
    - C. Sharing data with a contracted processor for the same purpose
    - D. Updating inaccurate contact information
11. What is the primary benefit of maintaining an up-to-date data flow diagram?
    - A. Improved encryption performance
    - B. Reduced storage requirements
    - C. Automated compliance certification
    - D. Better visibility into processing risks
12. Which attribute is most closely associated with data quality?
    - A. Confidentiality
    - B. Integrity
    - C. Availability
    - D. Purpose limitation

13. A centralized data lake increases privacy risk primarily because it:
    A. Eliminates classification controls
    B. Reduces data availability
    C. Consolidates data for broader secondary use
    D. Prevents analytics
14. Which of the following best supports the enforcement of data use limitation?
    A. Data classification labels
    B. Larger data retention windows
    C. Role-based access controls aligned to purpose
    D. Expanded analytics tools
15. Which technique reduces identifiability by combining records into groups?
    A. Tokenization
    B. Encryption
    C. Hashing
    D. Aggregation
16. A data inventory and data flow diagram are complementary because they do which of the following?
    A. Define retention periods
    B. Replace classification controls
    C. Eliminate need for audits
    D. Provide static and dynamic views of data
17. Which action best improves data quality during collection?
    A. Collecting all available data fields
    B. Validating inputs at the point of entry
    C. Extending retention periods
    D. Encrypting data in transit
18. A privacy professional reviewing AI training data should focus primarily on which of the following?
    A. CPU utilization
    B. Backup frequency
    C. Network throughput
    D. Dataset accuracy and representativeness

19. An organization aggregates customer transaction data for analytics. Which control best reduces privacy risk while preserving analytical value?

    A. Encrypting the aggregated dataset

    B. Removing all classification labels

    C. Applying minimum group size thresholds before aggregation

    D. Extending data retention periods

20. Which control best aligns analytics initiatives with data use limitation principles?

    A. Expanding data lake ingestion policies

    B. Requiring purpose-based approval for new analytics use cases

    C. Increasing storage capacity

    D. Reducing logging requirements

Answers to Review Questions

1. C. A data inventory documents what data the organization collects and processes, including its source, purpose, location, owner, and retention requirements. This structured catalog enables organizations to understand their data landscape and supports compliance, risk management, and lifecycle governance. Risk registers and control matrices track risks and controls, not data assets themselves.

2. B. Data flow diagrams illustrate how data is collected, transmitted, processed, stored, and shared. They help privacy professionals identify processing activities, third-party transfers, and potential risk points. While they might inform classification and retention, their primary purpose is to visualize data movement.

3. A. Data classification categorizes information according to sensitivity and regulatory requirements. These categories drive controls such as access restrictions, encryption, monitoring, and retention. Classification supports risk-based protection, ensuring that more sensitive data receives stronger safeguards.

4. B. Data quality refers to attributes such as accuracy, completeness, timeliness, and consistency. High data quality supports fair processing and reduces risks such as incorrect decisions about individuals. Encryption and classification relate to security and governance, not data quality.

5. A. Data use limitation is a core privacy principle requiring that data be used only for the purposes identified at the time of collection or otherwise permitted by law. This prevents function creep and unauthorized secondary uses. It does not mandate anonymization or centralization, though those might be used as supporting controls.

6. B. A data flow diagram shows how data moves between systems and external parties. By mapping transfers, privacy professionals can identify cross-border flows, vendor processing, and disclosure points. Retention schedules and access lists provide different types of governance information.

7. C. Improper aggregation or small sample sizes can allow individuals to be re-identified. Privacy professionals must evaluate aggregation thresholds and residual risk before treating aggregated data as non-personal or non-sensitive.

8. A. Data validation ensures that information remains accurate and up to date. Regular reviews, correction processes, and automated validation controls improve data quality. Authentication and storage capacity relate to security and infrastructure rather than data accuracy.

9. D. A data inventory typically documents attributes such as data owner, purpose, location, retention, and data categories. These attributes support governance and lifecycle management. Technical controls, such as encryption keys, are not core inventory elements.

10. A. Data collected for one purpose should not be repurposed without appropriate authorization or legal basis. Using order-related contact information for unrelated marketing is a classic example of function creep and violates the purpose limitation principle.

11. D. Data flow diagrams provide visibility into how data moves through systems and organizations. This visibility enables privacy professionals to identify risks such as excessive collection, unnecessary transfers, or uncontrolled processing.

12. B. Data integrity relates to accuracy and consistency, which are core aspects of data quality. While confidentiality and availability are important security objectives, integrity directly aligns with maintaining reliable and accurate data.

13. C. Data lakes aggregate large volumes of data from multiple sources. This consolidation increases the risk of secondary uses that might exceed original purposes. Strong governance controls are needed to enforce purpose limitation and access restrictions.

14. C. Access controls tied to job roles and approved purposes help ensure that users can only access data necessary for authorized activities. This operationalizes use limitation and reduces the risk of unauthorized secondary use.

15. D. Aggregation groups data into summary values such as averages or totals, reducing individual identifiability. While tokenization and hashing transform data, aggregation specifically combines records to produce less granular information.

16. D. A data inventory provides a static catalog of data assets, while a data flow diagram shows the dynamic movement and processing of data. Together, they provide a more complete understanding of the data lifecycle and support effective governance.

17. B. Input validation ensures that collected data meets expected formats and constraints. Early validation reduces errors and improves downstream data accuracy. Collecting excessive data increases risk and does not improve quality.

18. D. AI systems rely on the quality of training data. Inaccurate or biased datasets can produce harmful or unfair outcomes. Privacy professionals must evaluate whether training data is accurate, relevant, and appropriate for the intended use.

19. C. Minimum group size thresholds ensure that aggregated results represent sufficiently large populations, reducing the likelihood that individual data points can be inferred from small groups. This technique preserves analytical usefulness while reducing privacy risk.

20. B. Analytics platforms often encourage the reuse of existing data. Purpose-based approval ensures that new analytics activities are evaluated against original collection purposes and legal bases. This governance control prevents unauthorized secondary use and supports compliance with use limitation requirements.

Data Persistence and Destruction

This chapter covers CDPSE Domain 3, "Data Life Cycle Management," specifically the "Data Persistence and Destruction" subdomain.

This chapter covers these job practice elements:

✔ B—DATA PERSISTENCE AND DESTRUCTION

1. *Data Minimization*
2. *Data Disclosure and Transfer*
3. *Data Storage, Retention, and Archiving*
4. *Data Destruction*

The other subdomain in Domain 3, Data Life Cycle Management, is:

✔ A—DATA COLLECTION AND PROCESSING—covered in Chapter 5.

The CDPSE Task Statements relevant to this domain are:

3. *Advise on data life cycle policies and practices to ensure privacy considerations for data governance.*
4. *Design and evaluate the implementation of technical and operational controls for data classifications and data life cycle requirements.*

The topics in this chapter and in Chapter 5 account for 23% of the CDPSE examination.

Privacy programs rely on active and intentional management of personal information in an organization's databases and unstructured data stores. Privacy leaders need to identify and manage sometimes opposing needs through business practices, including data minimization, data retention, and data destruction. Privacy leaders need to be involved in large-scale data management and migration operations to ensure a balance among the needs of data subjects, regulators, and the organization itself.

Data Minimization

Data minimization refers to the practice of collecting and retaining *only* those specific data elements necessary to perform agreed-upon functions. In other words, organizations should be careful to collect or accept only the *personally identifiable information (PII)* required to perform the services they provide.

Just as double-entry accounting describes each item on a balance sheet as both an asset and a liability, personal and sensitive information can provide value to an organization as an asset but also represent a liability. While the asset value of personal and sensitive information might be clear, organizations are slower to realize that accumulating and retaining it also represents a liability.

Unfortunately, the financial liability associated with retained personal information rarely appears on an organization's balance sheet. And yet it is indeed a liability: the impact on an organization when cybercriminals steal that information or when the information is misused is real, in the form of breach response costs, the costs related to reducing harm inflicted on affected parties (think of credit monitoring services, a frequent remedy for stolen credit card numbers), fines from governmental regulators, and the occasional class-action lawsuit.

Data minimization has multiple dimensions:

- Collect only required fields
- Collect only required records
- Retain only as long as is needed
- Pseudonymize, tokenize, or anonymize as soon as possible
- Reduce accessibility

Each is described in detail in the following sections.

Collecting Only Required Fields

When collecting personal information directly from data subjects, organizations should collect only the data items required to fulfill the intended purpose of the collection. Every item collected must be rationalized, and the reason for collecting it must be documented. Data items that cannot be justified as necessary should not be collected.

Any data item proposed for collection that does not have a current business purpose should not be collected. Such a collection would impose liability on the organization with no corresponding benefit. For example, suppose an e-commerce company that sells books developed a customer portal where customers can select their favorite book categories and save their shipping addresses so they do not need to enter them for each order. An analyst proposes that the organization collect each customer's date of birth (including year) so a birthday discount code can be sent to customers during their birthday month. The privacy officer successfully argues that this function does not require the customer's year of birth, only the month. The organization decides not to collect the birth year and day for its customers because no identified purpose requires it (such as selling adults-only merchandise). Although there was a valid decision made in this case, more information might be required, such as a business record in the form of a detailed inventory of data items collected, including the collection purpose(s). This way, months or years later, a privacy professional can examine the records to discern the reasons for specific data-collection decisions without relying on workers' recollection.

There remains some inferred responsibility for providing personal information, which falls on the data subjects who provide it. Data subjects should be aware of the information they provide to an organization or government and attempt to withhold any information they believe is unnecessary for the organization to fulfill the intended purpose. For example, most e-commerce sites should not require a data subject's date of birth to complete transactions (the sale of products prohibited for minors is one exception; applying for credit is another). If an e-commerce site requests a date of birth, a data subject should avoid providing it unless there is some clear purpose that the data subject agrees with.

Providing False Information

Some privacy-conscious individuals known to the author take an interesting approach to sharing certain sensitive information with other organizations. They provide valid but deliberately false information to avoid revealing sensitive information about themselves. For instance, if an e-commerce site that sells tobacco products wants to confirm that visitors are over the age of 21, they enter a date of birth that indicates they are over 21, without entering their actual birth date. There are, however, a couple of complications to keep in mind if one chooses to do this. If the e-commerce site later wants to confirm a date of birth, the customer must keep track of the date they provided so they can enter the same value again (a password vault would be a handy way of storing this). If the e-commerce site later requests an image of a government-issued ID, the customer will have to "correct" the falsified date of birth to match their actual date of birth.

Understanding Linkage Attacks

A *linkage attack* occurs when an adversary combines multiple datasets: often one that is anonymized and one that is identified, to re-identify individuals or infer sensitive information by matching shared attributes.

For instance, an adversary obtains a public voter registry (containing names, postal codes, birth dates, and genders) and an anonymized medical records database containing postal codes and birth dates. The adversary can then attempt to re-identify the medical records data using the voter registration data to find matches in postal codes and dates of birth.

Collecting Only Required Records

If organizations acquire personal information in bulk (such as purchasing it from a data broker), only those records required to fulfill the intended business purpose should be collected. Any collection of records carries some liability for an organization, especially when the records provide no short-term value or benefit: if an intruder breaks in and steals this information, the organization that collected it might need to make reparations to all persons whose records were collected and stolen.

Organizations that purchase bulk PII data need to ensure they obtain only the records necessary to meet their business objectives. Sometimes, however, only large datasets are available, even if only certain records are requested or needed. In such cases, organizations should remove unnecessary records as soon as it's practical.

On a record-by-record basis, organizations should devise options to enable choices when collecting individual records. One example is e-commerce, where many online shopping sites permit customers to "check out as a guest." In this case, the buyer provides only enough information to complete the transaction, rather than being required to create a persistent user account, which usually involves collecting additional information such as a credit card number, billing address, shipping address, and other details.

One option for record removal is the pseudonymization or anonymization of selected records, which is discussed later in this section.

Discarding Data When No Longer Needed

Organizations that collect and retain personal data should understand the purposes of personal data fields to determine whether long-term retention is appropriate. For instance, an e-commerce website accepting credit card payments might collect the CVV (card verification value) from the customer and then discard it as soon as the transaction is approved or rejected.[1]

[1] The Payment Card Industry Data Security Standard (PCI DSS) prohibits the storage of CVV values after a transaction has been approved or declined.

In another example, a website that provides services only to adults aged 21 or older might require proof of age before any purchase can be made. This practice might involve uploading a government-issued ID or taking another action. Once the organization has verified that the subject is at least 21, it can discard the PII collected to verify the subject's age and simply indicate that the subject's age has been verified.

Minimizing Access

Data minimization is all about risk reduction by limiting the amount of data available for various functions. In "risk-speak," data minimization reduces the impact of improper data usage or a breach of personal information. An organization can achieve effective data minimization through access controls in several ways:

- **Reducing access volume** Organizations can limit the number of records that a worker can access, extract, or download in bulk operations. In B2C (business-to-customer) organizations, few people in the organization genuinely need access to the entire customer database; most should be restricted by various means.
- **Reducing personnel with data access** Organizations can limit the number of workers with access to customer data to those whose jobs require it.
- **Reducing access to sensitive fields** Organizations can limit the data fields accessible to their workers. For instance, most workers might not need to access customers' birthdays or full credit card numbers; therefore, the ability to view these or other sensitive fields should be limited.

Data *masking* can protect the contents of personal information from personnel who do not need to see it. A typical example is displaying a credit card number or a social insurance number. Although an information system might store the full contents of these values, some characters might be masked so that personnel cannot see them. Most often, programs display only the last four digits of a credit card number or a social insurance number.

Exam Tip

CDPSE candidates need to understand that encryption is another form of access control that might be applicable in some situations for limiting access to personal information.

Minimizing Storage

Organizations can significantly enhance the security of sensitive and personal information by limiting where and how workers can store such data. When workers use downloads or extracts from business applications, organizations can enact controls that limit where that data can be stored. Primarily, organizations should limit the storage of personal information about their customers, constituents, and employees to organization-managed systems.

Organizations can enact policies stating that all sensitive and personal information must be stored only on organizational file servers, not on laptops or desktop computers, mobile devices, removable storage devices, or personal cloud-based storage services. Further, sensitive and personal information can be blocked from being sent via company email or personal email. These controls are typically implemented with *data loss prevention (DLP)*, but *web content filtering* and *cloud access security broker (CASB)* capabilities can supplement DLP solutions.

The ultimate objective is to limit the storage of personal information to only those locations permitted by policy and controlled through tooling. However, privacy and security professionals need to tread carefully to avoid disrupting sanctioned business processes.

Minimizing Availability

Minimizing information availability is another option organizations can pursue to achieve data minimization. The most common approach is to migrate data from widely accessed systems to archival systems that only a few personnel can access. For example, suppose a regional hospital's patient care and billing systems contain medical records and billing records for the past 15 years. To reduce the risk of exposure, the hospital migrates all records older than two years to an archival system that only a few hospital personnel can access. This permits the hospital to comply with minimum data retention requirements while reducing risks associated with hospital personnel having access to large volumes of medical and financial information. Further, since the data archival system is accessible only from internal networks and by few personnel, there is a correspondingly lower risk of a break-in by intruders.

Organizations can implement additional controls to further protect the archival system, including *data loss prevention (DLP)*, *user behavior analytics (UBA)*, and *NetFlow*.

Minimizing Retention

Establishing a data retention schedule is an effective data minimization technique. By limiting the time data records reside in an organization, the risks associated with breaches and unauthorized disclosures are reduced.

Data retention is discussed in detail later in this chapter.

Minimization Through De-identification

Depending on the purpose of acquiring personal information, organizations can consider *de-identification* as a method to minimize the amount of PII they retain. For instance, if an organization acquires personal information for statistical purposes, it can pseudonymize or anonymize the records so that they no longer are associated with specific persons but can still provide statistical value.

When implemented correctly and from a privacy perspective, de-identification is as effective as the outright removal of records. When implemented correctly, an organization will continue to derive value from de-identified data through analytical value. For instance, after a database of user transactions has been de-identified, although the organization won't know precisely who performed individual transactions, it will still understand sales trends and other big-picture insights.

Three primary techniques are used in de-identification: pseudonymization, tokenization, and anonymization. While these techniques differ, the results are similar. If these techniques are not applied effectively, data subject identities might be determined through *re-identification*.

Pseudonymization

Pseudonymization is the substitution of data in sensitive data fields with alternate values to de-identify data records with specific persons. Pseudonymization is generally a reversible substitution technique: fields that identify actual persons are modified and replaced with pseudonym values. Here are some examples:

- *Peter Gregory* becomes *Qoem Rebnurvo*
- *118 Elm Street* becomes *539 Tlo Uepv*
- *peterhgregory@gmail.com* becomes *juwnfodpwlrmg@drep.com*

The substitution technique enables software to function correctly, while substitutions eliminate the association between the record and the actual person. However, this is different from anonymization because pseudonymization might still enable an individual to be singled out and linked across different datasets.

From a privacy perspective, de-identifying a record (when performed properly) is equivalent to its removal.

Tokenization

Tokenization involves replacing sensitive data elements with non-sensitive tokens, with the original values stored in a secure token vault. Tokenization is considered a form of pseudonymization but is discussed separately due to its architectural and operational characteristics.

For example, a healthcare organization chooses to tokenize its patients' Social Security numbers so that the patient database no longer includes them. Social Security numbers are needed for limited tasks and are visible to a few personnel. To tokenize a data field, such as a Social Security number field, the organization performs this procedure:

1. Create a new record in the secure token vault.
2. Copy the Social Security number to the new token vault record.
3. Copy the token vault record identifier to the Social Security field in the patient record.

The organization would then restrict access to the token vault to the few personnel who truly need it. The rest of the organization would see only the token value, not the Social Security number.

Anonymization

Anonymization is the process of irreversibly altering or removing sensitive data fields from records so that an individual cannot be identified, directly or indirectly. Anonymization can also be a simple removal technique: data fields that could associate a record with a specific person are removed. Here are some examples:

- *Peter Gregory* becomes (blanks)
- *118 Elm Street* becomes (blanks)
- *peterhgregory@gmail.com* (blanks)

Note that anonymization can cause software to behave in unexpected ways. Furthermore, database management systems might resist anonymization, as it could compromise *referential integrity*. To anonymize field data so that it works correctly, it might be necessary to copy records from a database to a separate database whose structure lacks the removed fields.

The challenge with de-identification is ensuring that data records can no longer be associated with natural persons, while retaining the information's value for other purposes.

Data Disclosure and Transfer

Data rarely resides within a single organization. Instead, data movement within and between organizations is inevitably a standard part of most organizations' business processes. Managing and tracking data movement is a critical and core activity in any privacy program.

When viewed together, data disclosure and transfer represent the movement of data from one system to another, one organization to another, or one jurisdiction to another. Table 6.1 illustrates the sometimes-subtle differences among the three.

The terms data disclosure, data transfer, and data migration are often confused and misused. The details of these must be known, when planning or discussing these activities.

Organizations must determine whether any existing or proposed data disclosure or transfer (particularly *cross-border data transfers*) complies with applicable privacy laws, which might require safeguards such as *standard contractual clauses, binding corporate rules*, or *business associate agreements*.

TABLE 6.1 Data Disclosure, Transfer, and Migration Compared

Aspect	Data Disclosure	Data Transfer	Data Migration
Primary concern	New access	Movement	System replacement
Introduces new recipient	Usually yes	Not necessarily	Usually no
Temporary vs permanent	Often temporary	Temporary or ongoing	Typically permanent
Scope	Sharing	Transmission	Structured relocation
Example	Send HR record to a vendor for background check	Send transaction data to a specialized service provider	Move legacy data to a new system
Privacy focus	Purpose limitation, least privilege	Cross-border and transmission safeguards	Data accuracy, minimization, retention

Data Disclosure

A *data disclosure* is an instance in which data is made accessible to another entity that did not previously have access to it. Typically, control of the data resides with the originating entity. However, the entity to which the data has been disclosed can view and process individual records, groups of records, or all records, in accordance with an agreement between the entities.

To borrow the GDPR terms for a moment, a *data controller* discloses data to a *data processor*. The two parties will have executed a *data processing agreement* that stipulates the services that the data processor will perform on behalf of the data controller. A data processor is a third party, necessitating due diligence and due care activities that are part of *third-party risk management (TPRM)*, as discussed fully in Chapter 2.

An example of data disclosure is the sharing of consumer credit records, credit scores, and histories from credit bureaus to other lenders considering extending credit to consumers. One would say that credit bureaus, acting as data controllers, disclose individual creditors' records to lenders, acting as data processors.

Data Transfer

Data transfer is the transfer of data from one organization to another, or from one jurisdiction to another within an organization. Regarding the transfer of data to another jurisdiction, privacy laws generally require that the protection of data in the new country meets or exceeds that in the originating country.

For example, a retail organization transmits daily transaction logs containing customer purchase details to a third-party fraud-detection service for post-facto analysis. The data originates in the retail company, the data controller, and is received by the fraud-detection service, the data processor, which might be located in another legal jurisdiction. This example also constitutes data disclosure because a new party gains access to personal information.

Data Migration

Data migration is a process of transferring data from one production system to another, generally *within an organization*. In the early days of information processing, data migration was a time-consuming, painstaking effort to move business information from an older (and perhaps unsupported) system to a newer one. A data migration was part of a greater effort, or conversion, which also involved updating business software (which, in those days, was often custom-written by in-house programmers) to ensure it would function in precisely the same way on the new system as on the old. Numerous rounds of testing would occur during a migration, which could take a year or longer for complex applications.

Modern data migrations include these concerns, although the context of migrations is more often the movement of data from one SaaS solution to another, or from an aging on-premises application to a SaaS system. The velocity at which data can be moved increases the risk of mishandling unless a proper data migration strategy is developed that accounts for security and privacy requirements. Some concerns during such a migration will include the following:

- **Business functionality** An organization needs to understand whether the new system performs its primary functions in the same way, providing the same results (or different results that the organization can deal with acceptably) as the old system.
- **Information format** When data is migrated from the old system to the new system, individual data fields might need to be manipulated or transformed, as the entire set of data fields in the old and new systems rarely match exactly. Furthermore, the format of data stored on the old system might differ from that of the new system, requiring that each data field be transformed. This process, called *extract, transform, load (ETL)*, simply means that extracted data must pass through a series of functions before being loaded into the target system. For example, if an old system stores a complex date field as *YYYYMMDD* and a new system uses the format *MMDDYYYY*, an ETL process will have to transform each date field's contents in each record as it is migrated from the old system to the new one.
- **Data types** An organization migrating data from an older system to a newer one needs to thoroughly understand how individual data fields are used, including both obvious and subtle differences in usage. For example, an older system might accept the inclusion of some special characters in data subjects' names, addresses, or other fields, while the newer system's rules for special characters differ.

- **Testing** An organization migrating data from an older system to a newer one needs to thoroughly test the conversion of data types and the migration of data from old to new systems. Often, techniques such as batch totals and checksums are employed, particularly on large datasets, to ensure that data is migrated properly and that all values are preserved.
- **Privacy** Organizations need to understand the controls and constraints built into both old and new systems to meet privacy requirements and controls in the new system. In some circumstances, organizations might need to develop compensating controls to manage those differences and to ensure the sustainment of privacy expectations.
- **Security** Organizations must understand how roles and data access techniques differ between the old and new systems and adjust their practices accordingly. For instance, the structure of access roles between the old and new systems might differ and be somewhat rigid. This would require the organization to remap job functions to the new system's roles so that personnel have the access they require to perform their jobs, but not so much that it increases risk.
- **Training** Persons using the older system will require training to understand how to use the new system properly. This should result in fewer errors and ensure better security and privacy.

A proper migration strategy will address these requirements and mitigate the risk of inadvertently exposing data in temporary storage locations that can (and have) resulted in data breaches. Additionally, an organization migrating to a newer system needs to understand whether it has capabilities not present in the older system. Examples include these:

- A newer system might integrate with federated identity services to support single sign-on.
- A newer system might send security events to a security information and event management (SIEM) system.
- A newer system might be able to integrate with a data loss prevention (DLP) system, thereby providing additional visibility and control over the use of personal information.

Data Storage

Organizations that process information, including sensitive and personal information, need to store that information temporarily or permanently. How sensitive and personal information is stored can make a vast difference in terms of privacy and security.

Flippantly, the decision-making process for storing information can come down to "put that data here" or "put that data there." However, organizations need to make data storage decisions with utmost seriousness and within the auspices of a formal data governance function. The stakes are high: the consequences of poor decision-making can reverse an organization's fortunes.

An organization must keep in mind several considerations for data storage, including these:

- **Data location and *data sovereignty*** Some privacy laws include stipulations regarding the geographic location where data about persons can be stored. Many countries shun or outright prohibit the export of personal information. While on the surface this concept is obvious, in practice it is sometimes difficult to determine the physical locations of data storage for many cloud-based services. Organizations are accountable for making sound decisions in the face of these uncertainties.
- **Data protection** Security specialists need to identify the security controls across the entire stack, from physical protection to human access and usage. This can be somewhat vague with cloud-based service providers, but it is often offset by external attestations such as *SSAE 18* or *ISAE 3402* audits.
- **Data access** Security and privacy specialists must identify the controls in place for data access, whether by machines or by workers. Organizations need to understand a cloud service provider's workers' ability to access their data and whether the organization would be notified if they do so.
- **Persistence** For as long as an organization intends to retain personal information (as well as all other types), organizations employ various means to ensure its continued availability through *backup* (copying to another location and/or other media), *snapshots* (point-in-time copy within a storage system), and *replication* (real-time copying of additions, changes, and deletions to data to another storage system, often in a different location). Personal information on backup media should be included in data lineage and considered when data is to be discarded at the end of its retention period.
- **Data retention** Organizations must determine how long various types of data should be retained. This is discussed further in the next section.
- **Access monitoring** The ability to monitor and log data access and changes to data access rights should be a significant consideration in any data storage decision. The lack of visibility and control effectively means that an organization has given up control over data protection and usage. Generally, data access visibility requirements mean that workers cannot store sensitive and personal data on removable (USB) storage devices or personally owned devices.

Exam Tip

CDPSE candidates need to understand the concept and purpose of cloud shared responsibility models.

Data Warehousing

A *data warehouse* is a set of data that has been copied from a production system and used for reporting, research, or archival purposes. Organizations create data warehouses when the size or transaction volume of their production databases makes using them infeasible for shared purposes, such as online transactions, research, and reporting. While it might sound similar to a data lake (discussed in Chapter 5), a data warehouse is a structured repository and typically supports defined business operational use cases.

Transaction processing in database management systems generally involves inserting records and simultaneously updating indexes. In contrast, research and reporting in database management systems involve searching for and retrieving records. The conflict is this: database management systems are generally tuned for optimum performance. Tuning a database management system for transaction processing results in poor performance for searching, while tuning a database for searching results in poor performance for inserting new records. Generally, the best course of action is to create a separate data warehouse tuned for searching, reporting, and research, and then periodically copy transaction data into it. This leaves the online transaction processing system ideally tuned for its purpose.

Data warehousing, data lakes, and big data are also discussed in Chapter 5.

If an organization is not required to retain personal information for long periods, moving records to a data warehouse can be an opportunity to de-identify them as they are removed from the production environment.

Data Retention and Archiving

Organizations are accustomed to retaining data for very long periods, often in perpetuity. For generations, the risks associated with long-term *data retention* have been quite low. Digital transformation has changed all of that: datasets that contain more details about data subjects (more fields with sensitive information and more records) are higher-value targets sought by cybercriminal organizations. Privacy professionals often call highly sensitive information "toxic data" because its theft can have dire consequences for the organization, including regulatory sanctions and class-action lawsuits. Finally, the liability of excess data retention is being felt, resulting in a greater emphasis on establishing data retention schedules to limit how long organizations retain sensitive information.

Put another way, the value of information that an organization accumulates has the "credit" and "debit" characteristics of double-entry accounting. Although the accumulation of sensitive data can bring more value to the organization, it also increases liability: the theft of a larger trove of sensitive data will incur greater costs than the theft of a smaller dataset. For example, suppose each of two similar e-commerce organizations has about five million customers. One of the organizations keeps only two years of transaction data and moves dormant customer data to an offline storage system. The other organization stores all customer data online, even for customers who have not patronized it for years. Suppose each organization's customer databases are stolen. In that case, the organization that reduced its customer database size will incur fewer costs than the organization that kept all its customer data online.

The approach to data retention is the development of a *data retention schedule*, a chart with the force of policy that specifies the minimum and maximum periods that the organization will retain specific types or sets of data. A data retention schedule is considered policy, and organizational departments are expected to comply with it. Security and privacy personnel can periodically conduct reviews or audits to determine whether the organization complies with its data retention policy and to require corrective action when violations are found.

Purging older records is not always as easy as it sounds. Several challenges can present themselves:

- **Database *referential integrity*** The design of relational databases can make the prospect of removing records a bit tricky. Primarily, a record cannot be removed if another record elsewhere in the database references it via a foreign key. The referential integrity concept refers to the restriction where a record (or "row" as it is often called) cannot be removed if another table has a row whose foreign key points to the record to be removed. The other table's row would first have to be modified or removed. This is typically a problem in older databases that were not designed with data retention in mind.
- **Comingling of data** Some storage media cannot be modified once created. For instance, magnetic tape is an "all or nothing" medium; it is impossible to remove specific data from a magnetic tape while retaining other data. If a system is backed up to magnetic tape and contains specific data that must be purged after two years, but also contains other data that must be retained for ten years, backing up all of this data to magnetic tape will create a conflict. The organization will not be able to conform to both of these retention requirements.
- ***Unstructured data*** Because *structured data* can be extracted from databases and further manipulated at users' workstations, it can be difficult to know whether individual workbooks contain information that has exceeded its retention period. The date stamp on a workbook does not indicate the transaction dates of rows in the workbook, which could be recent or far in the past. Variations in how data can be represented in workbooks make it infeasible to enforce effective transaction-level data retention in unstructured file stores.
- **Third parties** Organizations outsourcing business applications to third parties (through platform-as-a-service [PaaS] or software-as-a-service [SaaS] models) might find that one or more of their third parties cannot remove older records from their systems.

There might be referential integrity issues in their databases (discussed earlier), or they might simply lack the tools to remove older records from selected customers' databases. This kind of situation often arises when an organization, after selecting and using third-party applications, enacts a data retention policy only to discover that one or more third parties are unable to comply.

- **Email** In some organizations, workers send sensitive and personal information to one another via email. Searching for and removing specific email messages containing sensitive information might not be feasible; this problem is similar to the unstructured data problem discussed earlier. Removing all older email messages can be a viable approach. Still, the organization needs to fully understand the nature of its email use so that purging older email messages does not introduce unintended consequences, such as the destruction of other records that should be retained for long periods.

Data retention does not require an "all or nothing" approach, in which an organization will simply delete older records. Instead, organizations can define storage locations for business records that can be tightly managed and can establish a generic retention schedule for other storage locations. Additionally, records that have reached their expiration dates can be pseudonymized or anonymized, thereby removing personal information while retaining other aspects for historical purposes. Pseudonymization and anonymization are discussed earlier in this chapter.

As with other privacy practices, organizations should periodically review or audit their data retention policy to assess risk and compliance.

Industry Data Retention Laws

Privacy and security professionals need to work with business unit leaders and legal counsel to determine appropriate data retention periods for various data types. Often, laws in the context of said data need to be identified and understood. For instance, national, state, or provincial laws specify that organizations must retain employment "human resources" records for the duration of an employee's employment, plus several years afterward. Financial services and banking laws have similar requirements for minimum retention periods for financial transaction data.

Right to Be Forgotten

GDPR, CCPA/CPRA, and other privacy laws give data subjects a "right to be forgotten." In other words, data subjects can request that their data be removed. Still, such requests can be granted only to the extent that an organization can remove the information without violating other laws requiring its retention. For example, suppose Fred was unceremoniously fired from his job at Best State Bank. Thinking he can improve his employment prospects elsewhere, Fred asks Best State Bank to remove his employment record from its files under the "right to be forgotten" concept in applicable privacy laws. However, Best State Bank refuses to fulfill the request, citing employment laws requiring all employment records to be retained for the length of employment plus seven years after the end of employment.

Data Archival

In the early years of computing, data was often copied to magnetic tapes, which were kept in a vault for many years. Nowadays, with low data storage costs, organizations are increasingly likely to retain data in perpetuity, particularly business transactions and records about employees and customers. However, the risks associated with long-term retention have compelled organizations to consider alternatives; one is *data archival*, the process of preparing data for long-term storage. When organizations are bound by specific laws to retain data for many years, archival provides a viable opportunity to remove data from online transaction systems to other systems or media.

The terms "online," "near-line," and "offline" denote related approaches to archival storage. Online data remains in the primary processing system alongside current records. Near-line data can reside in a different system, such as a data warehouse, and can be accessed there or even returned to the primary transaction processing and storage system for a time. Offline data generally resides in another form—such as backup media (whether tapes, a virtual tape library (VTL), or disk storage)—but not in a form that is immediately available for normal processing.

Archiving can be a viable option for risk-averse organizations that want to rid themselves of older records systems but are required by law to store records long term. In this case, techniques such as pseudonymization and anonymization might not be available, because organizations are generally obligated to retain original information in business transactions, including subject names and other personal information.

The Data Retention Tug of War

Privacy professionals and business leaders are sometimes at odds, particularly over data retention. The core of the conflict is this: business leaders want to keep information for as long as possible, to mine every last morsel of value from it; on the other side, privacy professionals want data retained for the shortest possible time, if at all.

Neither side is entirely correct. Instead, business leaders and privacy professionals need to understand the facts, applicable laws, use cases, and options available to enable the organization to derive maximum value from its information, while applying techniques to reduce risks as much as possible.

Data Destruction

For all the effort organizations put into ensuring data availability, an equal amount of effort is required when they no longer need to retain data, even under adverse conditions. *Data destruction* is the intentional destruction of data so it cannot be recovered. Data destruction is invoked as a part of two processes: data classification and handling, and data retention.

Data destruction policy should include directives for the safe removal of data in numerous use cases, including data that is:

- Electronically stored on a laptop computer, desktop computer, tablet computer, smartphone, or USB drive
- Electronically stored on a server
- Electronically stored on a file server
- Electronically stored on a hard disk drive (HDD), solid-state drive (SSD), or optical disc
- Electronically stored by a cloud service provider
- Stored as a record in a database management system
- Stored as a record in a business application
- Stored on backup media
- Stored on printed paper

The rigor used to destroy data safely should depend upon the sensitivity of the affected data and a risk or threat assessment to determine the extent to which an adversary would attempt to reconstitute discarded or destroyed data.

Methods of data destruction include:

- ***Degaussing*** Used to erase data stored on magnetic media, including hard disk drives and backup tape
- **Destruction of encryption keys** Keys used to encrypt personal information, once destroyed, render personal information permanently inaccessible
- **Drilling** Used to render hard disk drives and solid-state drives unreadable
- **Incineration** Used to destroy backup media and hardcopy
- **Overwriting** Single or multiple passes of writing random data to fields to be destroyed
- **Shredding** Used to destroy hard drives, solid-state drives, optical discs, backup media, and hardcopy

Because cloud service providers manage many organizations' information systems and store data, most of these techniques are unavailable to them. Often, organizations need to request that certain data be destroyed, with a *certificate of destruction* provided as evidence.

Simple deletion of a file, directory, or database record is not destructive. The "deleted" data remains and is de-referenced and discoverable with simple tools.

Organizations must include the creation of evidence as part of their data destruction techniques, whether required by regulations or for other purposes.

Summary

Data minimization is the practice of collecting and retaining only the specific data elements necessary to perform agreed-upon functions. Organizations should be careful to collect or accept only the specific PII details required to perform whatever services they provide.

When collecting personal information directly from data subjects, organizations should collect only the data items required to fulfill the intended purpose of the collection. Every item collected must be rationalized, and the reason for collecting it must be documented.

Organizations should collect only information necessary to meet specific business objectives, and they should discard records that are no longer needed. Fields and records are required to perform specific functions, but those that are no longer needed should be discarded.

Another dimension of data minimization involves limitations on the number of personnel who can access specific fields, records, or databases. Only personnel with specific business needs should be able to access these items.

Pseudonymization is the process of replacing sensitive data in fields with alternate values (pseudonyms) to de-identify records about specific persons. Pseudonymization is a substitution technique: fields that identify actual persons are removed, and other values are used to replace those fields. *Anonymization* is the process of irreversibly altering or removing sensitive data fields from records so that an individual cannot be identified, directly or indirectly. Anonymization can be a simple removal technique: data fields that could associate a record with a specific person are removed. Tokenization involves replacing sensitive data elements with non-sensitive tokens, with the original values stored in a secure token vault.

Data disclosure is the act of making data in one organization accessible to another organization in a controller-processor relationship. Data transfer is the transfer of data from one organization to another, or within an organization from one jurisdiction to another. *Data migration* is the process of transferring data from one production system to another. Close attention is required to preserve data accuracy and integrity during a migration.

Privacy and security professionals should pay close attention to data storage environments to ensure that the organization can exert data protection, access control, and access usage controls on them.

Organizations should develop data retention schedules to limit how long sensitive data can be retained. A data retention schedule specifies the minimum and maximum retention periods for various types of data before they must be discarded or destroyed. Periodic checks and reviews should be performed to ensure compliance. Data destruction is the intentional destruction of data so it cannot be recovered. Data destruction is performed on fields, records, databases, and files that have reached the end of their retention period.

Exam Essentials

Apply data minimization throughout the data lifecycle. Data minimization requires collecting only necessary data, limiting its use to defined purposes, retaining it only as long as required, and reducing identifiability where possible. Minimization should be enforced through collection controls, retention schedules, and technical measures such as masking or aggregation.

Differentiate data disclosure, data transfer, and data migration. Data disclosure involves making data available to another party, often without transferring control. Data transfer refers to moving data between entities or jurisdictions where custody or control might change. Data migration is the movement of data between systems, typically within an organization, often for modernization or consolidation purposes.

Establish retention schedules based on legal, regulatory, and business requirements. Organizations should define retention periods for each data category, balancing operational needs with regulatory obligations and privacy principles. Retention schedules should be documented, consistently applied, and periodically reviewed.

Implement secure data storage and archiving controls. Persistent data must be protected through access controls, encryption, integrity mechanisms, and monitoring. Archived data requires equivalent protections, even when stored offline or in lower-cost storage tiers.

Ensure cross-border data transfers comply with applicable requirements. Transfers across jurisdictions can require safeguards such as contractual clauses, adequacy determinations, or other approved mechanisms. Organizations must assess applicable legal restrictions and ensure appropriate controls are in place before transferring personal data.

Use appropriate data destruction methods for media type and sensitivity. Logical destruction methods include cryptographic erasure and secure overwrite. Physical destruction methods include shredding, degaussing, drilling, or incineration. The selected method should render data unrecoverable based on risk level.

Document and verify destruction activities. Organizations should maintain records of destruction, including scope, method, and authorization. Verification steps, such as certificates of destruction or audit sampling, assure that retention limits and privacy requirements are enforced.

Review Questions

1. An organization implements a policy requiring business units to justify each data element collected in customer forms. Which principle is being applied?
   A. Data classification
   B. Data normalization
   C. Data anonymization
   D. Data minimization
2. Which of the following best distinguishes data disclosure from data transfer?
   A. Disclosure involves encryption; transfer does not
   B. Disclosure makes data accessible, while transfer moves custody or control
   C. Transfer is internal only; disclosure is external only
   D. Disclosure requires consent; transfer does not
3. A company keeps customer transaction data indefinitely "just in case" it might be useful. Which risk is most directly introduced?
   A. Reduced system availability
   B. Lower data accuracy
   C. Increased legal liability due to excessive retention
   D. Increased authentication complexity
4. Which activity is most appropriate when defining data retention requirements?
   A. Aligning retention periods with legal and business obligations
   B. Reviewing employee performance metrics
   C. Encrypting archived backups
   D. Implementing data classification labels
5. An organization moves historical data from production systems to lower-cost storage but still requires occasional access. This is best described as which of the following?
   A. Data destruction
   B. Data disclosure
   C. Data minimization
   D. Data archiving
6. Which control most directly supports secure data transfer between organizations?
   A. Data deduplication
   B. Data normalization
   C. Encryption in transit
   D. Data compression

7. A privacy program requires the removal of identifiers once they are no longer needed for operational purposes. This practice primarily supports which of the following?
   - **A.** Data minimization
   - **B.** Data classification
   - **C.** Data masking
   - **D.** Data migration
8. Which factor(s) should most strongly influence the selection of a data destruction method?
   - **A.** Storage cost
   - **B.** Vendor preference
   - **C.** Backup frequency
   - **D.** Media type and data sensitivity
9. An organization shares customer data with a service provider that processes it on behalf of the organization. This is an example of which of the following?
   - **A.** Data migration
   - **B.** Data destruction
   - **C.** Data disclosure and transfer
   - **D.** Data classification
10. Which of the following is the primary purpose of a retention schedule?
    - **A.** Define system uptime targets
    - **B.** Specify how long different data types should be kept
    - **C.** Determine encryption algorithms
    - **D.** Identify data owners
11. Which scenario best demonstrates data minimization during processing?
    - **A.** Encrypting all stored data
    - **B.** Replicating data across regions
    - **C.** Aggregating data to remove individual identifiers
    - **D.** Archiving inactive accounts
12. What is the primary risk of archiving data without applying security controls?
    - **A.** Reduced processing speed
    - **B.** Increased storage costs
    - **C.** Data duplication errors
    - **D.** Unauthorized access to long-term stored data

13. Which of the following best describes cryptographic erasure?
    A. Destroying encryption keys to render data unreadable
    B. Physically shredding storage media
    C. Overwriting data multiple times
    D. Compressing archived data

14. An organization moves customer records from an old CRM system to a new one within the same company. This is an example of which of the following?
    A. Data disclosure
    B. Data destruction
    C. Data archival
    D. Data migration

15. Which control assures that data destruction activities were completed properly?
    A. Data classification labels
    B. Data mapping diagram
    C. Certificate of destruction
    D. Encryption audit log

16. A company retains logs for regulatory compliance but deletes unnecessary fields within those logs. This approach reflects which of the following?
    A. Data minimization
    B. Data disclosure
    C. Data migration
    D. Data masking

17. Which is the most appropriate reason to archive data rather than delete it?
    A. Improve system performance only
    B. Reduce encryption overhead
    C. Maintain data for legal or historical requirements
    D. Simplify access control management

18. An organization transfers personal data to another country. Which consideration is most important?
    A. Data integrity
    B. Backup frequency
    C. Data compression efficiency
    D. Jurisdictional and regulatory requirements

19. Which destruction method is most appropriate for decommissioned solid-state drives containing sensitive data?
    A. File deletion
    B. Formatting the drive
    C. Data compression
    D. Physical destruction or cryptographic erasure

20. An organization shares anonymized analytics results with a partner without providing underlying data. This activity is best described as which of the following?
    A. Data transfer
    B. Data disclosure
    C. Data migration
    D. Data destruction

Answers to Review Questions

1. D. Data minimization requires organizations to collect only the data that is necessary for clearly defined purposes. Requiring justification for each data element forces business units to evaluate whether the information is actually needed. This reduces unnecessary collection, lowers privacy risk, and decreases the volume of data that must later be secured, retained, and potentially destroyed.

2. B. Data disclosure typically means making information available to another party, such as allowing viewing or limited use, without necessarily transferring ownership or control. Data transfer, by contrast, involves moving data between entities or jurisdictions, often changing custody, legal responsibility, or regulatory obligations. Understanding this distinction helps organizations apply appropriate governance and compliance controls.

3. C. Retaining data longer than necessary increases regulatory, legal, and breach exposure. Many privacy frameworks require organizations to retain personal data only for defined purposes and timeframes. Excessive retention expands the amount of data subject to discovery, increases the impact of a breach, and contradicts the principles of data minimization and retention limitation.

4. A. Retention schedules should be developed with consideration of regulatory mandates, contractual requirements, litigation hold obligations, and operational needs. By aligning retention periods with these factors, organizations avoid premature deletion and unnecessary long-term storage of sensitive information. This balance supports compliance and reduces risk.

5. D. Data archiving involves relocating inactive or infrequently used data to long-term storage while maintaining the ability to retrieve it when needed. Archiving reduces operational system load and storage costs but requires maintaining appropriate security controls, integrity protections, and retention policies for the archived information.

6. C. Encryption in transit protects data as it moves between systems or organizations by preventing interception or unauthorized disclosure. This control is especially important during transfers across networks, including public networks, where data might otherwise be exposed. Encryption helps ensure confidentiality and supports regulatory requirements for secure data movement.

7. A. Removing identifiers reduces the sensitivity of stored data and limits the risk of unauthorized disclosure. This practice reflects minimization by retaining only the information necessary for ongoing operations. It also reduces compliance obligations and lowers the impact of potential breaches.

8. D. Different storage media require different destruction approaches. For example, overwriting can be sufficient for magnetic media but not for solid-state drives. The sensitivity of the data also affects the level of assurance required. Selecting methods based on these factors ensures that data is rendered unrecoverable.

9. C. Providing data to a service provider typically involves both disclosure and transfer. The receiving organization gains access to the data, and custody can shift for processing purposes. This scenario requires contractual controls, data protection measures, and compliance with applicable privacy regulations.

10. B. A retention schedule establishes the duration for which specific categories of data must be stored. It also identifies when data should be archived or destroyed. This structured approach ensures consistent application of retention requirements across the organization.

11. C. Aggregation reduces the level of detail associated with individual data subjects. By using summarized or grouped data, organizations limit identifiability and reduce privacy risk. This aligns with minimization principles during data processing and analytics.

12. D. Archived data often contains sensitive or regulated information and might remain stored for extended periods. Without proper access controls, encryption, and monitoring, archived data can become a source of overlooked exposure. Attackers frequently target archival storage because it might have weaker protections.

13. A. Cryptographic erasure involves deleting or destroying encryption keys associated with encrypted data. Without the keys, the data cannot be decrypted and is effectively unrecoverable. This method is efficient for large volumes of encrypted data and is commonly used in cloud and storage environments.

14. D. Data migration refers to transferring data between systems, typically during upgrades, consolidation, or modernization efforts. The data remains within the organization, and the purpose is continuity of operations. Migration requires careful planning to preserve integrity, accuracy, and security.

15. C. A certificate of destruction documents that data or media have been securely destroyed using an approved method. This documentation supports audits, demonstrates compliance with retention requirements, and provides accountability for destruction activities.

16. A. Removing unnecessary fields limits the amount of personal or sensitive information retained. This allows the organization to meet compliance obligations while reducing privacy risk. Minimization can occur even when data must be retained for regulatory purposes.

17. C. Organizations often must retain certain records for statutory, contractual, or historical reasons. Archiving allows them to remove data from active systems while preserving it for required use. This approach balances operational efficiency with compliance obligations.

18. D. Privacy laws and regulations can restrict cross-border transfers. Organizations must evaluate whether appropriate safeguards, contractual clauses, or adequacy mechanisms are required. Failure to address jurisdictional requirements can result in regulatory violations.

19. D. Solid-state drives can retain data after traditional deletion or formatting due to wear-leveling mechanisms. Overwriting is often ineffective on solid-state drives. Physical destruction or cryptographic erasure provides higher assurance that data cannot be recovered. These methods are recommended for highly sensitive information.

20. B. Providing derived or aggregated results constitutes disclosure because information is being shared. However, the underlying dataset is not transferred, and custody remains with the originating organization. This distinction affects contractual and governance requirements.

Technology Stacks

This chapter covers CDPSE Domain 4, "Privacy Engineering," specifically the "Technology Stacks" subdomain.

This chapter covers these job practice elements:

✔ A—TECHNOLOGY STACKS

1. *Infrastructure and Platform Technology (e.g., legacy, cloud computing)*
2. *Devices and Endpoints*
3. *Connectivity*
4. *Secure Development Life Cycle*
5. *APIs and Cloud-native Services*

The other subdomains in Domain 4, Privacy Engineering, are:

✔ *B—PRIVACY-RELATED SECURITY CONTROLS*—covered in Chapter 8, and

✔ *C—PRIVACY CONTROLS*—covered in Chapter 9.

The CDPSE Task Statement relevant to this domain is:

7. *Collaborate with stakeholders to promote privacy principles (e.g., privacy by design) are followed during the design, development, and implementation of systems, applications, and infrastructure.*

The topics in this chapter and in Chapters 8 and 9 account for 39% of the CDPSE examination.

Technology infrastructure relates to privacy in this way: part of privacy involves governing the proper handling of stored personal information, and part involves protecting it—this is the discipline of information security. For a professional to be proficient in information security, they must understand how the underlying technology infrastructure works. It is often said that if you don't understand how the technology works, you cannot possibly know how to protect it.

Applications and software relate to privacy in this way: individual users interact with information technology primarily through business applications that track and record transactions and other activities. At times, this tracking is intrusive, and organizations sometimes fail to protect such tracking data. A privacy professional who wants to be proficient in information security must understand how business applications work. Privacy and security by design are not part of many organizations' business processes, which has led to serious flaws that result in invasions of privacy and breaches of personal information.

Infrastructure and Platform Technology

Effective privacy needs effective security. Effective security needs an IT architecture with integrity and protective controls. One common way IT architecture is discussed is as a *technology stack*, often referred to as a *service stack*. The technology stack is the set of *infrastructure* components that make up a system, often expressed in bottom-up notation, such as Linux-Apache-MySQL-Perl or Windows-IIS-SQL-ASP.NET. These are shorthand ways to describe the major building blocks of a system. There's an even shorter way to express technology stacks. For example, *LAMP* is Linux-Apache-MySQL-PHP/Perl/Python, and *WISA* is Windows-IIS-SQL-ASP.NET. More than a dozen such stack names are in use—IT people love their acronyms. Editorially, LAMP is exceedingly popular, in part because all its components are open source. Thus, the industry probably has tens of thousands of capable professionals familiar with the design and operation of dynamic web servers (of which the world has billions).

To round out the discussion of technology stacks, a similar term is used to describe the components of a software development environment: *development stacks*. For example, Eclipse-Subversion-Jenkins describes the components in a development stack. In this example, Eclipse is the desktop tool that developers use to write and debug code, Subversion is the source code repository, and Jenkins is the automated build and deploy environment. Look into the Certified Secure Software Lifecycle Professional (CSSLP) certification from ISC2[1] for more insight into secure software development.

Exam Tip

The CDPSE job practice touches on the secure development lifecycle and its concepts, but it provides no further discussion of development stacks in the job practice, and I don't discuss it further in this book.

Hardware

Hardware is the physical machinery used in IT computing and communications. Hardware comes in many forms, including *mainframes*, *servers*, network devices such as *routers* and *firewalls*, laptop computers, and smartphones. The fundamental concepts of hardware are discussed in this section.

As mentioned, security professionals can protect organizations only to the extent that they understand all of the underlying technology in use. This is an accurate assertion, because security professionals (and today, privacy professionals) lacking this knowledge will fail to recognize unsafe practices that can lead to the compromise of systems and the loss or exposure of sensitive and personal information.

This book covers the basics of hardware; more detailed explanations can be found in certification study guides written by this author for the CISA, CISM, and CISSP certifications.

Computers

Computers are general-purpose machines that run operating system software, which in turn runs subsystem or application software. Computers consist of the following components:

- *Central processing unit (CPU)* This is the component in which software instructions are decoded and executed. Many computers consist of multiple processors within a single CPU chip (those individual processors are known as *cores*), which improve performance.

[1] ISACA lacks a certification or certificate on secure software development, hence the mention of the ISC2 CSSLP. ISACA's CRISC and CISM address secure software development, but not in depth as does CSSLP.

- *Main storage* Commonly known as *random access memory (RAM)*, this is the high-speed memory used by the CPU to store the contents of programs currently being run. The computer's operating system will also occupy some of the computer's RAM. Main memory is generally volatile—that is, when power is removed from the computer, the contents of main memory are lost.
- *Secondary storage* This is a computer's permanent storage, traditionally on hard disk drives (HDDs), but more commonly on solid-state drives (SSDs) because of their superior performance. Secondary memory is used to store the operating system, programs, tools, and data within organized structures known as *file systems*. Unlike main storage memory, which is volatile, secondary storage memory is *persistent* and retains its contents even when power is removed from the computer.
- *Bus* This is the means of communication among various components of the computer, including its CPU, main storage, secondary storage, and adapters. Modern computers often have more than one bus—one or more for internal communications, and one or more for external communications via adapters. Bus standards in use include *Universal Serial Bus (USB)*.
- Adapters These plug-in devices connect other components (sometimes called *peripheral devices*, or peripherals) to a computer, such as additional storage, networks, printers, monitors, and keyboards. On larger computers (desktop, server, mainframe), adapters are separate components that plug into special connectors. In laptop computers, tablets, and smartphones, adapters are integrated into the computer's main logic board and are not removable.

Storage

Aside from storage within computers themselves, server and mainframe computers often employ separate storage systems for storing large amounts of data in database management systems, as well as unstructured storage. Storage systems are configured by organizing one or more *volumes*, within which file systems are created, and data of some kind is stored. Volumes can vary in size, and often their size can be adjusted dynamically.

Types of storage systems used include:

- *Storage area network (SAN)* This standalone storage system can be configured to contain several virtual volumes and can be connected to many servers through fiber-optic cables.
- *Network-attached storage (NAS)* This standalone storage system can be configured to contain multiple virtual volumes and connected to servers via a local area network (LAN).
- Cloud-based storage In this subscription service, a storage service provider employs large storage systems that organizations access over the Internet or dedicated communications connections.

Storage systems must be reliable. A common standard in place to ensure reliability is a *redundant array of independent disks (RAID)*. RAID ensures that data remains intact and available even if one or more hard drives fail within the storage system.

Networks

Networks are the means through which computers communicate with one another. Whether networked computers are in a single room or spread across the globe, and whether a telecommunications company is involved, networks facilitate all computer communications, both wired and wireless. Network technology is discussed later in this chapter and in Chapter 8.

Exam Tip

The CDPSE exam requires only a cursory understanding of computing and networking hardware.

Operating Systems

Computer *operating systems (OSs)* are large, general-purpose programs that control computer hardware and facilitate the use of software applications. Operating systems perform the following functions:

- **Access to peripheral devices** The operating system controls and manages access to all devices and adapters connected to the computer. This includes storage devices, display devices, and communications adapters.
- **Storage management** The operating system provides for the orderly storage of information on storage hardware. For example, operating systems provide file system management for storing files and directories on SSDs or hard drives.
- **Process management** Operating systems facilitate the existence of multiple *processes*, some of which are computer applications and tools. Operating systems ensure that each process has private memory space and is protected from interference and eavesdropping by other processes. These safeguards are collectively known as *process isolation*.
- **Resource allocation** Operating systems facilitate the sharing of resources on a computer, such as memory, communication, and display devices.
- **Communication** Operating systems facilitate communication with users via peripheral devices and with other computers through networking. Operating systems typically have drivers and tools to facilitate network communications.
- **Security** Operating systems restrict access to protected resources through process, user, and device authentication.

Examples of popular operating systems include Linux, Solaris, macOS, Android, iOS, Chrome OS, and Microsoft Windows.

The traditional context of the relationship between operating systems and computer hardware is this: one copy of a computer operating system runs on a computer at any given time. Virtualization, however, has changed all of that. Virtualization is discussed later in this section.

Server Clustering

Using special software, a group of two or more computers can be configured to operate as a *cluster*. This means the group of computers will *appear* as a single computer for the purpose of providing services. Within the cluster, one computer will be active, and the other computer(s) will be in passive mode. If the active computer experiences a hardware or software failure and crashes, the passive computer(s) will transition to active mode and continue providing service. This is known as *active-passive* mode. The transition is called a *failover*.

Clusters can also operate in *active-active* mode, where all computers in the cluster provide service; in the event of a computer failure, the remaining computer(s) will continue providing service.

Server clusters are often fronted with a *load balancer*, a network device that distributes incoming transactions across the cluster to maintain balanced utilization and prevent overload.

Grid Computing

Grid computing is a technique for distributing a problem or task across multiple computers, leveraging each computer's processing power to solve the problem or complete the task more quickly. Grid computing is a form of distributed computing, but in grid computing, the computers are coupled more loosely, and the number of computers participating in solving a problem can be dynamically expanded or contracted at will.

Virtualization

Virtualization refers to the set of technologies that enable two or more operating systems (of the same type or different types) to run on a single physical computer. Virtualization technology enables organizations to use computing resources more efficiently.

Before I explain the benefits of virtualization, I should first state one of the principles of computer infrastructure management: it is a sound practice to use a server for one single purpose. Using a single server for multiple purposes can introduce a few problems, such as these:

- Tools or applications that reside on a single computer could interfere with one another.
- Tools or applications that reside on a single computer could interact with one another or compete for shared resources.
- A tool or application on a server could, although rarely, cause the entire server to stop running; on a server with multiple tools or applications, it could cause the others to stop functioning.

Before virtualization, the most stable configuration for running many applications and tools was to run each on a separate server. This would, however, result in highly inefficient use of computers and capital, as most computers running a single operating system spend much of their time idle.

Virtualization allows IT departments to run multiple applications or tools on a single physical server, each within its own operating system, thereby making more efficient use of computers (not to mention electric power and data center space). Virtualization software emulates computer hardware so that an operating system running in a virtualized environment does not know that it is running on a *virtual machine*. Virtualization software, known as a *hypervisor*, includes resource allocation settings so that each *guest* (a running operating system) has a specific amount of memory, hard disk space, and other peripherals available for its use. Virtualization also facilitates the sharing of peripheral devices, such as network connectors, so that many guests can use an individual network connector. However, each will have its own unique IP address.

Virtualization is the basis of cloud-based infrastructure-as-a-service (IaaS) offerings from Amazon AWS, Google Cloud, and Microsoft Azure.

Virtualization software provides security by isolating each running operating system and preventing it from accessing or interfering with other operating systems. This is like the concept of *process isolation* within a running operating system, where a process is not permitted to access resources used by other processes.

A server with running virtual machines is depicted in Figure 7.1.

Many security issues need to be considered in a virtualization environment, including:

- **Access control** Access to virtualization management and monitoring functions should be restricted to those personnel who require it.
- **Resource allocation** A virtualization environment needs to be carefully configured so that each virtual machine is given the resources it requires to function correctly and perform adequately.

FIGURE 7.1 Virtualization.

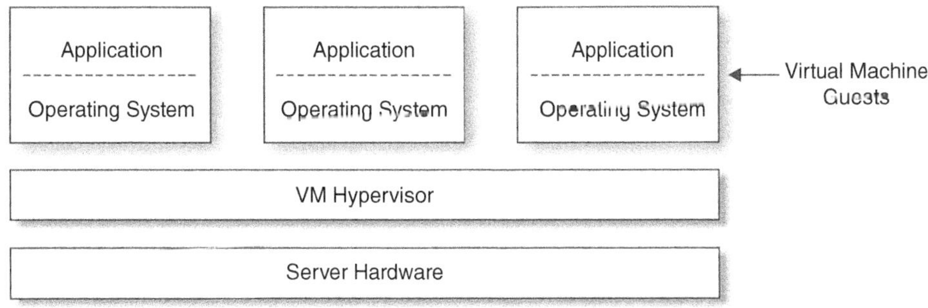

Source: Author.

- **Logging and monitoring** Virtual environments need to be carefully monitored so that any sign of security compromise will be quickly recognized and acted on.
- **Hardening** Virtual environments need to be configured so that only necessary services and features are enabled, and all unnecessary services and features are either disabled or removed.
- **Vulnerability management** Virtualization environments need to be monitored as closely as operating systems and other software so that the IT organization is aware of newly discovered security vulnerabilities and available patches.

Cloud Computing

Cloud computing refers to *cloud*-based, dynamically scalable, and usually virtualized computing resources that are used internally or provided as a service. Cloud computing services can be rented or leased, allowing an organization to have scalable application environments without the need for supporting hardware or a data center. Cloud computing can include networking, computing, and application services in an IaaS, software-as-a-service (SaaS), or platform-as-a-service (PaaS) model. Cloud computing is discussed in more detail later in this chapter.

Containerization

Containerization is a form of virtualization, whereby multiple applications run within a single operating system. Each such application is completely isolated from all others and can access only the resources allocated to its container.

Containerization is a different approach for providing isolated resources to applications in large environments. Suppose, for example, that an engineer wants to run ten isolated applications on a physical server. With virtualization, the engineer would create 10 virtual machines, each running a full operating system and one application. In containerization, the engineer would run a single OS instance with ten containers, one for each application.

The primary advantage of containerization over virtualization is the more efficient use of hardware resources. One disadvantage of containerization is that all containers run on a single version of the operating system, whereas in virtualization, multiple operating systems can run in virtual machines.

File Systems

A *file system* is a logical structure that facilitates the storage of data on a digital storage medium such as a hard drive, SSD, optical disc, or flash memory device. The structure of the file system facilitates the creation, modification, expansion and contraction, and deletion of data files. A file system can also be used to enforce access controls, determining which users or processes are permitted to access, alter, or create files.

It can also be said that a file system is a special-purpose database designed for storing and managing files.

Modern file systems employ a storage hierarchy that consists of two main elements:

- **Directories** A *directory* is a structure that is used to store files. A file system can contain one or more directories, each of which can contain files and subdirectories. The topmost directory in a file system is usually called the "root" directory. A file system can exist as a hierarchy of information, in the same way that a building can contain several file rooms, each containing several file cabinets, which contain drawers that contain dividers, folders, and documents. Directories are called *folders* in some computing environments.
- **Files** A *file* is a sequence of zero or more characters that are stored as a logical whole. A file can be a document, a spreadsheet, an image, a sound file, a computer program, or data that is used by a program. A file can be as small as zero characters in length (an empty file) or as large as many gigabytes (trillions of characters). A file occupies units of storage on storage media (which could be a hard disk, SSD, or flash memory device, for example) that can be called blocks or sectors; however, the file system hides these underlying details from the user so that the file can be known simply by its name, the directory in which it resides, and its contents.

Well-known file systems in use today include the following:

- ***File Allocation Table (FAT)*** This file system has been used in MS-DOS and early versions of Microsoft Windows, and it is often used as the file system on portable media devices such as flash drives. Versions of FAT include FAT12, FAT16, and FAT32. FAT does not support security access controls, including the specification of access permissions for files and directories. FAT also does not include any journaling (the process of recording changes made to a file system, which aids in file system recovery) features, making it more vulnerable to corruption if power is removed during write operations.
- ***NT File System (NTFS)*** This is used in newer versions of Windows, including desktop and server editions. NTFS supports file- and directory-based access control and file system journaling.
- ***Resilient File System (ReFS)*** This file system is available on Windows Server 2012 and later versions and is complementary to NTFS for large-scale storage.
- ***EXT4*** This journaled file system is used by the Linux operating system.
- ***Hierarchical File System Plus (HFS+)*** This file system has been used on computers running the Apple macOS operating system.
- ***Apple File System (APFS)*** This file system is used on computers running the Apple macOS operating system and replaced HFS+ starting with Mac OS X 10.13 (High Sierra).
- ***ISO/IEC 9660*** This file system is used by CD-ROM media.
- ***Universal Disk Format (UDF)*** This optical media file system is considered a replacement for ISO/IEC 9660. UDF is widely used on rewritable optical media such as DVDs and Blu-ray.

Database Management Systems

A *database management system (DBMS)* is a software program or collection of programs that facilitates the storage and retrieval of potentially large amounts of structured information residing in a *database*. Controlled by a *database server*, a DBMS provides methods for inserting, updating, and removing data; computer programs and applications can use these functions to manipulate data in the database. A DBMS also usually includes authentication and access control, thereby enabling control over which users and programs can access which data.

DBMS Organization

Most DBMSs employ a *data definition language (DDL)* to define the structure of the data in a database. The DDL defines the types of data stored in the database as well as relationships between different portions of that data.

DBMSs employ a *data dictionary (DD)* or directory system (DS) to store information about the internal structure of databases. To understand how they relate to each other, you can think of the DDL as the instructions for building a database's structure and data relationships; the DD or DS is where the database's structure and relationships are stored and used by the DBMS.

DBMSs also employ a data manipulation language (DML) for inserting, deleting, and updating data in a database. SQL is a popular DML that is used in the Oracle and SQL Server DBMSs.

DBMS Structure

Three principal types of DBMSs are in use today: relational, *object*, and *hierarchical*. Each is described in this section.

Relational Database Management Systems

The *relational database management system (RDBMS)* represents the most popular model used for DBMSs. A relational database permits the design of a structured, logical representation of information.

Many relational databases are accessed and updated using the *Structured Query Language (SQL)*. Standardized by ISO/IEC and ANSI, SQL is used in many popular relational DBMS products, including Oracle Database, Microsoft SQL Server, MySQL, and IBM DB2.

RDBMS Basic Concepts

A relational database consists of one or more *tables*. A table can be thought of as a simple list of records, such as lines in a data file. The records in a table are often called *rows*, and the different data items that appear in each row are usually called *fields*.

A table often has a *primary key*, which is simply one of the table's fields that contains values that are unique within the table. For example, a table of healthcare patients can include each patient's identification number, which can serve as the table's primary key.

One or more indexes can be built for a table. An *index* facilitates rapid searching for specific records in a table based on the value of a field other than the primary key. For instance, a table that contains a list of assets and their serial numbers can have an index of the table's serial numbers. This will enable a rapid search for a record with a specific serial number; without the index, RDBMS software would have to examine every record in the table sequentially until the desired record was found.

One of the most powerful features of a relational database is the use of foreign keys. A *foreign key* is a field in a record in one table that can reference a primary key in another table. For example, a table that lists sales orders includes fields that are foreign keys, each referencing records in other tables. This is shown in Figure 7.2.

Relational databases enforce *referential integrity*. This means the database will not permit a program (or user) to delete a row from a table if any records in other tables reference the row to be deleted via foreign keys. The database will instead return an error code that signals to the requesting program that rows in other tables would be "stranded" if the row were deleted. Using the example in Figure 7.2, a relational database will not permit a program to delete salesperson #2 or #4 from the Salesperson table, because records in the Orders table reference those rows.

FIGURE 7.2 Fields in a sales orders table point to records in other tables.

Orders Table

date	cust #	salesperson #	
09152009	461	4	
09152009	277	4	
09152009	16	8	
09152009	129	9	
09162009	849	4	
09162009	97	2	

Customers Table

cust #	last name	first name
15	Jones	Christopher
16	Turner	Dell
17	Freeland	Brad
18	Green	Byron

Salesperson Table

salesperson #	last name	first name
2	Crawford	Bill
3	Ramos	Tom
4	Tavernia	Paul

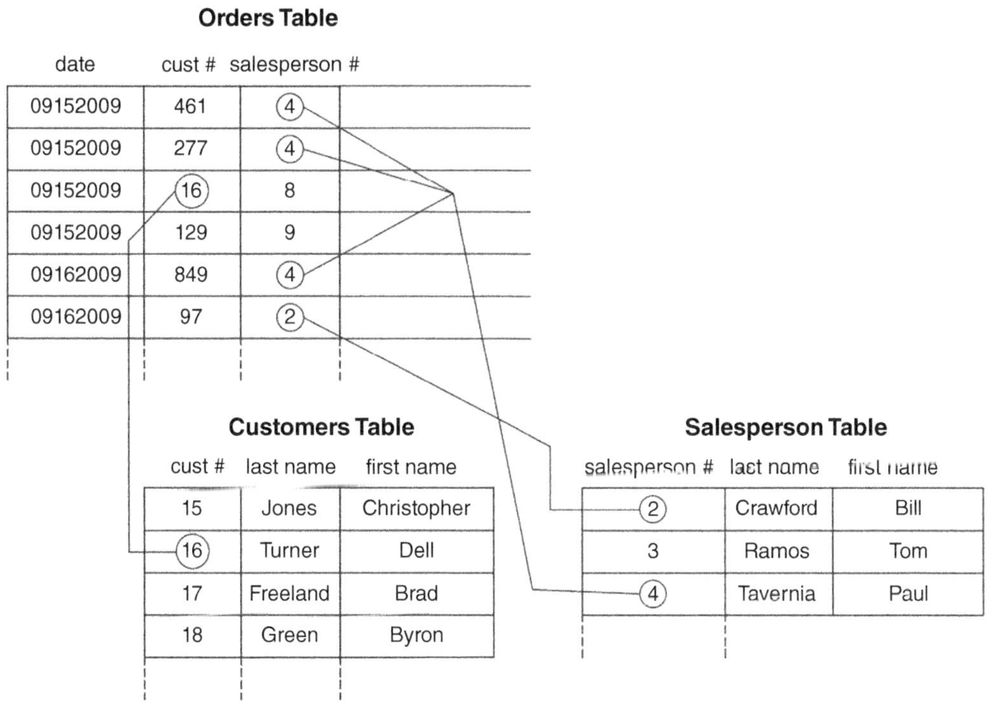

Source: Author.

The power of relational databases comes from their design and from SQL. Queries are used to find one or more records from a table using the `SELECT` statement. An example statement is

```
SELECT * FROM Orders WHERE Price > 100 ORDER BY Customer
```

One powerful feature of relational databases is a special query called a *join*, which retrieves records from two or more tables in a single query. An example join query is

```
SELECT Salesperson.Name, count(*) AS Orders FROM Salesperson JOIN
Salesperson_Number ON Salesperson.Number = Orders.Salesperson GROUP BY
Salesperson.Name
```

This query will produce a list of salespersons and the number of orders they have sold.

Relational Database Security

Relational databases in commercial applications need to have some security features, including these three primary security features:

- **Access controls** Most relational databases have access controls at the table and field levels, so that a database can permit or deny a user the ability to read data from or write data to a specific table or even a specific field. To enforce access controls, the database needs to authenticate users so that it knows the identity of each user making access requests. DBMSs employ a *data control language (DCL)* to control access to data in a database.
- **Encryption** Sensitive data, such as financial or medical records, might need to be encrypted. Some relational databases provide field-level encryption, allowing a user or application to specify which fields should be encrypted. Encryption protects the data by making it difficult for an intruder to read the contents of the database if the database is obtained by illicit means.
- **Audit logging** DBMSs provide audit logging features that enable an administrator or auditor to view some or all activities that take place in a database. Audit logging can show precisely what activities take place, including details of database changes and the users who made them. The audit logs themselves can be protected so they resist tampering, making it difficult for someone to modify data and erase their tracks.

Database administrators can also create *views*, which are virtual tables created via stored queries. Views can simplify viewing data by aggregating or filtering data. They can improve security by exposing only certain records or fields to users.

NoSQL

NoSQL DBMSs are nonrelational and designed to support large, sometimes disparate, datasets across multiple systems. Several types of NoSQL databases are in use, including Column, Document, Key-Value, and Graph. The motivation for using NoSQL databases is primarily their applicability and usefulness: relational databases are not always the best choice for every application.

Application Servers

An *application server* is a system that runs one or more business software applications that are designed to support one or more business processes. The application(s) run under the control of a server operating system (such as Linux, Windows, Solaris, AIX, IBM I, or z/OS), which in turn either runs directly on server hardware, under the control of a hypervisor as a virtual machine, or in a container.

Modern business applications communicate with a DBMS where business records are stored and processed. These DBMSs can reside on the same operating system or, more typically, on a separate server.

Business applications that interact with humans typically communicate with a *web server* (which might be on the same operating system) or via APIs with companion mobile apps running on tablets and smartphones.

More details about software applications are found later in this chapter.

Devices and Endpoints

An *endpoint* is any of several types of end-user devices, including desktop computers, laptop computers, *tablet computers*, and *smartphones*. The term can also refer to *connected devices*, which are discussed later in this chapter.

In some organizations, endpoints include connected devices in the categories of *Internet of Things (IoT)*, *industrial control systems (ICS)*, and *supervisory control and data acquisition (SCADA)*. Other organizations use the terms IoT, ICS, SCADA, and so on, to distinguish these endpoints from those used by end users. Industry lexicons are still developing in this area, and there is no final consensus yet on the precise definitions of these terms.

Laptop and Desktop Computers

Laptop and desktop computers are the mainstays of end-user computing in most organizations. For the most part, IT departments issue laptops or desktop computers to employees and use a service desk to support end users with questions or problems about their computers. Microsoft Windows remains the dominant laptop and desktop operating system, with Apple macOS also widely used. Some organizations also support ChromeOS on Chromebooks as well as the Linux operating system.

Configuration Management

Configuration management refers to the process of determining configuration settings on various types of devices, and of recording and maintaining these configurations. Organizations often develop *configuration management standards* that define the required configuration settings for systems and devices. Configuration management is critical for information security, as properly and consistently configured systems and devices are more resilient than those whose configurations are not well managed, if at all.

For improved efficiency and security, most organizations employ standard computer *images*, which are preconfigured operating systems with all configurations, security, agents, and tools preinstalled. Using images saves considerable time compared to installing all the tools and applications manually, which typically takes several hours.

IT departments generally use management tools to centrally manage the configuration of laptops and desktops across the organization. With a mouse click, an IT administrator can change a configuration setting on many or all the laptops and/or desktops in the organization.

Security and Privacy

Security configurations and tools on endpoints are critical. Without robust security architectures and effective security operations, endpoints would be quickly compromised by attackers, resulting in malware that will cause a variety of harmful issues, including theft of login credentials, theft of stored data, *spam*, *viruses*, *spyware*, and *ransomware*.

Organizations generally implement essential security capabilities on endpoints:

- **Antimalware** Whether they are traditional *antivirus* software or more advanced *antimalware* programs, these tools detect, block, and remove most virus and malware attacks when they occur.
- **Firewall** These are especially important for laptop computers, which are often used away from the corporate network and its firewall(s) protecting all endpoints.

In addition, many organizations also employ one or more of these security tools on endpoints:

- ***Intrusion prevention system (IPS)*** Similar to an enterprise network IPS, this detects and blocks attacks.
- ***Data loss prevention (DLP)*** These tools have a variety of capabilities, including monitoring and controlling the handling of sensitive information. DLP is an important tool that provides organizations with specific visibility and control over the handling of data containing personal information.
- ***Application allowlisting*** Formerly known as application whitelisting, this is used to restrict which applications are permitted to run on an endpoint.
- ***Web content filtering*** This is used to protect endpoints from malicious websites in *watering-hole attacks* and to block access to websites based on their subject matter.
- ***Endpoint detection and response (EDR)*** These tools are used to monitor, detect, investigate, and respond to threats on endpoint devices. EDR represents continued innovation on what started as simple antivirus tools.

Further, in many organizations, end users are not local administrators on their laptops and desktops. This helps to reduce the number and impact of end user support issues and the impact of successful malware attacks.

Support

In all but the smallest organizations, IT departments use tools that enable *service desk* personnel to access end-user laptops and desktops remotely. This kind of administrative access takes two forms: First, an end user can "share their screen" with an administrator who can temporarily take control of the computer to troubleshoot an issue or show a user how to operate a program. Second, an administrator can access a user's computer *without* the user's knowledge or consent. The latter method can be used as part of an investigation or in other circumstances where IT must better understand either the contents of the computer or the actions taking place on it, without the user's knowledge.

Virtual Desktop Infrastructure

While the desktop computing paradigm has been popular for decades, *virtual desktop infrastructure (VDI)* technology is gaining in popularity. In VDI, the programs and storage are on centralized servers that use a remote display protocol to give end users the appearance of local computing. VDI offers operational, security, and privacy advantages:

- Central control of desktop operating systems
- Less expensive endpoint computers, since they are not storing any data or running applications
- Improved security through network access restriction—endpoints can be permitted to communicate only with their VDI servers
- Better control of sensitive and personal information, since it is never stored on endpoints

The primary disadvantage of VDI is that a network connection is always required to run programs and access data. However, hybrid environments can also be engineered to allow occasional local storage of data.

Mobile Devices

The power and ubiquity of *mobile devices* make them excellent candidates for conducting business while away from the workplace or home office. Virtually every office worker owns a *smartphone* capable of connecting to company email, running browsers and applications, and storing copious amounts of data.

Allowing workers to use personally owned mobile devices to access company email and apps can make them far more productive. Workers often check their email before and after work, on weekends, and even on vacation. The flexibility of always being connected means workers are no longer tethered to workplaces or home offices.

To mitigate risks, including data leakage and credential theft, many organizations actively manage mobile devices with *mobile device management (MDM)* systems that enforce security configurations and further protect sensitive and personal information. Some MDM products can prevent end users from inadvertently leaking company information by restricting local file storage and handling. *Mobile application management (MAM)* systems are similar to MDM and focus on securing applications rather than the entire device. Of particular interest to privacy professionals, some MDM or MAM systems include *data loss prevention (DLP)* capabilities, or DLP tools are used separately, to monitor and control the flow of personal information.

The problem with personally owned mobile devices, however, is that they are not the organization's property, meaning the organization does not have complete control over them. This poses a problem for organizations that need visibility into and control over data usage and movement.

Bring Your Own ...

The phenomenon of *bring-your-own-device (BYOD)* began in the early 1990s when organizations first created "remote access." BYOD accelerated in the 2000s with the Apple iPhone and its native ability to connect directly with organizations' email servers, thereby bringing business email to personally owned devices without the consent, assistance, or visibility from company IT departments. Although organizations slowly responded by restricting such access, they had no choice but to accept the trend and manage it accordingly.

Another significant hotbed of BYOD lies in the remote access capability. Most organizations' VPN services do not verify whether the computer requesting remote access is a company-owned, company-managed machine. Consequently, many workers accessing company networks and systems remotely from home use their personally owned computers rather than their corporate-issued laptops. This, too, represents a significant data leakage risk, as organizations will be completely blind to what their workers do with sensitive data once it leaves their control.

BYOD is like *bring-your-own-apps (BYOA)*; in this case, an organization's employees load personally owned applications onto their company-issued computers, or even use free or nominal-cost cloud apps to store or process sensitive and personal information.

To counter BYOD and BYOA, IT departments must implement additional controls, including the following:

- *Network access control (NAC)* This protocol controls which devices are permitted to connect to a wired or wireless network, as well as by remote access. MAC address filtering can also be used, but it does not scale well for larger organizations.
- *Application allowlisting* This tool permits only approved programs to execute on a computer.
- *Cloud access security broker (CASB)* This tool manages and controls users' access to cloud servers, preventing interactions with cloud services not permitted by the organization. Web content filtering can also perform this function in many cases.
- *Data loss prevention (DLP)* These tools observe and restrict the movement of files containing sensitive and personal information. This can help prevent data from being exported to cloud-based services not permitted by the organization.
- *User behavior analytics (UBA)* These tools observe network and system patterns over time and generate alerts when anomalous events occur.

Zero-trust Architecture

The concept of *zero-trust (ZT)* represents a new way of thinking about information security. Traditionally, information security focused on protecting and controlling an entire computing and network ecosystem, including servers and data, endpoints, and the networks that connect them. The perimeter was vast and included everything in the organization's control.

Zero-trust changes all of that. First, it changes the definition of the perimeter from that of the entire enterprise to microperimeters near the actual information being protected. These concepts are part of zero-trust:

- **Untrusted endpoints** With regard to the protection of sensitive and personal information, end-user computing is considered untrusted, as though the organization's users were on the Internet with unmanaged, untrusted endpoints.
- **Untrusted data center systems** With regard to the protection of data in DBMSs, database servers no longer blindly trust all systems in the data center, but instead require any system (such as an application server) to authenticate itself.
- **Untrusted networks** With regard to the security of application servers, these servers no longer accept incoming connections from endpoints on enterprise networks without first requiring strong authentication. Also, from the perspective of data center networks, all other networks, including end-user networks and the Internet, are considered untrusted and hazardous.

Connected Devices and Operational Technology

If the endpoints, mobile devices, servers, *appliances*, and network devices in the IT ecosystem are the "visible part of an iceberg," then the world of *connected devices*, ICSs, and SCADA systems is located "below the surface." In many industries, including energy, public utilities, manufacturing, air traffic control, medical research, and more, legions of devices of all kinds communicate with one another over data networks. And many of these devices have been in use for decades.

There has been an explosion of connected devices in the consumer world as well. Doorbells, televisions, thermostats, kitchen appliances, light switches, barbecue grills, security cameras, medical devices, and automobiles—nearly everything is connected to networks, and much is connected to the Internet itself.

Privacy and security are often overlooked in the design and implementation of many of these so-called "smart" devices, but these issues abound and are not easily managed or mitigated. Consider the following:

- Poorly designed security, or no security at all
- Lack of security update capability—no way to patch devices already in use
- Devices running outdated and unsupported versions of operating systems and subsystems
- Troves of backend data containing biometric information, images, location data, financial data, and medical data—all waiting to be compromised and stolen

- Poorly designed security controls protecting critical infrastructure, including power generation and distribution, water supply and treatment, vital manufacturing facilities, air traffic control, and more
- Increased connectivity between these control networks, with office worker networks and the Internet itself, exposes these control networks to attacks

The heightened importance and inherent weaknesses of connected devices compel organizations to implement additional protective controls, such as network segmentation, to isolate these devices from the rest of the organization. Tight access controls restrict access to and from these networks, and diligent monitoring of communications within them is used to detect anomalies that can be signs of tampering or intrusion.

The other side of the problem of connected devices is the information they gather, some of which relates to individual people. This information includes:

- Location history—detailed accounts of the individual's whereabouts
- Facial recognition
- Financial transactions
- Medical information, including vital signs and health history

Arguably, numerous benefits are derived from collecting this information, including improvements in the quality of life for the people using the devices. But the accumulation of this information also increases the risk of major breaches if it is not fully protected against all threats.

The other dimension of the problem with these vast information stores, with myriad details about individuals' personal lives, is the potential misuse of this information. Without proper governance, organizations tend to "push the envelope" in how this personal information can be used.

Finally, there are abuses by government agencies that, through various means (legal and otherwise), can obtain all or parts of these information stores as a part of the "surveillance state."

Smart Devices: Back to the Security Stone Age

Just as major vendors were making security important in their products, and many organizations were getting their vulnerability management acts together, along came so-called smart devices. From a security perspective, most of them are simply awful: they use outdated, vulnerable libraries and operating systems, are poorly configured, and cannot be patched in the field. These devices are everywhere—in homes and businesses—and they are turning the world of infosec upside down because of their poor design and utter lack of support. They are a menace on networks today due to their poor security. Better organizations are taking matters into their own hands and either blocking them outright or placing them on well-defended, isolated networks, where their weaknesses can't hurt the rest of the organization.

In homes, these devices are spying on users, eavesdropping on conversations, leaking personal data, and joining botnets. Unlike with better organizations, most home users don't know or fully appreciate the hazards posed by these devices.

Connectivity

Connectivity refers to the ability for applications and systems to communicate with other applications and systems over network connections. Connectivity is a big topic, and it's covered in this book as follows:

- **Network media** Chapter 8
- **Network protocols (TCP/IP)** Chapter 8
- **Network architecture** Chapter 8
- **Remote access** In the next section

Remote Access

Remote access is the means of providing connectivity to an internal corporate network through a secure data link. Many organizations provide remote access so that employees who are temporarily or permanently off-site can access internal network resources from their remote locations.

Remote access was initially provided via dial-up modems with authentication. While remote dial-up is still available in some instances, most remote access is provided over the Internet. It typically uses an encrypted tunnel, or virtual private network (VPN), to protect transmissions from eavesdroppers. VPNs are so prevalent in remote access technology that the terms VPN and remote access have become synonymous. Remote access architectures are depicted in Figure 7.3.

Two security controls are essential for remote access:

- **Authentication** It is necessary to know who is requesting access to the corporate LAN. Authentication might use the same user ID and password personnel use on-site, or multifactor authentication might be required.
- **Encryption** Many on-site network applications do not encrypt sensitive traffic because it is all contained within the physically and logically protected corporate LAN. However, because remote access serves the same function as being on the corporate LAN, and because the applications themselves usually do not provide encryption, the remote access service typically provides encryption.

Authentication and encryption are needed because they serve as a substitute (or *compensating control*) for the physical access controls typically in place to control which personnel can enter the building to use the on-site corporate network. When personnel are on-site, their identity is confirmed through keycard or other physical access controls. When personnel are offsite using remote access, because the organization cannot "see" the person on the far end of the remote access connection, the authentication used is a substitute.

Credential-stealing malware is a significant problem. As a result, organizations are implementing multifactor authentication for access to internal resources, regardless of users' location—whether they are on a corporate network, working from home, in the field, or traveling.

FIGURE 7.3 Remote access architectures.

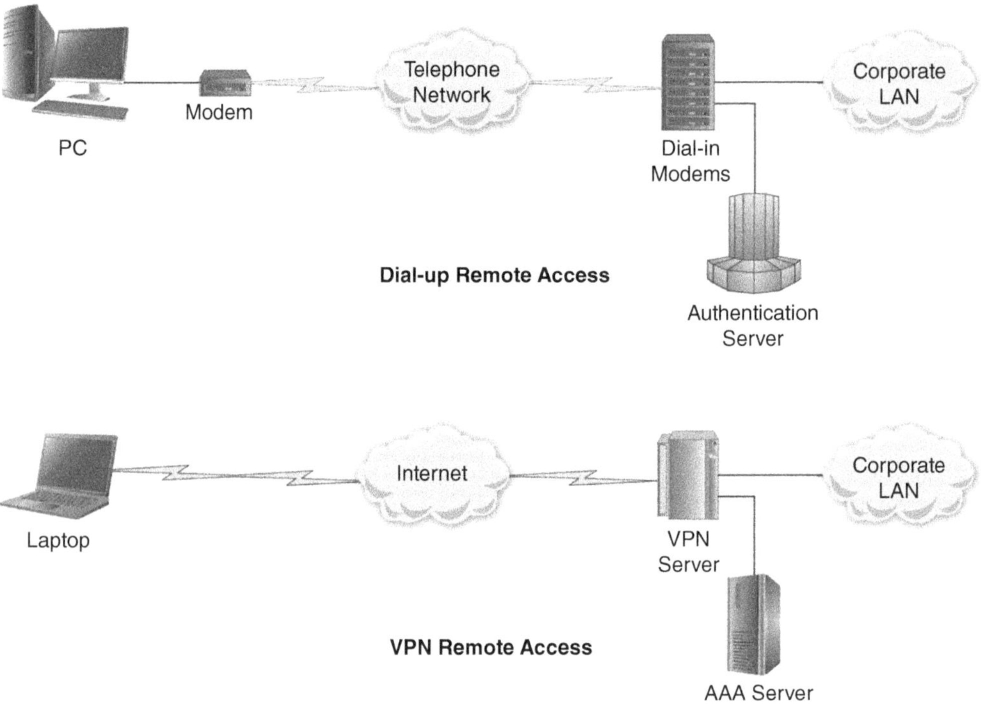

Source: Author.

The New Remote Access Paradigm

As organizations migrate their business applications to colocation centers and *XaaS* providers, and after the last internal resource is moved to the cloud, what is the point of remote access? Remote access to *what*?

If we think about this in terms of VPN and the protection afforded by encryption, VPN makes good business sense by protecting network traffic from potential eavesdroppers (whether human or malware). For this reason, it's preferred to use "VPN" instead of "remote access."

Organizations still need to address several subtopics when considering their VPN architectures considering cloud migration, such as split tunneling, Internet backhauling, and whether VPN should always automatically activate on workstations away from internal corporate networks.

Client VPN

A client VPN connection can be established using *VPN client* software. A VPN client is generally installed on an endpoint system like any other program, and it can be configured with settings, so that end users do not need to type in the name or IP address of the VPN server every time they want to establish a connection. Further, some VPN clients can be configured by organizations' IT departments with settings such as group passwords that end users cannot see.

A VPN connection can be initiated at will when an end user is ready to access internal network resources within the organization. Some organizations configure their endpoints so that VPN connections are "always on" whenever endpoints are connected to any network.

Clientless (SSL) VPN

Clientless VPN is so-called because no software—such as a VPN client—needs to be installed on endpoints. Instead, the endpoints' built-in networking capabilities are sufficient for setting up VPN connections. In these cases, a user will navigate to a special URL in a browser (such as `https://remote.company.com` or, hopefully, something not so easily guessed). The browser will facilitate the establishment of the VPN connection.

Clientless VPN is limited to web protocols such as HTTP and HTTPS. If other protocols, such as Remote Desktop Protocol (RDP) or Secure Shell (SSH), are required, additional technologies might need to be deployed, or a VPN client must be used to access these resources within internal networks.

Split Tunneling

Many VPN connections can establish a *split tunnel*, a characteristic of a VPN connection in which network traffic destined to the organization's internal network will traverse the VPN connection, while network traffic destined to the Internet will proceed directly to the Internet, bypassing the VPN connection. Split tunnels are sometimes preferred by organizations that do not care to carry high-bandwidth Internet traffic through their VPN infrastructures. However, a split tunnel—by design—will bypass an organization's network-based protective controls, potentially permitting an end user (or malware on the endpoint) to exfiltrate sensitive and private information.

Organizations that are more privacy or security-conscious will not permit split tunneling, and if they are concerned with high-bandwidth network services (such as streaming movies or music), they will direct their workers not to use these services while on VPN (if ever).

Secure Development Lifecycle

Civil engineers design bridges before their construction. Engineers first obtain requirements, which specify details such as the number of lanes on the bridge and the weight it is expected to carry. These engineers then consider other factors, such as wind, rain, snow, ice, heat, and cold, as well as potential weight loads on the bridge and environmental factors, such as landslides and soil instability, that threaten the integrity of the bridge pilings and other support structures.

Once the bridge is built, it must be maintained. This includes painting, checking and retightening fasteners, repairing the road surface, checking the foundations and abutments, and making careful measurements to ensure it remains in place and performs as designed.

Software development is not so different from designing and building bridges. Organizations gather requirements for the proposed software application (or operating system, tool, or other), including security and privacy requirements and any applicable compliance requirements. Design of the software program should not commence until all of these requirements are known. Likewise, development should not commence until the design is complete and reviewed and approved by stakeholders.

This section describes the end-to-end software development process, including well-known models such as Waterfall, DevOps, and DevSecOps.

The "S" in SDLC Now Stands for "Systems"—Or Does It?

IT and security professionals who have been in the business for more than ten years will sooner or later notice the switch in the well-known SDLC acronym. Originally, and for decades, SDLC referred to the *software development lifecycle*, as many organizations developed their own business applications and spent considerable effort maintaining and customizing them over many years.

Today, because of two changes that have occurred, the *S* in SDLC has been changed to *systems* to represent a broader perspective than just that of software applications: First, fewer organizations develop their own business application software and instead purchase off-the-shelf applications or (more often) subscribe to software-as-a-service (SaaS) services for their primary business applications. Second, the SDLC has been expanded to encompass projects such as infrastructure development.

The acronym SDLC also stands for *secure development lifecycle*, which is a way of expressing security by design in the systems/software development lifecycle. Terminology in IT has a way of changing quickly at times, and slowly at times. Since "SDLC" can mean any of the three (software, systems, secure), it's hard to say how this one will settle out.

SDLC Phases

The *systems development lifecycle (SDLC)* describes the end-to-end process for developing and maintaining information systems. A common structure for SDLC is a *waterfall*-style framework that consists of several distinct phases:

- Feasibility study
- Requirements definition
- Design
- Development
- Testing
- Implementation
- Post-implementation
- Maintenance
- Retirement

Organizations often employ a *gate process* approach to their SDLCs, requiring a formal review at the end of each phase before the next phase can begin. The review is usually a formal meeting where project managers and other participants present the project's status. Management, if satisfied that the current phase of the project has been completed successfully and that all requirements have been met, will then permit the project to proceed to the next phase.

In addition to the waterfall SDLC model, iterative and spiral models are used in SDLC processes. The iterative and spiral models both operate in (visually) circular modes, as opposed to the linear waterfall model. The *spiral* model consists of developing requirements, designing, and building one or more prototypes, followed by additional requirements and design phases until the entire design is complete. Similarly, the *iterative development* model progresses through one or more loops of planning, requirements, design, coding, and testing until development and implementation are considered complete.

The *DevOps* model is also often used for systems development processes. DevOps is an iterative development-and-operations model discussed later in this chapter. *DevSecOps* is a DevOps model that incorporates essential security and privacy measures.

SDLC in this section is described from the perspective of the waterfall model. The activities discussed in this section in the waterfall model are quite similar to those in the iterative and spiral models.

Feasibility Study

The *feasibility study* is an intellectual effort to determine whether a specific change or set of changes in business processes and underlying systems is practical to implement.

Often, the purpose of a feasibility study is not to answer the question, "Can a specific type of change be made to the business?" but rather, "Is a specific type of change to the business feasible from a cost and benefit perspective?" In other words, the feasibility study is an analysis of proposed changes to business processes and supporting applications, including the costs associated with those changes and the expected benefits. Although there is often a qualitative aspect in the feasibility study, there is almost always a quantitative aspect that states, "These specific changes will cost XXX to build, YYY to maintain, and are anticipated to make a ZZZ impact on revenue."

Organizations don't always make changes to business processes to increase revenue or reduce costs. However, revenue and costs are nearly always the quantitative elements that are considered. For example, if an organization is implementing changes to processes and systems to comply with new regulations, management will still be interested in the cost and revenue impacts the changes will have.

A feasibility study is not always done as a part of a "*Should* we comply with this new law?" but rather, "*How* will we comply with this new law?" In other words, a feasibility study can be used to explore various options for complying with new regulations.

A feasibility study should seek to uncover every reasonable issue and risk associated with the new system. The study should appear impartial and should not reflect the biases or preferences of those taking part in the study or its outcome.

A feasibility study will inform the creation of a *business case*, an explanation of the expected benefits to be realized from the new or changed system.

A feasibility study can also include or reference a formal business plan for the proposed new activity. A *business plan* is a formal document that describes the new business activity, its contribution and impact to the organization, the resources required to operate the activity, the benefits from operating the activity, and any risks associated with the activity.

When the feasibility study has been completed, a formal management review should take place so that senior management fully understands the study's results and recommendations and can determine whether (or how) the project should proceed, or whether any changes to the plan should be made.

Performing the Feasibility Study: Imagination for Improvement

A feasibility study is performed when management has decided that a new process is needed or that significant changes are needed to an existing process. By "instantiation," I mean that management has decided to initiate the process of developing a new system or updating an existing system to support the process change. Management makes such a decision as a response to an event, which could be any of the following:

- **Changes in market conditions** For example, the entry of a new competitor or the development of a new product or service feature by a competitor might spur management to respond by matching the competitor's capabilities. A competitor can also create a new market through innovation in products or services; such a move sometimes prompts an organization to make changes to maintain parity with the competitor. Or perhaps *your* organization is creating a new market through a groundbreaking innovation in how it does business or what it delivers to its customers.

- **Changes in costs or expenses** Dramatic shifts in capital or expense costs might force an organization to make changes. For instance, higher fuel costs might prompt the organization to reduce field service calls, but doing so might require stronger remote diagnostics and self-healing capabilities. In the 1990s, for example, the shift to outsourcing software development required changes in development methodologies, prompting organizations to build or buy better defect-management applications. And dropping telecommunications costs and higher bandwidth meant that online service providers began to ratchet up their offerings, most of which required enhancements to existing online service applications, and sometimes brand-new ones.
- **Changes in regulation** The rise in dependence on technology has led to negative outcomes, which in turn have prompted new legislation or changes to existing legislation. Relatively recent privacy regulations, including the European Union General Data Protection Regulation (EU GDPR) and the California Consumer Privacy Act (CCPA), have upended industries that store and process personal information for marketing and other purposes. Other examples of relatively recent and updated regulations include Sarbanes-Oxley, GLBA (Gramm-Leach-Bliley Act), HIPAA (Health Insurance Portability and Accountability Act), FERC/NERC (Federal Energy Regulatory Commission/North American Electric Reliability Corporation) regulations, PCI DSS (Payment Card Industry Data Security Standard), and many others. Many of these regulations require organizations to implement additional safeguards, controls, recordkeeping, and data governance for business processes and information systems. Sometimes this results in an organization opting to discontinue using an older information system in favor of developing or acquiring a newer application that can more effectively comply with applicable laws.
- **Changes in risk** New types of vulnerabilities are discovered regularly, and new threats are developed in response to vulnerabilities, as well as to changes in economic conditions and organizational business models. In other words, hackers find new ways to attack systems for profit within the growing cybercrime enterprises worldwide. Applications that were considered safe just a few years ago are now known to be too vulnerable to operate. Reducing risk sometimes means changing application logic, and sometimes it requires discontinuing the application altogether.

Recent privacy and security regulations have highlighted the concept of *compliance risk*. Organizations increasingly need to track their compliance with applicable laws and regulations and determine the potential consequences for failing to do so.

- **Changes to business processes** Privacy laws such as GDPR and CCPA have compelled organizations to change their business models and processes. Often, this will require organizations to alter their business applications so that they continue to support those changed processes. For example, a change in how marketing reaches its customers requires changes to business processes and supporting applications.

- **Changes to legal agreements** Changes in legal agreements between organizations can compel an organization to make changes to its software applications. There are several possible reasons for this, including changes in risks or regulations imposed upon customer or partner organizations.
- **Changes in customer requirements and expectations** Changes such as those just discussed will often prompt customers and customer organizations to ask for new features or changes to existing features in the products and services they buy. Often, this requires changes in processes and applications to meet these customers' needs.

It is important to understand that *innovation* is also a valid and frequent reason an organization chooses to change a business process or software application. Generally, in this case, an organization has developed new features or methods within a business process, along with supporting software applications, to gain a competitive advantage.

Internal and external events prompt management to act by initiating changes in business processes, product designs, service models, and, frequently, the software applications used to support and manage them. What begins as an informal discussion turns to more formal actions and eventually to the initiation of a project to make changes.

Requirements Definition

Requirements describe the necessary characteristics of a new system or changes to an existing system. They describe how the application should work and the technologies it should support. The types of requirements used in software projects include the following:

- Business functional requirements
- Technical requirements and standards
- Privacy requirements
- Security and regulatory requirements
- Disaster recovery and business continuity requirements

Business Functional Requirements

Nearly every systems development project will include *functional requirements*. These statements describe the required characteristics that the system must have to support business needs. This includes both how the system accepts, processes, and produces information, and how users interact with the software in terms of technology, appearance, and user interface functionality.

Functional requirements should be part of new system acquisitions as well as system modifications or updates.

Example functional requirements include the following:

- Application supports payroll tax calculations for U.S. federal, states, counties, and cities
- Application supports payment by credit card, electronic check, and virtual currency
- Application encrypts credit card numbers, social insurance (e.g., U.S. Social Security) numbers, and driver's license numbers in storage, and when transmitted

Notice that the preceding examples do not specify *how* the system is to accomplish these things. Business requirements are interested in *what* the system does; the system architect or designer will determine *how* the system will support those requirements.

In a few circumstances, new business requirements are not needed for a system modification. For example, if a software interface is being upgraded, an existing software program might need to be modified to work with the new interface. A change like this should be transparent to users, and the system should not differ in how it supports existing business requirements. So, in a way, it can be argued that business requirements still apply in this case: the system must adhere to existing business functional requirements.

Many organizations are tempted to seek technical solutions before defining the business problem and how to solve it.

It is not unusual for a formal requirements document to span many hundreds of pages. This will be the case especially for larger and more complex systems such as customer relationship management (CRM), enterprise resource planning (ERP), manufacturing resource planning (MRP), or service management systems.

Technical Requirements and Standards

To help the organization remain efficient, any new application or system should use the same basic technologies already in use (or planned for long-term use). The details related to maintaining the required consistency constitute most *technical requirements* and standards. These and other requirements are known as *nonfunctional requirements*.

An organization of any appreciable size should have formal technical and *architecture standards* in place. These standards are policy statements that specify the technologies, protocols, vendors, and services that comprise the organization's core IT infrastructure. The purpose of standards is to increase technological consistency across the IT infrastructure, which helps simplify the environment and reduce costs.

When an organization is considering acquiring a new system, the requirements for the new system should align with the organization's IT and security standards. This will help the organization select a system with the lowest possible impact on capital and operational costs over its lifetime.

In addition to IT standards, many other technical requirements will define the desired new system. These requirements will describe several characteristics of the system, including:

- How the system will accept, process, and output data
- Specific data layouts for interfaces to other systems
- Support of specific modules or tools that will supplement or support application functions (for example, the type of tax table that will be used in an invoicing or payroll system)
- Language support
- Specific middleware support
- Client platform support

The entire body of technical requirements should accomplish two sweeping objectives: ensure that the new system will blend harmoniously with the existing environment, and ensure that the new system will operate as required at the technical level.

Privacy Requirements

In the broadest sense, privacy concerns two distinct issues. First, privacy concerns the *protection* of personal information so that unauthorized parties cannot access it. This aspect of privacy neatly falls into the umbrella of security: security requirements that require access controls or encryption of personal information can be developed. Regulations such as GDPR and CCPA have forced new paradigms upon organizations regarding the handling of personal information in many industry sectors. Organizations that were once free to do practically anything they wanted with personal information have found themselves constrained and forced to be transparent about how they handle it.

Second, privacy is the prevention of the *proliferation and misuse* of personal information. This has less to do with security and more to do with how the organization collects, handles, and uses personal information, and whether it permits this information to be shared with other organizations for their own purposes. In this regard, privacy is about business functionality related to how the application collects and handles personal information, and to ensuring that only the information needed to perform the intended business function is collected.

For example, if a system includes canned reports about customers that are sent to third parties, those reports should be configurable so that they can contain (or omit) certain fields. For instance, customers' dates of birth can be omitted from a report sent to a third-party organization to reduce the risk of the third party using or abusing the information to the detriment of individual customers. The rule, in this case, is this: you can't abuse or misuse the information you do not possess or cannot access. Indeed, regulations such as the EU GDPR require that organizations collect sensitive data only as needed to perform services and retain it for only as long as necessary.

Privacy requirements are not always easy to discern from the language of privacy regulations; this has compelled many organizations to seek outside counsel for interpretation and guidance. In the absence of case law and other precedents, many organizations have adopted a "wait and see" attitude before making sweeping changes to business processes and supporting information systems.

Security Requirements

Security requirements must be developed to ensure that the new or updated system includes appropriate controls and characteristics to protect personal information and other sensitive information, such as intellectual property and internal financial data.

Organizations should have an existing *security requirements* document that can be readily applied to any systems development or acquisition project. These requirements should describe the business and technical controls that address several security topics, including the following:

- **Authentication** This broad category includes many specific requirements related to how system users authenticate to the system. For systems that perform autonomous authentication, this will include all the password quality requirements (minimum length, expiration, complexity, and so on), account lockout settings, password reset procedures, user account provisioning, and user ID standards. Authentication standards can also include requirements for machine and system accounts to support automated functions within the application. For systems that use a network-based authentication service, such as LDAP (Lightweight Directory Access Protocol), Kerberos, or a single sign-on (SSO) solution, security requirements should specify how the application must interface with the authentication service.
- **Authorization** This category includes requirements related to how different users are granted access to different functions and data in the application. Authorization requirements can include how roles are established, maintained, and audited. An organization might require that the application support several *roles*, which are templates that contain authorization details that can be applied to a user account.
- **Access control** This category has to do with how the system is configured to permit access for users and/or roles. Unlike authorization, which assigns roles to users, access control concerns the assignment of permissions to objects such as application functions and data stores. Depending on how a system is designed, permission assignment might be user-centric, object-centric, role-based, or a combination of these.
- **Encryption** Really another form of access control, encryption is used to hide data that, for whatever reason, might exist in "plain sight" in some contexts and yet must still be protected from those who do not have the authorization to access it. Encryption standards fall into two broad categories: data requiring encryption in certain settings and contexts, with specific encryption algorithms and key lengths, and key management handled in specific ways that permit the system to be operated similarly to other systems in the IT environment.

- **Data validation** Systems should not blindly trust that all input and output data are properly formed and formatted. Instead, a system should perform validation checks against input and output data, whether a user enters data into a system input form or the application receives the data via a batch feed from a trusted source. Data validation includes not only input data but also the results of intermediate calculations and output data. Requirements should also specify what the system should do when it encounters data that fails a validation check.
- **Audit logging** This is the characteristic whereby the system creates an electronic record of events. These events include changing system or application configuration settings, adding and deleting users, changing user roles and permissions, resetting user login credentials, changing access control settings, and, of course, the actions and transactions that the system is designed to handle. Requirements regarding audit logging will concern the configuration used to control which event types are written to the audit log, as well as the controls that protect the audit log from tampering (which, if permitted, could allow someone to "erase their tracks").
- **Security operational requirements** Management of passwords, encryption keys, event logs, patching, and other activities is required to maintain a system's confidentiality, integrity, and availability.
- **Misuse and abuse requirements** This category needs to include the full range of use (and misuse) cases through which a user might—deliberately or not—misuse or abuse the system. This includes malicious input and other methods that might cause the system to malfunction, resulting in *privilege escalation*, exposure of or tampering with sensitive data, and exhaustion of system resources. The list of requirements should not merely match the capabilities of the organization's automated or manual testing tools.

Regulatory Requirements

Regulatory requirements must be identified and tabulated to ensure the new or updated system includes appropriate controls and characteristics that facilitate compliance with applicable regulations.

Identifying applicable laws and regulations is not an easy undertaking. Organizations need to understand which laws and regulations apply in which circumstances. Considerations include the following:

- Location of the organization's legal entity headquarters, as well as the locations of other parts of the organization, and what operations take place there
- Location(s) where data is stored
- Location(s) where data is processed
- Countries, states, and provinces where data subjects reside
- Industry sector

Taking all of these considerations into account, larger organizations find themselves subject to the jurisdiction of many countries, states, and provinces across different aspects of their business operations and various segments of their employee or customer base.

Organizations need to identify various classes of business requirements, which include:

- **Information technology requirements** For instance, some laws and regulations are specific about controls, such as encryption
- **Business process requirements** Some regulations define requirements for business processes, such as security incident response
- **Organization requirements** For example, Article 37 of the GDPR defines requirements for the role of a data protection officer

An organization's legal counsel typically tracks the laws and regulations that the organization is obligated to comply with. Often, legal counsel will rely on subscription services that periodically issue bulletins announcing new regulations, as well as articles on case law and other developments that help them better understand how to interpret regulations and translate them into business requirements.

Disaster Recovery and Business Continuity Requirements

Systems that do—or might in the future—support critical business functions included in an organization's disaster recovery plans need to have certain characteristics, described as *disaster recovery and business continuity requirements*, which could be shortened to *resilience requirements*. Depending on recovery targets specified for the business process supported by the system, these requirements might include the ability for the system to run in the public cloud, on a server cluster, on a virtual machine, or in a load-balanced mode; to support data replication; to facilitate rapid recovery from backup tape or database redo logs; or to be installed on a cold recovery server without complicated, expensive, or time-consuming software licensing issues. Requirements could also dictate the system's ability to be easily recovered from a server or virtual machine image on a storage area network (SAN), to operate correctly in a virtual server environment, and to operate correctly in a cloud environment such as AWS or Azure. A system might also be expected to work with a different brand or version of a database management system, or to coexist with other systems, even though it is usually configured to run on a server by itself.

Organizing and Reviewing Requirements

In a systems acquisition or development project in which many individuals contribute requirements, the project manager or another person should track each requirement to a specific individual, enabling that person to justify or explain it if needed. When all requirements have been collected and categorized, the project manager should check with each contributor to ensure that each requirement is truly a *requirement* and not merely a "nice-to-have" feature. Perhaps each requirement can be weighted or ranked by importance. This will help, especially in a *request for information (RFI)* or *request for proposals (RFP)* situation, where analysts need to evaluate suppliers' conformance to individual requirements. This helps project personnel determine which vendors are best able to meet the requirements that matter most.

The teams that develop requirements need to ensure that requirements are measurable and verifiable, because the requirements developed in this phase of the project should flow directly into user acceptance testing plans (for functional requirements) and system testing plans (for technical requirements).

Design

After all functional, technological, security, privacy, regulatory, and other requirements have been finalized and approved, the system design can begin. It is assumed that a high-level design was developed in the feasibility study, since an elementary design is necessary to estimate costs and compute the system's financial viability; if not, the high-level design should be developed first.

The design effort should be a top-down process, starting with the system's major components and then decomposing each module into increasingly detailed components.

It is important that *data flow diagrams (DFDs)*, *entity-relationship diagrams (ERDs)*, or some other high-level depiction of the system be developed first. Data privacy laws such as the GDPR and CCPA obligate organizations to know and determine where personal information is stored, how it is processed, and how and where it moves between systems and into and out of the organization. Design should start at a high level and progress to increasingly complex levels, to the point where database designers and developers have sufficient detail to begin development.

Project team members who represent business owners/operators/customers should review the application design to confirm that the analysts' and designers' concept of the application agrees with that of the business owners. Reviews should be conducted at each design level, not just at the top level. Business experts should be able to read and understand both a high-level and a detailed design, and confirm whether the design is appropriate.

Design reviews by privacy and security specialists help the organization understand whether the system's design will comply with policies and applicable regulations. For this reason, design documents must specify not only the technology components and controls in the design, but also the physical locations where personal information will be stored and processed.

Customer design reviews can be a point in the process where business customers and designers do not see eye to eye and might disagree on the design; any disagreements can be attributed either to differences in understanding technology or to practical versus abstract thinking. To end the design review prematurely could have costly consequences. The potential consequences of failing to come to an agreement on design are vividly depicted in the classic illustration shown in Figure 7.4.

FIGURE 7.4 The potential consequences of failing to agree on design.

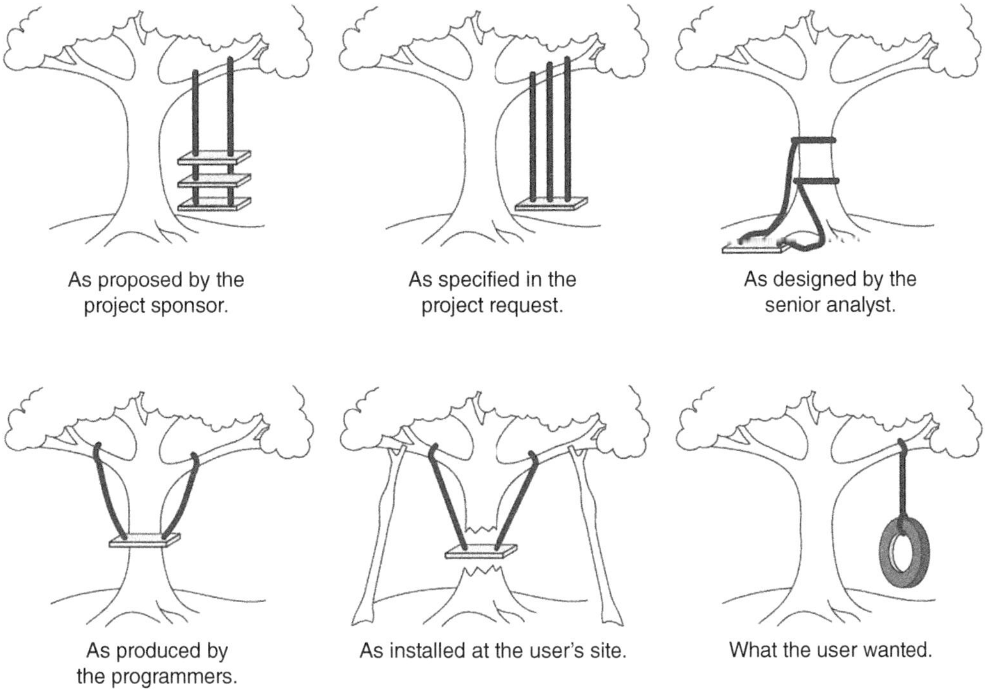

As proposed by the project sponsor.

As specified in the project request.

As designed by the senior analyst.

As produced by the programmers.

As installed at the user's site.

What the user wanted.

Source: Image obtained from *The Oregon Experiment* by Christopher Alexander; Copyright © 1975 by The Center for Environmental Structure; Reproduced with permission of the Licensor through PLSClear.

Key activities in the system design phase include:

- The use of a structured software design tool or methodology that records details of data flow and processing flow from high-level to detailed levels
- Data flow diagrams that identify the locations of storage and processing, as well as third parties to whom data is sent or received from
- Generalized and detailed database design at the logical and physical levels
- Storyboards showing user interaction with the system
- Details on reports that the system can generate

The system design effort should also include developing test plans for use during the project's development and testing phases. Test plans need to be developed no later than the design phase, because developers will need to perform unit testing during development to verify that they have coded software modules properly (and they might need to consult test plan documents to confirm that they are developing software correctly). If test plans are not developed until the test phase, developers will have to figure out tests on their own, or they might not perform enough testing, resulting in many more defects being discovered during the formal testing phase of the project.

When design reviews have concluded that the design is complete, a "design freeze" should be instituted, after which no further changes to any level of the design will be permitted. With a design freeze in effect, both designers and users are more inclined to think through all the details and do a better job confirming whether the design is correct. An organization that does not institute a design freeze will find the design changing throughout the development phase, resulting in different parts of the system conforming to different "versions" of the ever-changing design. This will cause chaos during development and testing and will lead to many more reported defects during user acceptance testing and after implementation. Management should strongly assert a design freeze, since changing the design during the development phase will drive up development costs when developers are forced to rework code written in conformance with earlier versions of the design.

Organizations with internal IT auditors should include them in design reviews to confirm that the system design will result in a system whose integrity can be verified through auditing. Organizations that incur external audits might want to invite external auditors to review the design documents for this same purpose.

Development

Developers and engineers take the detailed design documents from the design phase and begin building the system. One or more of these activities are included in the development phase:

- **Coding the application** Using tools selected for the project, developers will build the application code. Newer development tools can include design elements, code generators, debuggers, or testing tools that will make developers more productive.
- **Designing systems** Engineers will design the systems on which applications, database management systems, and other components will reside, ensuring they have the necessary resources to function properly.
- **Developing program- and system-level documents** During development, developers document technical details such as program logic, data flows, and interfaces. This aids other developers later when modifications to the application are needed.
- **Developing user procedures** As they develop user interfaces, developers can write the procedure documents and the help text that system users will read. In a more extensive, formal environment, developers might write the essential core of these documents, which tech writers will complete. A better idea: end-user documentation is written by

tech writers who derive procedures from requirements. The software developer and engineers will use the technical requirements and the completed end-user documentation to guide the development of end-user systems.

- **Working with users** As they develop the parts of the system that interface with users, developers will need to work with them to ensure that the forms, screens, and reports they build meet users' needs.

Development in a Software Acquisition Setting

In a software acquisition situation where an organization purchases or leases software rather than developing it in-house, development activities might still be required. In a software acquisition project, software development is often needed to facilitate several needs:

- **Customizations** Larger off-the-shelf applications require customizations that must be developed. These customizations can take many forms, including application code modules, XML documents, and configurations.
- **Integrations with other systems** Applications rarely standalone. Instead, they accept data from various sources and, in turn, provide data to other systems. Sometimes, "bridge programs" or integration gateways need to be written that serve to move and transform data from one environment to another. All these integrations should have been identified in the design phase.
- **Authentication** In an effort to improve security or make system adoption easier, organizations often require that new applications use a system- or network-based authentication service. The primary advantage of this approach is that users do not need to remember yet another user ID and password. An application's authentication can often be tied to LDAP or Microsoft Active Directory, or it can be part of a federated identity environment.
- **Reports** Complex applications can include a report writer module for creating custom reports. Depending on the underlying technology, a developer might be needed to develop these reports. Even if a report authoring tool is intuitive and easy to use, a developer might still be needed to help users design reports.

An organization considering acquiring software should develop and enforce policies on the extent to which customizations will be permitted. Customizations can be costly when off-the-shelf software is upgraded, because they might need to be rewritten to work with the upgraded software. The cost savings of using off-the-shelf software can be negated by the additional time required to manage and upgrade customizations.

Source Code Management

In any development effort, whether the team is a single developer or hundreds, an organization should implement *source code management* using a *source code repository*. Such a tool has several purposes:

- **Protection** A source code management tool often includes access controls so that only authorized personnel can access the application source code. This helps protect the organization's intellectual property and prevents others from learning the application's inner workings or performing unauthorized changes to source code, either of which could lead to fraud or misuse of the application later.
- **Control** A source code management system utilizes "check-out" and "check-in" functions so that only one developer at a time can work on a specific part of the application. This helps to ensure the integrity of the application's source code.
- ***Version control*** A source code management system tracks each version of the code as it is checked in by developers. The system tracks changes from version to version, shows code differences between versions, and permits reverting to an older version if application problems arise later.
- **Recordkeeping** A source code management system maintains records related to check-outs, check-ins, and modifications to source code. This makes it possible for management to know which changes are being made to the source code and who is making them.

Organizations that outsource some of their software development to third parties need to determine the business rules governing those third parties' access to source code. Some portions of a software application might be considered intellectual property or might constitute trade secrets. Further, there might be security-related sections. In such cases, organizations should consider enacting and enforcing business rules that restrict outsourced developer access to these more sensitive portions of code.

Source code management is not limited to the period when the application is first developed; on the contrary, it is a vital activity that must continue throughout the application's lifespan.

Testing

During the requirements, design, and even development phases of a software project, various project team members develop specific facts and behavioral characteristics (reflecting the requirements) about the application. Each of those characteristics must be verified before the application is approved for production use. This concept is depicted in a V-model in Figure 7.5. The *V-model* is sometimes used to depict the increasing levels of detail and complexity in the SDLC.

FIGURE 7.5 Requirements and design characteristics must all be agreed upon and verified through testing.

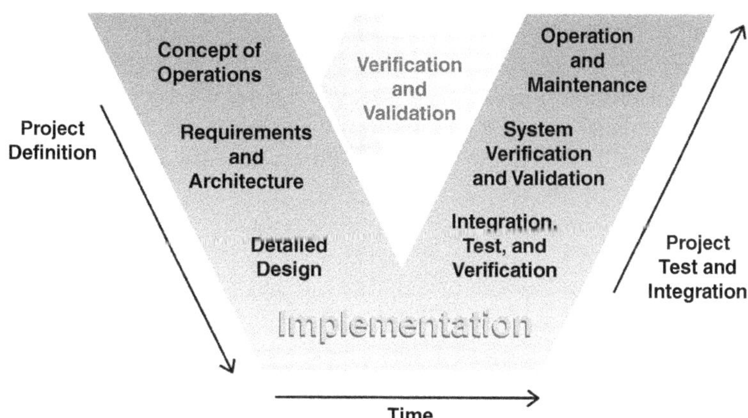

Source: U.S. Federal Highway Administration.

The stages of testing in a systems development project are unit testing, system testing, functional testing, quality assurance testing, and user acceptance testing. Each stage will be addressed in turn, following a brief overview of test plans.

Test Plans

Before testing can take place, test plans must be *created*. Testing, at the overall project level and at the detail level, should be a methodical, repeatable process, not subject to the skills and experience of any individual performing tests.

Test plans are primarily derived directly from requirements developed prior to development. There might, however, be other sources or types of testing that are not explicitly stated in the requirements, including:

- Adequacy of business use cases
- Resistance against misuse and abuse cases
- The degree to which a program's operation and functions are self-evident to the user

Because of the volume and/or complexity of test cases, it might be necessary to create formal test plans. Test plans can be developed for several reasons, including:

- The volume of tests that need to be distributed to several individuals in some logical manner
- Testing performed by one or more outside parties or organizations
- Tests allocated based on the availability of individual testers or test teams
- Tests allocated based on the knowledge or skills of individual testers or test teams
- Tests allocated based on the tools required to perform testing (for example, workload testing or security defect testing)

Unit Testing

Unit testing is usually performed by developers during the coding phase of the software development project, or by engineers as they assemble and integrate various system components. When each developer or engineer is assigned to build a section of a system, they are given specifications that include test plans or test cases to verify that the system components work properly. This is true regardless of whether the part of the system that the developer is working on will be seen and used by end users or will be buried deep within the bowels of the system and never seen by anyone.

In a formal development environment, unit test plans should be precise and list each test the developer should perform. The developer then performs each test and records the results (usually the actual output). Those test results are then archived for later reference if needed.

Archiving unit testing records can be valuable when later phases of testing are underway, and a problem is found. Developers trying to isolate the cause of later testing problems can refer to test plans and results from the unit testing phase to determine whether the test plans and other unit testing activities were performed correctly or contained appropriate test cases. This evidence can save the project team a lot of time by eliminating the need to repeat unit testing.

Unit testing should be a part of the development of each module in the application. When a developer is assigned a programming task in a software development project, unit testing should be performed immediately after coding and debugging are complete. In some organizations, developers work in pairs—the senior developer writes code, and the junior developer performs testing. This allows junior developers to learn more about advanced development by observing the senior developer and testing their code.

It can be argued that unit testing for a software module should not be performed by the developer who wrote it. The developer might be under time pressure to complete development and testing and might overlook test cases or gloss over errors as irrelevant. Also, a developer can be too familiar with their code to objectively test it. The methodology of "written by one and tested by another" has the advantage of objective testing. Still, it can be more difficult to implement in smaller organizations where a single developer is writing all the code.

System Testing

As various parts of a system are developed and unit-tested, they will be installed into a test environment. When enough modules or components have been completed, it will eventually become possible to begin end-to-end (or at least partial end-to-end) *system testing*. In this way, it will be possible to test several components to verify whether they work together properly.

System testing includes *interface testing* to confirm that the system is communicating properly with other systems. This will include real-time interfaces as well as batch processing.

System testing also includes *migration testing*. When one system replaces another, data from the old application is often imported into the new system to eliminate the need for both systems to operate simultaneously. Migration testing ensures that data is being properly formatted and imported into the new system. This testing is often performed several times before the real, live migration at cutover time.

As with unit testing, system testing should have pre-prepared test plans developed during the system design phase. As with unit testing, system testing should not be performed by the developers and engineers who developed the modules under test or by the integrators who set them up in the test environment. Further, system testing results should be formally documented and archived for later reference.

Functional Testing

Functional testing primarily verifies functional requirements developed earlier in the project.

Each functional requirement must be expressed in a way that makes it inherently verifiable. When each functional requirement is developed, one or more tests should also be developed and conducted during the functional testing phase of the project.

Functional tests should be formally recorded, including test input and test results. All of this should be archived in case it's needed if the application is suspected of malfunctioning. Often, functional test results can verify whether the malfunction was present during the functional testing before the application went live.

User Acceptance Testing

Before business users formally approve and begin using a new (or updated) system, *user acceptance testing (UAT)* often occurs. UAT should consist of a formal, written body of specific tests that permits system users to determine whether the system will operate properly.

The detailed output of user acceptance testing should be archived, as it might be needed in the future.

UAT is often a stage in the acceptance of a leased or purchased system, as well as of a system developed by a third-party organization. User acceptance testing determines whether the customer organization will accept (and pay for, as the case may be) the system and begin its formal use.

Acceptance criteria for UAT should be developed by end users, not by developers or designers; otherwise, internal or external customers can end up with a system that does not function as desired or expected.

Quality Assurance Testing

Quality assurance testing (QAT) is a formal verification of system specifications and technologies. Users are usually not involved in QAT; instead, this testing is typically performed by IT or IS departments.

Like UAT, QAT should be a "gatekeeper" test in any situation where the organization is purchasing off-the-shelf systems or the system is being developed by an external organization. The results of QAT should also determine whether the organization will formally accept, pay for, and use the system.

Implementation

In the *implementation* phase of the project, the completed system is placed into the production environment and started. Implementation must start before UAT and QAT begin. UAT and QAT should be performed in the environment anticipated to become the in-use production environment once approvals to use the system are obtained.

From the very day construction of the implementation environment begins, it should be as controlled as a production environment. This means that all changes to the environment should go through a change management process. Also, administrative access to the production environment should be restricted to personnel who will support it after it goes live. The implementation timeline relative to other phases of the software development project is depicted in Figure 7.6.

Because the production environment is where UAT and QAT testing often take place, it must be pristine and inaccessible to developers and other personnel. This reduces the likelihood of unauthorized changes to the system that could compromise its security or privacy.

FIGURE 7.6 Implementation involves preparing the production environment before UAT and QAT.

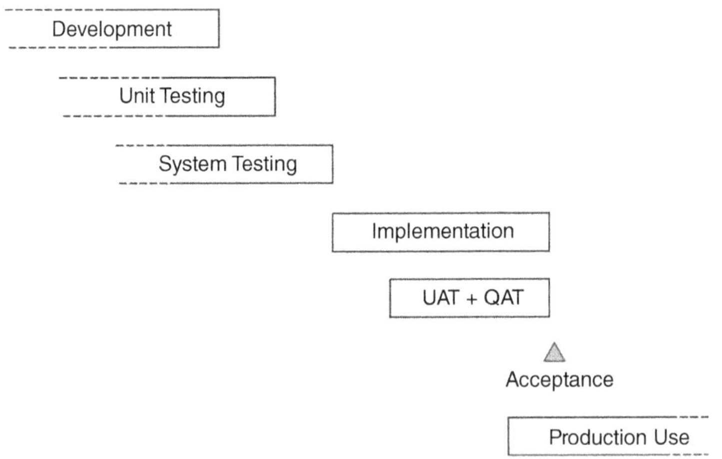

Source: Author.

Implementation Planning

Implementation is a complicated undertaking that requires planning. Some activities can have long lead times, requiring implementation to begin during development or earlier.

- **Prepare physical space for on-premises production systems** For organizations implementing a system on physical servers, an existing data center can be used for a system's servers and other equipment. But if there isn't room, or if an existing data center's available space is insufficient, the organization might need to consider expanding an existing data center or using a colocation center. More often, however, an organization will implement its system in a hosted cloud environment, where the service provider offers virtual machines on which the organization will build and configure operating systems.
- **Build production systems** The actual servers (whether physical or virtual) that the application will use must be built and configured. If the organization does not have the necessary servers available, the hardware systems must be leased or purchased; depending upon the type of hardware, considerable lead time might be required. If the public cloud will be used, the organization needs to select a public cloud vendor (this should be done at design time or earlier!) and implement server operating systems there. Once the hardware or virtualization platform is available, personnel will need to install and configure operating systems and possibly other subsystems such as database or application management systems. Supporting infrastructure such as configuration management systems, monitoring systems, routers, switches, firewalls, and so forth (whether physical or virtual) will also be implemented at this time.
- **Install application software** Once the systems are ready for the application software, it can be installed and configured.
- **Migrate the data** For environments in which an existing system will be retired, data from the former environment usually needs to be transferred to the new environment. Often, this procedure requires developing one or more custom programs to extract, convert, and insert data into the new environment. This procedure is usually performed more than once: it must be rehearsed at least once to ensure it works properly. Also, migrated data is often needed for functional testing, UAT, and training before the actual cutover.

As each phase of implementation is completed, the newly completed component should be locked down immediately and treated as though it is already in production. Usually, this is the only way to ensure the integrity of the entire environment.

Training

The success of the entire development or acquisition project hinges on the knowledge and skills of several different people in the organization. The following are among those who might need training:

- **End users** Personnel who will be using the system need to be trained so that they will know how to operate it properly.
- **Customers** If outside customers will be using the new system, they will need an appropriate amount of information so that they will understand how to use it. In other cases, customers will not be using the system directly, but a new system can still influence how they interact with the organization. If customer service or sales personnel are using a new system for taking orders or for looking up customer data, they might be asking different questions or presenting different information to the customer.
- **Support staff** Personnel who provide customer service to users and customers need to be trained in the workings of the system, as well as on administrative "back office" tools that they can use to assist users.
- **Trainers** Organizations that employ a training organization will need to "train the trainers" so that, in turn, they can train users and customers correctly.

The purpose of a system might require that others also receive training. This could include internal or external auditors or regulators who have oversight over the organization.

Data Migration

In the context of the SDLC, the purpose of a data migration is to transfer data from an older, soon-to-be-retired system to a new system. Depending on the nature of the old and new systems, the purpose of the data migration might be to make historical records originating in the older system available in the newer system. From a privacy perspective, the organization must track data movement and ensure that any temporary copies are indeed temporary and deleted once no longer needed.

In some cases, an organization will continue to run the older system to maintain access to historical data. In some circumstances, it might require fewer resources to keep the old system running than to migrate the historical data to the new system.

Data migration often requires developing programs that extract data from the old system, perform required transformations, and format it for import into the new application. This is frequently a complex task, as there might be differences so significant between the data models of the old and new systems that the *meaning* of stored data differs between them. In some cases, it will be necessary to create certain parts of the database in the new system by extracting data from the old system and then performing calculations to generate the data required for the new system. Careful analysis is required in all cases to ensure that the *meaning* of the data in each system is understood, so that the migration is done properly.

The following are some techniques and considerations that ensure a successful migration:

- **Record counts** Programs or utilities should be used to count the number of records in counterpart tables in the old and new environments. This will confirm the completeness of the migration programs that move data from the old environment to the new one.
- **Batch totals** Data records with numeric values can be added together in the old and new databases. This will help confirm the integrity of key data elements in the old and new environments.
- **Checksums** Programs that compute checksums can be run against old and new databases to ensure the accuracy of migrated data. Developers do need to be aware of the methods used to store data, which could lead to differences in checksums. For instance, an address field in one system might pad it with spaces, but in the other, it might pad it with nulls. Also, the way that dates are stored can vary between systems. While using checksums can be valuable, developers and analysts must be familiar with any differences in data representation between the old and new environments.

Like other software projects, the migration programs themselves must be carefully designed and tested, and test results analyzed to ensure they are working properly. Often, it is necessary to perform a test migration—well in advance of the scheduled cutover date—to ensure that the migration programs have been properly written.

Executing the Cutover

When the production system has been constructed, applications loaded, data migrated, and all testing performed and verified, the project team has reached the *cutover* milestone. Often, management review and approval are required to verify that all necessary steps have been completed correctly.

Depending on the nature of the system as well as external influences such as regulation or business requirements, an organization can transfer processing to the new environment in one of several ways:

- **Parallel cutover** The organization can operate both the old and new systems in parallel for a time, making careful comparisons between the two to ensure that the new system is working properly.
- **Geographic cutover** In an application used across large geographic regions, such as a retail point-of-sale system, the organization can migrate individual locations to the new system instead of moving all locations at once.
- **Module-by-module cutover** The organization can migrate different parts of the system at different times. In a financial management system, for instance, the organization could move accounts receivable to the new environment, then move accounts payable, and finally move the general ledger. During and between each of these phases, the organization must keep track of exactly which business information resides in which system.

- **User segment cutover** In a system with many users of different kinds, the organization could migrate groups of users to the new system, based on logically contextual criteria. For instance, an organization could migrate newer customers first and older customers later.
- **All-at-once cutover** An organization can elect to migrate the entire environment at one time.

The project team must analyze all available methods for the cutover and choose the one that balances risk, efficiency, and cost-effectiveness.

Analysts might discover data problems in the old environment that necessitate cleanup prior to the migration or as part of the migration. Examples of problems include duplicate records, incomplete records, or records containing values that violate one or more business rules. Analysts who discover data inconsistencies such as these need to alert the project team and then help them decide how to remedy the situation.

In complex migrations, organizations can use *Extract, Transfer, Load (ETL)* tools to facilitate data migration and transformation. ETL tools can be less costly than manual efforts.

Rollback Planning

A *rollback* is a serious undertaking and would be considered only when a problem in the new environment is so serious that it cannot be easily remedied. *Rollback planning* is recommended in environments where a system's availability and integrity are critical to the organization, even if a rollback is never needed.

To ensure the project's success, rollbacks should also be designed and tested in advance to ensure that this lifeline will function if needed.

Post-implementation

The software project is not completed when the system cutover has taken place. Several other activities still must take place before the project is closed. This section describes these final tasks.

Post-implementation Review

After the implementation of a new system, one or more formal reviews must take place. The purpose of these reviews is to collect all known open issues and to identify and discuss the project's performance. Because the organization is likely to undertake similar projects in the future, it is valuable to identify which parts of the project went well and what could have been improved. The implementation review should consider the following:

- **System adequacy** The project team should work with the users of the new system to collect issues and comments, which are then discussed during the implementation review. Any issues requiring further attention should be identified.
- **Privacy reviews** The system's privacy features and controls need to be discussed and any problems identified. Any temporary copies of data should be purged once the stability of the new environment is confirmed.
- **Security reviews** The system's access controls and other security controls should be discussed and any issues or problems identified.
- **Audit review** The system's ability to be audited, as well as any early audit results, should be discussed.
- **Issues** All known problems regarding the new environment should be identified, including user feedback, operations feedback, and the accuracy and completeness of documentation and records. The project team needs to discuss each issue and assign it to one or more individuals to address and remedy.
- **Return on investment** If the purpose of implementing the application was to establish or improve *return on investment (ROI)* or efficiency, then initial measurements need to be taken. The project team needs to recognize that several business cycles might be required before an accurate ROI can be determined.

More than one post-implementation review might be needed. To hold a single post-implementation review shortly after going live and then calling it good is probably inadequate for most organizations. Instead, a series of reviews might be needed, perhaps stretching over years.

IS auditors should be involved in every phase of the SDLC, including post-implementation reviews, to ensure that the system is functioning in accordance with the control or regulatory requirements auditors are responsible for. Auditor feedback must be included in the body of issues and comments reviewed during the initial and subsequent reviews.

Maintenance

Immediately after implementation, the system enters the maintenance phase. From this point forward, all changes to the environment must be performed under formal *IT service management* processes, including *incident management*, *problem management*, defect management, *vulnerability management*, *change management*, and *configuration management*. All these processes should have been developed and modified as necessary to accommodate the new application when the cutover was completed.

Retirement

Retirement, also known as decommissioning or disposal, is the set of activities undertaken when a system or application reaches the end of its service life. The reasons that an organization will retire an application or system include:

- System no longer meets business needs
- Vendors no longer support one or more components

The retirement of a system often follows one of two paths, explained here.

Migration to Another System

Here, the organization has decided that the existing system or application no longer meets its needs, and that a different system or application will support business processes. There are several potential reasons to migrate to another system, including:

- Vendors no longer support the current system (or some of its components)
- New functionality required by business processes or regulations is not available or cost-effective
- The cost of operating the current system is too high

When deciding to migrate to another system, an organization needs to determine whether historic data will be migrated to the replacement system or if the retired system will be placed in a "read-only" mode to retain historic records and support historical reporting. If this approach is not cost-effective, the organization can migrate all historical data to the replacement system or generate reports that will serve as the historical record.

Cessation of Supported Business Processes

Here, the organization has chosen to discontinue the business process(es) supported by the system. In their lifecycles, organizations sometimes make small and large adjustments to their mission and goals, and at times this involves discontinuing some business processes and retiring the systems that support them.

Refer to the "Data Migration" subsection earlier in this chapter for a detailed discussion on migrating data from a retired system.

Software Development Risks

Software and systems development are not risk-free endeavors. Even when management provides adequate resources for a software development project and supports a viable methodology, there are still many more paths to failure than to success.

Several specific risks are associated with software development projects:

- **System inadequacy** The system might fail to support all business requirements. During the requirements and specifications phases of a software development project, some business requirements might have been overlooked, disregarded, misunderstood, or unappreciated. For whatever reason, if a system falls short of meeting all business requirements, it might be underutilized or even abandoned.
- **Security and privacy defects** The system might contain security or privacy defects that permit various forms of misuse and abuse, including denial-of-service, privilege escalation, data disclosure, and data corruption.
- **Project risk** If the system development (or acquisition) project is not well run, the project might exceed spending budgets, time budgets, or both. This can result in significant delays and even the abandonment of the project altogether if management considers it a failure.
- **Business inefficiency** The system might fail to meet business efficiency expectations. In other words, the system itself might be difficult to use, might be exceedingly slow, or might require additional manual work to meet business needs. This can result in critical business tasks taking too long or requiring additional resources to complete.
- **Regulatory changes** In the time between the development of requirements (reflecting regulations at that time) and the implementation of a system, new regulations might have been enacted, requiring significant design changes to the system. In the modern world of extraterritorial regulations, this can include laws passed outside of the city, state, province, or country where the organization is located.
- **Market changes** Between the time a software development project is approved and when it is completed, sudden or unexpected changes in market conditions can spell disaster for the project. For instance, drastic supply or price shocks in the macro environment can adversely affect costs, making a new business activity no longer viable. Changes in the market can also result in reduced margins on products and services, which can turn a project's ROI upside down.

Management is responsible for the business decisions that it makes; in ideal situations, management makes these decisions with sufficient information at hand. Usually, however, there are some unknowns.

Alternative Software Development Approaches and Techniques

For decades, the waterfall approach to software development was used by most organizations. Breakthroughs and changes in technology and practices in the 1970s and 1980s led to new approaches in software development that can be every bit as effective as the waterfall model and, in many cases, more efficient and faster.

DevOps

DevOps is a growing movement that uses an Agile development methodology, coupled with tighter integration among development teams, software QA, and IT operations. DevOps isn't complete without tools facilitating more effective (often automated) testing.

In DevOps, the lines between software development, QA, and IT operations are somewhat blurred. Organizations need to ensure that access control models and capabilities continue to support regulatory and compliance requirements, such as:

- **Data segregation** Developers should never have access to production data.
- **Separation of duties** Critical processes, such as change control, still require administrative and technical controls so that no one person (such as a developer) can make unauthorized changes in production environments.

The relationship between development, software QA, and IT operations is depicted in Figure 7.7.

DevSecOps

DevSecOps is an offshoot of (or, others would say, an improvement on) DevOps. DevSecOps represents the best of DevOps and includes security design and testing capabilities that are a part of the rapid development and automated testing process. Often, static and/or dynamic code-scanning capabilities are integrated into the software build environment to identify security defects as early as possible. Further automated testing can be performed in production environments to reveal exploitable defects that developers can remediate in subsequent sprints.

FIGURE 7.7 DevOps is the integration of development, software QA (testing), and IT operations.

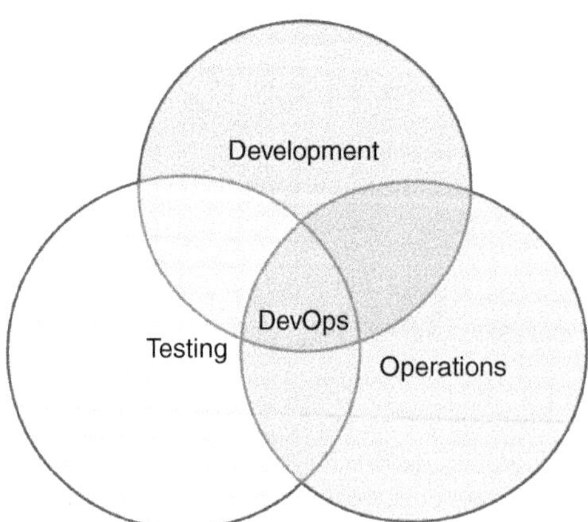

Source: Author.

Continuous Integration/Continuous Deployment

Continuous integration/continuous deployment (CI/CD) combines continuous integration (where developers' code is integrated into a single shared mainline several times each day) and continuous deployment (where software updates are delivered iteratively through automated deployments). The result is similar to DevOps, where software applications undergo a near-constant stream of small updates, whereas the traditional waterfall methodology can involve just a few updates per year.

Agile Development

The *Agile* development model is an alternative methodology appropriate for some organizations. The Agile methodology uses the Scrum framework. In an Agile development project, a larger development team is broken into smaller teams of five to nine developers and a leader, and the project deliverables are divided into smaller pieces that can be achieved in just a few weeks.

Exam Tip

Agile is one of several techniques developed as an alternative to the traditional waterfall methodology, which was considered too slow and deprived organizations of agility.

Agile, DevOps, DevSecOps, and CI/CD can all be considered rapid development methodologies in which small, incremental changes are made to applications on a near-continuous basis, as opposed to the traditional waterfall methodology, where significant updates are made to applications only once or twice per year.

Web-based Application Development

The creation of the HTML content-display standard and the HTTP communications protocol has revolutionized *web-based application* development. The web browser is ubiquitous, has become the universal client platform, and is not unlike intelligent display terminals or client-server architectures from earlier eras.

The Web, as it is popularized now, came along just in time: two-tier and three-tier client-server computing, the great new application development paradigm developed in the 1990s, was not living up to its promise, particularly in network performance and client software maintenance. Web software has dramatically simplified software development from the perspective of the user interface (UI). Though developers have a little less control over what and how data will be displayed on a user's workstation, the trade-off of not having to maintain client-side software is viewed as an acceptable compromise.

From a development methodology perspective, *web-based application development* can be performed within virtually all of the development frameworks, including waterfall, DevOps, Agile, RAD (rapid application development), DOSD (data-oriented software development), CI/CD, and OO (object-oriented) (some of which were discussed in this chapter). Primarily, it's the target technology that differentiates web-based application development from its alternatives.

Protocol standards have been developed to facilitate communication between web-based applications, including JSON-RPC, SOAP (Simple Object Access Protocol), and *Web Services Description Language (WSDL)*. JSON-RPC is a stateless remote procedure call (RPC) protocol coded in JavaScript Object Notation (JSON) to encode requests and responses, allowing a client to invoke methods on a remote system over a transport such as HTTP or WebSocket.

SOAP is an XML-based application programming interface (API) specification that facilitates real-time communication between applications over HTTP and HTTPS. Functionally, SOAP operates similarly to RPC, in which one application transmits a query to another, and the other responds with a result. SOAP messages are based on the XML standard.

Web services description language (WSDL) serves as a specification repository for the SOAP services available in a particular environment. This enables an application to discover what services are available on an application server.

System Development Tools

Application developers can create *programming language* source code using tools ranging from simple text editors to advanced tools such as computer-aided software engineering (CASE), fourth-generation languages (4GLs), and vibe coding. While there's little reason to discuss text editors such as vi, Notepad, or Emacs, advanced development tools are worthy of attention and are discussed in this section.

Integrated Development Environment

Integrated development environments (IDEs) are a class of desktop software development tools that incorporate source code editing, version control, compilation, and debugging in a single tool. An IDE enables a developer to write, test, and debug code without switching between programs.

IDEs typically have multiple windows, or panes, that enable the software developer to view and edit code, run code, observe execution, and view the source code library. Other functions might be available as well.

Some IDEs offer integration with external tools, such as source code scanners that detect security and quality defects.

Computer-aided Software Engineering

CASE represents a broad variety of tools used to automate various aspects of application software development. CASE tools cover three basic realms of development:

- **Upper CASE** This includes activities ranging from requirements gathering to the development of data models, data flow diagrams, and interfaces.
- **Middle CASE** This involves the development of detailed designs, including screen layouts, report definitions, data design, and data flows.
- **Lower CASE** This involves the creation of program source code and data schemas.

These terms are loosely used to classify various CASE tools. Some CASE tools are strictly Upper CASE, while others include Middle CASE and/or Lower CASE; many cover the entire range of functionality and can be used to capture specifications, create data structures and flow diagrams, define program functions, and generate source code.

CASE tools do not usually produce source code ready for implementation and testing. Instead, they are used to generate the majority (in the best cases) of the code for a given program; then the developer(s) would add details and specific items that the CASE tool did not cover. CASE tools are not meant to replace developer work, but they help reduce the time required for coding in a development project, improve consistency, and enhance program quality.

CASE tools often contain *code generators* that create the actual program source code.

CASE tools do not eliminate the need for any of the essential phases of the SDLC. With or without CASE tools, it is still necessary for a project team to create requirements, specifications, and design. CASE does help automate some of these activities, however.

Vibe Coding

Vibe coding is a software development practice assisted by AI large language models (LLMs) that, when issued one or more prompts, will generate source code automatically.

Strictly speaking, development experience is not required for vibe coding; however, the code generated by an AI LLM must be examined and tested to ensure proper functionality and confirm it is free of exploitable defects. These assurances require development experience and tooling, to ensure that vibe coding results in source code that meets an organization's business needs.

Applications and Software Hardening

The concept of resilience is not always considered in the design, development, and management of software applications. *Resilience*, however, is an essential characteristic of any software program that is to run in the real world, with the potential for users who use the program correctly or incorrectly, or attackers who attempt to trick the application into performing in ways not intended by its designers.

Hardening at the application layer is not altogether different from hardening at the network or system layer. The concept is the same: hardening refers to techniques intended to make systems more resistant to misuse and attack, or, to put it another way, to prevent unintended consequences resulting from unexpected stimuli.

Hardening is not an activity that should be applied to a system once it has been implemented, but as a part of its initial design.

Security professionals need to pay close attention to hardening in the entire technology stack. Refer to the "Hardening" section in Chapter 8.

Application Hardening Principles

Application layer hardening addresses several perspectives about software applications, including the following:

- ***Input validation*** Software programs must carefully examine all input before acting upon it. Input attacks are among the most popular because of their ease of implementation and because many software programs inadequately examine input data. The types of attacks that can occur because of inadequate input checking include:
  - *Buffer overflow* Input data deliberately exceeds the program's input storage capacity and attempts to overwrite the program's instructions with code of the attacker's choice, usually to take over control of the program.
  - *Injection attack* Input data is crafted to execute arbitrary commands sent to the backend database management system (a SQL injection attack) or to an end-user's browser (a JavaScript injection attack).
  - *Denial-of-service (DoS) attack* Input data is crafted to cause the target program or system to malfunction, causing it to cease operations.
  - *Data corruption* A program that does not perform boundary and type checking on input data might malfunction or attempt to process invalid data.
- **Authentication and session management** Software applications need robust authentication mechanisms to resist authentication bypass attacks. For logged-in users, software applications must have layers of defense against attempts to break into other users' sessions.
- **Temporary files** As part of routine operations, programs might create temporary files that contain sensitive data. An attacker might be able to easily access a temporary file and steal sensitive data, or alter its contents, disrupting data processing.
- **Logging and monitoring** Software applications need to generate security events that are sent to an *audit log*, a central log repository, or an SIEM. Events such as logins (successful or not), creation of new privileged accounts, changes in configuration settings, creation of new customers (in SaaS environments), and others should result in event messages sent to a log management and alerting system. Someone should be monitoring these logs and have detailed instructions to follow when alerts are generated.

- **Verbose error messages** Software application developers need to be careful when creating error messages so they are not overly verbose. For instance, a credit card payment function should not display the full details of a failed transaction or log them in an event log; instead, sensitive data such as names and credit card numbers should be truncated or omitted entirely. Also, in user interfaces, error messages should not reveal too much about the inner workings of software programs and the databases behind them. Error messages that are overly verbose could give attackers vital information that helps them conduct an attack on the application.
- **Improper encryption** Application developers should avoid outdated encryption algorithms, poor key management (such as easily found keys and hard-coded encryption keys in apps), and unsalted hashes, and they should avoid improper uses of cryptography. Also, websites should use HTTPS instead of HTTP to avoid transmitting sensitive information without encryption.
- **Components with known vulnerabilities** Software applications often use components that originate from other organizations. Examples include open-source code libraries, unsupported operating systems (as well as subsystems and network devices), insecure and unsafe browser extensions, and outside SaaS services with unpatched vulnerabilities.
- **Cross-site scripting and cross-site request forgery** These two common web application vulnerabilities can give attackers control of sessions and inject malware into users' computers.

The Open Web Application Security Project (OWASP), at `https://owasp.org`, is an excellent resource for web developers and cybersecurity professionals seeking information on web application security.

Testing Applications

To ensure that applications are free of exploitable vulnerabilities that could compromise personal information or cause them to malfunction, application testing tools and techniques should be used regularly. Application hardening testing is used to confirm that an application is reasonably free of exploitable vulnerabilities that could allow an attacker to compromise it. Functional testing—that is, confirming that design requirements were properly implemented—is separate from hardening testing.

The following types of application hardening testing are available:

- **Code reviews** A *code review* is a manual review of application source code that has been updated recently. Generally, when a developer is given a task to make a change to an application's source code module(s), another developer will examine the code to confirm that the code changes have not introduced any new vulnerabilities. Code reviews are not performed solely for vulnerability analysis; other reasons include compliance with the organization's coding policies.

- **Static code scans** *Static application security testing (SAST)* is an automated scan of source code that intends to determine whether there are any exploitable defects in the application's source code. Code scans can be performed in at least three ways:
  - In the IDE, as a developer is working on source code
  - On demand, as directed by someone who is running a source-code scanning tool
  - As a part of a daily build cycle in the build system
- **Dynamic code scans** *Dynamic application security testing (DAST)* is an automated scan of a running application. A dynamic code-scanning program "runs" the application as though it were a human user, clicking on pages, filling in forms, and observing the effects of stimuli such as form submissions and cookie manipulation. Dynamic code scans are typically run on demand on all or part of an application. They are also integrated into an application's build environment, where all or parts of an application can be scanned automatically, usually overnight.
- ***Software composition analysis (SCA)*** The practice of analyzing application source code to detect open-source software and determine whether it is up to date, free of vulnerabilities, and complies with applicable license requirements.
- **Manual tests** Various tools can be used to test individual web forms, fields, and cookies, as dynamic code scanners do, but on a "one page at a time" or even "one field at a time" basis. Many such tools exist for manually testing various types of exploits and application components. Penetration tests use these tools to go beyond the capabilities of automated scanning tools.
- ***Penetration test*** Also known as a "pen test," this involves engaging an external party to conduct a broad range of tests against a target application. External parties are often used because most organizations lack this expertise internally; they are also generally more objective and unafraid to conduct tests and report results without being concerned with internal politics.
- ***Bug bounty*** In this arrangement, an organization will solicit external security researchers to perform security tests on a target system. Researchers will be compensated for identifying exploitable vulnerabilities, with higher rates paid for more serious vulnerabilities. There are several "bug bounty as a service" organizations that organize the effort into a security testing "marketplace," bringing together organizations that need testing and security researchers who want to earn additional income.

Discussed earlier in this chapter, organizations must develop formal test plans at every level of development, derived (at least in part) from requirements.

APIs and Cloud-native Services

APIs and services are the means through which applications communicate with each other, both within an environment and between organizations.

APIs and Services

In addition to human-interactive systems, there are legions of software applications and tools that perform automated tasks without any human interaction. Whether these tools and applications handle regularly scheduled batch jobs or run on demand, they work quietly on systems, doing whatever processing, data transfer, or gateway services are needed.

An *application programming interface (API)* is an automated computer interface developed to perform a dedicated function. An API is generally running on a computer, listening for incoming messages or transactions that it can process in a predetermined way. An API is a part of a software program that is designed to accept input data through a communications interface. It processes that data in some way, perhaps storing it, performing calculations, converting it to a different format, or performing another task.

From a privacy and security perspective, these backend systems are every bit as important as human-interactive systems, and they store and process potentially vast amounts of data, including personal information. Here are some examples of these types of systems:

- **Bulk file transfer** Data feeds from one organization to another, copied with the old standby, File Transfer Protocol (FTP), or hopefully the secure version of file transfer—FTPS or SFTP
- **Month/quarter/year-end financial processing** Automated programs that perform financial period closes and other tasks
- **Callouts to other software platforms** Mobile apps that integrate with social media programs, mapping applications, messaging applications, and more
- **Backend calculation services** Commercial applications that perform tasks such as calculating sales tax and shipping costs, and location services
- **Banking services** Commercial applications that process fund transfers and payments
- **Payment services** Commercial applications that accept credit cards and other forms of payment on behalf of organizations that sell products and services

All of these and more use various interfaces to communicate with other systems on demand, in bulk, or both. Many of these services use the global Internet to communicate with other organizations' and users' systems. However, some highly sensitive services between companies are still transmitted over private, dedicated communication channels.

Many different technologies are used to operate these services, including FTP and related batch file transfer protocols, *web services*, and somewhat older interfaces such as CORBA and SOAP.

Contrary to what many believe, there are plenty of security- and privacy-related issues associated with the use of these services that need to be addressed. Among them are the following:

- **Application, interface, and system security** These interfaces are backed by applications and run on operating systems over networks. They are subject to many of the same kinds of attacks that human-interactive systems endure. Secure development processes, monitoring, and testing are required. A skilled hacker can inflict just as much damage hacking an API as they can hacking a human-interactive application. Both are windows into backend data that might prove valuable on the black market. Many of the same tools are used to test software security in APIs and human-interactive systems.

- **Authentication** APIs and web services must enforce authentication and authorization to ensure that only trusted systems and endpoints can make connections and transmit or receive data. Authentication can also enforce *field-level access control*, where systems making an incoming API connection are permitted access only to certain data fields.
- **Rate-limiting** APIs and web services must employ rate-limiting mechanisms to prevent unintended bulk data transfers, a potential indicator of data exfiltration, in which an attacker uses an API to steal sensitive information.
- **Input validation** Also known as *data filtering*, APIs and web services must employ input validation when receiving data to ensure that the received data types and ranges match expectations.
- **Privacy** These interfaces are often part of other processing ecosystems. Organizations that use outside services need to understand how the organizations that run those services protect and use personal information.
- **Data sovereignty** Organizations using other parties' interfaces for processing personal information need to understand the physical locations where this processing occurs so they can comply with privacy laws governing cross-border data transfers.

From a business process perspective, all API implementations and changes should be managed through established change management processes. And in instances where APIs introduce new data into the environment, data governance should include *input controls* and enforce an *input authorization* process to ensure that all new data is vetted and approved by management. And, of course, *input validation* must be a part of every instance where new data is introduced into a system, regardless of the method.

Microservices

Microservices represents an architectural approach in which an application is built as a collection of small, independent services that each perform a specific business function and communicate with one another through well-defined interfaces. Each service operates as a separate component, typically with its own codebase, runtime environment, and often its own data store. This contrasts with *monolithic architectures*, where all functionality is implemented within a single, tightly coupled application.

A typical microservices deployment uses containerization technologies to package services and orchestration platforms to manage scaling and availability. Requests from users are often routed through an API gateway, which directs traffic to the appropriate service.

Services can also communicate asynchronously through event-driven architectures, allowing one service to publish events that other services consume.

For example, an e-commerce platform might implement separate microservices for product catalog management, shopping cart functionality, payment processing, and order fulfillment. When a user places an order, the shopping cart service sends order details to the payment service. After successful payment, an event is generated, triggering the fulfillment service to initiate the shipment.

Cloud Services and Infrastructure

The term *cloud* is an abstraction that can refer to one or more of these:

- Computers made available to customers as a service
- A collection of virtual machines located on premises or at a remote location
- Software applications (including those that emulate hardware devices such as firewalls) made available to customers as a service
- Data storage made available to customers as a service
- Network connectivity made available to customers as a service

Fairly standard models describing types of *cloud service providers (CSPs)* have been developed, including IaaS, PaaS, and SaaS, which are described in the remainder of this section.

Infrastructure-as-a-service (IaaS)

Infrastructure-as-a-service (IaaS) refers to servers in which computing, networking, or storage infrastructure is offered as a service to customers. IaaS solutions are generally accessed via the Internet, but they can also be accessed via dedicated network connections. All forms of IaaS employ virtualization technology to make services accessible to customers. (Virtualization was discussed earlier in this chapter.)

Often, IaaS is consumed as customer-managed operating systems that customer organizations build, configure, and maintain. This represents a direct replacement for traditional on-premises servers. Customers manage their IaaS environments through a management interface that enables them to build, start, stop, or destroy individual server operating systems. IaaS environments also enable customers to arrange their servers in a designed virtual network, which can include firewalls and other security devices, resulting in a network architecture not unlike that of an on-premises or *colocation* environment.

Elasticity

A favorite feature of IaaS environments is *elasticity*, in which the cloud service provider automatically instantiates additional copies of running operating systems (with their respective business applications) to meet demand. The rules, parameters, and limits regarding elasticity are configurable by customers. For instance, an e-commerce organization might employ 20 web servers and 20 database servers to manage demand. The customer can configure the cloud to add up to 10 additional web and database servers during peak demand periods. Since cloud service providers charge their customers based on the number of servers used and the work they perform, these limits ensure that excessive demand will not result in excessive charges.

Types of IaaS Services

IaaS services are designed and delivered in various ways. Common terms have been adopted for these services, including the following:

- *Public cloud* The use of infrastructure that is managed and accessed over the public Internet
- *Virtual private cloud* A portion of a public cloud environment that is logically separated between customers
- *Private cloud* The use of IaaS with its management and virtualization capabilities, dedicated to a single customer and hosted by the IaaS provider, a colocation provider, or on-site
- *Hybrid cloud* The use of a combination of public cloud and private cloud

Notable IaaS providers include Amazon Web Services (AWS), Microsoft Azure, Google Cloud, and Oracle Cloud Infrastructure (OCI).

Organizations typically employ a private cloud to meet regulatory or contractual requirements that forbid the use of the public cloud.

Platform-as-a-service (PaaS)

Platform-as-a-service (PaaS) is a service platform hosted by a service provider and available over the Internet. Service platforms typically have a core service that resembles software-as-a-service (SaaS), but with the ability for other organizations to attach or integrate their own software programs and/or databases into the core platform. Examples of PaaS services include Salesforce, SAP Concur, and Heroku.

Software-as-a-service (SaaS)

Software-as-a-service (SaaS) is the model through which software vendors make their applications available to customers. Rather than making the software available for customers to install on their own servers, software vendors run it on their own computers and make it available to customers under a leasing arrangement

SaaS vendors typically run very large instances of their applications in a multitenant architecture, whereby multiple customers use the application concurrently. SaaS vendors implement logical controls that partition customer data so customers can access only their own data, not that of other customers.

Application vendors have found that supporting only their own running instances of their software is far more efficient and effective than supporting customers running the software on their own servers. Further, the growth of IaaS means fewer organizations maintain their own server environments, making SaaS a more attractive prospect for many customers.

SaaS reduces the complexity of application management for organizations. Instead of building and maintaining server operating systems and database management systems, and installing application patches, organizations log in to SaaS applications hosted by the software companies themselves, who are the true users of business applications, without having to do any of the work supporting their infrastructure.

Serverless Computing

Serverless computing is a cloud service model in which a customer organization deploys its software applications to a cloud service provider that manages the underlying operating systems. The term "serverless computing" does not imply the absence of a server, but rather the absence of the need for the customer organization to manage it. Examples of serverless computing services include AWS Lambda, Google Cloud Functions, Azure Functions, and IBM Cloud Functions.

Mobile Backend-as-a-service

A relatively new concept, *mobile backend-as-a-service (MBaaS)*, is a cloud-based platform that facilitates the development of data-backed mobile apps. These platforms commonly include user management, APIs, and notifications. Some MBaaS services feature integration with social media platforms such as Facebook, Twitter, and Instagram.

Shared Responsibility Models

Many organizations adopt cloud-based services under the belief that cloud service providers handle all aspects of information security. This errant thinking has led to many breaches over the years. A *shared responsibility model* defines the parties that are responsible for various aspects of information security. Having a clear understanding of your responsibilities and capabilities for managing the cloud environment is critical to upholding privacy and security requirements. For example, in a SaaS model, the SaaS provider manages network and operating system security, while the SaaS customer is responsible for user access management. In an IaaS model, the IaaS provider handles physical security, but the IaaS customer is responsible for configuring and patching operating systems. The following illustrates a typical shared responsibility model:

Responsibility	SaaS	PaaS	IaaS	On-Prem
Data governance and rights management	Customer	Customer	Customer	Customer
Client endpoints	Customer	Customer	Customer	Customer

Responsibility	SaaS	PaaS	IaaS	On-Prem
Account and access management	Customer	Customer	Customer	Customer
Identity and directory infrastructure	Both	Both	Customer	Customer
Application software	Vendor	Both	Customer	Customer
Network controls	Vendor	Both	Customer	Customer
Operating system	Vendor	Vendor	Customer	Customer
Physical hosts	Vendor	Vendor	Vendor	Customer
Physical networks	Vendor	Vendor	Vendor	Customer
Physical data center	Vendor	Vendor	Vendor	Customer

Regardless of the cloud model that is chosen, the organization needs to understand many details that are related to the way the cloud provider provides its services to the organization, such as the following:

- **Access control** The cloud service provider must have an effective access control plan to ensure that only authorized personnel have access to infrastructure components and virtual machines. Often, the organization using cloud services will manage access control in the upper layers (such as operating systems, database management systems, and applications it might install and maintain on cloud servers). In contrast, the cloud provider will manage access control at lower levels (such as virtual machine hypervisors and physical access).
- **Environment segregation** The cloud service provider must effectively separate systems and data between customers so that no cloud customer can access the systems and/or data of other customers.
- **Physical security** The cloud services provider must provide adequate physical security so that only authorized personnel will have physical access to all cloud environment infrastructure and facilities.
- **Regulation** The cloud service provider must provide controls that meet applicable regulatory requirements for its customers. However, customers must also identify applicable regulations that they must implement in a cloud environment. For example, an organization that manages end-user profiles in a SaaS environment is accountable for its use of that user profile information and must disclose those uses in its privacy policies.

- **Privacy** The cloud service provider (and, indeed, the customer organization using cloud services) must implement safeguards to ensure the appropriate protection and handling of personally identifiable information (PII) stored in cloud environments.
- **Legal jurisdiction** The cloud service provider and its customers must have a firm understanding of the physical location of stored data relative to the data subjects' locations. This will enable legal counsel to understand the applicability of security and privacy laws governing the use of stored data. This is particularly important in the context of data privacy and data sovereignty laws, some of which are extraterritorial.
- **Availability** The cloud services provider must deliver service availability to customers at a level that meets their expectations. This applies not only to the steady availability of services, but also to on-demand availability.
- **Audit** Many standards, regulations, and legal agreements require some level of auditing of systems, applications, and supporting controls. The cloud environment must be verifiable in this regard.

The "Shared Responsibility Models" sidebar earlier in this section shows a typical cloud responsibility model that illustrates which party is responsible for implementing and operating specific security aspects in a cloud environment.

The Cloud Security Alliance (`https://cloudsecurityalliance.org`) is a high-quality resource for controls and guidance for cloud service providers and organizations using cloud-based services.

Cloud Service Advantages and Disadvantages

The appeal of cloud-based services is compelling, as they potentially allow organizations to increase their agility in implementing systems and infrastructure. There are also drawbacks, however. Table 7.1 highlights some of these factors.

Shadow IT and Citizen IT

The advent of cloud computing and SaaS made it all too easy for organizational departments to procure their own applications directly. Often, this occurred without consulting or even informing the IT department. Most often, corporate departments are simply trying to "do the right thing" by streamlining business processes to reduce cost or increase competitiveness. However, without IT, security, or privacy professionals involved, *shadow IT* (sometimes called citizen IT) is fraught with security and privacy risks, as there might be few or no people in these departments who are aware of these risks and the techniques used to mitigate them.

Often, shadow IT occurs when an organization's IT department is out of step with, or misaligned with, its internal users. Frustrated that their IT departments are not supporting them, they bypass IT to solve their information-processing problems.

Shadow IT can be difficult to detect, but tools such as a cloud access security broker (CASB), data loss prevention (DLP), and web content filtering systems can help identify it.

TABLE 7.1 Cloud Service Advantages and Disadvantages

Aspect	Self-Managed	Cloud-Managed
Control	Total control of networks, hardware, and operating systems	Partial or no control, depending on the platform used (SaaS, PaaS, IaaS)
Deployment	Slower, requiring hardware and software procurement and implementation	Faster, as infrastructure is in place and need only be configured
Agility	Lower	Higher
Scalability	Low: additional infrastructure must be procured	High, through elasticity
Security	Organization responsible for all aspects	Shared responsibility between CSP and customer
Cost	Easier to control	Harder to control
Skillsets	Full stack skillsets required	Full stack skillsets not required; cloud skillsets required
Internet dependency	Partial, depending on architecture and integrations	Full
Assurance	Internal Audit can test controls directly, as often and as rigorously as required	Must rely on audit reports such as SSAE18, ISAE3402, SOC 1, SOC 2
Privacy	Organization has total visibility and control on the use of personal information	Organization has partial visibility and control on the use of personal information

Summary

Effective privacy needs effective security. Effective security needs an IT architecture with integrity and protective controls.

The technology stack is the set of technologies that make up a system. It's often expressed in bottom-up notation, such as Linux-Apache-MySQL-Perl (LAMP), or Windows-IIS-SQL-ASP.NET (WISA).

Hardware is the physical machinery of computing and communications in IT. Hardware comes in many forms, including mainframes, servers, network devices such as routers and firewalls, laptop computers, and smartphones.

Computers are general-purpose machines that run operating system software, which in turn runs subsystem or application software. Computers consist of a CPU, main storage, secondary storage, one or more buses, and adapters for communicating over networks or with humans.

Storage systems are configured by organizing one or more volumes, within which file systems are created, and data of some kind is stored. Volumes can vary in size, and often their size can be adjusted dynamically.

Networks are the means through which computers communicate with one another. Whether networked computers are in a single room or spread across the globe, and whether a telecommunications company is involved, networks facilitate all computer communications, both wired and wireless.

Network devices carry network traffic. The arrangement of network devices leads to the architecture of a network. Security devices on a network protect systems from unwanted traffic.

Computer operating systems are large, general-purpose programs that control computer hardware and facilitate the use of software applications and tools. They also facilitate access to peripheral devices, manage storage, allocate resources, facilitate communications, and protect data. Computers can be combined in various ways, including clusters and grids.

Cloud computing refers to dynamically scalable, usually virtualized computing resources used internally or provided as a service by a third party.

Virtualization refers to the set of technologies that enable two or more operating systems (of the same type or different types) to run on a single physical computer. Virtualization technology enables organizations to use computing resources more efficiently.

Containerization is a form of virtualization, whereby multiple applications can run within a single operating system. Each such application is completely isolated from all others and can access only the resources allocated to its container.

A file system is a logical structure that facilitates the storage of data on a digital storage medium such as a hard drive, SSD, optical disc, or flash memory device. The structure of the file system facilitates the creation, modification, expansion and contraction, and deletion of data files. A file system can also be used to enforce access controls that determine which users or processes are permitted to access, alter, or create files.

A database management system, or DBMS, is a software program or collection of programs that facilitates the storage and retrieval of potentially large amounts of structured information. A DBMS contains methods for inserting, updating, and removing data; computer programs and software applications can use these functions to manipulate data in databases.

An application server is a system that runs one or more business software applications that are designed to support one or more business processes. The application(s) run under the control of a server operating system, which in turn runs either directly on server hardware, as a virtual machine under a hypervisor, or in a container.

An endpoint is any of several types of end-user devices, including desktop computers, laptop computers, tablet computers, and smartphones.

Laptop and desktop computers are the mainstays of end-user computing in most organizations. For the most part, IT departments issue laptops or desktop computers to employees and use a service desk to support end users with questions or problems about their computers.

Security and configuration management tools are used to manage the configuration, health, and security of endpoints. Security on endpoints includes antimalware, firewalls, intrusion prevention systems, data loss prevention, application allowlisting, and web content filtering.

A virtual desktop infrastructure (VDI) employs central, server-based desktop operating systems that use remote interaction protocols that give end users the appearance of local computing.

Mobile devices, including tablets and smartphones, provide convenient, on-the-go computing capabilities for users. Mobile device management (MDM) systems are used by organizations to control mobile devices that are used for business purposes.

Bring-your-own-device (BYOD) is a growing trend in which an organization's workers can use their personal devices to conduct business. Some organizations permit BYOD; others allow it with some degree of control; and others forbid it altogether.

Zero-trust is an architectural approach in which devices and users are not trusted by default but are trusted only when they meet specific context-based requirements.

Connected devices are nonhuman interaction computers and devices used in residential, office, and industrial environments to monitor and control equipment and machinery. Connected devices are sometimes less configurable and more difficult to secure than servers and endpoints; thus, organizations often isolate them on separate networks with strict access controls.

Remote access provides connectivity to an internal corporate network via a data link. Many organizations use it to enable employees who are temporarily or permanently off-site to access internal network resources from their remote locations.

Remote access is facilitated by virtual private networks (VPNs) that encapsulate and encrypt network traffic and require authentication. VPN clients are the programs used on endpoints to establish VPN connections. Clientless VPN is used when only web access to internal networks is required.

The systems development lifecycle (SDLC) describes the end-to-end process for developing and maintaining information systems. The phases of the traditional waterfall SDLC are feasibility study, requirements definition, design, development, testing, implementation, and post-implementation.

The feasibility study is an intellectual effort to determine whether a specific change or set of changes in business processes and underlying systems is practical to implement.
A feasibility study is an analysis of proposed changes to business processes and supporting applications, including the costs associated with those changes and the expected benefits.

Requirements describe the necessary characteristics of a new system or changes to an existing system. They describe how the application should work and the technologies it should support. In addition to developing functional requirements, organizations need to develop security and privacy requirements to ensure that information systems will continue to comply with applicable regulations.

While a conceptual design might have been developed during the feasibility study, the design phase requires more detail, enough that engineers and developers can build the entire system.

Data flow diagrams (DFDs) and entity-relationship diagrams (ERDs) should be included in system design documentation to ensure the protection and proper use of personal information.

Development takes place when requirements and designs have been completed and approved. Development takes on many forms, from software development to software integration and infrastructure implementation.

Test plans are directly derived from requirements. Formal testing is performed to ensure that all requirements are met in the new or updated system. Tests are performed in layers, including unit, integration, system, functional, and user acceptance testing.

Implementation is a complicated undertaking that requires planning. Some activities have long lead times, requiring implementation to begin during development or earlier.

Training is needed for personnel who will use, operate, monitor, and support new systems and applications. Training content needs to be recorded so that personnel who join the organization after implementation can receive the same training as those who were present for initial training.

In the context of the SDLC, the purpose of a data migration is to transfer data from an older, soon-to-be-retired system to a new system. Depending on the nature of the old and new systems, the purpose of the data migration is to make historical records originating in the older system available in the newer system.

When the production system has been constructed, applications loaded, data migrated, and all testing performed and verified, the project team has reached the cutover milestone. Often, management review and approval are required to verify that all necessary steps have been completed correctly.

A rollback is a serious undertaking and is considered only when a problem in the new environment is so serious that it cannot be easily remedied. Rollback planning is recommended in environments where a system's availability and integrity are critical to the organization, even if a rollback is never needed.

Sometime after implementation, a post-implementation review should be conducted for a new system to discuss the project and its expected benefits.

Retirement, also known as decommissioning and disposition, is the set of activities undertaken when a system or application reaches the end of its service life.

Software development is not a risk-free endeavor. Even when management provides adequate resources for a software development project and supports a viable methodology, there are still many more paths to failure than to success.

The waterfall SDLC model contains all the elements found in other development methodologies, although the structure, sequence, and roles vary across methodologies.

DevOps is a growing movement that uses the Agile development methodology, coupled with tighter integration among development teams, software QA, and IT operations. DevOps isn't complete without tools facilitating more effective (often automated) testing.

Continuous integration/continuous deployment (CI/CD) combines continuous integration (where developers' code is integrated into a single shared mainline several times each day) and continuous deployment (where software updates are delivered iteratively through automated deployments).

Integrated development environments (IDEs) are a class of desktop software development tools that incorporate source code editing, version control, compilation, and debugging in a single tool. An IDE enables a developer to write, test, and debug code without switching between programs.

CASE tools and vibe coding are development tools that generate source code from a set of inputs.

Hardening at the application layer is not altogether different from hardening at the network or system layer. The concept is the same: hardening refers to techniques intended to make systems more resistant to misuse and attack, or, to put it another way, to prevent unintended consequences resulting from unexpected stimuli.

To ensure that applications are free of exploitable vulnerabilities that could compromise personal information or cause applications to malfunction, various application testing tools and techniques need to be used regularly. The types of testing include code reviews, static and dynamic code scanning, manual tests, penetration testing, and bug bounties.

An API, or application programming interface, is an automated computer interface developed to perform a dedicated function. An API is generally running on a computer, listening for incoming messages or transactions that it can then process in a predetermined way.

Infrastructure-as-a-service (IaaS) refers to servers in which computing, networking, or storage infrastructure is offered as a service to customers. IaaS solutions are generally accessed via the Internet, but they can also be accessed via dedicated network connections.

Platform-as-a-service (PaaS) is a service platform hosted by a service provider and available over the Internet. Service platforms typically have a core service that resembles software-as-a-service (SaaS), with the ability for other organizations to attach or integrate their own software programs and/or databases into the core platform.

Software-as-a-service (SaaS) is the model through which software vendors make their applications available to customers. Rather than making the software available for customers to install on their own servers, software vendors run it on their own computers and make it available to customers under a leasing arrangement.

Mobile backend-as-a-service (MBaaS) is a cloud-based platform that enables the development and deployment of data-driven mobile apps.

Shadow IT is the phenomenon whereby an organization's departments (or individual end users) procure their own IT services, bypassing corporate IT.

Organizations often choose to acquire a business application hosted in a cloud or SaaS environment, rather than hosting it on their own systems. Their choices include software-as-a-service (SaaS), platform-as-a-service (PaaS), and infrastructure-as-a-service (IaaS).

Cloud responsibility models depict the distribution of security- and privacy-related responsibilities in a cloud environment between the cloud service provider and the customer.

Exam Essentials

Understand how infrastructure choices affect privacy risk. Legacy systems, on-premises environments, and cloud platforms differ in data visibility, logging capability, encryption options, and control boundaries. Privacy engineering must evaluate how infrastructure architecture influences data protection, residency, isolation, and monitoring capabilities.

Recognize privacy implications of devices and endpoints. Endpoints such as laptops, mobile devices, IoT systems, and operational technology often collect, cache, store, or transmit personal data. Privacy engineering requires controls such as endpoint encryption, event monitoring, local data minimization, secure configuration, and lifecycle management.

Account for connectivity as a privacy exposure surface. Networks, APIs, wireless communications, and inter-system integrations create pathways for the movement of personal data. Privacy engineering must address secure transmission, segmentation, in-transit encryption, and monitoring of data flows across connectivity layers.

Integrate privacy into the systems development lifecycle (SDLC). Privacy requirements should be defined during design, validated during development, and tested before deployment. Activities include data flow mapping, privacy threat modeling, privacy-by-design principles, and verification of data minimization and retention controls.

Evaluate APIs as controlled interfaces for the exchange of personal data. APIs frequently expose personal data to external partners and other services. Privacy engineering must enforce authentication, authorization, rate limiting, data filtering, schema validation, and logging to reduce overexposure of personal data.

Understand privacy risks in cloud-native architectures. Microservices, containers, serverless functions, and orchestration platforms distribute data processing across components. Privacy engineering must ensure consistent enforcement of encryption, identity management, secrets handling, and data governance across services.

Ensure consistency of privacy controls across the entire technology stack. Privacy engineering requires coordinated controls across infrastructure, endpoints, networks, development practices, and service interfaces to prevent gaps through which personal data could be exposed or processed beyond defined purposes.

Review Questions

1. Which infrastructure characteristic most directly affects data residency and sovereignty requirements?
   A. Geographic location of data centers
   B. Load balancing configuration
   C. CPU utilization levels
   D. Application response time
2. Which control is most effective in minimizing privacy risk on endpoint devices?
   A. Increasing device processing speed
   B. Installing additional applications
   C. Expanding storage capacity
   D. Enabling local data encryption
3. What is the primary privacy risk associated with unsegmented network connectivity?
   A. Reduced bandwidth utilization
   B. Increased hardware costs
   C. Unauthorized lateral data movement
   D. Improved system performance
4. In the systems development lifecycle (SDLC), when should privacy requirements be first defined?
   A. During deployment
   B. During testing
   C. During design
   D. During maintenance
5. Which API control best prevents excessive exposure of personal data?
   A. Implementing data filtering and field-level access
   B. Increasing API response time
   C. Returning full datasets by default
   D. Disabling logging
6. Which cloud-native characteristic introduces additional privacy complexity?
   A. Distributed microservices processing
   B. Centralized architecture
   C. Static resource allocation
   D. Single application deployment

7. Which endpoint scenario presents the highest privacy risk?
   A. Centrally managed corporate laptop
   B. Unmanaged personal device accessing sensitive data
   C. Encrypted mobile device
   D. Virtual desktop infrastructure session
8. What is the primary purpose of network encryption in privacy engineering?
   A. Protect data in transit from interception
   B. Improve transmission speed
   C. Reduce storage requirements
   D. Simplify application design
9. Which SDLC activity specifically identifies how personal data moves through a system?
   A. Data inventory
   B. Data flow mapping
   C. Performance tuning
   D. Input validation
10. What is the primary privacy concern with poorly secured APIs?
    A. Reduced system uptime
    B. Increased latency
    C. Unauthorized data access and leakage
    D. Higher infrastructure cost
11. Which infrastructure model provides the least direct control over underlying hardware?
    A. On-premises infrastructure
    B. Public cloud
    C. Private cloud
    D. Dedicated hosting
12. Which endpoint control best supports data minimization?
    A. Limiting local data caching
    B. Expanding local storage
    C. Increasing application permissions
    D. Disabling updates

13. What is the primary function of an API gateway in a microservices architecture?
    A. Store application data
    B. Replace backend services
    C. Manage user authentication centrally
    D. Eliminate network traffic
14. Which connectivity-related practice best supports privacy when transmitting personal data between systems?
    A. Sending data in plain text over internal networks
    B. Using encrypted communication protocols such as TLS
    C. Compressing data before transmission
    D. Increasing packet size to reduce overhead
15. Which SDLC practice ensures that privacy controls are functioning as intended before release?
    A. Code documentation
    B. Configuration management
    C. Privacy testing and validation
    D. Version tracking
16. In a cloud-native environment, what is the primary privacy risk associated with misconfigured identity and access management (IAM)?
    A. Reduced system scalability
    B. Unauthorized access to distributed services and data
    C. Increased processing latency
    D. Higher storage costs
17. Which scenario best illustrates a privacy-by-design principle in SDLC?
    A. Adding encryption after a breach
    B. Disabling logging to improve performance
    C. Increasing system complexity
    D. Implementing access controls during development
18. Which device category typically introduces the most challenges for privacy engineering due to limited control and visibility?
    A. Enterprise-managed servers
    B. Virtual machines in a data center
    C. Internet of Things (IoT) devices
    D. Cloud-based storage systems

19. Which architectural pattern most complicates consistent enforcement of privacy controls across services?
    - A. Monolithic architecture
    - B. Microservices architecture
    - C. Single-tier application
    - D. Standalone application

20. Which of the following is the best example of a basic privacy control?
    - A. Encrypting data at rest
    - B. Increasing server capacity
    - C. Adding additional processors
    - D. Expanding network bandwidth

Answers to Review Questions

1. A. Data residency and sovereignty requirements depend on where data is physically stored and processed. The geographic location of data centers determines which legal and regulatory regimes apply, making it a primary privacy consideration in infrastructure design.

2. D. Local data encryption protects personal data stored on endpoint devices from unauthorized access, particularly in cases of device loss or theft. It is a foundational privacy and security control for endpoints.

3. C. Lack of network segmentation allows data and access to move laterally across systems without restriction, increasing the likelihood of unauthorized access to personal data and expanding the impact of a breach.

4. C. Privacy requirements must be established during the design phase to ensure that systems are built with appropriate controls from the outset. Late-stage integration of privacy controls is less effective and more costly.

5. A. Data filtering and field-level access ensure that only necessary data elements are returned in API responses, supporting data minimization and reducing the risk of overexposure.

6. A. Microservices distribute processing across multiple components, increasing the number of data flows and interfaces. This creates additional complexity in enforcing consistent privacy controls across services.

7. B. Unmanaged personal devices lack standardized controls, monitoring, and enforcement mechanisms, making them more susceptible to data leakage, malware, and unauthorized access to personal data.

8. A. Encryption in transit ensures that data cannot be read or altered by unauthorized parties during transmission across networks, which is essential for protecting personal data flows.

9. B. Data flow mapping identifies how personal data is collected, processed, stored, and transmitted within a system, enabling identification of privacy risks and control points.

10. C. APIs expose system functionality and data. Without proper authentication, authorization, and validation, they can become entry points for unauthorized access to personal data, resulting in data loss and potential harm.

11. B. In public cloud environments, the cloud provider manages the underlying hardware and infrastructure, reducing the organization's direct control and requiring reliance on shared responsibility models.

12. A. Limiting local data caching reduces the amount of personal data stored on devices, thereby minimizing exposure in case of compromise or loss.

13. C. An API gateway acts as a centralized entry point for requests, often enforcing authentication, authorization, and routing. It helps control access to services and reduces direct exposure of internal components.

14. B. Encrypted communication protocols such as TLS protect personal data in transit by preventing interception and unauthorized disclosure during transmission. Connectivity between systems often crosses internal and external networks, and encryption ensures confidentiality and integrity regardless of the underlying transport. This aligns with privacy engineering principles by safeguarding personal data as it moves across components of the technology stack.

15. C. Privacy testing verifies that implemented controls, such as data minimization, consent enforcement, and retention rules, operate correctly before deployment.

16. B. Misconfigured identity and access management can result in excessive permissions across multiple services, enabling unauthorized access to personal data in a distributed environment where services interact dynamically.

17. D. Privacy by design requires integrating privacy controls early in development. Implementing access controls during development ensures that privacy protections are built into the system from the outset.

18. C. IoT devices often lack standardized security controls, have limited update mechanisms, and might continuously collect sensitive data. Their distributed nature and limited manageability create significant privacy risks.

19. B. Microservices architectures distribute functionality across multiple independent services, each with its own interfaces and data handling processes. This increases the complexity of maintaining consistent privacy controls, such as access management, logging, and data minimization.

20. A. Encrypting data at rest is a fundamental privacy and security control that protects stored personal data from unauthorized access, especially in cases of system compromise or physical theft.

Chapter

8

Privacy-related Security Controls

This chapter covers CDPSE Domain 4, "Privacy Engineering," specifically the "Privacy-related Security Controls" subdomain.

This chapter covers these job practice elements:

✔ B—PRIVACY-RELATED SECURITY CONTROLS

1. *Asset Management*
2. *Identity and Access Management*
3. *Patch Management and Hardening*
4. *Communication and Transport Protocols*
5. *Encryption and Hashing*
6. *Monitoring and Logging*

The other subdomains in Domain 4, Privacy Engineering, are:

✔ A—TECHNOLOGY STACKS—covered in Chapter 7, and

✔ C—PRIVACY CONTROLS—covered in Chapter 9.

The CDPSE Task Statement relevant to this domain is:

4. *Design and evaluate the implementation of technical and operational controls for data classifications and data life cycle requirements.*

The topics in this chapter and in Chapters 7 and 9 account for 39% of the CDPSE examination.

This chapter covers a variety of technical subjects related to the security of networks and systems that store, process, or transmit personal information. These complex topics are presented in summary form. Several references are included that direct the reader to more complete discussions of these topics.

This chapter includes a lengthy discussion of controls. While not explicitly a part of this domain, a discussion of controls is important, as they represent the safeguards organizations put in place, often in the form of technical safeguards such as firewalls and log monitoring.

Asset Management

Assets are the things of value that an organization protects in an information security program. They consist of tangible things, including the following:

- **Information systems hardware** Servers, laptops, tablets, mobile devices, and network devices of various sorts
- **Software** Operating systems, subsystems, applications, and tools—regardless of location, as well as *software licenses*
- **Virtual assets** Operating system guests, containers, and so on
- **Information** Structured databases and *unstructured data*
- **Facilities** Data centers, development centers, operations centers, business offices, sales offices, retail locations, and so on
- **Personnel** Staff, contractors, temporary workers

Asset management is the collection of activities used to manage the *asset inventory*, including the classification, use, and disposal of assets. It is a foundational activity, without which several other activities could not be effectively managed, including vulnerability management, device hardening, incident management, data security, and some aspects of financial management.

Asset Identification and Valuation

In a typical organization, and in the context of information processing, assets consist of information and the information systems that support and protect it.

Hardware Assets

Hardware assets can include server and *network* hardware, user workstations, office equipment such as copiers, printers, scanners, and Wi-Fi access points. Some organizations also include assets in storage and replacement components.

Accurately identifying hardware assets can be challenging, and many organizations do a subpar job of building and maintaining inventory information. Accounting might have an asset inventory in its accounting system, but this would not account for assets not in use or retired assets that have been reverted to storage. Further, asset inventory in accounting often does not cite the business applications they support. Tools used by IT for security scans or patch management are another source of inventory information, though it is often incomplete for many reasons. Even purpose-built asset inventory systems are plagued by inaccuracies because maintaining the data is not always a high priority.

An organization responsible for managing information and information systems must know what its assets are. More than that, IT needs to acquire and track several characteristics of every asset, including the following:

- **Identification** This includes the make, model, serial number, asset tag number, logical name, and other means of identifying the asset.
- **Value** Initially, this can signify the purchase price, but it might also reflect its depreciated value if an IT asset management program is associated with the organization's financial asset management program.
- **Location** The asset's location needs to be specified so that its existence can be verified in a periodic inventory.
- **Security classification** Security management programs almost always include a plan for classifying the sensitivity of information and/or information systems. Example classifications include secret, restricted, confidential, and public.
- **Asset group** IT assets can be classified into a hierarchy of asset groups. For example, servers in a data center that support a large application can be assigned to an asset group known as "Application X Servers."
- **Owner** This is usually the person or group responsible for the operation of the asset.
- **Custodian** Occasionally, the ownership and operation of assets will be divided between two bodies, where the owner owns them, but a custodian operates or maintains them.

Because hardware assets are installed, moved, and eventually retired, it is important to periodically verify the asset inventory by physically inspecting the assets. Depending on the value and sensitivity of systems and data, this inventory reconciliation, or "true-up," might be performed as often as monthly or as seldom as once per year. Discrepancies in actual inventory must be investigated to verify that assets have not been moved without authorization or stolen.

Subsystem and Software Assets

Software applications, such as development tools, drawing tools, and security scanning tools, and subsystems such as application servers and database management systems, are all considered assets. Like physical assets, software assets have tangible value and should be periodically inventoried. Some purposes for inventorying software include compliance with *software licensing* agreements, business continuity planning, and disaster recovery planning. If an organization tracks the return on investment of information systems, then, certainly, the value of software assets constitutes the full value of the assets that support or enable key business processes and activities.

Information Assets

Information assets are less tangible than hardware assets, because they are not easily observed. Information assets take many forms:

- **Customer information** Most organizations store information about people, whether employees, customers, constituents, beneficiaries, or citizens. The information can include sensitive details such as contact information, personal details, transactions, and order history.
- **Intellectual property** This type of information can take the form of trade secrets, source code, product designs, policies and standards, and marketing collateral.
- **Business operations** This generally includes merger and acquisition information and other types of business processes and records not mentioned earlier.
- **Virtual assets** Most organizations are moving their business applications to the cloud, eliminating the need to purchase hardware. Organizations that use infrastructure-as-a-service (IaaS) have virtual operating systems that are another form of information. Even though IaaS operating systems are not purchased, but rented or leased, there is nonetheless an asset perspective: they take time to build and configure, and therefore have a replacement cost. The value of assets is discussed more fully later in this section.

Cloud-based Information Assets

One significant challenge related to information assets lies in the nature of cloud services and how they work. A significant portion of an organization's information assets might be stored in other organizations' cloud-based services. Some of these assets will be overlooked unless an organization has exceedingly good business records. The main reason is how cloud services work: it's easy to sign up for a zero- or low-cost service and immediately begin uploading business information. Unless the organization has advanced tools such as a *cloud access security broker (CASB)*, it will be nearly impossible to know all the cloud-based services in use.

The nature of *shadow IT* implies that not all assets can be identified. This is particularly true of cloud-based assets and virtual assets.

Virtual Assets

Virtualization technology, which enables an organization to run multiple, separate operating systems on a single server, is a popular practice, whether on hardware servers in their data centers or in hosting facilities. Organizations that use IaaS are also employing virtualization technology.

IaaS and virtualization make it far easier to create and manage server assets, but maintaining an accurate inventory of *virtual machine* assets is even more challenging than for physical assets, and greater discipline is required to track and manage them properly. Unlike physical servers, which require different stakeholders to initiate and approve a purchase, virtual servers can be created with a click of a button, often at no additional cost to the organization and without approval. The term *virtualization sprawl* reflects this tendency.

The creation/use of virtual servers and other virtual machines is not limited to manual techniques. Virtual machines can also be created automatically. A typical example of this is through a cloud services feature known as *elasticity*. Additional virtual machines can be automatically created and started during heavy workloads when more servers are needed.

Containerization is another form of virtualization in which multiple software instances execute on a running operating system. The existence of these running instances might be a part of a virtual asset inventory.

Software-defined networking (SDN), the class of technologies that facilitate the creation and management of virtual network devices, poses the same challenge to organizations. Additional devices can be created at will or automatically. Managing them requires more discipline and potentially greater effort. SDN and virtualization technology are a part of *infrastructure-as-code (IaC)*, in which an organization's entire virtual environment is defined in machine-readable files.

Asset Classification

In asset classification, an organization assigns an asset to a category that represents its usage or risk. In an information security program, the purpose of asset classification is to determine each asset's level of criticality to the organization.

In the context of information privacy, asset criticality can be related to information sensitivity. For instance, a customer information database that includes contact and payment information would be considered highly sensitive and could significantly impact present and future business operations in the event of compromise.

Criticality can also be related to operational dependency. For example, a database of virtual server images might be considered highly critical. If an organization's server images were compromised or lost, it could adversely affect its ability to continue operations.

These and other criticality measures form the basis for information protection, system redundancy and resilience, business continuity planning, disaster recovery planning, access management, and privacy. Scarce resources in the form of information protection and resilience need to be allocated to the assets that require it the most, because it doesn't usually make sense to protect all assets to the same degree; instead, more valuable and critical assets should be more fully protected than those deemed less valuable and critical. (To illustrate this point, the late McGeorge Bundy, former U.S. National Security Advisor, is known to have said, "If we guard our toothbrushes and diamonds with equal zeal, we will lose fewer toothbrushes and more diamonds.")

The best approach to asset classification in most organizations is to identify and classify *information* assets first, then classify systems. One area often overlooked or not addressed to a satisfactory level is dealing with *unstructured data* and data residing outside the organization's approved systems.

Data Classification

Data classification is a process by which different datasets and collections within an organization are analyzed for value, criticality, integrity, and sensitivity. There are different ways to understand these characteristics, ranging from monetary value to sensitivity to operational criticality.

Data classification is explored in detail in Chapter 5.

System Classification

Once an organization is satisfied that its information classification is in order, it can embark on *system classification*. Like various information assets, information systems can also be classified according to various security and operational criteria. The purpose of system classification is similar to that of information criteria: to identify and categorize system assets according to the classification of information they store, process, or transmit, so that an appropriate level of protection can be determined and implemented.

Once a system is classified according to the highest level of information stored, processed, or transmitted through it, the measures used to protect the information system might well protect the information, or, in some cases, protect only the system. Both means are utilized, and both are essential.

A typical approach to system classification and protection is as follows: for each level of classification and each system type, a system-hardening standard is developed that specifies the features and configuration settings to apply to the system. These settings help make the system resistant to attack, and in some cases, the settings will help protect the information being stored, processed, or transmitted by the system.

Some examples will help illustrate these points:

- **Database management server** A database management server is used to store information, perhaps credit card data, at the Restricted level of classification. The system itself will be classified as Restricted, and the organization will develop system-hardening standards for the operating system and database management systems.

- **Demilitarized zone (DMZ) firewall** A firewall protects servers located in a DMZ from threats on the Internet. It protects the organization's internal assets from the DMZ if an attacker compromises an asset in the DMZ. Though the firewall does not store information, it protects it by restricting the types of traffic permitted to flow from the Internet to the systems on which it resides. The organization will develop and implement hardening standards for the firewall.
- **Internet time server** A server provides precise time clock data to other servers, network devices, and end-user workstations. Although the time server itself does not store, process, or transmit sensitive information, it is classified as Restricted because it has direct access (via time protocols and possibly other protocols) to assets classified as Restricted. This server will be hardened in accordance with the organization's hardening standards.

This final example introduces the concept of zones of protection. In the architecture of typical information-processing environments, information systems directly store, process, and transmit information at various classification levels, and are themselves classified accordingly. The other servers and assets in the same environment that access these servers or are accessed by them typically need to be classified at the same level. If one of these support servers were compromised by an attacker, the attacker would have direct, and perhaps unrestricted, access to an asset that stores, processes, or transmits sensitive or valuable data.

In a large, flat network, this logic could result in an organization classifying many, or even all, of its systems at the same level as the highest-classified system. This could require an organization to implement costly, complex protective and administrative measures across large numbers of systems. For this and other reasons, organizations often employ *network segmentation*, which divides a large, flat network into multiple zones, with firewalls and other protective measures implemented at the boundaries between these zones.

Figure 8.1 depicts a typical network segmentation scheme.

Facilities Classification

Data, asset, and systems classification can often be extended to facilities classification in larger organizations. *Facility classification* is a method for assigning risk levels to work centers and processing centers based on their operational criticality or other risk factors. Facilities classification aims to develop more consistent security controls for facilities with similar risk levels.

For instance, an information processing center will likely have extensive video surveillance and layers of multi-factor physical access controls. In contrast, a sales office will have minimal (if any) video surveillance and simpler access controls.

Personnel Classification

In some organizations, additional requirements are imposed on individuals with access to particularly sensitive information. Whether this information consists of trade secrets, government secrets, personal information, or other information, organizations might be

FIGURE 8.1 Example network segmentation scheme.

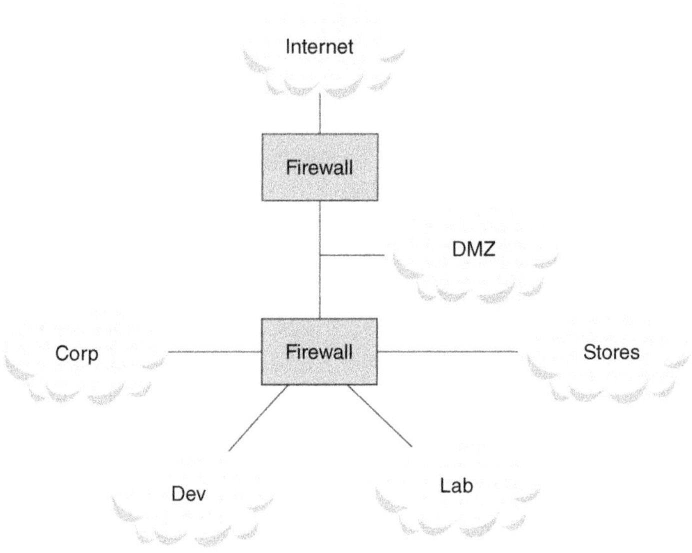

Source: Author.

required to comply with specific requirements, such as more thorough or more frequent *background checks*.

Because of the higher cost of these background investigations (to continue this example), it makes more sense to establish a classification scheme for personnel in the organization. For instance, the usual personnel classification requires a standard background check at the time of hire. A higher classification, required for access to specific information, might require a more rigorous background check at the time of hire. The highest classification might require this rigorous background check to be performed annually. Organizations in a situation like this might want to classify their employees to track the requirements for initial and ongoing background checks to ensure compliance with applicable laws, regulations, or contracts.

Organizations with no legally imposed requirements for personnel classification might still have good reasons to do so. Such circumstances can include:

- Specific policy and standards with additional sign-off/acknowledgment, as well as more robust awareness and security training
- Personnel with access to the most sensitive information (trade secrets and other intellectual property)
- Personnel with access to sensitive functions (domain administrators and personnel with other privileged system access)
- Personnel being promoted to an executive-level position, such as vice president

Thus far, only background investigations have been mentioned as variables applied to personnel in various classification levels. Other differences in the treatment of personnel at higher security levels can include:

- Assigned devices have a higher level of security protection.
- Access reviews occur more frequently or be more rigorous.
- Authentication requirements are more stringent (such as multi-factor authentication for every login).
- A different badge color outwardly signifies a higher security level
- Personnel are assigned to work in a facility (or portion thereof) with more stringent physical security controls, such as biometrics, mantraps, security guards, or additional video surveillance.

Personnel Are More Than a Number

I hope readers are not offended by my use of the term "personnel" as "assets" in an organization. Certainly, people are more than just a number; they are the soul and essence of an organization, through which its culture is personified, and valuable activities are accomplished. People are of value and warrant protection—hence, the emphasis on workplace safety and employee assistance programs (EAPs). In some organizations, personnel will also be classified into two or more security levels—for example, to limit the number of authorized persons who can access certain classified assets.

Asset Valuation

A key part of asset management is identifying an asset's value. In the absence of an asset's value, it is more difficult to classify the asset or calculate the risks associated with an asset. Without a known valuation, the impact of harm can be more difficult to know.

Asset valuation is essential for risk analysis and risk management, which are discussed in Chapter 3.

Qualitative Asset Valuation

For purposes such as asset classification and risk analysis, establishing asset valuation in qualitative terms is common across many organizations. Instead of assigning a dollar (or other currency) value to an asset, the organization can assign a value using a low-medium-high scale or a numeric scale such as 1 to 5 or 1 to 10. By using qualitative asset valuation, an organization can determine which assets are more or less valuable relative to others. This can be highly useful in an organization with many assets, as it provides a view of its high-value assets without the "noise" of lower-value assets.

Quantitative Asset Valuation

Many organizations opt to surpass qualitative asset valuation and assign a dollar (or other currency) valuation to their assets. This is common in larger or more mature organizations that want to understand all the costs associated with risk and with loss events.

In a typical quantitative valuation of an asset, its value can be calculated in one of several ways, including:

- **Replacement cost** The valuation for a hardware asset is determined to be the cost of purchasing (and deploying) a replacement. For a database, its replacement cost can be the operational costs required to restore it from backup or the costs to recover it from its source, such as a service provider.
- **Book value** This represents the value of an asset in the organization's financial system, typically the purchase price less depreciation.
- **Net present value (NPV)** If the asset directly or indirectly generates revenue, this valuation method can be used.
- **Redeployment cost** The value of a virtual machine might be determined by the cost of setting it up again. This is typically a soft cost if it is set up by internal staff, but it could be a hard cost if another company is hired to redeploy it. Remember to include any software licensing costs.
- **Creation or reacquisition cost** If the asset is a database, its cost might be determined by the cost of creating it again. If the asset is intellectual property, such as software source code, its valuation might be determined by the effort required to re-create it.
- **Consequential financial cost** The valuation of a database containing sensitive data might be measured by the financial costs resulting from its theft or compromise. Though the cost of recovering that database might be relatively low, the consequences of its compromise could run into the hundreds of dollars per record. This is a typical cost when measuring the full impact of a breach.

Organizations need to carefully determine the appropriate method for setting the value of each asset. While some instances will be fairly straightforward, others will not. In many cases, an individual asset will have more than a single valuation category. For example, a credit card database might primarily be valued on its consequential costs (because of the potential fines plus remediation costs associated with consumers who have been harmed) and also redeployment costs, although, in this case, this can be a small fraction of the total valuation.

Organizations should document their rationales and valuation methods, particularly for sensitive information assets, whose valuations can vary widely depending on the method used. Better yet, larger and more mature organizations will have guidelines that specify methods and formulas for information asset valuation.

Controls

Before we dive into the topic of security and privacy controls, it's first necessary to discuss the concept and application of controls in general. This section contains a brief discussion of controls; a comprehensive discussion of controls and control frameworks can be found in this author's books on the CISM (Certified Information Security Manager), CISA (Certified Information Systems Auditor), and CRISC (Certified in Risk and Information Systems Control) certifications.

Policies, procedures, mechanisms, systems, and other measures designed to reduce risk are collectively known as *controls*. An organization develops controls to ensure that its business objectives are met, risks are reduced, and errors are prevented or corrected. Controls are used in two primary ways in an organization: to ensure desired outcomes and to avoid unwanted outcomes. In the context of privacy and information security, controls should be defined and implemented to ensure the protection and proper handling of personal information.

The broad objective of controls, both technical and procedural, is *attack surface reduction*, the purposeful reduction in the number of entry points, interfaces, and exposures that an attacker could exploit.

Control Objectives

Control objectives are statements of desired states or outcomes from business operations to mitigate risks. When building a security program, and preferably before selecting a control framework, you need to establish high-level control objectives. Example control objective subject matter includes the following:

- Protection of IT assets
- Accuracy of transactions
- Confidentiality and privacy of sensitive information
- Availability of IT systems
- Controlled changes to IT systems
- Compliance with corporate policies
- Compliance with applicable regulations and other legal obligations

Control objectives are the foundation for one or more controls. For each control objective, one or more control activities will be implemented to ensure its realization. For example, the "availability of IT systems" control objective could be implemented via several control activities, including the following:

- IT systems will be continuously monitored, and any interruptions in availability will trigger alerts to the appropriate personnel.
- IT systems will have resource-measuring capabilities.

- IT management will review capacity reports monthly and adjust resources accordingly.
- IT systems will have antimalware controls monitored by the appropriate staff.

Together, these four (or more) controls contribute to the overall control objective of IT system availability. Similarly, other control objectives will include one or more controls that will ensure their realization.

After establishing control objectives and defining the control activities that will support the objective, your next step is to design controls. This can be a considerable undertaking when done in a vacuum. A better approach is to use one of several high-quality, industry-accepted control frameworks discussed later in this section as a starting point.

If an organization elects to adopt a standard control framework, the next step is to perform a risk assessment to determine whether controls in the control framework adequately meet each control objective. Where there are gaps in control coverage, additional controls must be developed and implemented.

An IT organization supporting many applications and services will generally have some controls that are specific to each application. However, IT will also have a set of controls that apply across all applications and services. These are usually called its *IT general controls (ITGCs)*.

Privacy Control Objectives

Privacy control objectives resemble ordinary control objectives but are set in the context of privacy and information security. The following are some examples of privacy control objectives:

- Protection of personal information from unauthorized personnel
- Protection of personal information from unauthorized modification
- Integrity of personal information
- Controlled use of personal information
- Operational compliance with the privacy policy

An organization will probably create several additional information systems control objectives on other basic topics, such as malware, availability, and resource management, many of which directly or indirectly contribute to the protection and proper use of personal information.

Control Frameworks

A *control framework* is a collection of controls that are organized into logical categories. Well-known control frameworks such as ISO/IEC 27001, NIST SP 800-53, and the CIS Controls are intended to address a broad set of information risks common to most organizations. The standards bodies that publish these frameworks are now publishing privacy-centric frameworks that build on the information security frameworks, such as ISO/IEC 27701 and the NIST Privacy Management Framework (PMF).

Standard control frameworks have been developed to streamline the process of control development and adoption within organizations. If there were no standard control frameworks, organizations would have to assemble their controls using other, inferior sources, such as the following:

- Gut feeling
- Prior experience in another organization
- A security practitioner in another organization
- An Internet search
- A deficient or incomplete risk assessment

A security manager could perform a comprehensive risk assessment and develop a framework of controls based on identified risks; indeed, this would not be considered unacceptable. However, with a variety of high-quality control frameworks freely available (apart from the ISO/IEC and COSO standards, which must be purchased), an organization could start with a standard control framework to simplify and accelerate its efforts.

Selecting a Control Framework

Several high-quality control frameworks are available for organizations that want to start with a standard framework rather than starting from scratch or using other approaches. Table 8.1 lists commonly used control frameworks. Some of these frameworks are described in more detail later in this section.

TABLE 8.1 Commonly Used Control Frameworks

Control Framework	Description	Industry Use
ISO/IEC 27001/27002	Broadly adopted international controls	All
ISO/IEC 27701	Published in August 2019 as an extension to ISO/IEC 27001 and 27002; updated in October 2025 as a standalone standard	All
NIST SP 800-53	Broadly adopted U.S.-based controls	Government, private industry
CIS Controls	Broadly adopted U.S.-based controls	All
Payment Card Industry Data Security Standard (PCI DSS)	Controls for protection of credit card data	Retail, restaurants, entertainment, banking, credit card processing

(Continued)

TABLE 8.1 (Continued)

Control Framework	Description	Industry Use
NIST Cybersecurity Framework (CSF)	Emerging U.S.-based controls	All
NIST Privacy Framework	Published in January 2020 and a draft update published for public comment in April 2025 as a companion of the NIST CSF	All
Health Insurance Portability and Accountability Act (HIPAA)	Controls for the protection of electronic protected health information (ePHI)	Medical services including delivery, billing, and insurance
COBIT 2019	Broadly adopted international controls	All
Committee of Sponsoring Organizations of the Treadway Commission (COSO)	Controls for preserving the integrity of financial information and financial statement reporting	All U.S. public companies, as well as private companies requiring similar controls
North American Electric Reliability Corporation (NERC) Reliability Standards	Controls for the protection of electric generation and distribution infrastructure	Electric utilities
Cloud Security Alliance (CSA) Controls	Controls for use by cloud-based service providers	All
SOC 1 (System and Organization Controls Report)	Bespoke controls for use by financial service providers	All
SOC 2 (System and Organization Controls Report)	Standard controls for use by cloud-based service providers	All
SIG (Standardized Information Gathering)	Controls used in the assessment of third parties	All

There is ongoing debate regarding which control framework is best for an organization. In the author's opinion, the debate on the topic reveals that many do not understand the purpose of a control framework or the risk management lifecycle. The common belief is that once an organization selects a control framework, it is "stuck" with a set of controls and will not make changes to them. Instead, as discussed throughout this book, the selection of a control framework is a starting point, not a perpetual commitment. Once a control framework is selected, the risk management lifecycle is used to understand risks within the organization, resulting in changes to the organization's controls. In fact, it can be argued that an organization practicing effective risk management will eventually arrive at a more or less similar set of controls, regardless of the starting point.

A different and valid approach to control framework selection has more to do with the structure of controls than the controls themselves. Each control framework consists of logical groupings based on control categories. For instance, most control frameworks include sections on identity and access management, vulnerability management, and incident management. Some control frameworks' groupings are more sensible in certain organizations based on their operations or industry sector.

There is also nothing wrong with a security manager selecting a control framework based on their familiarity and experience with it. This is valid to a point; however, selecting the PCI DSS control framework for a healthcare delivery organization might not be the best choice.

Exam Tip

CDPSE candidates are not required to memorize COBIT or other frameworks, but familiarity with them will help them better understand how these frameworks contribute to effective privacy and security governance and control.

ISO/IEC 27002

The international standard, *ISO/IEC 27002*, "*Information security, cybersecurity and privacy protection—Information security controls*," is a well-known security controls framework. The categories of controls are as follows:

- Operational controls
- People controls
- Physical controls
- Technological controls

ISO/IEC 27002 costs about $300 per single-user copy and is available from `www.iso.org/`.

CIS Controls

The *Center for Internet Security Critical Security Controls (CIS CSC)* is a control framework that traces its lineage to the SANS Institute. The framework was formally referred to as the "SANS Top 20" or "SANS 20 Critical Security Controls." The categories of controls are as follows:

1. Inventory and control of enterprise assets
2. Inventory and control of software assets
3. Data protection
4. Secure configuration of enterprise assets and software
5. Account management
6. Access control management
7. Continuous vulnerability management
8. Audit log management
9. Email and web browser protections
10. Malware defenses
11. Data recovery
12. Network infrastructure management
13. Network monitoring and defense
14. Security awareness and skills training
15. Service provider management
16. Application software security
17. Incident response management
18. Penetration testing

CIS CSC controls available from `www.cisecurity.org/controls/` (registration required).

PCI DSS

The *Payment Card Industry Data Security Standard (PCI DSS)* is a global control framework specifically for protecting credit card numbers and related information when stored, processed, and transmitted on an organization's networks. The PCI DSS was developed by the PCI Security Standards Council, a consortium of the world's dominant credit card brands, namely Visa, MasterCard, American Express, Discover, and JCB.

PCI DSS is mandatory for all organizations that store, process, or transmit credit card data. Organizations with larger volumes of card data are required to undergo annual on-site audits. Many organizations use the controls and the principles in PCI DSS to protect other types of financial and personal data, such as account numbers, Social Security numbers, and dates of birth.

The control objectives of PCI DSS are as follows:

1. Install and maintain network security controls
2. Apply secure configurations to all system components
3. Protect stored account data
4. Protect cardholder data with strong cryptography during transmission over open, public networks
5. Protect all systems and networks from malicious software
6. Develop and maintain secure systems and software
7. Restrict access to system components and cardholder data by business need to know
8. Identify users and authenticate access to system components
9. Restrict physical access to cardholder data
10. Log and monitor all access to system components and cardholder data
11. Test security of systems and networks regularly
12. Support information security with organizational policies and programs

PCI DSS is available from `www.pcisecuritystandards.org` (registration and license agreement required).

HIPAA

The *Health Insurance Portability and Accountability Act (HIPAA)* established requirements for protecting ePHI. These requirements apply to virtually every corporate or government entity (a *covered entity*) that stores or processes ePHI. HIPAA requirements fall into three main categories.

- Administrative safeguards
- Physical safeguards
- Technical safeguards

Several controls reside within each of these three categories. Each control is labeled as "Required" or "Addressable." Controls that are *Required* must be implemented by every covered entity. *Addressable* controls are considered optional for each covered entity, meaning the organization does not have to implement an Addressable control as stated if a documented risk assessment concludes that an equivalent alternative is in place, or that the stated control or an equivalent alternative does not apply or poses negligible risk if not implemented.

HIPAA is available from `www.gpo.gov/fdsys/pkg/CRPT-104hrpt736/pdf/CRPT-104hrpt736.pdf`.

NIST SP 800-53 and NIST SP 800-53A

NIST SP 800-53, *Security and Privacy Controls for Federal Information Systems and Organizations*, is one of the most well-known and adopted security control frameworks. NIST SP 800-53 is required for all U.S. government information systems, as well as all information systems in private industry that store or process information on behalf of the U.S. government.

Even though the NIST SP 800-53 control framework is required for U.S. federal information systems, many organizations that are not required to employ it have utilized it, primarily because it is a high-quality framework with in-depth implementation guidance and is available at no cost.

NIST SP 800-53A, *Assessing Security and Privacy Controls in Federal Information Systems and Organizations: Building Effective Assessment Plans*, is the companion standard to NIST SP 800-53 that defines techniques for auditing or assessing each control in that standard.

The structure of NIST SP 800-53 and 53A controls is as follows:

- Security Control Families
  - AC—Access Control
  - AT—Awareness and Training
  - AU—Audit and Accountability
  - CA—Assessment, Authorization, and Monitoring
  - CM—Configuration Management
  - CP—Contingency Planning
  - IA—Identification and Authentication
  - IR—Incident Response
  - MA—Maintenance
  - MP—Media Protection
  - PE—Physical and Environmental Protection
  - PL—Planning
  - PS—Personnel Security
  - RA—Risk Assessment
  - SA—System and Services Acquisition
  - SC—System and Communications Protection
  - SI—System and Information Integrity
  - SR—Supply Chain Risk Management

- Privacy Control Families
  - AP—Authority and Purpose
  - AR—Accountability, Audit, and Risk Management
  - DI—Data Quality and Integrity
  - DM—Data Minimization and Retention
  - IP—Individual Participation
  - SE—Security
  - TR—Transparency
  - UL—Use Limitation

NIST SP 800-53 and NIST SP 800-53A are available from `http://csrc.nist.gov/publications/PubsSPs.html`.

Mapping Control Frameworks

Frequently, organizations find themselves in a position where more than one control framework needs to be selected and adopted. The primary factors driving this are as follows:

- Multiple applicable regulatory frameworks
- Multiple operational contexts

Organizations with multiple control frameworks often crave a simpler organization for their controls. Often, organizations will "map" their control frameworks together, resulting in a *crosswalk*, which is a chart with controls from each framework present. Mapping control frameworks together can be time-consuming and tedious, though in some instances the work has already been done. Some mappings must be built manually if reliable online sources cannot be found.

Table 8.2 shows selected controls from PCI DSS and NIST SP 800-53 mapped together.

When mapping control frameworks or reviewing prewritten control framework mapping, it's important to note that the detailed requirements between control frameworks can still differ. For instance, one control framework might stipulate password rotation every 90 days, while another might allow the organization to choose the rotation frequency. In other words, even though two control frameworks have statements on individual items, those items might not always agree.

Working with Control Frameworks

Once an organization selects a control framework and multiple frameworks are mapped together (if the organization has decided to do so), security managers will need to organize a set of activities around the selected/mapped control framework.

TABLE 8.2 Selected PCI DSS and NIST SP 800-53 Control Mappings

Description	PCI DSS 4.x	NIST SP 800-53
Implement audit logging	10.2	AU-2, AU-12
Record audit log details	10.3	AU-3
Time synchronization	10.4	AU-8
Log review	10.6	AU-6
Audit log retention	10.7	AU-11

Risk Assessment

Before a control can be designed, the privacy or security manager needs to have some idea of the nature of risks that a control is intended to address. In a running risk management program, a new risk might have been identified during a risk assessment, leading to the creation of an additional control. In this case, information from the risk assessment is needed to properly design the control to handle these risks.

If an organization implements a control prior to a risk assessment, it might not design and implement the control properly. Here are some examples:

- A control is not rigorous enough to counter a threat.
- A control is too rigorous and costly (in the case of a moderate or low risk).
- A control does not counter all relevant threats.

In the absence of a risk assessment, the likelihood of one of these undesirable outcomes is quite high. If an organization is implementing a control, a risk assessment must be conducted. If an organization-wide risk assessment is not feasible, a risk assessment focused on the control area should be performed. Hence, the organization knows which risks the control is intended to address.

Control Design

An early step in control use is its design. In a standard control framework, the control language itself appears, along with some degree of guidance. The privacy or security manager, together with personnel responsible for relevant technologies and business processes, needs to determine which activities should occur. In other words, they need to figure out how to operationalize the control.

Proper control design will potentially require one or more of the following:

- New or changed policies
- New or changed business process documents

- New or changed information systems
- New or changed business records

Control Implementation

After a control has been designed, it needs to be put into service. Depending on the nature of the control, this could involve operational impact in the form of changes to business processes and/or information systems. Changes with greater impact will require greater care so that business processes are not adversely affected. For instance, an organization might implement a control that requires production servers and other devices to be hardened against attacks to comply with recognized standards such as the CIS Benchmarks. After the hardening standards are developed (no easy task, by the way), they need to be tested and implemented. If a production environment is affected, it could take quite a bit of time to ensure that none of the hardening standard items adversely affects the performance, integrity, or availability of affected systems.

Control Monitoring

After an organization implements a control, it needs to monitor it. For this to happen, the control needs to have been designed to enable monitoring. In the absence of monitoring, the organization will lack methodical means to observe the control and determine whether it is being operated correctly and is effective.

Some controls are not easily monitored. For instance, a control addressing abuse of intellectual property rights includes the enactment of new *acceptable use policies (AUPs)* that prohibit employees from violating intellectual property laws such as copyrights. Many forms of abuse cannot be easily monitored.

Control Assessment

Any organization that implements controls to address risks should periodically examine those controls to determine whether they are working as intended and as designed. There are several available approaches to control assessment:

- **Security review** One or more information security staff members examine the control along with any relevant business records.
- **Control self-assessment (CSA)** Control owners answer questions and include any relevant evidence.
- **Internal audit** The organization's internal auditors (or information security staff) perform a formal examination of the control.
- **External audit** An external auditor formally examines the control.

An organization will select one or more of these methods, guided by any applicable laws, regulations, legal obligations, and results of risk assessments.

Control audits are discussed in Chapter 4.

Identity and Access Management

Identity and access management comprises a collection of activities in an organization that are concerned with the following:

- *Identity management* Management of an accurate inventory of workers in the organization, whether full-time employees, part-time employees, temporary workers, contractors, consultants, or employees of other organizations performing services requiring access to networks, systems, or data
- *Access management* Management of all of these workers' access rights into networks, systems, data, applications, and places where business operations take place

Identity and access management is getting more difficult. As organizations shift from on-premises to cloud-based computing, the traditional fallback controls of building access and network firewalls are no longer relevant. Often, only identity and access management processes are available to distinguish persons authorized to access systems and data from those who are not.

Part of the duality of privacy is security. Increasingly, identity and access management is becoming central to security and, therefore, to privacy as well.

There are several access control models that contain structure and rules for building access control systems. The two most common models found in government and industry are as follows:

- *Discretionary access control (DAC)* Often implemented on file servers, access rights are governed by the owners of files and directories.
- *Mandatory access control (MAC)* Access rights are set by system administrators so that the system enforces access based on security labels and a centrally defined access control policy. End users who want permissions to be changed must make formal requests to system administrators.

Access Controls

Access controls determine whether and how *subjects* (usually persons, but also running programs, computers, and devices) can access *objects* (usually systems and/or data). Logical access controls work in a few different ways:

- **Subject access** A logical access control uses some means to determine the *identity* of the subject requesting access. Once the subject's identity is known and verified beyond a reasonable doubt, the access control performs a function to determine whether the subject should be allowed to access the object. If access is permitted, the subject can proceed; if denied, the subject cannot proceed. An example of this type of access control is an application that first authenticates a user by requiring a user ID and password before granting access.

- **Service access** A logical access control is used to control the types of messages allowed to pass through a control point. The logical access control is designed to permit or deny messages of specific types (and might also permit or deny them based on origin and destination) to pass. Examples of this type of access control include a firewall, screening router, intrusion protection system (IPS), *web content filter*, or CASB that makes pass/block decisions based on the type of traffic, its content, origin, and destination.

These two types of access are like a concert hall with a parking garage. The parking garage (the service access) permits cars, trucks, and motorcycles to enter, but denies entry to oversized vehicles. Upstairs at the concert box office (the subject access), persons are admitted if they possess a photo identification with a name that matches a list of prepaid attendees. Further, certain persons are granted "backstage access" if they possess the required credentials and are not carrying dangerous objects such as weapons.

Broadly, access controls are designed and implemented in accordance with an organization's *access control policy*, which defines principles, processes, roles, and responsibilities for managing access.

Access Control Concepts

In discussions about access control, security and privacy professionals often use terms that are not used in other disciplines, including these:

- **Subject, object** These pronouns refer to access control situations. A *subject* is usually a person, but it could also be a running program, a device, or a computer. In typical security parlance, a subject is someone (or some*thing*) that wants to access something. An *object* (which could be a computer, application, database, file, record, or other resource) is the thing that the subject wants to access.
- **Fail open, fail closed** This refers to the behaviors of automatic access control systems when they experience a failure of some kind. For instance, if power is removed from a keycard-based building access control system, will all doors be locked or unlocked? The term *fail closed* means that all accesses will be denied if the access control system fails; the term *fail open* means that all accesses will be permitted upon its failure. Generally, security and privacy professionals like access control systems to fail closed, because it is safer to admit no one than to admit everyone. But there will be exceptions now and then where fail open might be better; for example, building access control systems might need to fail open in some situations to facilitate the emergency evacuation of personnel or the entry of emergency services personnel.
- **Least privilege** According to the concept of *least privilege*, an individual user should have the lowest privilege possible that will still enable them to perform required tasks.
- **Segregation of duties** The concept of *segregation of duties* specifies that no single individual should have a combination of privileges that would permit them to perform high-value operations on their own. The classic example is a business accounting department where the functions of creating a payee, requesting a payment, approving a payment, and making a payment should be performed by two or more separate

individuals. This will prevent any one person from embezzling funds from an organization without notice. In the context of information technology, functions such as requesting and provisioning user accounts should be performed by two different individuals so that no single individual can create user accounts on their own.

- **Split custody** The concept of *split custody* is the practice of dividing knowledge of a specific object or task between two or more persons. One example is splitting a critical encryption key's password between two parties: one person has the first half and the other has the second half. Similarly, the combination to a bank vault can be split so that two persons have the first half of the combination while two others have the second half. In some industries, this practice is known as *dual control*.
- *Role-based access control (RBAC)* The task of managing users' access to systems and information, particularly in larger organizations, is daunting, labor-intensive, and error-prone. One approach to streamline access management is to implement role-based access control. Here, user accounts are assigned to *roles*, which themselves are given access rights. When business changes occur, and users' access rights need to be updated, only the role needs to be changed; all users assigned to the role will have their access updated by virtue of the role's change.

Access Control Threats

Because access controls are often the only means of protection between protected assets and users, access controls are often vigorously attacked. Indeed, many attacks against computers and networks containing valuable assets are against access controls in attempts to trick, defeat, or bypass them. Threats represent the intent and ability to harm an asset. In the context of privacy, these threats represent an adversary's desire to access personal information and steal, expose, corrupt, or destroy it.

Threats to access controls include social engineering, *malware*, *eavesdropping*, *logic bombs*, *backdoors*, *keyloggers*, and *scanning*.

The potency and frequency of threats to a system are directly proportional to the perceived value of the assets it contains or protects.

Social Engineering Is the Initial Attack Vector

Research and numerous surveys reveal that most successful cyberattacks begin with *social engineering*—when personnel in an organization are tricked into performing actions that enable an adversary to attack the organization successfully. The most common form of social engineering is phishing, but several other techniques are used as well. The attack types listed in the previous section are almost always preceded by an initial social engineering attack that provides the adversary with the beachhead needed to break into the environment.

Access Control Vulnerabilities

Vulnerabilities are weaknesses in a system that enable a threat to be carried out more easily or to have a greater impact. Vulnerabilities alone do not bring about actual harm. Instead, threats and vulnerabilities work together. Most often, a threat exploits a vulnerability, because it is easier to attack a system at its weakest point. Common vulnerabilities include:

- **Unpatched systems** Security patches are designed to remove specific vulnerabilities. An unpatched system still has vulnerabilities, some of which are easily exploited. Attackers can easily enter and take over systems that lack important security patches.
- **Default system settings** Default settings often include unnecessary services that increase the chances that an attacker can break into a system. The practice of *system hardening* involves removing unnecessary services and making security configuration changes to make a system as secure as possible.
- **Default passwords** Some systems are shipped with default administrative passwords that make it easy for a new customer to configure the system. One problem with this arrangement is that many organizations fail to change these default passwords. Hackers have access to extensive lists of default passwords for practically every kind of computer and device that can be connected to a network.
- **Incorrect permissions settings** If the permissions for access to files, directories, databases, application servers, or software programs are incorrectly set, this could permit access—and even modification or damage—by persons who should not have access.
- **Vulnerabilities in utilities and applications** System utilities, tools, and applications that are not part of the base operating system could have exploitable weaknesses that could allow an attacker to compromise a system.
- **Application logic** Software applications—especially those that are accessible via the Internet—that contain inadequate session management, resource management, and input-testing controls can permit an intruder to take over a system and steal or damage information.

Identification, Authentication, and Authorization

Access to computing resources is protected by mechanisms that ensure only authorized subjects can access protected information. Generally, these mechanisms first identify who (or what) wants to access the resource, then determine whether the subject is permitted to access it, and either grant or deny access.

Several terms, including *identification*, *authentication*, and *authorization*, are used to describe various activities and are explained here.

Identification

Identification is the act of asserting an identity without providing any proof of it. This is analogous to one person walking up to another and saying, "Hello, my name is ______."

Because it requires no proof, identification is not usually used alone to protect high-value assets or functions.

Websites often use identification to remember someone's profile or preferences. For example, a bank's web application might use a cookie to store the name of the city in which the customer lives. When the customer returns to the website, the application will display some photos or news that are related to the customer's location. But when the customer is ready to perform online banking, this simple identification is insufficient to prove the customer's actual identity.

Identification is the *first* step in gaining access to a system or application. The next steps are authentication and authorization, which are discussed next.

Authentication

Authentication is similar to identification, where a subject asserts an identity. In identification, no proof of identity is requested or provided; in authentication, some form of proof of the subject's identity is required. That proof is usually provided in the form of a secret password or a more sophisticated means of authentication, such as a token, biometric, *smart card*, or digital certificate. Each of these is discussed later in this section.

When the user presents their *user ID* plus a second factor, such as a password, *token*, biometric, or other factor, the system will determine whether the login request will be granted or denied. Regardless of the outcome, the system will record the login event in an event log.

Multi-factor authentication is quickly becoming the norm for all human subjects authenticating to networks and systems containing sensitive information.

Authorization

After a subject has been authenticated, the next step is *authorization*. This is the process by which the system determines whether the subject should be permitted to access the requested resource in the requested manner. To determine whether the subject is permitted to access the resource, the system will perform some lookup or other reference to a business rule. For instance, an access control table associated with the requested resource might contain a list of users permitted to access it. The system will read through this table to determine whether the subject's identity appears in the table. If so (and if the type of requested access matches the type permitted in the table), the system will permit the subject to access the resource. If the user's identity does not appear in the table, the user will be denied access. Whether the login is successful or not, an access attempt (and its disposition) is logged in an event log.

Typically, permissions are centrally enforced by the operating system and administered by system administrators (mandatory access control), although some environments allow resource owners to manage user access (discretionary access control).

Exam Tip

The terms *identification, authentication,* and *authorization* are often misused by business professionals who might not realize the differences between them. Privacy and security professionals need to understand the differences.

User IDs and Passwords

User IDs and passwords are the most common means for users to authenticate to a resource—whether it is a network, server, or application.

User IDs

In most environments, a user's user ID will not be a secret; in fact, user IDs might be derived from the user's name or an identification number. Some of the common forms of a user ID include combinations of the user's first and last name or an employee ID number.

Confidential numbers, such as social insurance (Social Security in the United States) or driver's license numbers, should not be used as user IDs, as these identifying numbers are generally meant to be kept confidential.

Passwords

Whereas a user ID is not necessarily kept confidential, a password *always* is. A *password*, also known as a *passphrase*, is a secret combination of letters, numbers, and other symbols known only to the actual user. End users are typically advised the following about passwords:

- Select a strong password or passphrase that is easy to remember but difficult for others to guess.
- Passwords must never be shared or used by others.
- Passwords must never be transmitted in cleartext over any network.
- Passwords should be stored in a secure password vault.
- Each system should have a unique password.
- Passwords used for personal accounts should not be used for any work-related account.

Given their vital importance, many organizations' information security policies devote considerable attention to passwords, including details such as:

- *Password length* The minimum and, sometimes, the maximum length of passwords
- *Password complexity* The types of characters required in a password (lowercase letters, uppercase letters, numerals, and symbols, such as @#$%&?)

- *Password expiration* The length of time that a password is considered valid before it must be replaced
- *Password reuse* Whether a user can reuse a password used in the past
- *Password lockout* The automatic disabling of a user account after a set number of unsuccessful login attempts (an indication of an attack)
- *Password reset* Procedures and safeguards concerning the reset of a password in various circumstances, including forgotten passwords and password lockouts
- *Password vaulting* Whether password vaults are optional, required, and which ones to use
- *Default password* A policy requiring default passwords to be changed on all systems before their production use

There is no single combination of password length, complexity, expiration, lockout, reset, and reuse that can be applied to all organizations. Instead, organizations must consider applicable regulations, risks, risk appetite, and other factors to determine their password policies.

User Account Provisioning

When a user is issued a new computer or system user account, they need to know the password to access the resource. Generating and transmitting an initial password to a user can be tricky because passwords should never be sent via email. A sound practice for initial user account *provisioning* would involve using a limited-time, *one-time password* securely provided to the user; upon first use, the system would require the user to change the password to a value known only to them.

Ideally, users will be required to change their password as soon as they have their new user account, but some systems don't even permit this. Privacy and security professionals should understand an environment's capabilities as well as the risks and value of the assets being protected. Any recommendations should reflect system capabilities and asset value.

Risks with User IDs and Passwords

Password-based authentication is among the oldest in use in information systems. Although password authentication remains prevalent, several risks are associated with its use due to the various ways passwords can be discovered and reused by others. Some of these risks involve the following:

- Eavesdropping
- Key logging
- *Phishing*
- Finding a password written down
- Finding a stored password
- Exploiting a browser's password store

These follow the same theme: user IDs and passwords are static and, if discovered, can be used by others. For this reason, other, more secure means of authentication have been developed, including biometrics, tokens, smart cards, and certificates, all of which are collectively *multi-factor authentication*, discussed next.

Multi-factor Authentication

Multi-factor authentication (MFA), formerly known as strong authentication, is so-called because it relies not only on "something you know" (namely, a password), but also upon "something you have" (such as a key card or smart card) and/or "something you are" (such as a fingerprint). MFA requires a user's user ID and password, but the user must also possess something or use a biometric to complete the authentication. Several technologies are used for MFA, including tokens, soft tokens, SMS tokens, smart cards, digital certificates, and biometrics.

Users of MFA systems need to be trained on their proper use. For example, they need to be told not to store their tokens or smart cards with their computers, and to keep their smartphones or mobile devices locked except when in use.

SMS-based MFA is increasingly considered unsafe due to the risks associated with *SIM fraud*. Other methods are therefore preferred.

Biometrics

Several *biometric* authentication technologies share a common theme: they all measure a unique physical characteristic of the person authenticating. Some of the technologies in use are as follows:

- Fingerprint
- Handprint
- Voice recognition
- Iris scan
- Facial scan
- Signature
- Gait

Organizations considering the use of biometrics must carefully assess the logistics of its use, including initial registration, ease and cost of use, use cases (local access, remote access, offline access), and cultural considerations. Some personnel will consider the use of biometrics an invasion of their privacy, whether or not those fears are well-founded.

Reduced Sign-on

In a *reduced sign-on* environment, several applications use a centralized directory service such as *Lightweight Directory Access Protocol (LDAP)*, *Remote Authentication Dial-in User Service (RADIUS)*, *Diameter*, or *Microsoft Active Directory (AD)* for authentication. The term comes from the result of changing each application's authentication from standalone to centralized, and the reduction in the number of user ID–password pairs each user is required to remember.

> **Exam Tip**
>
> The terms "reduced sign-on" and "single sign-on" are often used interchangeably. Many times, a reduced sign-on environment is labeled as single sign-on. For the exam, remember that they are *not* the same.

Single Sign-on

In a *single sign-on (SSO)* environment, applications are logically connected to a centralized authentication server that is aware of each user's logged-in/logged-out status. At the start of the workday, when a user logs in to an application, they will be prompted for login credentials. When the user logs in to another application, the application will consult the central authentication server to determine whether the user is already logged in; if so, the second application will not require the user's credentials. The term refers to the fact that a user needs to sign on only once, even in a multi-application environment.

SSO is more complicated than reduced sign-on. In an SSO environment, each participating application must be able to communicate with a centralized authentication controller and act accordingly by requiring a new user to log in, or not.

Remote Access

Remote access provides connectivity to an organization's internal networks. Remote access is discussed in detail later in this chapter.

Access Control Lists

Access control lists (ACLs) are a common means of administering access controls. ACLs are used by many operating systems and other devices, such as routers, as a simple means to control access to resources, such as servers or networks.

On many devices and systems, the list of packet-filtering rules (which gives a router many of the characteristics of a firewall) is known as an ACL. In the UNIX operating system, for instance, ACLs can control which users are permitted to access files and directories and run tools and programs. ACLs in these and other contexts are often simple text files that can be edited with a text editor.

Privileged Access Management

Privileged access management (PAM) comprises an organization's policies, procedures, and tools for managing privileged user and *service accounts*.

Because of the higher risks associated with privileged accounts, organizations often implement additional policies and procedures beyond those that govern non-privileged users. Some of the differences in processes and tooling include:

- Additional approvals required for assigning privileged accounts to personnel
- More frequent access reviews for privileged accounts
- More rigorous authentication, including longer passwords, more sensitive lockout settings, and more frequent expiration
- Logging of activities performed
- Service accounts configured to be non-interactive
- The use of a password vault to broker interactive sessions, such that the administrators do not possess passwords
- On-the-spot approvals required for privileged access to production environments

Access Control Processes

Sound business processes must be in place for access controls to manage user access effectively and protect critical systems and sensitive information. These business processes should be documented, and detailed business records must be kept that document all related activities. Formal roles and responsibilities must be defined so that only authorized persons can perform various functions. Access control processes generally fall into two categories: processing access requests and conducting periodic access reviews.

Access Requests

Formal access request processes should be used to control the provisioning of user access. Using the principle of separation of duties, the actions of requesting access, approving access, and providing access should be performed by different individuals.

Each step in an access request process should be recorded. These business records permit audits of access request processes to confirm that only properly issued and processed access requests result in the granting of user access.

The approver of an access request should be the system owner, typically an individual in a business unit or department. IT personnel, who act as stewards of information systems, should not approve access requests.

Access requests should only be granted to subjects who have completed a *background check*, which is typically managed by Human Resources at the time of hire.

Access Transfer and Termination

Access rights for employees *transferring* to a different position need to be reviewed and updated. Often, employees transferred to another position will no longer require the access rights unique to their former position. There are, however, exceptions, such as a transferred employee who is still performing all or part of their former position or training a replacement.

Access rights for former employees and contractors should be removed as quickly as possible after *termination*. For so-called "friendly" terminations, access rights should be removed within 24 hours. For "hostile" terminations (when an employee is being terminated), access rights should be removed at the time the employee is being notified.

In both instances, removing access rights protects the organization from an employee exacting revenge. It also removes the temptation for any former employee to log in for any reason.

Many organizations lack centralized management of contractors, resulting in IT departments not being notified of contractors whose contracts expire or are terminated early.

Access Reviews

The rate of change in organizations creates the need for *access reviews*—periodic reviews of access rights to ensure that all subjects who have access to systems and sensitive data still require that access. Several types of reviews ensure that provisioning and deprovisioning processes are effective, accurate, and timely.

Reviews are warranted even in organizations with automation and workflow in their identity and access management processes. Reviews are even more critical in organizations that use manual processes. The objectives of access reviews ensure that access management processes remain effective and accurate, and that access rights remain valid and justified.

Several types of access reviews are performed:

- **Access certifications** System owners review access rights for subjects and confirm that each subject still requires access rights. Any subjects that no longer require access rights are flagged, and their access is removed.
- **Provisioning certifications** Access management personnel examine subjects' access rights and confirm that there is valid evidence of properly executed requests, reviews, approvals, and execution for each.

- **Deprovisioning certifications** Security personnel obtain lists of terminated personnel from human resources and confirm that deprovisioning was properly and timely executed for each.
- **Activity reviews** Security personnel examine systems to determine whether subjects have logged into them recently. Inactive user accounts can be flagged for removal if subjects have not logged in for extended periods, as they likely no longer require access.
- **Segregation of duties (SOD) matrix reviews** Periodic reviews of SOD matrices help to determine whether all disallowed combinations of access are represented in SOD matrices. This is only a review of the roles themselves, not of the people who hold them.
- **Segregation of duties reviews** Reviews of subject accesses to detect SOD exceptions confirm whether any persons have access rights that violate the segregation of duties policy.
- **Temporary worker reviews** In organizations lacking centralized management of temporary workers, additional reviews will be needed to ensure that no active user accounts exist for temporary workers who are no longer active in the organization.
- **Privileged account reviews** All of the reviews listed here should be performed at a higher frequency for privileged accounts. This higher frequency is warranted due to the additional powers associated with privileged accounts and the greater damage that can result from abuse or compromise.
- **Service account reviews** These reviews determine whether service accounts are still being used, where and how they are used, and who manages them to ensure that there is no unauthorized use of service accounts.

In the absence of access governance tools, some of these reviews can be labor-intensive. Because of these, organizations will perform reviews on a risk basis: more critical systems will be reviewed more frequently than others.

Access certifications and reviews help prevent the *accumulation of privileges* (also known as *access creep*), where long-term personnel slowly accumulate access rights.

Access Monitoring

Since many cyberattacks begin with attempts to compromise individual user and system accounts, continuous monitoring of user and system account activity is considered an essential practice in cybersecurity. This monitoring is typically achieved through the real-time transmission of user account events from *access control logs* to a centralized log server, or, better yet, to a SIEM system, so that alerts on suspicious behavior can be generated and such matters investigated.

The events that should be sent to a log server or SIEM include the following:

- **All successful logins** Ideally these will include the originating IP address and geolocation of the login event.
- **All unsuccessful logins** This also needs to include IP address and location.
- **All user account permission changes** This should include the IP address and/or user account that performed the change.
- **All user account creations** This should include the IP address and the user account performing the change.
- **Privileged account changes** This includes permission changes and password changes.
- **Service account changes** This includes the creation of and modification to any service account.

Organizations need to develop "use cases" in their SIEM systems to alert security personnel of events that warrant investigation and action. For instance, if a user account logs in from the United States, and then a short time later, there is a login for the same user account in another country (known as an *impossible login*), an investigation should immediately commence to determine whether the user account has been compromised, resulting in an adversary logging into the account from the foreign location.

Identity Proofing

Many requests to an IT *service desk* are access related. Thus, organizations must employ sound *identity proofing* procedures, which are steps to confirm the identity of the requestor. For critical systems such as financial accounting applications, IT departments might perform a segregation of duties (SOD) check to determine whether the access request, if approved, would create a segregation of duties problem. For instance, many accounting departments separate critical functions such as vendor creation, payment request, and payment approval to separate individuals as a measure of fraud prevention. If a user with payment request privileges requests payment approval privileges, the SOD check should flag this and recommend that the requested access not be granted.

Patch Management and Hardening

Organizations managing information technology must employ processes and procedures to ensure their systems are resistant to attack and abuse. These processes are as follows:

- Vulnerability management
- Patch management
- Hardening

These processes are implemented with tooling and automation to improve efficiency and consistency. These processes are discussed in this section.

Patch management, vulnerability management, and hardening play a significant role in reducing the attack surface.

Vulnerability Management

Vulnerability management is a business process for identifying and mitigating vulnerabilities in IT systems, devices, applications, networks, and cloud environments. Vulnerability management is a policy-driven, lifecycle process consisting of these activities:

- **Vulnerability scanning** The use of *vulnerability scanning* tools to identify vulnerabilities in systems, devices, and applications. Scanning tools are configured to perform scheduled, automated scans of the IT environment (or portions of it). Well-known vulnerability scanning tools include Nessus, Rapid7, and Qualys.
- **Vulnerability confirmation** Analysts running vulnerability scanning tools need to examine vulnerability scan results and validate each finding (or at least those that the organization plans to act upon), because vulnerability scanning tools sometimes report false positives.
- **Assign severity level** It's imprudent to rely on the vulnerability scanner's severity rating, as any rating is produced out of context.
- **Risk analysis** Once confirming that identified vulnerabilities are genuine, analysts will perform a light risk analysis to determine the risk posed by the vulnerabilities to the organization.
- ***Remediation*** For those vulnerabilities the organization chooses to remediate, it performs remediation, which can take the form of a patch, configuration change, or architecture change. Remediation usually follows guidelines in the vulnerability management policy, which specify the required timeframe for remediation at each severity level. When remediation is performed as a patch, the patch management process (discussed in the next section) is used. When remediation is performed as a configuration change, the configuration management process (see Chapter 7) is used.
- **Remediation confirmation** Once remediation has been completed, it is prudent to confirm that remediation is successful, often with a re-scan.

Vulnerability scanning tools might identify thousands, tens of thousands, or even more vulnerabilities in an IT environment. Since an IT department, even with automation, might not be able to remediate all vulnerabilities, it will need to rely on policies that direct personnel to concentrate on the most important vulnerabilities.

Patch Management

Patch management is the process of applying functionality and security patches to systems, devices, and applications. Patch management is considered part of the broader vulnerability management process, which includes identification and analysis, whereas patch management focuses on installing patches.

The patch management process is closely linked to other processes, including:

- **Configuration management** The formal process for managing the configuration of systems and devices in an IT environment. See Chapter 7.
- **Hardening** The process of configuring systems and devices to make them more resistant to abuse and attack. This is discussed in the next section.
- **Change management** The formal process for managing change in an IT environment. See Chapter 7.
- **Vulnerability management** This is discussed here in this section.

All but the smallest organizations employ automation for patch installation to drive efficiency and consistency.

When driven by the vulnerability management process, organizations generally develop a *service-level agreement (SLA)* that defines the timeframe for installing patches.

Hardening

System *hardening* techniques are used to make systems and devices more resistant to attack. Hardening is considered essential, particularly for systems that communicate over the Internet. Mainly, hardening refers to a set of configuration settings that are applied to a system. Although these configuration settings can be applied manually, most organizations use tooling to automate their application, enabling hardening to occur more quickly and accurately.

Hardening Principles

System hardening principles are general principles describing several configuration practices that can be employed to make systems more resistant to attack. The primary principles on the topic of hardening include the following:

- **Single purpose** Systems should perform a single function or purpose, rather than having multiple roles. For instance, web, application, and database servers should reside on separate systems. This principle need not be taken to extremes, however: for instance, a DNS server can also serve as an NTP server.
- **Unnecessary subsystems and programs** Systems should be installed with only the programs and subsystems necessary for the system's purpose. For example, a web server should not have DBMS software installed on it.
- **Listeners** System utilities should not be placed in network listen mode unless necessary for their function. For instance, a UNIX server that occasionally needs to send email might need to have the Sendmail program installed, but Sendmail should not be in listen mode (awaiting inbound email).

- **Permitted connections** Systems should be configured to permit inbound connections only from authorized systems or networks. For example, inbound administrative SSH connections should be permitted only from administrative workstations or VLANs. Also, production servers should not be able to access the Internet via a browser, FTP, or other protocols, except for those necessary for their function.
- **Unnecessary data** Systems should have only the data necessary for their present function on the system. For example, application servers should not have the application's source code stored on the system. Demo or test data should not be present on any production system.
- **Necessary user accounts** Only those user accounts necessary for the function and maintenance of a system should be present on the system.
- **Default passwords and identifiers** All *default passwords* and identifiers on a system should be changed to non-default values. For example, the SNMP community string should be changed from "public" to a value not easily guessed by an outsider.
- **Rename privileged accounts** Privileged accounts, such as root or administrator, should themselves be renamed. Direct brute-force login attacks will be more difficult for attackers to carry out successfully if they do not know the names of administrative accounts.
- **Up-to-date software** The operating system and all software programs should be currently supported and up to date. Outdated and unsupported software should not be used, particularly on mission-critical systems.

Hardening Standards

Developing specific configuration settings to support hardening principles can be time-consuming and might not cover all circumstances. Further, system administrators might lack detailed expertise to apply all needed hardening configuration changes competently. For these reasons, organizations might choose to adopt one of a few good hardening standards that are available:

- **Device and system manufacturers** Better manufacturers, realizing that many of their business customers will want to harden their systems, will publish principles and/or sets of configuration standards that can be used to harden systems to protect them from attack.
- **The Center for Internet Security benchmarks** The Center for Internet Security (CIS) has published numerous excellent hardening standards for practically every type of system under the sun, from mainframes to smartphones. These benchmarks are available free of charge from `www.cisecurity.org/cis-benchmarks/`. CIS also provides tools and images that support these standards.
- **DoD Cyber Exchange guides** The DoD Cyber Exchange publishes numerous Security Technical Implementation Guides (STIGs) that include high-quality hardening standards for numerous types of systems. STIGs and other information are available at `https://public.cyber.mil/stigs/`.

Exam Tip

CDPSE candidates do not need to memorize hardening standards, but they are expected to understand the concepts of system hardening.

Real World Scenario

The Relative (In)Security of Connected Devices

A manufacturing company assembles products for direct sales to retail customers. The company utilizes industrial control systems (ICS) to manage its manufacturing line machinery, and has found that most of its ICS equipment does not support hardening or patching. This means a privacy breach could originate from its vulnerable, unpatched ICS equipment.

A security consultant recommends that the company segment its internal networks and use firewalls and IPS to limit network traffic between its corporate and manufacturing networks, to reduce the possibility of a breach in the manufacturing network from spreading to its corporate network, where its customers' personal information is stored.

Communication and Transport Protocols

Networks are the means through which computers communicate with one another. Whether the computers are across the room or halfway around the world, networks facilitate all computer communications, whether wired or wireless, and whether telecommunications services are used or not. This section presents a brief overview of network technology.

Network Media

Network media is the material through which network traffic travels, whether wired or wireless. That is, the network connection uses copper wires or fiber-optic cables for wired connections, or a radio-frequency (RF) protocol for wireless.

Another perspective on network media is whether it's provided by the user organization or by a telecommunications provider. For instance, a home or office user would set up a wireless Wi-Fi network, and a telecommunications provider would set up a 5G or LTE network.

Network media types include the following:

- *Twisted-pair* This ubiquitous network cabling is used in homes and businesses to connect systems.
- *Fiber-optic* Used by larger businesses in their data centers as well as telecommunications providers to connect businesses, data centers, and private residences to the Internet, this high-capacity glass fiber media carries signals in the form of light pulses and is impervious to magnetic and electric field interference.
- *Digital subscriber line (DSL)* The technologies used to deliver data connections over telephone lines.
- *Broadband cable* The mainstay of television signals for decades, cable is used as the medium for residential and business Internet connections.
- *4G/5G/LTE/CDMA* These over-the-air wireless protocols are provided by telecommunications carriers the world over. Our smartphones and, occasionally, tablets use these carrier protocols to communicate online. These protocols are provided as part of a fee-based voice and/or data service.
- *Wi-Fi* This ever-popular wireless network standard is used in homes, businesses, and even outdoors in urban areas. These days, devices in homes are usually connected to a residential Wi-Fi network that, in turn, is connected to a telco-provided Internet connection delivered over DSL, cable, or fiber.
- *Bluetooth* This short-range wireless protocol is a handy replacement for formerly wired connections for devices such as printers, keyboards, mice, and headphones.
- *Near-field communication (NFC)* This ultra–short range (up to 4 cm) protocol is used for contactless payment and other uses.

This list represents contemporary media types. Many others—too numerous to mention in this book—are still in use or have been entirely deprecated.

Network Protocols

Generally, the term *network protocols* refers to numerous individual standards, as well as families and suites of standards, by which information is carried over the network media discussed in the preceding section. For simplicity, this section discusses lower-level protocols first, followed by higher-level protocols.

Notable low-level protocols include these:

- *Ethernet* This is the dominant protocol used for wired home and office networks, carried over twisted-pair cable. Data in the Ethernet protocol is transported over *frames*, which are individual messages being sent from one station to another.
- *T-Carrier* and *E-Carrier* These telecommunications standards are used to transport voice and data over telecommunications cables. These families include scores of individual protocols, such as *T-1* (with a data rate of 1.544 Mbps), that can be multiplexed into 24 voice or data channels or into a single logical data pipe.

- *Digital subscriber line (DSL)* This is broadband Internet delivered over copper telephone landlines.
- *Synchronous optical networking (SONET)* This family of telecommunications standards is used to transport voice and data over long-distance optical fiber. Individual protocols such as OC-1 and OC-3 carry voice and/or data at 51.84 Mbps and 155.52 Mbps, respectively.

High-level protocols in use today are all part of the TCP/IP suite of protocols. Invented in the 1970s as a resilient, long-distance, packet-carrying network, TCP/IP is the foundation for virtually all data networking everywhere, including the global Internet.

The *TCP/IP network model* and protocol suite employs a technique known as *encapsulation*, whereby messages in higher-level protocols are encapsulated within messages in lower-level protocols, which in turn are encapsulated in messages in the physical network medium. For example, when a user loads a web page in their browser, the HTTPS protocol is encapsulated within the TCP protocol, which is encapsulated within the IP protocol, which is encapsulated within Ethernet frames, which are carried over electrical signals on twisted-pair network cable. Figure 8.2 illustrates this encapsulation.

Notable protocols used in the TCP/IP suite include:

- **IPv4 and IPv6** These are the lowest-level protocols in the TCP/IP suite, notable for their schemes for assigning numeric addresses to devices. When TCP/IP was first invented, the base IP protocol was designed for a maximum of about 4.3 billion devices worldwide. In the 1990s, it was realized that this was no longer sufficient, leading to the IPv6 standard, which can accommodate 2^{128}, or $3.4 \times 10^{\wedge 38}$, addresses. Numerous other security and functionality improvements are included in IPv6.

FIGURE 8.2 TCP/IP network encapsulation.

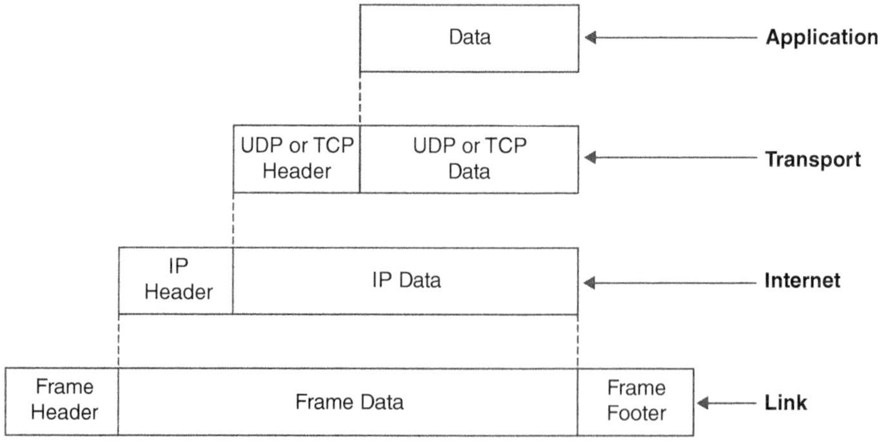

Source: Author.

- **Routing protocols** These protocols are used by routers, network devices that organize and keep network traffic moving toward its respective destinations. These protocols include Routing Information Protocol (RIP), Border Gateway Protocol (BGP), Intermediate System-to-Intermediate System (IS-IS), Open Shortest Path First (OSPF), Interior Gateway Routing Protocol (IGRP), and Enhanced Interior Gateway Routing Protocol (EIGRP).
- ***Hypertext Transfer Protocol (HTTP)*** **and** ***Hypertext Transfer Protocol Secure (HTTPS)*** These two protocols are used by web browsers to request and receive information from web servers.
- ***DNS (Domain Name System)*** This is a key protocol used to translate domain names into numeric addresses needed to determine the endpoints of all network communications in TCP/IP.
- ***FTP (File Transfer Protocol)*** This and newer versions (*File Transfer Protocol Secure [FTPS]* and the alternative protocol *Secure File Transfer Protocol [SFTP]*) are used for bulk file transfers between systems.
- **SSH and Telnet** *Secure Shell (SSH)* and *Telnet* are *command-line interface (CLI)* protocols often used by administrators to manage systems and devices.
- ***Simple Mail Transport Protocol (SMTP)*** This protocol is used to transport email between email servers.
- ***Network Time Protocol (NTP)*** This protocol is used to ensure that the time clocks on systems and devices are accurate to the millisecond. This is important because computer clocks tend to "drift."
- ***Voice over IP (VoIP)*** This family of protocols is used for transporting live "telephone" and video communications over TCP/IP networks.

This section has barely scratched the surface of network technology. For a complete explanation of network protocols, readers are referred to any of the classic network texts, such as *TCP/IP Illustrated* (Addison-Wesley Publishing).

Remote Access

Remote access is the means of providing connectivity to a corporate LAN through a data link. Many organizations provide remote access so that employees who are temporarily or permanently working off-site can access LAN-based resources from their remote locations.

Remote access was initially provided using dial-up *modems* that included authentication. Although remote dial-up is still available in some instances, most remote access is provided over the Internet. It typically uses *encapsulation* and encryption to build an encrypted *tunnel*, or *virtual private network (VPN)*, to protect transmissions from eavesdroppers. VPNs are so prevalent in remote access technology that the terms *VPN* and *remote access* have become synonymous. Remote access architectures are depicted in Figure 7.3.

Two security controls are essential for remote access:

- **Authentication** It is necessary to know *who* is requesting access to the corporate LAN, and with *what* device. Authentication can use the same user ID and password personnel use on-site, or multi-factor authentication might be required. Authentication might also include a digital certificate or other means to authenticate the device, thereby preventing remote access to assets not owned by the organization.
- **Encryption** Many on-site network applications do not encrypt sensitive traffic because it is all contained within the physically and logically protected corporate LAN. However, because remote access serves the same function as the corporate LAN and because the applications themselves sometimes do not provide encryption, the remote access service usually provides encryption. Encryption can use *Transport Layer Security (TLS)*, *Internet Protocol Security (IPsec)*, *Layer 2 Tunneling Protocol (L2TP)*, or *Point-to-Point Tunneling Protocol (PPTP—now deprecated)*.

These controls are needed because they serve as a substitute (or *compensating control*) for the physical access controls usually present, which control which personnel can enter the building to use the on-site corporate LAN. When personnel are on-site, their identity is confirmed through a keycard or another physical access control. When personnel are offsite using remote access, because the organization cannot "see" the person on the far end of the connection, the authentication used is the next best option.

The migration of corporate resources from internal networks to cloud-based networks is changing the notion of remote access. Organizations are implementing multi-factor authentication for access to their cloud-based resources, regardless of users' location—whether they are on a corporate LAN, working from home, in the field, or traveling.

The New Remote Access Paradigm

As organizations migrate their business applications to colocation centers and XaaS providers, and after the last internal resource is moved to the cloud, what is the point of remote access? Remote access to *what*?

If we think about this in terms of VPN and the protection afforded through encryption, VPN still makes good business sense for the purpose of protecting network traffic from potential eavesdroppers (whether human or malware). For this reason, it's preferable to say "VPN" rather than "remote access."

Organizations still need to address several subtopics when considering their VPN architectures, considering cloud migration, such as *split tunneling*, Internet backhauling, and whether VPN should always automatically activate on workstations away from internal corporate networks.

Network Devices

Various network devices are used to build networks that connect computers and other devices to the *Internet*. These devices include:

- *Router* A device used to connect networks to each other.
- *Switch* A device used to connect computers and other devices to a *local area network (LAN)*.
- *Modem* A device that converts data in digital format into an analog format for transmission over a transmission medium such as a telephone line or radio.
- *Access point* A device that connects Wi-Fi devices to a LAN.

Some security-related devices are also used in networks, including:

- *Firewall* A security device used to control the transmission of data between networks.
- *Intrusion detection system (IDS)* A security device used to detect potentially malicious network traffic.
- *Intrusion prevention system (IPS)* A security device used to block potentially malicious network traffic.
- *Gateway* A device used to convert or transform data from one format to another.
- *Spam filter* A device used to block and, optionally, quarantine, incoming spam email messages. When a quarantine is used, users have an opportunity to review and, optionally, release legitimate messages.
- *Network access control (NAC)* A device used to determine whether individual devices are permitted to communicate on a LAN. This capability is often built into network switches.
- *NetFlow* A network protocol that collects metadata about traffic flows, which analytics tools can then analyze to detect and alert on anomalous activity.

In cloud infrastructure-as-a-service (IaaS) environments, network devices are often virtual machines rather than physical devices.

Network Architecture

Metaphorically, networks are like roads, with varying capacities and with intersections and controls such as traffic signals. Organizations design their internal data networks so that workers using laptops, desktops, smartphones, or tablets can communicate with key business applications.

Network architecture has less to do with where the cabling is, and more to do with a network's logical design. Some organizations build large, "flat" networks in which every computer can freely communicate with every other computer. In contrast, other organizations employ *network segmentation*, in which the network is divided into security zones, and controls between them (such as *firewalls*) restrict network traffic only to that which is considered necessary. *Microsegmentation* is another means for protecting systems and critical systems, in which individual systems employ firewalls that block all but essential communications with other systems. Network architecture is a component of *enterprise architecture*.

The concept of *zero-trust (ZT)* can be viable for many organizations with sizable mobile or remote workforces, as well as for organizations with large numbers of customers or constituents. Zero-trust is a model in which portions of the network (or systems outside the network) are considered untrusted. Zero-trust is a way of thinking about the network that enables the implementation of appropriate security controls to protect highly sensitive or secretive systems and information.

Encryption and Hashing

Encryption is the technique used to hide information in plain sight. It works by scrambling the characters in a message using a method known only to the sender and receiver, making it useless to any party that intercepts it. Encryption plays a crucial role in protecting personal information. In some situations, it is not practical or feasible to prevent third parties from having logical access to data—for instance, data transmissions over public networks.

This technique can also be used to *authenticate* information that is sent from one party to another. This means that a receiving party can verify that a specific party did, in fact, originate a message and that it is authentic. This enables a receiver to know that a message is genuine and that it has not been forged or altered in transit by any third party.

With encryption, best practices call for system designers to use well-known, robust encryption algorithms. Thus, when a third party intercepts encrypted data, it can determine which algorithm is being used, but still cannot read the data. What the third party does not know is the *key* that is used to encrypt and decrypt the data. How this works is explained later in this section.

Encryption can be thought of as another layer of access protection. Like user ID and password controls that restrict data access for everyone but those with login credentials, encryption restricts access to (plaintext) data to everyone but those with encryption keys.

Encryption

Encryption is a reversible process, whereby plaintext can be converted to illegible ciphertext and back to plaintext. Only those who possess an encryption key can read the ciphertext.

Terms and Concepts Used in Cryptography

Several terms and concepts used in *cryptography* are not used outside of the field. Privacy and security professionals must be familiar with these to be effective in understanding, managing, and auditing information systems that use cryptography:

- *Plaintext* An original message, file, or stream of data that can be read by anyone who has access to it
- *Ciphertext* A message, file, or stream of data that has been transformed by an encryption algorithm and rendered unreadable
- *Encryption* The process of transforming plaintext into ciphertext, as depicted in Figure 8.3
- *Hash function* A cryptographic operation on a block of data that returns a fixed-length string of characters used to verify the integrity of a message
- *Message digest* The output of a cryptographic hash function
- *Digital signature* The result of encrypting the hash of a message with the originator's private encryption key, used to prove the authenticity and integrity of a message, as depicted in Figure 8.4
- *Algorithm* A specific mathematical formula that is used to perform encryption, decryption, message digests, and digital signatures
- *Decryption* The process of transforming ciphertext into plaintext so that a recipient can read it
- *Cryptanalysis* An attack on a *cryptosystem* in which the attacker is attempting to determine the encryption key that is used to encrypt messages
- *Encryption key* A block of characters used in combination with an encryption algorithm to encrypt or decrypt a stream or blocks of data; also used to create and verify a digital signature
- *Key encrypting key* An encryption key used to encrypt another encryption key
- *Key length* The size (measured in bits) of an encryption key; longer encryption keys can take considerably more effort to attack a cryptosystem successfully

FIGURE 8.3 Encryption and decryption use an encryption algorithm and a key.

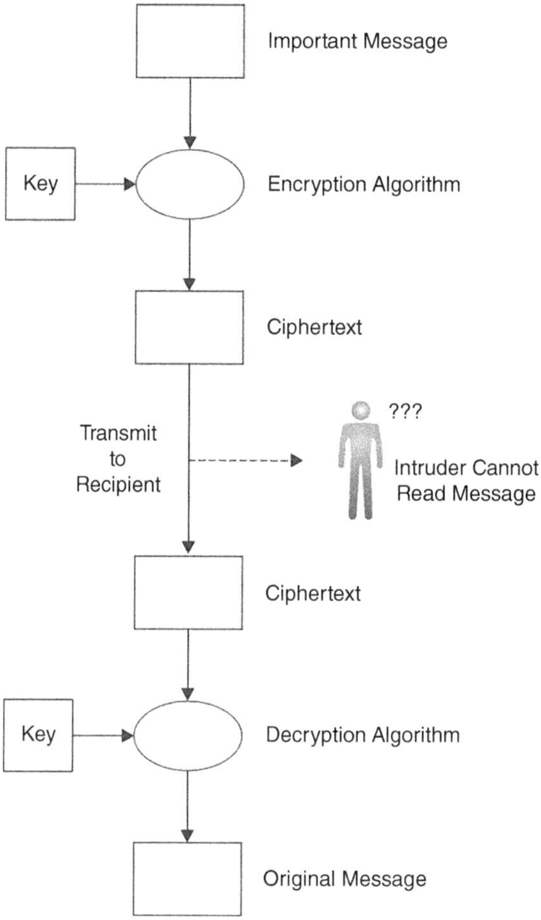

Source: Author.

- ***Block cipher*** An encryption algorithm that operates on blocks of data
- ***Stream cipher*** A type of encryption algorithm that operates on a continuous stream of data, such as a video or audio feed
- ***Initialization vector (IV)*** A random number that is needed by some encryption algorithms to begin the encryption process

FIGURE 8.4 Digital signature used to verify the integrity of a message.

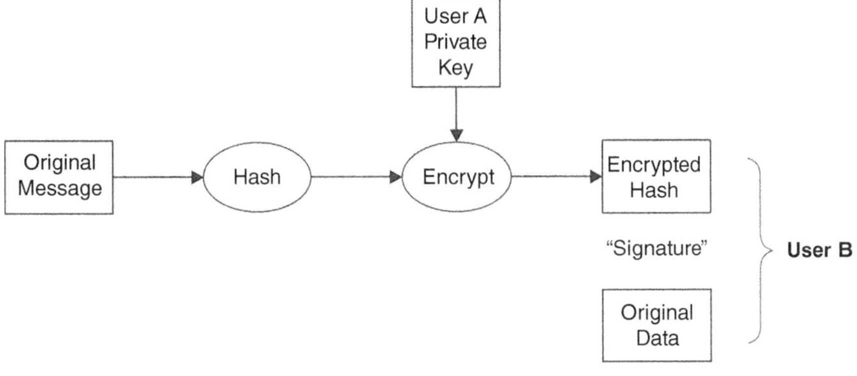

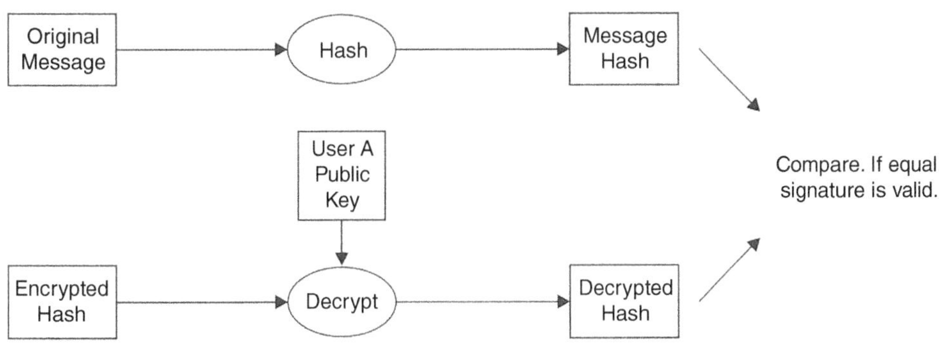

Source: Author.

- ***Symmetric encryption*** A method for encryption and decryption in which it is necessary for both parties to possess a common encryption key
- ***Asymmetric encryption*** or ***public-key cryptography*** A method for encryption, decryption, and digital signatures that uses key pairs, consisting of a *public key* and a *private key*
- ***Key exchange*** A technique used by two parties to establish a symmetric encryption key when no secure channel is available

- *Nonrepudiation* The property of digital signatures and encryption that can make it difficult or impossible for a party to deny having sent a digitally signed message, unless they admit to having lost control of their private encryption key

Poor implementations of cryptography can result in insufficient protection, leading to the compromise of personal information. Privacy and security professionals should be sufficiently familiar with cryptography to recognize whether a cryptosystem was properly designed and appropriately managed.

Symmetric Key Cryptosystems

A *symmetric key cryptosystem* is based on a symmetric cryptographic algorithm. The primary characteristic of a private-key cryptosystem is the necessity for both parties to possess a common encryption key that is used to encrypt and decrypt messages.

The two main challenges with private-key cryptography are as follows:

- **Key exchange** An "out-of-band" method for exchanging encryption keys is required before any encrypted messages can be transmitted. This key exchange must occur over a secure channel; if the encryption keys were transmitted over the primary communications channel, anyone who intercepted them would be able to read any messages, provided they could determine the encryption algorithm used. For instance, if two parties want to exchange encrypted email, they would need to exchange their encryption key first via telephone or fax, provided they are confident that their telephone and fax transmissions are not being intercepted.
- **Scalability** Private-key cryptosystems require that each sender-receiver pair exchange an encryption key. For a group of 4 parties, 6 encryption keys would need to be exchanged; for a group of 10 parties, 45 keys would need to be exchanged. For a large community of 1,000 parties, many thousands of keys would need to be exchanged.

Some well-known private key algorithms in use include AES (Rijndael), Serpent, and Twofish. Other algorithms, such as RC4, Skipjack, Triple DES (3DES), and Blowfish, are considered legacy and are deprecated.

Secure Key Exchange

Secure key exchange methods are used by two parties to establish a symmetric encryption key without actually transmitting it over a channel. Secure key exchange is needed when two parties that are previously unknown to each other need to establish encrypted communications where no out-of-band channel is available.

With the right method, two parties can perform a secure key exchange even if a third party intercepts their entire conversation. This is because algorithms used for secure key exchange rely on information known only by the two parties that is not transmitted between them.

The most popular algorithm is the *Diffie-Hellman* Key Exchange Protocol. Another algorithm in limited use is quantum key distribution (QKD).

Public-key Cryptosystems

Public-key cryptosystems are based on *asymmetric*, or *public key*, cryptographic algorithms. These algorithms use two-part encryption keys that are handled differently from those in symmetric-key cryptosystems.

Key Pair

In public-key cryptography, *public* and *private* encryption keys are used. Each user of a public-key cryptosystem has these two keys. Together, the public and private keys are known as a *key pair*. The two keys require different handling and are used together but for different purposes, as explained in this section.

When a user generates their key pair, it will exist as two separate files. The user is free to publish or distribute the public key openly; it could even be posted on a public website. This contrasts with the private key, which must be well protected and never published or sent to any other party, as in a private-key cryptosystem. Most public-key cryptosystems use a password mechanism to protect the private key; without its password, the private key is inaccessible and cannot be used. A *public key infrastructure (PKI)* system can be used to publish public keys and make them accessible to users.

Message Security

Public-key cryptography is an ideal application for securing messages, particularly email, because users do not need to establish and communicate symmetric encryption keys through a secure channel. With public-key cryptography, users who have never contacted each other can immediately send secure messages to each other. Public-key cryptography is depicted in Figure 8.5.

FIGURE 8.5 Public-key cryptography used to transmit a secret message.

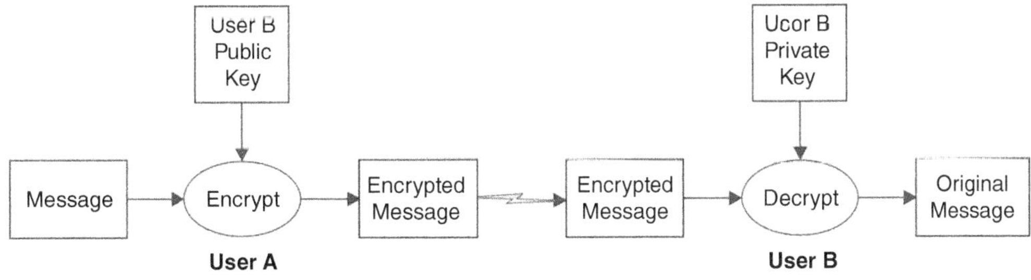

Source: Author.

Every user is free to publish their public encryption key, so it is easily retrievable. PKI servers on the Internet can make public keys available to anyone in the world. Public-key cryptography is designed so that open disclosure of a user's public key does not compromise the secrecy of the corresponding private key: a user's private key cannot be derived from the public key.

When User A wants to send an encrypted message to User B, the procedure is as follows:

1. User B publishes their public key to the Internet at a convenient location.
2. User A retrieves User B's public key.
3. User A creates a message and encrypts it with User B's public key and sends the encrypted message to User B.
4. User B decrypts the message with their private key and can read it.

Note that only User B's encryption key is used in this example. This method protects the message from eavesdroppers and is not used to verify its authenticity.

Public-key cryptography can also be used to verify the authenticity and integrity of a message. This is used to verify that a specific party did, in fact, create the message. The procedure is as follows:

1. User A publishes their public key to the Internet at a convenient location.
2. User B retrieves User A's public key and saves it for later use.
3. User A creates a message, digitally signs it with their private key, and sends the signed message to User B.
4. User B verifies the digital signature using User A's public key. If the message verifies correctly, User B knows that the message originated from User A and has not been altered in transit.

In this example, only the authenticity and integrity of a message are assured. The message is not encrypted, which means any party that intercepts it can read it.

Public-key cryptography can be used *both* to encrypt and to digitally sign a message, thereby guaranteeing its confidentiality and authenticity. The procedure is as follows:

1. User A and User B publish their public encryption keys in convenient places.
2. User A retrieves User B's public key, and User B retrieves User A's public key.
3. User A creates a message, signs it with their private key and encrypts it with User B's public key, and then sends the message to User B.
4. User B decrypts the message with their private key and verifies the digital signature with User A's public key.

Public-key cryptography also supports the encryption of a message with more than one user's public key. This enables a user to send a single encrypted message to several recipients, each encrypted with their respective public keys. This method does not compromise the secrecy of any user's private key, since a user's private key cannot be derived from the public key.

Elliptic Curve Cryptography

Elliptic curve cryptography (ECC) is attracting interest for use in public-key cryptography applications. ECC requires less computational power and bandwidth than other cryptographic algorithms and is considered more secure as well. Because of its low power requirements, it is used extensively in mobile devices.

Verifying Public Keys

A fraudster can assume another person's identity and even publish a public key associated with that identity. Four methods are available for verifying a user's public key as genuine:

- ***Certificate authority (CA)*** A public key that has been obtained from a trusted, reputable certificate authority can be considered genuine.
- **Email address** Public keys used for email will include the user's email address. If the email address is part of a corporate or government domain (for example, *adobe.com* or *seattle.gov*), then some credence can be given to the successful exchange of messages with that address. However, since email addresses can be spoofed, this should be considered a weak method at best.
- **Directory infrastructure** A directory services infrastructure, such as Microsoft Active Directory, LDAP, or a commercial product, can be used to verify a user's public key.
- ***Key fingerprint*** Many public-key cryptosystems employ a method for verifying a key's identity, known as the key's fingerprint. If users want to verify a public key, they retrieve it and calculate its fingerprint. The user then contacts the claimed owner of the public key, who runs a function against their private key that returns a string of numbers. The user also runs a function against the owner's public key, also returning a string of numbers. If both numbers match, the public key is genuine.

When issuing a public key, the requestor must be authenticated, for example, by presenting a government-issued ID or contacting the owner at a publicly listed telephone number.

Hashing and Message Digests

Hashing is the process of applying a cryptographic algorithm to a block of information that results in a compact, fixed-length *digest*. The purpose of hashing is to provide a unique "fingerprint" for the message or file—even if the file is very large. A message digest can be used to verify the integrity of a large file, thus assuring that the file has not been altered.

Some of the properties of message digests that make them ideally suited for verifying integrity include:

- Any change made to a file—even a single bit or character—will result in a significant change in the digest.
- It is computationally infeasible to modify a file without changing its digest.
- It is computationally infeasible to create a message or file that will result in a given digest.
- It is computationally infeasible for any two messages to have the same digest.

One common use of message digests is on software download sites, where the computed hash for a downloadable program is available so that users can verify that the software program has not been altered (provided that the posted hash has not also been compromised).

Unlike encryption, where ciphertext can be transformed back into plaintext (provided one has the encryption key), hashing is a "one-way" algorithm, in which the message digest cannot be transformed back into the original plaintext.

Digital Signatures

A *digital signature* is a cryptographic operation in which a sender "seals" a message or file using their identity. The purpose of a digital signature is to authenticate a message and to guarantee its integrity. Digital signatures do not protect the confidentiality of a message; the message remains readable by anyone who intercepts it. However, encryption is one of the operations performed to verify integrity.

Digital signatures work by encrypting message hashes; recipients verify the integrity and authenticity of messages by decrypting the hashes and comparing them to the original messages. In detail, a digital signature works like this:

1. The sender publishes their public key on the Internet at a location easily accessible to recipients.
2. The recipient retrieves the sender's public key and saves it for later use.
3. The sender creates a message (or file), computes a message digest (hash), and then encrypts the hash with their private key.
4. The sender sends the original file plus the encrypted hash to the recipient.
5. The recipient receives the original file and the encrypted hash. The recipient computes a message digest (hash) of the original file and stores the result. They then decrypt the hash with the sender's public key. The recipient compares the hash of the original file and the decrypted hash.
6. If the two hashes are identical, the recipient knows that the message in their possession is identical to the message the sender sent, that the sender is the originator, and that the message has not been altered.

The use of digital signatures is depicted earlier in this chapter in Figure 8.4.

Digital Envelopes

Two aspects of symmetric (private key) and asymmetric (public key) cryptography that have not been discussed yet are the computational requirements and performance implications of these systems. In general, public-key cryptography requires far more computing power than private-key cryptography. The practical implication is that public-key encryption of large datasets can be highly compute-intensive, making its use infeasible on some occasions.

One solution to this is a *digital envelope* that leverages the convenience of public-key cryptography while maintaining the lower overhead of private-key cryptography. This practice is known as *hybrid cryptography*. The procedure for using digital envelopes works like this:

1. The sender and recipient agree that the sender will transmit a large message to the recipient.
2. The sender selects or creates a symmetric encryption key, known as the *session key*, and encrypts the session key with the recipient's public key.
3. The sender encrypts the message with the session key.
4. The sender sends the encrypted message (encrypted with the session key) and the encrypted session key (encrypted with the recipient's public key) to the recipient.
5. The recipient decrypts the session key with their private key.
6. The recipient decrypts the message with the session key.

Encryption Applications

Several applications utilize encryption algorithms. Many of these are well-known and in everyday use.

Secure Sockets Layer/Transport Layer Security (SSL/TLS)

These encryption protocols are used to encrypt web pages requested with HTTPS (Hypertext Transfer Protocol Secure). *Secure Sockets Layer (SSL)* and its successor, *Transport Layer Security (TLS)*, have become de facto standards for encrypting web pages as they traverse the Internet between web servers and web browsers. TLS is also commonly used to encrypt email between email servers, so that messages sent from one organization to another will be encrypted as they transit the Internet.

Privacy and security professionals still use the term "SSL." However, the term "SSL" implies the use of TLS unless specifically stated otherwise.

Secure/Multipurpose Internet Mail Extensions (S/MIME)

The *Secure/Multipurpose Internet Mail Extensions (S/MIME)* protocol provides sender and recipient authentication and encryption of message content and attachments. S/MIME is most often used to encrypt email messages.

Secure Shell (SSH)

The *Secure Shell (SSH)* protocol is used to create a secure channel between two systems. The most popular use of SSH is to replace the Telnet and R-series protocols (rsh, rlogin, and so on), but it also supports tunneling for protocols such as the X Window System and FTP.

Internet Protocol Security (IPsec)

The *Internet Protocol Security (IPsec)* suite of protocols is used to create a secure, authenticated channel between two systems. IPsec operates at the Internet layer in the TCP/IP suite; hence, all IP traffic between two systems protected by IPsec is automatically encrypted. IPsec has two primary protocols, 1) Authentication Header (AH), which provides authentication and data integrity, and 2) Encapsulating Security Payload (ESP), which provides confidentiality. Each protocol can operate in either transport mode or tunnel mode. Transport mode leaves the original IP header in place and only encrypts the data payload. Transport mode is used to secure direct host-to-host communication (e.g., VoIP). Tunnel mode encrypts the entire IP packet (header and payload) and adds a new header. Tunnel mode is commonly used to secure virtual private network (VPN) connections.

Blockchain

Blockchain is a distributed ledger used to record cryptographically linked transactions in a peer-to-peer network. Once recorded, transactions in a blockchain cannot be altered or removed. Blockchain is decentralized by design. Implementations of blockchain include the Bitcoin cryptocurrency as well as emerging uses in financial services and supply chain management.

Exam Tip

CDPSE candidates must understand the differences between encryption and hashing, and how they contribute to effective privacy. It's essential to know whether encryption or hashing would be a better control in particular use cases.

Key Management

Key management refers to the processes and procedures used by an organization to generate, protect, use, and dispose of encryption keys throughout their lifecycle. Several common key management practices are described in this section.

The integrity of a cryptosystem and the confidentiality of the information it encrypts are only as strong as the management of its encryption keys.

Key Generation

The start of an encryption key lifecycle is *key generation*. At first glance, this process should require little scrutiny, but further study shows it is critical and requires safeguards.

The system on which key generation takes place must be highly protected. If keys are generated on a compromised system or one of questionable integrity, it would be difficult to determine whether a bystander could have electronically observed the key generation. In many situations, it would be reasonable to require that systems used for key generation be highly protected, isolated, and used by as few persons as possible. Regular integrity checks would need to take place to ensure that the system continues to be free of any anomalies.

Furthermore, the key generation process needs to include some randomness (or, as some put it, *entropy*) so that it cannot be easily duplicated elsewhere. If key generation were not a random event, it could be possible to duplicate the conditions related to a specific key and then regenerate a key with the very same value. This would instantaneously compromise the integrity and uniqueness of the original key.

Key Protection

Private keys used in public-key cryptosystems and keys used in symmetric cryptosystems must be continuously and vigorously protected. At all times, they must be accessible *only* to parties authorized to use them. If *key protection* measures for private encryption keys are compromised (or suspected to be compromised), a key compromise can occur, enabling the attacker to view messages encrypted with these keys. In commercial environments, keys are often protected in a *hardware security module (HSM)*.

A *key compromise* occurs when a private encryption key is disclosed to an unauthorized third party. When a key compromise occurs, it will be necessary to re-encrypt all data encrypted with the compromised key using a new encryption key.

In many applications, an encryption key is protected by a password. The length, complexity, distribution, and expiration of passwords protecting encryption keys must be well designed so that the strength of the cryptosystem (based on its key length and algorithm) is not compromised by a weak password scheme protecting its keys.

Key Encrypting Keys

Applications that utilize encryption must obtain their encryption keys in some way. In many cases, an intruder might be able to examine the application to discover an encryption key, allowing them to decrypt communications used by the application. A common remedy for this is the use of encryption to protect the encryption key. This additional encryption requires a key of its own, known as a *key encrypting key*. Of course, this key also must reside somewhere; often, features of the underlying operating system can be used to protect an encryption key as well as a key encrypting key.

Key Custody

Key custody refers to the policies, processes, and procedures for managing keys. This is closely related to key protection but is focused on *who* manages keys, *where* they are kept, and *how* they are used.

Key Rotation

Key rotation is the process of issuing a new encryption key and re-encrypting data protected with the new key. Key rotation can occur when any of the following occur:

- **Key compromise** When an encryption key has been compromised, a new key must be generated and used.
- **Key expiration** In some situations, encryption keys are rotated on a schedule, according to an encryption key's *cryptoperiod*.
- **Rotation of staff** In some organizations, if any of the persons associated with the creation or management of encryption keys transfer to another position or leave the organization, keys must be rotated.

Key Disposal

Key disposal refers to the process of decommissioning encryption keys. This can occur upon receipt of an order to destroy a dataset encrypted with a specific encryption key—destroying the encryption key can be as effective (and a whole lot easier) as destroying the encrypted data itself. Key disposal can present some challenges, however. If an encryption key is backed up to tape, for instance, disposing of the key will require destroying the backup media as well. Hence, it is crucial to dispose of an encryption key *only* after it is determined that it is no longer needed.

A novel method for data disposal is the destruction of encryption keys.

Public Key Infrastructure

One issue with public-key cryptography is the secure storage and distribution of public encryption keys. Although individuals are free to publish public keys online, doing so securely and under centralized control requires some central organization. A PKI is designed to fulfill this and other functions.

A PKI is a centralized system used to store and publish public keys and other information. Some of the services provided by a PKI are as follows:

- *Digital certificates*
- Certificate authority (CA)
- *Registration authority (RA)*

- *Certificate revocation list (CRL)*
- Certification practice statement (CPS)

> **Exam Tip**
>
> CDPSE test takers are not expected to memorize key management procedures, but you should understand these concepts.

Monitoring and Logging

Logging security-related events, centralized collection of these logs, and proactive monitoring with correlation engines are considered essential practices in cybersecurity. These activities help an organization detect a range of threats, from misbehavior by its workers to active attacks by cybercriminal organizations.

Monitoring activities related to data access can help an organization identify improper uses of personal information. This is a newer branch of cybersecurity practiced by a few organizations, although it is gaining popularity due to new privacy laws such as GDPR and CCPA/CPRA.

Event Monitoring

Event monitoring is the practice of examining the events occurring on information systems, including applications, operating systems, database management systems, end-user devices, file servers, and every type and kind of network device, and being aware of what is going on throughout the entire operating environment. The types of events of interest to privacy and security managers include the following:

- Successful and unsuccessful logins
- Unexpected system or device reboots
- Changes made to security configurations
- Changes made to operating system files
- Accesses and changes to personal data
- Queries to databases
- Changes made to access permissions of sensitive files on a file server
- Anomalous movement of sensitive files

Historically, it was considered sufficient to review system *event logs* and *audit logs* daily. Mainly, this was a review of yesterday's events (or the weekend's events on a Monday) to ensure that no privacy or security incidents warranted further investigation. Those days are mostly gone, however.

Today, most organizations perform *real-time* event monitoring. This means organizations need to have systems in place that will immediately inform them if events are occurring anyplace in the environment that warrant attention. Although the technology available today for real-time event monitoring is impressive, the vast amounts of information collected and analyzed can produce meaningless alerts if the systems are not properly tuned. Staff must understand the logs being collected and take the time to define the use cases that warrant alerts and investigations. Organizations that do not invest the time and resources required to tune the system will find their teams overwhelmed with alerts, which are often ignored.

Log Reviews

A *log review* is an examination of an event log in an information system to determine whether any privacy, security, or operational incident has occurred in the system. A log review is an examination of yesterday's activities in a system. Most organizations, however, conduct *continuous log reviews* by sending log data into a security information and event management (SIEM) system, which is discussed later.

Centralized Log Management

Centralized log management involves sending event logs on various systems over the network to a central collection and storage point, called a *log server*. There are two primary uses for a log server: for archival storage of events that might be used later in an investigation, and for storage of events to be reviewed daily or in real time. Generally, real-time analysis is performed by a SIEM system.

Security Information and Event Management

A *Security Information and Event Management (SIEM) system* collects and analyzes log data from many or all systems in an organization and produces alerts to inform personnel of specific events. A SIEM has rules to correlate events from one or more devices to provide additional detail about an incident. For instance, an attacker performing a brute-force password attack on a web server might generate alerts on the web server itself and also on the firewall and intrusion detection system. A SIEM would portray the incident using events from these and possibly other devices to give personnel a richer depiction of the incident.

For a SIEM to be effective, the timestamps in log entries from various devices must be complete and accurate. The SIEM must be able to discern the actual sequence of events, which is based on each log entry's timestamp. Because computer time clocks are notoriously inaccurate on their own, configuring computers to perform *time synchronization* to synchronize their clocks with a standard *time source*, or time server, is an essential practice.

Despite its name (*security* information and event management), a SIEM system is often used not only to inform personnel of security events, but also to inform them of operational and privacy-related events.

Orchestration

In the context of security information and event management systems, *orchestration* refers to a scripted, automated response that is automatically or manually triggered when specific events occur. Orchestration systems can be standalone systems (such as a *security orchestration, automation, and response (SOAR)* system) or might exist as part of the SIEM itself.

For example, suppose an organization has developed "run books," or short procedures for personnel who manage the SIEM for actions to perform when specific types of events occur. The organization, desiring to automate some of these responses, implements an orchestration tool that includes scripts that can run automatically when specific events occur. The orchestration system can be configured to run some scripts immediately, while other scripts can be set up and run when an analyst "approves" them.

The advantage of orchestration is twofold: first, repetitive and rote tasks are automated, relieving personnel of boredom and improving accuracy, and second, response to some types of events can be performed much more quickly, thereby blunting the impact of certain types of incidents.

Some SOAR tools now employ agentic AI capabilities to reduce response time and improve efficiency regarding the response to security-related events.

Threat Intelligence

Modern SIEMs can ingest *threat intelligence* feeds from various external sources. This enables the SIEM to better correlate events in an organization's systems with various threats experienced by other organizations.

Organizations can subscribe to one or more machine-readable threat intelligence sources that help the organization better understand which security events in their environment might represent intrusions. Some of these sources are open source, while others are fee-based commercial services. Often, these feeds are managed by a *threat intelligence platform (TIP)* that receives, parses, and processes threat intelligence data.

For example, suppose another organization is attacked by an adversary from a specific IP address in a foreign country. This information is included in a threat intelligence feed that arrives in your organization's SIEM. This helps your SIEM be more aware of activity of the same type or from the same IP address. This can alert the organization to incidents occurring elsewhere that could occur in the organization's network.

Threat Hunting

For many organizations, it's no longer sufficient to wait for attacks to manifest themselves in their SIEM or other monitoring systems. Instead, organizations go on the offensive to look for clues of possible intrusions in their environment. *Threat hunting* is the practice of conducting searches—typically in SIEM logs and configuration management databases—to see whether traces of intrusions, known as *indicators of compromise (IoC)*, are present in their systems.

For example, an organization might have received an advisory from a national law enforcement organization with specific intelligence on a new strain of malware. The advisory contains the filenames of some of the malware's artifacts. Threat hunters in the organization can scan log files or configuration management databases (CMDBs) in a search for the presence of those files on their systems to determine whether a similar attack in their own network might be occurring.

Security Advisories

Numerous organizations, including law enforcement, publish human-readable advisories on various cybersecurity events. Security teams in companies often subscribe to one or more of these advisories to be better informed on events occurring around the world. Sometimes these advisories compel security teams to request that their IT departments take action, which could include any of the following:

- Blocking specific IP addresses on external firewalls
- Installing specific security patches
- Making configuration changes to systems or devices
- Threat hunting to look for signs of intrusion
- Blocking email from specific domains, IP addresses, or accounts
- Issuing advisories to the workforce to be on the lookout for signs of suspicious activities

Organizations should actively subscribe to security advisories from the manufacturers of the hardware and software products they use in their environments. Organizations should also subscribe to two or more non-vendor advisory sources.

Sources for security advisories include:

- **Product vendors** Microsoft, Cisco, Oracle, Apple, Google, and so forth
- **CISA** Known Exploited Vulnerabilities (KEV) and other alerts
- **NIST** National Vulnerability Database (NVD)
- **CERT Coordination Center** Vulnerability notes database
- **MITRE** CVE database
- **ENISA** Threat landscape and advisories

Monitoring Has Little Value Without an Incident Response Plan

It is not enough for an organization that has comprehensive event and audit logging, a SIEM, SOAR, Tip, and alerts to let personnel be aware of potential privacy breaches. Such an organization has little hope of success, unless it also has an incident response plan, with playbooks to guide personnel to quickly respond to privacy incidents and breaches.

Incident response planning is discussed in detail in Chapter 2.

Summary

Assets are the things of value that an organization protects in an information security program. In a typical organization, assets will consist of information and the information systems that support and protect those information assets.

Identification and valuation contribute to an organization's asset inventory. There are several types of assets relevant to privacy and information security, including hardware, software, information (both on-premise and cloud-based), virtual assets, facilities, and personnel.

Asset classification is an activity whereby an organization assigns an asset to a category representing usage or risk. In an information security program, the purpose of asset classification is to determine, for each asset, its level of criticality to the organization.

Once an organization is satisfied that its information classification is in order, it can embark on system classification. Like various types of information assets, information systems also can be classified according to various security and operational criteria.

In some organizations, additional requirements are imposed on persons who have access to particularly sensitive information. Whether this information consists of trade secrets, government secrets, or other information, organizations might be required to meet specific requirements such as more thorough or frequent background investigations.

Controls are the policies, procedures, mechanisms, systems, and other measures designed to reduce risk. Control objectives are statements of desired states or outcomes from business operations. When building a security program, and preferably prior to selecting a control framework, the organization must establish high-level control objectives.

It takes time (at least one full risk management cycle) for an organization to establish a framework of controls that address all identified risks, and additional time for control assessment is needed to determine whether all controls are effective. Often, organizations start with a standard control framework that aligns with their industry sector. Some organizations find they are required to implement multiple control frameworks; they map controls to form a crosswalk that helps them better understand all the controls that are required.

Identity and access management is a collection of activities in an organization that is concerned with the inventory of an organization's workers and their access rights in information systems and applications.

Access controls are used to determine whether and how subjects (usually persons, but also running programs and computers) are able to access objects (usually systems and/or data).

Because access management is central to information protection, privacy professionals need to become familiar with access management techniques and their terminology, including terms such as subject, object, fail open/fail-closed, least privilege, segregation of duties, and split custody.

Identification is the act of asserting an identity without providing any proof of it. Authentication is similar to identification in that a subject asserts an identity, but it also requires proof of identity using a password or access token. Authorization is the process through which a system determines what access rights an authenticated user will be given.

Multi-factor authentication (MFA) is so-called because it relies not only on "something you know" (namely, a password), but also upon "something you have" (such as a key card or smart card) and/or "something you are" (such as a fingerprint).

Reduced sign-on (RSO) and single sign-on (SSO) refer to authentication and authorization mechanisms intended to streamline users' access to multiple business applications.

Privileged access management (PAM) is the policies, procedures, and tooling to manage higher-risk administrator and service accounts.

Access request processes need to be carefully designed so that only valid access requests are fulfilled. Access review processes ensure that access request processes are effective and confirm that users still require access to do their jobs. Access monitoring helps an organization detect anomalous behaviors that can be signs of malicious activities that could lead to a breach.

Identity proofing ensures that subjects are who they claim to be. This is of particular importance to curb fraud and social engineering.

Vulnerability management is the overall process to ensure that systems, devices, and applications are reasonably free of exploitable vulnerabilities. Vulnerability scanners are used to identify vulnerabilities. Risk analysis helps understand the urgency for specific vulnerabilities. Patch management is the process of applying security and functionality patches to systems—often in response to vulnerability management findings.

System hardening refers to techniques used to make systems and devices more resistant to attack. Mainly, hardening refers to a set of configuration settings that are applied to a system. Hardening principles include the removal of unnecessary programs, utilities, data, and user accounts; renaming administrative user accounts; permitting only required connections; changing default passwords; and using only up-to-date software. Hardening standards are available from the Center for Internet Security and the DoD Cyber Exchange.

Whether networked computers are located across the room or halfway around the world, networks facilitate all computer communications, both wired and wireless, whether telecommunications services are used or not.

The TCP/IP protocol suite employs a technique known as encapsulation, whereby messages in higher-level protocols are encapsulated within messages in lower-level protocols, which in turn are encapsulated in messages in the physical network medium.

Some organizations employ network segmentation, in which the network is divided into security zones, and controls between them (such as firewalls) restrict network traffic to only what is necessary.

Remote access is defined as the means of providing remote connectivity to a corporate LAN through a data link. Remote access is provided by many organizations so that employees who are temporarily or permanently working off-site can access LAN-based resources from their remote location.

Encryption is used to hide information in plain sight. It works by scrambling the characters in a message using a method known only to the sender and receiver, making it useless to any party that intercepts it.

A private-key cryptosystem relies on an encryption key known to both parties, whereas a public-key cryptosystem uses public-private key pairs. The selection of a private versus public-key cryptosystem depends on how it will be used, and by whom.

Hashing is the process of applying a cryptographic algorithm to a block of information that results in a compact, fixed-length "digest." A message digest can be used to verify the integrity of a large file, thus assuring that the file has not been altered.

A digital signature is a cryptographic operation where a sender "seals" a message or file using their identity. The purpose of a digital signature is to authenticate a message and to guarantee its integrity.

The term key management refers to the processes and procedures used by an organization to generate, protect, use, and dispose of encryption keys throughout their lifecycle.

Event monitoring is the practice of examining events occurring on information systems, including applications, operating systems, database management systems, end-user devices, file servers, and all types of network devices, and being aware of what is happening throughout the entire operating environment.

Monitoring of activities related to data access can help an organization identify improper uses of personal information.

A security information and event management (SIEM) system collects and analyzes log data from many or all systems in an organization and produces alerts to inform personnel of specific events. A security orchestration, automation, and response (SOAR) system improves responsiveness to SIEM alerts. Agentic AI can further improve responsiveness.

Threat hunting is the practice of conducting searches—typically in SIEM logs and configuration management databases—to see whether traces of intrusions are present in their systems. Threat intelligence feeds, whether machine- or human-readable, aid in event detection. A threat intelligence platform (TIP) automates the ingestion of incoming threat intel feeds.

Exam Essentials

Understand the role of asset management in privacy engineering. Asset inventories identify systems, applications, and data repositories that process personal data. Accurate classification and ownership assignment enable organizations to apply appropriate privacy safeguards, enforce retention requirements, and reduce unauthorized data exposure.

Recognize how identity and access management (IAM) protects personal data. IAM enforces authentication, authorization, and least-privilege access to systems containing personal data. Role-based and attribute-based controls help ensure that only authorized individuals can view, modify, or transfer personal information. Privileged access management controls protect high-risk privileged administrative and service accounts.

Apply patch management and system hardening to reduce privacy risk. Timely patching and secure configuration minimize exploitable vulnerabilities that could lead to unauthorized disclosure of personal data. Hardening removes unnecessary services, enforces baseline configurations, and reduces the attack surface of privacy-relevant systems.

Understand the importance of secure communication and transport protocols. Protocols such as TLS, HTTPS, and secure VPNs protect personal data during transmission. Secure transport prevents interception, tampering, and unauthorized access when data moves between systems, users, or organizations.

Distinguish between encryption and hashing for privacy protection. Encryption protects confidentiality by transforming data into unreadable form that can be reversed with a key, while hashing provides integrity and non-reversible transformation. Both techniques support privacy by safeguarding stored and transmitted personal data.

Recognize the role of monitoring and logging in privacy assurance. Logging captures access and processing activities involving personal data. Continuous monitoring enables detection of unauthorized access, supports incident response, and provides audit trails for compliance and accountability.

Integrate security controls into privacy engineering processes. Privacy-related controls should be applied throughout system design and operation. Coordinated implementation of asset management, IAM, encryption, and monitoring supports privacy-by-design principles and reduces risk across the data lifecycle.

Review Questions

1. Which asset management activity most directly supports privacy engineering objectives?
   A. Tracking software license costs
   B. Maintaining an inventory of systems that store personal data
   C. Monitoring CPU utilization
   D. Measuring application performance
2. Which IAM principle is most effective in reducing unnecessary exposure to personal data?
   A. Role-based access control
   B. Separation of duties
   C. Least privilege
   D. Multi-factor authentication
3. What is the primary privacy benefit of timely patch management?
   A. Reducing exploitable vulnerabilities
   B. Improving application performance
   C. Lowering operational costs
   D. Enhancing audit reporting
4. Which protocol is specifically designed to protect data in transit over the web?
   A. SSL
   B. HTTP
   C. TLS
   D. SNMP
5. Which statement best describes hashing in a privacy context?
   A. It encrypts data using a reversible key
   B. It compresses data for storage efficiency
   C. It masks data for display only
   D. It transforms data into a non-reversible value
6. Why are monitoring and logging important for privacy engineering?
   A. They detect unauthorized access to personal data
   B. They reduce storage requirements
   C. They automate system backups
   D. They improve network bandwidth

7. Which asset management practice best supports data minimization?
   - A. Increasing storage capacity
   - B. Implementing multi-factor authentication
   - C. Identifying unused systems containing personal data
   - D. Enabling network segmentation
8. Which IAM control most directly prevents unauthorized access when credentials are compromised?
   - A. Multi-factor authentication
   - B. Single sign-on
   - C. Role-based access control
   - D. Privileged access review
9. What is the primary objective of system hardening in privacy engineering?
   - A. Removing unnecessary services and configurations
   - B. Increasing application availability
   - C. Expanding logging capabilities
   - D. Encrypting database backups
10. Which transport control best protects personal data transmitted between microservices?
    - A. Plain HTTP
    - B. FTP transfer
    - C. Telnet session
    - D. TLS-secured API communication
11. Encryption primarily supports which privacy objective?
    - A. Availability
    - B. Accountability
    - C. Auditability
    - D. Confidentiality
12. Which logging practice best supports privacy incident investigations?
    - A. Logging only system errors
    - B. Logging access to personal data repositories
    - C. Logging CPU usage
    - D. Logging disk capacity thresholds

13. Which asset attribute is most important for applying privacy controls?
    A. Hardware vendor
    B. Physical location
    C. Data classification
    D. Warranty expiration date
14. Which IAM activity supports ongoing privacy compliance?
    A. Periodic access reviews
    B. Password length enforcement
    C. Network segmentation
    D. Password complexity enforcement
15. Why should organizations encrypt personal data backups?
    A. To improve backup speed
    B. To reduce storage costs
    C. To simplify restoration
    D. To protect data if backup media are compromised
16. Which monitoring capability best supports the detection of insider misuse of personal data?
    A. Network bandwidth monitoring
    B. User activity monitoring on sensitive systems
    C. Hardware temperature monitoring
    D. Patch compliance reporting
17. Which control ensures that personal data transmitted between organizations is protected from interception?
    A. Data retention policy
    B. Asset lifecycle management
    C. Access recertification
    D. Secure transport protocol
18. Which hashing use case most directly supports privacy engineering?
    A. Encrypting database connections
    B. Protecting stored passwords
    C. Securing network routing
    D. Compressing log files

19. An organization maintains strong encryption but does not manage cryptographic keys properly. What is the greatest privacy risk?
    A. Increased storage consumption
    B. Unauthorized data access due to key exposure
    C. Reduced application performance
    D. Incomplete logging records

20. A privacy engineer wants to detect unauthorized bulk downloads of personal data. Which control is most appropriate?
    A. Asset inventory update
    B. Patch deployment
    C. Behavioral monitoring and logging
    D. Password complexity enforcement

Answers to Review Questions

1. B. Maintaining an inventory of systems that store personal data allows organizations to identify where personal information resides across infrastructure, applications, and repositories. This visibility enables privacy engineers to apply appropriate safeguards such as access restrictions, encryption, retention policies, and monitoring. Without an accurate inventory, personal data might exist in unknown locations, increasing the risk of unauthorized exposure, inconsistent control implementation, and non-compliance with regulatory obligations.

2. C. The principle of least privilege ensures that users receive only the access necessary to perform their assigned duties. By limiting permissions to the minimum required, organizations reduce the number of individuals who can view or manipulate personal data. This directly lowers the risk of accidental disclosure, misuse, or malicious access. Least privilege is particularly important in privacy engineering because excessive access often leads to unnecessary data exposure across systems and environments.

3. A. Timely patch management addresses known vulnerabilities in operating systems, applications, and firmware. Attackers often exploit unpatched systems to gain unauthorized access to sensitive information, including personal data. By promptly applying security patches, organizations reduce the likelihood that vulnerabilities can be leveraged for data exfiltration or unauthorized processing. This directly supports privacy objectives by maintaining confidentiality and reducing the attack surface associated with systems that handle personal data.

4. C. Transport Layer Security (TLS) encrypts data transmitted between clients and servers, ensuring confidentiality and integrity during communication. When personal data is transmitted over networks, particularly the Internet, it is vulnerable to interception or modification. TLS prevents eavesdropping and tampering by encrypting the communication channel and validating endpoints. This protection is essential for privacy engineering, as many privacy risks arise from insecure data transmission between systems or users.

5. D. Hashing converts data into a fixed-length value using a one-way mathematical function. Unlike encryption, hashing is not reversible, meaning the original data cannot be reconstructed from the hash value. This property is useful in privacy engineering for protecting sensitive elements such as passwords or verification tokens. Even if a system is compromised, hashed values do not directly reveal the original personal data, reducing the risk of exposure.

6. A. Monitoring and logging provide visibility into who accessed personal data, when access occurred, and what actions were performed. This information enables detection of suspicious or unauthorized activity, supports incident response, and helps organizations meet accountability requirements. Effective logging also supports forensic analysis after a privacy incident, allowing organizations to determine the scope of exposure and take corrective action. Without monitoring, unauthorized access to personal data can go undetected.

7. C. Identifying unused systems containing personal data allows organizations to eliminate unnecessary data storage locations. Decommissioning or sanitizing these assets reduces the volume of retained personal information and limits exposure. Data minimization is a core privacy principle, and asset management supports it by ensuring that personal data is only stored where necessary. Removing redundant or obsolete systems reduces both operational complexity and privacy risk.

8. A. Multi-factor authentication (MFA) requires users to provide multiple forms of verification, such as something they know, have, or are. Even if an attacker obtains a user ID and password, the attacker is unlikely to possess the additional factor required for access. This significantly reduces the likelihood of unauthorized entry into systems containing personal data. MFA is therefore a critical privacy-related security control, especially for privileged accounts and systems that process sensitive information.

9. A. System hardening involves turning off unused services, removing default accounts, enforcing secure configurations, and limiting functionality to only what is necessary. By reducing the number of potential entry points, organizations reduce the attack surface that could be exploited to access personal data. Hardening complements patch management and helps prevent unauthorized access or system compromise that could lead to privacy violations.

10. D. Microservices architectures often involve frequent data exchanges between components. Using TLS-secured API communication ensures that these exchanges are encrypted and authenticated. Without encryption, personal data transmitted internally could be intercepted or manipulated. TLS provides confidentiality and integrity protections, making it an essential control for protecting personal data moving within distributed systems.

11. D. Encryption protects confidentiality by transforming readable data into ciphertext that can only be accessed using a decryption key. This ensures that even if storage media, backups, or network transmissions are compromised, personal data remains protected. Encryption is widely used for data at rest, in transit, and sometimes in use, making it one of the most fundamental controls for safeguarding personal information.

12. B. Logging access to personal data repositories provides a record of who accessed sensitive information and what actions were performed. This information is critical for identifying unauthorized access, determining the scope of exposure, and supporting forensic analysis. Logs also provide evidence for regulatory reporting and compliance verification. Without such logging, organizations might be unable to determine whether personal data was improperly accessed.

13. C. Data classification identifies the sensitivity level of information stored or processed by an asset. Assets containing personal data require stronger controls such as encryption, restricted access, and enhanced monitoring. By classifying data, organizations can apply appropriate safeguards based on risk. Without classification, privacy controls can be inconsistently applied, leaving sensitive data insufficiently protected.

14. A. Periodic access reviews ensure that users continue to require access to personal data as roles change. Over time, individuals can accumulate permissions that are no longer necessary. Regular reviews identify and remove excessive access, reducing privacy risk and supporting least privilege. This process also helps organizations demonstrate compliance with privacy regulations that require access governance.

15. D. Backup media can be stored offsite, transported, or handled by third parties, increasing the risk of unauthorized access. Encrypting backups ensures that personal data remains unreadable even if media are lost, stolen, or improperly accessed. This protects confidentiality and aligns with privacy requirements for safeguarding stored personal information.

16. B. User activity monitoring tracks actions performed by individuals on systems containing personal data. This includes access patterns, data exports, and unusual behavior. Such monitoring can detect insider threats, such as employees accessing data outside their job responsibilities. Detecting these behaviors early helps prevent unauthorized disclosure and supports incident response.

17. D. Secure transport protocols such as TLS encrypt communications between organizations. When personal data is transmitted externally, it is particularly vulnerable to interception. Encryption ensures confidentiality and integrity, preventing unauthorized parties from accessing or altering data during transmission.

18. B. Hashing stored passwords ensures that actual values are not retained in plaintext. If a database is compromised, attackers obtain hashed values rather than usable credentials. Strong hashing algorithms with salting further reduce the likelihood of recovery. This approach protects user credentials and limits privacy exposure.

19. B. Encryption is only effective when keys are securely generated, stored, and managed. Poor key management, such as storing keys alongside encrypted data or failing to rotate keys, can allow unauthorized individuals to decrypt personal data. This undermines confidentiality and creates significant privacy risk. Effective privacy engineering requires strong key lifecycle management.

20. C. Behavioral monitoring analyzes patterns of system usage and data access. Detecting unusually large downloads or abnormal access patterns can indicate potential data exfiltration. Combined with logging, this control enables organizations to identify and respond to privacy incidents involving unauthorized transfer of personal data.

Privacy Controls

This chapter covers CDPSE Domain 4, "Privacy Engineering," specifically the "Privacy Controls" subdomain.

This chapter covers these job practice elements:

✔ C—PRIVACY CONTROLS

1. *Consent Tagging*
2. *Tracking Technologies (e.g., cookie management)*
3. *Anonymization and Pseudonymization*
4. *Privacy-enhancing Technologies (PETs)*
5. *AI/Machine Learning (ML) Considerations*

The other subdomains in Domain 4, Privacy Engineering, are:

✔ A—TECHNOLOGY STACKS—covered in Chapter 7.

✔ B—PRIVACY-RELATED SECURITY CONTROLS—covered in Chapter 8.

The CDPSE Task Statements relevant to this domain are:

4. *Design and evaluate the implementation of technical and operational controls for data classifications and data life cycle requirements.*
13. *Evaluate changes in regulatory landscape, emerging threats to privacy, and privacy-enhancing technologies (PETs).*

The topics in this chapter and in Chapters 7 and 8 account for 39% of the CDPSE examination.

Privacy engineering requires implementing technical controls that directly enforce privacy requirements across systems and data processing workflows. This chapter examines several categories of privacy controls commonly applied in modern architectures. Consent tagging enables systems to track and enforce the permitted use of personal data based on user authorization. Tracking technologies, such as cookies and similar mechanisms, require careful management to ensure transparency, user choice, and compliance with regulatory obligations. Anonymization and pseudonymization techniques reduce identifiability while supporting operational needs. Privacy-enhancing technologies provide advanced methods for analyzing and sharing data while reducing the exposure of personal information. Finally, AI and machine learning pose unique privacy risks, including consent withdrawal, re-identification, and data leakage, which require additional safeguards. Together, these controls support privacy-by-design principles and help organizations operationalize privacy requirements throughout the data lifecycle.

Consent Tagging

A cornerstone of modern privacy law and discussed throughout this book, *consent* is freely given permission granted by a data subject for the collection and/or processing of their personal data. *Consent tagging* is the assignment of metadata to personal data or processing activities that records the scope, purpose, and status of a data subject's consent, so that permitted uses and restrictions can be enforced. But of course, consent is much more than a simple yes-no. *Granular consent* permits data subjects to select which controls or uses they agree with. Instead, any collection of consent should include several data points, including:

- **Data subject identifier** A unique identifier that distinguishes the data subject from all others. This identifier should not include government-issued identifiers, such as Social Security or driver's license numbers.
- **Date and time** The date and time that the consent was collected.
- **Consent status** Whether consent is granted, revoked, modified, or expired.

- **Date or version of consent language** Any identifier that specifies the language of the consent. Since organizations change their privacy policy language from time to time, it's essential to capture the version or date of the privacy policy or other consent language that the data subject agreed to.
- **Legal basis** The stated legal reason for which the personal information is collected.
- **Purpose** The purpose of collection and/or use that the data subject consented to (or revoked).
- **Context** Whether the consent was collected at a website, mobile site, mobile app, by telephone, in writing, in person, or some other means.
- **Retention or expiration** The time period for which the consent was given, or when the consent is to expire.
- **Sharing restrictions** Any details on whether the data subject's personal information can be shared, including which personal details, for which purpose(s), or to which external party(ies).

These and other fields should be captured and saved in a database or audit log, with restrictions on subsequent modifications to this data. The data collected and the method of storage should support *nonrepudiation*, so that a data subject cannot later credibly deny having provided consent.

As implied in these descriptions, many jurisdictions accommodate a data subject's desire to withdraw or modify consent. Organizations must comply with these requests and capture evidence of the consent change, as well as the operations performed as a result.

The use of personal information to train AI/ML models presents some challenges. The section, "AI/ML Considerations," later in this chapter, explains these challenges.

Exam Tip

The term "consent tagging" is an ISACA term not found in major frameworks. The concept is known under other names, including consent metadata, consent labels, consent attributes, purpose-based tagging, and privacy labels.

Tracking Technologies

Web and mobile applications are the engines of commerce in many industries. Today, measuring business is all about measuring what happens in information systems. In their zeal for insight, some of these measurements intrude into persons' privacy. This section describes a variety of techniques for tracking individual users' activities, as well as ways to limit tracking.

The 2020–2021 COVID-19 pandemic, with its lockdowns and work-from-home (WFH) shift, accelerated the transformation of many organizations into digital businesses, resulting in a proliferation of usage-tracking data.

Advertising Tracking

An old joke in the advertising business goes like this: "Did you hear about the marketers who could not sleep at night? They were worried that they were wasting half of their advertising budget, but they didn't know which half." Cue rim shot.

In the traditional advertising world, when companies purchased ad space on billboards, buses, airports, and radio and television commercials, there was no direct way of knowing whether their ads were influential, never mind which individual persons were responding to those ads. The Internet changed all of that. With ads served to individuals on their laptops, tablets, and smartphones, it is now simple to distinguish individuals from one another, deliver data-driven targeted advertising, and know the outcomes with more certainty based on shared tracking data.

This leap in technology has led citizens to say, "Enough!" and prompted laws to curb tracking, its uses, and potential abuses. Indeed, the existence of this book and your interest in it are a result of tracking, plus the accumulation and abuse of personal information that has gone too far in many cases.

Tracking Techniques and Technologies

Numerous techniques and technologies are used to track the activities and locations of Internet-connected devices and their owners. Information systems log various types of events that give system owners better insight into how, how much, and by whom their systems are used. Some of this logging is highly detailed and often includes, directly or indirectly, the identities of the persons using these devices; this can be considered unnecessary and can represent an invasion of privacy.

IP Addresses

Every endpoint—smartphone, tablet, laptop, desktop computer, or connected device such as a home surveillance camera, voice assistant, printer, and more—has an *IP address*. As briefly discussed in Chapter 8, an IP address is a unique numeric value assigned to a network and to the devices within it. In today's broadband Internet, an IP address can be associated with a data subject. Indeed, some jurisdictions consider an IP address as a part of personal information.

Most websites, as well as many mobile applications, log basic activities such as authentication and meaningful transactions. Because IP addresses on the public Internet are unique and provide approximate geographic location information (sometimes no better than an entire country), they are often part of these log entries.

Techniques such as network address translation mean that a public IP address will represent an organization's network or a residential network, but not the individual devices within that network. This means that separate individuals, each on their own device, visiting the same website will share the same public IP address. To the uninformed, these could appear to be a single user unless log entries include other uniquely identifying information.

In some jurisdictions, including California, Germany, and the UK, an IP address is considered an element of personal information.

Device Identifiers

Individual devices such as laptop computers, tablet computers, and smartphones have internal device identifiers that uniquely identify them. Device serial numbers are stamped on these devices and are also available electronically. Also, mobile phones have an IMEI (International Mobile Equipment Identity) number that mobile network service providers use to uniquely identify devices worldwide. Some of the activity tracking performed by mobile network operators and Internet service providers includes identifiers like these. Often, these identifiers can be associated with their owners, giving network operators unique insight into the detailed usage of their devices.

Web Tracking

Web tracking refers to general practices associated with measuring and observing users who visit websites. Website operators track individual user sessions on their websites for three primary reasons:

- **Session integrity** The nature and design of Internet protocols and multi-user applications require that each user's session be uniquely identified. This is necessary to distinguish each user from every other. For instance, e-commerce sites need to properly and uniquely identify individual user sessions, so that each user can browse and purchase products and services. This session integrity also gives each user a sense of relative privacy, knowing that no other user can see which products they are viewing or purchasing.
- **Usage statistics** Websites and applications want to collect analytics on their usage: how many users are visiting (and at what times of day, days of the week, and so on), what pages they are viewing in what sequence, and how long they remain on individual pages. This information helps organizations design websites and applications that are easier and simpler to use.
- **Advertising tracking** Advertising and its revenue fuels a significant portion of the Internet. Thus, advertisers and website operators track not only the number of visitors but also uniquely identify them to distinguish one from another. The technologies in

play here give rise to the "creepy factor." For example, when a person searches the Internet for a specific thing, and then, for days afterward, on every page they visit, they see advertisements from various companies for those very things.

Cookies

Cookies are small pieces of data that websites create and store in a user's browser. Generally, a cookie is used by the website to uniquely distinguish users from one another and to remember unique users' preferences, such as preferred language and display or usage settings. Several types of cookies are used for various purposes, including:

- ***Session cookies*** These are used to uniquely identify a user's session. A session cookie is assigned when a user logs in to a website and is removed when the user logs off or closes the browser.
- ***Persistent cookies*** These cookies remain on a user's browser and are sometimes used to remember users' preferences, such as preferred language, country, and preferred landing page. Persistent cookies are also known as *advertising cookies* because they are used to distinguish users from one another.
- ***First-party cookies*** These cookies are placed by the domain the user is visiting and identified with that domain. For instance, if a user is visiting `www.company.com`, a first-party cookie will be associated with the domain company.com.
- ***Third-party cookies*** These cookies are placed by the domain the user is visiting, where the cookie is associated with a different domain. For example, if a user is visiting `www.company.com`, that web server could attempt to place a cookie from `www.cooltracking.com` for advertising purposes.
- ***Super cookies*** These are cookies with an origin of a top-level domain such as `.com` or `.co.uk`. They are used for tracking users across many domains.
- ***Zombie cookies*** These cookies are created by various means and designed to be difficult or impossible to detect or delete; they regenerate themselves when possible.
- **HTML5 Web storage** The popular HTML5 standard includes specifications for local storage of information. One such use mimics the function of cookies.

Web Beacons

A *web beacon* is a technique used by web servers to track how web pages and email messages are viewed. Web beacons generally take the form of a transparent 1 × 1 pixel image that is invisible to users. Because web servers log details of every object download, including images, web beacons can function much like cookies and enable the collection of information, such as whether the recipient has opened an email and whether it was opened by others (presumably after being forwarded). This is particularly true if a website utilizes uniquely named web beacon image files that are each sent only to one specific user.

Web beacons are also sometimes used in email to provide a sender with detailed information about the recipient when the recipient reads the message.

Device Information and Name

When a user visits a website, the site's web servers can obtain a limited amount of information about the user's device, including:

- **Device manufacturer and model** The name of the device manufacturer and the model
- **Device name** The name that the user assigned to the device when the data subject purchased it and set it up
- **Browser** The name and version of the browser used to visit the site
- **Operating system** The name and version of the operating system (for example, Windows, macOS, Linux, iOS, Android)
- **Viewport width** The width of the device's display in pixels

The collection of this type of data is known as *digital fingerprinting*.

Location

Virtually all mobile devices, as well as many laptops, have built-in GPS receivers and, thus, make precise locations available to applications. Many mobile apps utilize location information directly for navigation, but also often for business reasons. For instance, many websites and e-commerce apps from organizations with "brick-and-mortar" stores show users the location of the nearest stores. Other uses for location information support the delivery of location-relevant advertising to users.

With location tracking enabled, some of these apps and websites collect detailed location histories for users. This becomes a point of contention among citizens who believe it constitutes overreach—perhaps this information could be used against them in some way. Many also believe that manufacturers of mobile devices accumulate detailed location histories that include excessive amounts of personal information, which could lead to misuse or abuse.

Other devices, such as *GPS trackers* that can be covertly affixed to vehicles, and *Apple AirTags* and similar devices, can also be used to track the location of objects, which can imply the location of persons, with or without their knowledge. Figure 9.1 shows an Apple AirTag, and Figure 9.2 shows a GPS tracker.

For devices without location services, the user's approximate location can be inferred from their device's IP address.

RFID

Radio frequency identification (RFID) refers to a family of similar technologies used to track the presence or movement of objects. Such objects have RFID tags affixed to them, or the capability might be embedded in them. The types of objects using RFID technology include credit and debit cards, building entrance badges, and inventory tags.

Eavesdropping

A growing concern among privacy and security professionals is the increase in consumer devices and mobile apps that *eavesdrop* on their users in various ways. Many mobile apps

FIGURE 9.1 Apple AirTag.

Source: Author.

FIGURE 9.2 GPS vehicle tracker.

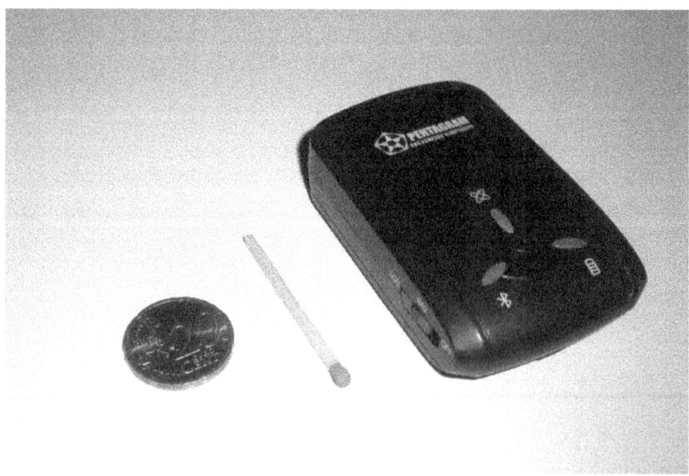

Source: Mock5 via Wikimedia Commons.

access sensitive data on users' mobile devices, often with no good reason, and many "smart" consumer devices collect more information from us than seems reasonable. For instance, there is no reason for a camera or photo-editing app to access a user's contact list; when installing such an app, users often "click through" the permission dialogue without thinking about what they're being asked to permit.

Similarly, some apps can sneak around a mobile device's controls to obtain such information anyway. The operators of mobile app stores (primarily Apple and Google) do a pretty good job of preventing illicit eavesdropping. Still, some app developers are clever and find ways around the controls.

Applications can access and abuse users' privacy and security in the following ways:

- **Camera** Many apps for both mobile devices and laptops request access to the device's camera. For "honest" applications, it's evident when the camera is in use, but apps could access it at other times as well. On many laptop computers, a small indicator light illuminates when the camera is in use, but not all mobile devices have this feature. (Personally, I am suspicious about whether new "smart" televisions have built-in cameras in their bezels. I also believe it is possible to activate the camera without also illuminating its indicator.)
- **Photos** Many apps request access to stored photos on mobile devices. Although there is a legitimate need for photo-editing and social media apps for posting photos or updating profile pictures, users should pay attention to permission requests to access stored photos.
- **Microphone** Apps that need to record a user's voice or other sounds must request access to the device's microphone. This includes videoconferencing and audio calling applications. Others, such as health apps (for observing sleep, for example), can also request mic access. Remember that any voice-activated product has a built-in microphone that is essentially listening all the time (likely even when the product is switched off).
- **Location** Some applications need to know the device's location to be useful to users. While mapping, navigation, and travel-related applications obviously require location services, others might not.
- **Contacts** Mobile device users might be asked whether certain applications can access stored or cloud-based contact lists. Users should be especially careful with this permission, as unscrupulous vendors' applications can harvest others' contact information for marketing purposes.
- **Voice assistant** Many mobile devices and laptop computers are equipped with "Siri," "Alexa," and "Hey Google" voice assistants. Users need to be aware that, when activated, these voice assistants might be listening and potentially uploading all speech within range of the device.
- **Local and cloud storage** Mobile device users should be wary of applications that request permission to access local and cloud-based storage. Miscreant apps can attempt to exfiltrate those contents for who knows what purposes.
- **Social media accounts** Many mobile apps provide "value add" services as an adjunct to popular social media services such as Facebook, Twitter, LinkedIn, and Instagram.

Those apps request permission to log in to users' social media accounts to provide their services. Sometimes this access is misused or abused, with more personal information being sent to these other services than most users would consider reasonable.

- **Smart devices** Many smart devices, particularly TVs, track everything done on the TV, including taking screenshots of the screen, listening and capturing audio (for voice-powered remotes), and even some with covert cameras. Certain manufacturers of TVs, smartphones, and other devices aggregate this tracking data to build a detailed profile of one's activities. For instance, one brand of smart TVs advises that customers should not have conversations on sensitive topics in the presence of the television!
- **Paste buffer (clipboard)** The paste buffer (known as the clipboard) on Apple mobile devices can, at times, contain highly sensitive information such as passwords, URLs, email addresses, and phone numbers. Apps on some mobile devices have free access to the paste buffer, resulting in leakage of sensitive information.
- *Key logger* A hardware device or software program that intercepts keys typed and mouse clicks, in attempts to harvest passwords and other sensitive data from targeted users.

Is Big Tech the New Big Brother?

Companies like Apple, Google, Microsoft, Samsung, Vizio, and scores of others have designed numerous high-tech products that are revolutionary in how they make our work and personal lives easier and richer. But in recent years, we're learning about some practices that might represent overreach in their capabilities. Here are some examples:

- Samsung suggests that owners of its smart televisions should take sensitive conversations away from the television lest voice-recognition software overhear what's said.
- Several brands of children's smart toys, including toys from Mattel and Genesis Toys, eavesdrop on children and their families' conversations—by design.
- Google keeps a detailed dossier on the specific movements of users of Android devices or Google Maps and other navigation apps.
- Employees of Amazon's Ring doorbell and ADT's security systems have been caught eavesdropping on customers' homes.
- And, finally, voice assistants hear everything.

Consumers are growing wary of big tech and the potential for overreach. Privacy professionals have long been concerned. The pendulum of acceptable tracking versus intrusions into privacy continues to swing, even as new technologies reveal even more about the lives of the people using them.

Facial Recognition

Combined with advancements in mobile device and CCTV optical capabilities, *facial recognition* software is going mainstream. Many products from Apple, Samsung, Google, Microsoft, and others use facial recognition to log in to mobile devices. Commercial facial recognition products are also enabling corporations and law enforcement to identify people, including wanted criminals.

Privacy rights advocates are vigorously opposing facial recognition capabilities in public places such as airports, shopping malls, and city streets out of concerns that it could be abused by authorities seeking to create a surveillance state. Some cities, states, provinces, and countries are passing laws forbidding the use of facial recognition capabilities in public places, and some larger technology organizations are refusing to sell these capabilities to governments. Public-facing facial recognition cannot, however, be "uninvented," and it is likely to continue being used secretly by corporations and governments despite regulations forbidding its use.

License Plate Tracking

Many local jurisdictions employ video surveillance systems to capture license plate numbers from cars, trucks, and motorcycles, and to track the location and movement of citizens. Mitigating this risk is difficult and often illegal, including through license plate coatings and shields, alterations, and removal.

Biometrics

Aside from facial recognition, other forms of *biometrics* have been in use for decades. Numerous companies manufacture fingerprint and palm-scan readers for use on mobile devices, as well as for building and secure-zone entrance control. Iris scanning is also fairly common, as high-resolution cameras can obtain a quality image from a few feet away. Facial recognition can be thwarted with dark eyeglasses, hats, scarves, and other measures.

Static signature recognition, which is the task of verifying whether a signed document is genuine, has been used for centuries and is still used in banking to confirm signatures on checks. More intrusive biometric techniques, such as retinal scanning and dynamic handwriting scanning, are no longer in common use.

Contact Tracing

Contact tracing has been used for disease control for decades. Historically, contact tracing has been a manual process involving interviews with confirmed cases to identify their recent contacts. Being highly manual, it has not been the most efficient tool for reducing the spread of disease. However, the proliferation of smartphones capable of providing proximity information can prove useful for contact tracing. As a result of the COVID-19 pandemic, Apple and Google introduced support for "COVID-19 apps" that could use their smartphone's Bluetooth radio signals to notify a user who comes into proximity with someone who is also using a "COVID-19 app" and has recorded in the app as testing positive for an infectious disease.

FIGURE 9.3 Contact tracing was built into Apple mobile devices.

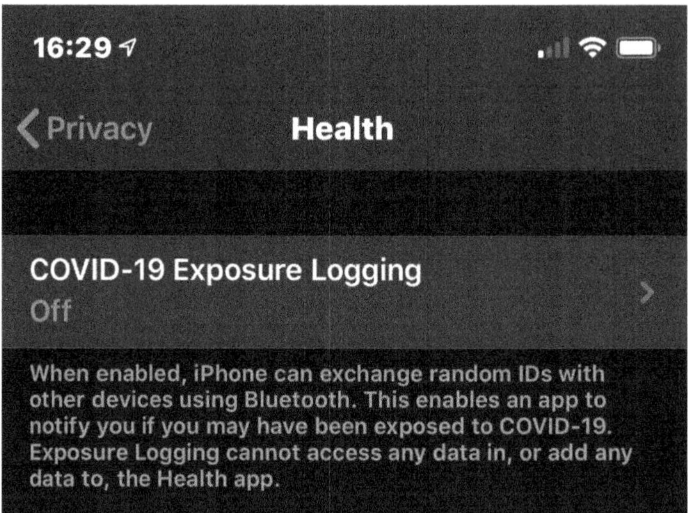

Source: Author.

While health authorities view contact tracing as a valuable tool for infectious disease control, privacy advocates consider it an overly intrusive process that is subject to abuse by police states. Indeed, contact tracing can be used to discover associations between people who meet only face-to-face. Critics of contact tracing point to numerous "false positives" that would result. For instance, two hotel guests sleeping in adjacent rooms might be considered in proximity for several hours.

In mid-2020, Apple and Google included contact tracing capabilities as a standard feature in iOS and Android; this feature was not activated by default and must be explicitly enabled (see Figure 9.3). While removed in 2023, such capabilities could be reintroduced in the future.

Tracking in the Workplace

Organizations that conduct part or all of their business with computers need to enact a variety of controls to reduce the likelihood and impact of attacks. Indeed, this is the whole point of cybersecurity, as well as a substantial portion of information privacy.

Some cybersecurity controls involve managing and logging activities on computing devices (laptops, desktops, tablets, and smartphones) used by its workers. After all, anomalous behavior on any of these devices can be a sign of an attack. To detect and prevent such attacks, it is necessary to track and centrally log many types of activities on computers, including the following:

- Websites visited
- Files created, viewed, updated, transferred to other media, and deleted
- Email messages sent and received
- Contents of network communications
- Location of said devices (for device theft detection and remote data destruction)

Organizations with more mature cybersecurity programs will track and log most or all of these activities and use analytics on these records to detect anomalies that might indicate security or privacy breaches.

Organizations undertaking such tracking and recording often include notices on these devices and in company policy, stating that such measures are taken in the name of data protection, and that any personal use of these devices (or networks) is subject to these practices, resulting in "no expectation of privacy."

In many countries, security tracking must be approved by *works councils* and similar employment bodies, even if the organization claims a legitimate interest in protecting its information.

Internet Access History

Web content filtering is used to prevent users from visiting websites known to be malicious, which, when visited, will attempt to install malware or spyware on visitors' computers, and it's used to prevent users from visiting websites whose subject matter is not business-related (such as weapons, gambling, and pornography sites). Many such web content filtering systems log the websites and web pages viewed by organization personnel, often associating web activity with specific workers by name. This log data can prove invaluable in an investigation into a security or privacy breach. *Cloud access security brokers (CASBs)* are implemented to prevent the use of unauthorized cloud services. Logging capabilities in these systems are frowned upon or even illegal in some countries.

SSL/TLS Decryption

To detect and prevent the leakage of the company's sensitive information, some organizations undertake a practice known as *TLS Inspection.* Encrypted network traffic is decrypted so that its contents can be examined for evidence of a security or privacy breach. Because so much Internet traffic is encrypted, organizations lacking SSL decryption are blind to many types of threats.

Legal problems with SSL decryption arise when workers occasionally use organization-issued computers to conduct personal business, such as accessing personal email, making personal purchases, accessing healthcare services, conducting personal banking, and so on. Though a small number of organizations prohibit and actively block all such personal uses, most permit a minimal amount of personal use and will make an effort not to decrypt traffic from sites believed to be low business risk that could transmit personal information; however, they warn workers that all activities, whether business or personal, are monitored for security and privacy purposes.

Some organizations "allow list" personal banking and similar activities, so that an employee's personal use of organization-issued computers is not examined in some cases. Indeed, personal banking is an unlikely path for exfiltrating sensitive data and represents a low risk for security and privacy breaches.

Decades ago, SSL was replaced by TLS. Still, many of us use "SSL" to mean session encryption, fully aware that TLS is the technology used.

Email Archiving

Internal email represents an ongoing conversation in most organizations. For this reason, many organizations continuously archive all email communication on separate email archive servers. If the organization receives a legal request for specific email messages, search capabilities on email archive servers streamline the data collection effort. Any personal use of organizational email accounts will naturally be included in such archiving. Again, employees are generally cautioned through visible notices that monitoring is taking place.

Tracking Prevention

Users of mobile devices and smart products have limited abilities to prevent tracking and eavesdropping. Various tracking prevention remedies are discussed in this section.

Cookie Opt-out

Visitors to websites are often informed about the use of cookies to track their preferences. Users are free to decline the use of cookies. Sometimes this means that a user's preferences won't be remembered between visits; if the cookie opt-out includes session cookies, however, a visitor might be unable to conduct transactions with the organization in their browser. Although many browsers provide a function to remove all cookies, some browsers permit users to remove individual cookies.

Cookie Blocking

Third-party cookies are blocked by default on most browsers and users are permitted to reject first-party cookies. Rejecting first-party cookies can sometimes disrupt the normal functioning of some websites, depending on their architecture. Some browsers allow users to permit and/or block cookies from specific domains, giving them more granular control over cookie-based web tracking.

Cookie Removal

Web browsers on mobile devices and laptop computers allow users to remove all cookies. This will result in all logged-in sessions being effectively logged out, and any website preferences, such as preferred language or postal code, will be removed.

Firewall Rules

In cases where unique domain names are used to manage third-party cookies, firewall rules can be implemented that block access to those domains. As this is a potentially complex effort, the assistance of network or security engineers might be needed.

Do Not Track

The *Do Not Track* web browser setting can be used to disable web server tracking for a user. Note that Do Not Track is a request that lacks specific controls for enforcement; website operators must voluntarily implement features that result in the user's visits not being tracked. Do Not Track has not been widely adopted by the industry, in part because of the lack of legal mandates for its use. Do Not Track is the web version of the U.S. Do Not Call legislation enacted in 2003 in response to the scourge of annoying telemarketing calls.

Privacy Mode Browsing

Many browsers have a *privacy mode*, sometimes called *incognito mode*, in which website visit tracking is not included in the browsing history. This might be useful on shared computers if a user does not want other users to know about their browsing history. Many people are unaware that privacy mode browsing does not diminish or affect the full logging performed by web content filters, cloud access security brokers, and websites themselves. Indeed, websites make no distinction between privacy-mode browsing and regular browsing in their activity logs.

Tor Browsers

Users who don't want their locations tracked online can use a Tor browser, which routes traffic through the Tor network and utilizes aggressive anti-fingerprinting capabilities. The Tor network is designed to conceal the IP address and, thus, the physical location of the device using the Tor browser. Tor browsers also do not retain cookies or browsing history between sessions. Use of the Tor network is limited to the Tor browser. Users who want to anonymize their IP addresses for other programs turn to private VPN services.

It is generally believed that many of the "exit nodes" of the Tor network have been identified by government law enforcement or intelligence agencies, making Tor use less anonymous than it once was.

Private VPN Services

Persons concerned about protecting their network traffic or who want to anonymize their IP address can use a private VPN service. These services, available on mobile devices as well as laptop and desktop computers, enable users to "hide" behind a relatively anonymous IP address, which helps conceal their location.

VPN services do not anonymize a user's web browser. For instance, if an email user logs in to their webmail service and then activates a VPN, their webmail session will likely continue uninterrupted, since the user's identity is authenticated via session cookies. That said, websites with stronger security measures can alert users or even block access if they detect attempts to log in from faraway countries. In a similar vein, my online banking app on my smartphone blocks the VPN function because the GPS location and the VPN IP address location conflict.

Faraday Bags

Users of mobile phones and other small devices can purchase *Faraday bags*, which are small pouches made of metallic material that block RF signals. Placing a mobile device into a Faraday bag essentially causes it to "disappear" from cellular, Wi-Fi, and Bluetooth networks.

Mobile device Faraday bags can also be used to protect access cards, preventing them from being cloned by attackers. Smaller versions of Faraday bags are made for key fobs used to lock, unlock, and remotely start automobiles. Because of the relatively poor security of key fobs, people concerned about automobile theft use these bags. Figure 9.4 shows a mobile device and

FIGURE 9.4 Faraday bags protect mobile devices and key fobs from eavesdropping and tracking.

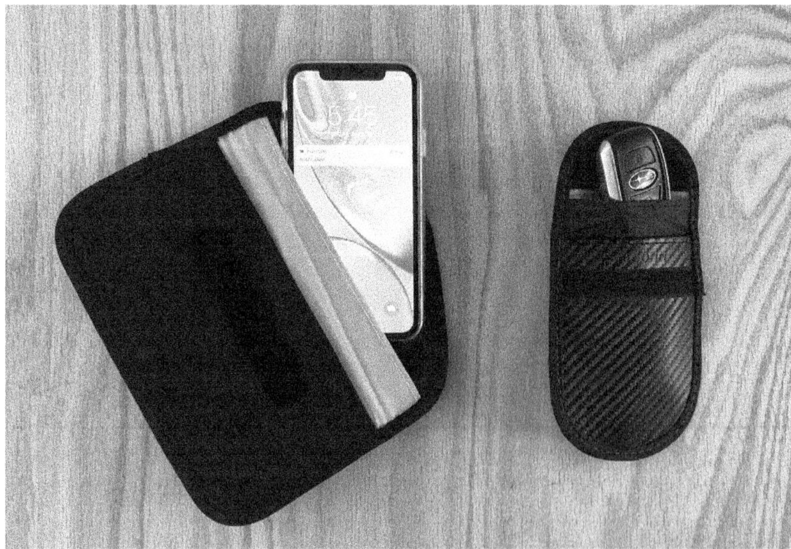

Source: Author.

key fob Faraday bag. A disadvantage of a Faraday bag is that the mobile device is unavailable for any use while inside the bag.

Anonymization and Pseudonymization

De-identification refers to any of several techniques that all serve a single purpose: to remove from business records any traceable reference to a specific natural person. De-identification is a key concept in data privacy because it is an effective means of reducing risks associated with storing large amounts of personally identifiable information (PII).

For several valid reasons, organizations might not completely remove older business records containing PII. Often, significant value can be derived from older records, including the charting of long-term trends. However, in many cases, it is no longer necessary for organizations to continue relating older business records to specific individuals. This is where organizations can use de-identification techniques to remove specific references to individuals while retaining other aspects of these records.

Techniques often used in de-identification include the following:

- **Anonymization** ISO 25237 (Health Informatics—Pseudonymization) defines *anonymization* as any "process by which personal data is irreversibly altered in such a way that a data subject can no longer be identified directly or indirectly, either by the data controller alone or in collaboration with any other party." PII fields can be removed or hashed so that the data cannot be associated with specific data subjects.
- ***k-anonymization*** In this technique, specific identifying fields in a data subject record are altered through *generalization*. For example, specific subject ages are changed to age ranges (42 becomes 40–45) or postal codes (99349 becomes 993**), so that individual data records are more resistant to re-identification. The name comes from the technique whose goal is for a record in a dataset to be indistinguishable from at least *k-1* other records.
- **Pseudonymization** In the European Union, General Data Protection Regulation (GDPR) Article 4 defines *pseudonymization* as "the processing of personal data in such a manner that the personal data can no longer be attributed to a specific data subject without the use of additional information, provided that such additional information is kept separately and is subject to technical and organisational measures to ensure that the personal data are not attributed to an identified or identifiable natural person." Here, specific identifying fields such as name, address, phone number, email address, and financial account numbers are removed and replaced with pseudonyms.
- **Masking** Data *masking* is a privacy protection technique in which sensitive information is concealed from view, such as on a screen or in a report. With masking, the sensitive information still resides in source data files, but is not displayed. A common example of masking is the hiding of all but the last four digits of a credit card or Social Security number.

- **Tokenization** *Tokenization* is a de-identification technique in which sensitive information is replaced by a token, which is often a pointer to a database where the original information can be found.
- **Encryption** *Encryption* as a pseudonymization technique involves the scrambling of sensitive data that can be converted to plaintext by anyone possessing the encryption key; it's explored in detail in Chapter 8.

Privacy professionals need to understand an organization's de-identification techniques to ensure that records cannot be re-identified with specific individuals.

Privacy-enhancing Technologies

Privacy-enhancing technologies (PETs) are a variety of techniques that enable the processing, analysis, and sharing of personal information while minimizing exposure and reducing re-identification risk. Examples of PETs include:

- **Data transformation** Techniques discussed earlier in this chapter, including anonymization, k-anonymization, masking, pseudonymization, and tokenization.
- ***Homomorphic encryption*** An encryption and data processing technique in which encrypted data can be processed without decryption. When the processor does not possess the decryption key, it cannot access the plaintext data.
- ***Trusted execution environment*** Also known as *confidential computing*, personal and sensitive information is isolated during processing so that other system components cannot access it.
- ***Differential privacy*** A technique for releasing information about datasets while protecting the privacy of individual data subjects, by injecting noise into results. This helps to limit what can be inferred about any individual in the data.
- ***Synthetic data*** The creation of artificial datasets that preserve the statistical properties of the original dataset.
- ***Federated learning*** A machine learning training technique in which several entities contribute training data, which is kept decentralized. In federated learning, models are trained locally with model updates shared with other entities, rather than the personal information itself.

Privacy-enhancing technologies provide organizations with technical mechanisms to analyze and share data while reducing exposure of personal information. Their effectiveness depends on selecting approaches that align with the specific processing objective, risk profile, and regulatory requirements. Some techniques, such as anonymization or masking, are appropriate for data release, while others, such as federated learning, are better suited for collaborative analytics. Selection should consider data sensitivity, acceptable accuracy trade-offs, scalability, and operational complexity.

AI/ML Considerations

Artificial intelligence (AI) and *machine learning (ML)* encompass a range of capabilities that simulate human analytical capabilities. Generative AI, through tools such as ChatGPT, Claude, and Grok, can analyze large datasets and provide insights into them.

In the context of privacy, the most significant risk related to the organizational use of AI and ML concerns how these models are trained. Organizations that produce and sell products and services to customers are apt to train their AI/ML models with customer data to learn more about their preferences. Similarly, organizations can purchase large datasets of prospective customers to identify those to whom they will market their products.

The main problem with using personal information to train AI and ML models is that those models cannot be "untrained" by removing individual records.

Opt Out and Consent Withdrawal

When personal information is used to train an AI model, opting out or withdrawing consent creates significant technical and governance challenges. During training, individual data points are not retained as discrete records; instead, they are absorbed into model parameters in a distributed manner. This transformation makes it difficult to isolate and remove the influence of a specific individual after consent is withdrawn. Deleting the original training record does not eliminate its effect, because patterns learned from that data are entangled with information from many other sources.

Operationally, organizations can struggle to determine whether a person's data was included in training, which model versions were affected, and where those models have been deployed. Retraining a model without the withdrawn data might be required, but this can be costly and time-consuming, especially when models are large or frequently updated. Derived artifacts, such as embeddings, fine-tuned models, or synthetic datasets, might also propagate the influence of the original data.

From a compliance perspective, consent withdrawal typically requires cessation of further processing and, where feasible, removal of previously used data. Mitigation strategies include maintaining data lineage, tagging datasets by consent status, retraining models, and applying privacy-preserving techniques. However, complete removal of an individual's influence might remain technically impractical.

Given these challenges, it is recommended that organizations that want to train their AI/ML models with personal information first process the training data using data minimization and de-identification techniques, so that the withdrawal of consent does not force an organization to retrain its models.

Re-identification Risk

Re-identification risk in AI and ML arises when individuals whose data contributed to training, testing, or inference can be identified directly or indirectly from model behavior or outputs. Although datasets can be anonymized, models can still encode patterns that reflect unique or rare characteristics. Attackers can exploit this through techniques such as *membership inference*, which attempts to determine whether a specific individual's data was included in training, or *model inversion*, which reconstructs approximate input data from predictions. *Linkage attacks* can also occur when model outputs are combined with external datasets to identify individuals.

This risk increases when models overfit training data, when datasets include small or distinctive populations, or when model interfaces allow repeated probing. Embeddings, synthetic data, and derived artifacts can also preserve identifiable traits, even when raw data is not exposed. The consequences include disclosure of sensitive attributes, erosion of anonymization assurances, and regulatory or contractual non-compliance.

Mitigation strategies include applying differential privacy, reducing overfitting through regularization, limiting the level of detail in outputs, restricting access to model interfaces, and performing privacy-focused testing. However, re-identification risk cannot always be eliminated, particularly when models are widely accessible or trained on highly distinctive data.

Mitigating AI-related Risks

AI and ML represent perhaps the biggest technical innovation since the Industrial Revolution, the invention of the personal computer, or the Internet. AI and ML can profoundly transform organizations and entire industries, and indeed, this transformation is already underway. While organizations are not going to stop using AI because of privacy risks, those risks can be mitigated through several means discussed in this book, and summarized here:

- **Privacy governance and management**
  - Privacy policy
  - Privacy controls
  - Privacy by design
  - De-identification
  - *Input authorization* and *input controls*
  - Automated opt-out, consent capture, and fulfillment
  - Legal basis for processing
  - Privacy incident management
  - Privacy training

- **Data governance and management**
  - Data classification
  - Data inventory
  - Data provenance
  - Data lineage
  - Management approvals for all new uses of personal information
  - Data management training
- **Security governance and management**
  - Information security policy
  - Acceptable use policy
  - Security by design
  - Risk management
  - Attack surface reduction
  - Event and incident logging
  - Security incident management
  - Sound identity and access management
  - Third-party risk management
  - Security awareness training
- **Organizational culture**
  - Code of conduct and ethics policy
  - Accountability

Summary

Consent tagging, also known as consent metadata, consent labels, and privacy labels, represents the data that should be collected when a data subject provides, modifies, or withdraws consent to the use of their personal information.

Tracking schemes are established so that website, API, and application providers can monitor and measure their systems and enrich the website or application experience for users. Some of the logging and other techniques can represent overreach and an invasion of privacy.

Tracking identifiers include IP addresses, device identifiers, HTML cookies, web beacons, location data, RFID tags, eavesdropping, and digital fingerprinting.

Facial recognition and biometrics have some useful purposes, although there is growing concern that these capabilities will be misused to the detriment of private citizens. Several prominent organizations and governments have sought to ban their use.

Contact tracing represents an attempt to track the spread of infectious diseases. However, contact tracing data can also be misused for political and nefarious purposes.

Organizations use internal tracking tools and techniques to reduce the probability and impact of attackers and malware. Tools include web content filters, cloud access security brokers, email archiving, and SSL decryption.

Attackers can obtain sensitive information through keyloggers, cameras, photo libraries, microphones, location data, and other means, including malware and social media attacks.

End users can limit some tracking through several techniques, such as opting out of cookies, blocking and removing cookies, blocking cookies with firewalls, using Tor browsers, using VPN services, using Faraday bags, and setting the Do Not Track flag in their browsers.

De-identification refers to any of several techniques available that all serve a single purpose: to effectively remove from business records any traceable reference to a specific natural person. Techniques include anonymization, k-anonymization, pseudonymization, masking, tokenization, and encryption.

Privacy-enhancing technologies can reduce privacy risks. Techniques include homomorphic encryption, trusted execution environments, differential privacy, synthetic data, and federated learning.

Organizations using and training AI and ML systems on personal data face additional challenges, primarily the need to remove individual training records when data subjects opt out or withdraw consent. Further, AI and ML can make re-identification easier, which can make de-identification somewhat more challenging.

Mitigating AI- and ML-related risks depends on the entire privacy stack, including privacy governance and management, data governance and management, security governance and management, and organizational culture.

Exam Essentials

Understand consent tagging and its purpose. Consent tagging assigns metadata to personal data indicating the scope, purpose, and status of user consent. This enables systems to enforce permitted uses, support withdrawal of consent, and provide audit evidence for regulatory compliance.

Recognize the privacy implications of tracking technologies. Tracking technologies such as cookies, device fingerprints, and beacons collect behavioral data that can be used to identify individuals or profiles. Privacy controls include notice, consent management, purpose limitation, and mechanisms for opt-out or preference management.

Distinguish anonymization from pseudonymization. Anonymization irreversibly removes identifiers so individuals cannot be re-identified, whereas pseudonymization replaces identifiers with tokens while retaining the ability to relink data under controlled conditions. Pseudonymized data remains subject to privacy regulations.

Identify common privacy-enhancing technologies (PETs). PETs include techniques such as differential privacy, federated learning, homomorphic encryption, trusted execution environments, and synthetic data. These technologies enable analysis while minimizing exposure of personal information.

Understand trade-offs when selecting PETs. PET selection requires balancing privacy protection, data utility, performance overhead, implementation complexity, and scalability. No single PET eliminates risk, and governance controls must complement technical measures. All measures must comply with applicable regulations.

Recognize AI/ML-specific privacy risks. AI systems introduce re-identification risk, model inversion, membership inference, and unintended memorization of sensitive data. These risks can persist even when training data is anonymized.

Apply privacy-by-design principles to AI/ML use. Privacy controls for AI include data minimization, consent management, secure training practices, output limitation, differential privacy, and testing for leakage. These measures reduce the likelihood of exposing personal data through model behavior.

Review Questions

1. Which of the following best describes consent tagging?
   - A. Encrypting personal data fields before storage
   - B. Removing identifiers from datasets
   - C. Logging user authentication events
   - D. Associating metadata with data to record permitted uses and restrictions
2. A cookie banner that allows users to accept analytics cookies but reject advertising cookies demonstrates which of the following?
   - A. Granular consent management
   - B. Data masking
   - C. Tokenization
   - D. Differential privacy
3. Which technique replaces identifiers with reversible substitutes that require a separate lookup table?
   - A. Tokenization
   - B. Anonymization
   - C. Hashing with no salt
   - D. Aggregation
4. Which of the following is the primary risk associated with anonymized datasets?
   - A. Encryption failure
   - B. Data retention violations
   - C. Lack of access controls
   - D. Re-identification through linkage attacks
5. Which of the following is considered a privacy-enhancing technology (PET)?
   - A. Network segmentation
   - B. Differential privacy
   - C. Patch management
   - D. Multi-factor authentication
6. Consent tagging is most useful in which scenario?
   - A. Enforcing user-specific data processing restrictions across systems
   - B. Limiting administrator privileges
   - C. Encrypting backups
   - D. Detecting malware

7. Which tracking technology is most commonly used to monitor user behavior across websites?
   - A. Third-party cookies
   - B. Session tokens
   - C. TLS certificates
   - D. DNSSEC

8. Which anonymization technique reduces risk by grouping individuals into broader categories?
   - A. Tokenization
   - B. Encryption
   - C. Generalization
   - D. Hash chaining

9. Federated learning improves privacy by doing which of the following?
   - A. Centralizing all training data
   - B. Encrypting cookies
   - C. Training models locally and sharing model updates instead of raw data
   - D. Removing audit logs

10. Which control ensures that tracking technologies operate only after user consent?
    - A. Data retention policy
    - B. Access control list
    - C. Key escrow
    - D. Consent enforcement mechanism

11. Which scenario represents pseudonymization rather than anonymization?
    - A. Removing all identifying attributes permanently
    - B. Aggregating data into statistical summaries
    - C. Deleting records entirely
    - D. Replacing names with unique identifiers stored separately

12. Which PET allows computations on encrypted data without decrypting it?
    - A. Tokenization
    - B. Homomorphic encryption
    - C. Hashing
    - D. Data masking

13. A model inversion attack attempts to do which of the following?
    A. Corrupt training data
    B. Deny service to ML systems
    C. Extract sensitive information from trained models
    D. Modify consent records
14. Which control best mitigates excessive data collection by tracking technologies?
    A. Data minimization configuration
    B. Backup rotation
    C. Patch management
    D. Network load balancing
15. Which technique adds statistical noise to protect individual privacy in datasets?
    A. Tokenization
    B. Pseudonymization
    C. Differential privacy
    D. Hashing
16. Which combination most effectively reduces re-identification risk in AI training datasets?
    A. Differential privacy and aggregation
    B. Encryption and access control
    C. Pseudonymization and audit logging
    D. Data retention limits and patching
17. Consent tagging primarily supports which privacy principle?
    A. Accountability and purpose limitation
    B. Availability
    C. Nonrepudiation
    D. Data portability
18. Which tracking technology operates without storing data on the user's device?
    A. First-party cookies
    B. Pixel tracking
    C. Device fingerprinting
    D. Session cookies

19. Anonymization differs from pseudonymization because anonymization does which of the following?
    A. Uses encryption keys
    B. Eliminates the ability to identify individuals
    C. Allows re-identification
    D. Requires consent

20. Which of the following is an example of a privacy-enhancing technology?
    A. Firewall
    B. Antivirus software
    C. Differential privacy
    D. Load balancer

Answers to Review Questions

1. D. Consent tagging involves attaching metadata to data elements that reflects the data subject's consent preferences, lawful basis, and permitted uses. This enables systems to enforce processing restrictions automatically and ensures that downstream uses of data remain consistent with the individual's consent.

2. A. Granular consent management allows users to selectively permit different categories of tracking technologies. This supports privacy regulations that require specific and informed consent rather than blanket acceptance. The banner enforces user preferences at a category level, aligning data collection with declared purposes.

3. A. Tokenization replaces direct identifiers with tokens or pseudonyms while maintaining the ability to re-identify individuals using additional information stored separately. This reduces the risk of exposure but does not eliminate identifiability, so the data remains personal data under most privacy regulations.

4. D. Even when identifiers are removed, anonymized datasets can be re-identified by correlating them with other datasets. This is known as a linkage or re-identification attack. Proper anonymization requires assessing this risk and applying techniques such as aggregation, suppression, or noise addition.

5. B. Differential privacy is a PET that introduces statistical noise into datasets or query outputs to prevent the identification of individuals while still allowing meaningful analysis. It is specifically designed to balance data utility with privacy protection.

6. A. Consent tagging allows organizations to propagate user consent preferences alongside data. This ensures that downstream systems honor permitted purposes and prevents unauthorized processing that conflicts with original consent.

7. A. Third-party cookies are placed by domains other than the one the user is visiting. They enable cross-site tracking and profiling, leading to increased regulatory scrutiny and browser restrictions.

8. C. Generalization reduces data precision, for example, by replacing exact ages with age ranges. This increases the size of anonymity sets and reduces the likelihood of identifying individuals.

9. C. Federated learning keeps data on local devices and shares only model parameters or gradients. This reduces exposure of raw personal data and supports privacy-preserving machine learning workflows.

10. D. Consent enforcement mechanisms block or enable tracking technologies based on user selections. This is typically implemented through consent management platforms that control script execution.

11. D. Pseudonymization retains the ability to re-identify individuals using a separate mapping. Tokenization is a form of pseudonymization. This distinguishes it from anonymization, where re-identification should not be reasonably possible.

12. B. Homomorphic encryption enables the processing of encrypted data while preserving confidentiality. This supports privacy-preserving analytics without exposing underlying personal data.

13. C. Model inversion attacks exploit trained models to infer information about individuals in the training dataset. This is a key privacy risk associated with machine learning systems.

14. A. Configuring tracking technologies to collect only necessary data supports data minimization principles and reduces privacy risk. This includes limiting fields, retention periods, and tracking scope.

15. C. Differential privacy introduces mathematically calibrated noise to outputs, ensuring that the presence or absence of any individual has minimal impact on results, reducing re-identification risk.

16. A. Differential privacy reduces the ability to infer individual contributions, while aggregation increases the size of anonymity sets. Together, these techniques significantly reduce re-identification risk in AI training datasets.

17. A. Consent tagging ensures that data processing aligns with declared purposes and provides traceability for compliance. This supports both accountability and purpose limitation.

18. C. Device fingerprinting collects attributes such as browser type and screen resolution to uniquely identify users without storing cookies. This raises privacy concerns due to a lack of transparency and control.

19. B. Anonymization removes or transforms data so that individuals cannot be identified using reasonably available means. Pseudonymization retains a reversible link, whereas anonymization aims to remove it entirely.

20. C. Differential privacy is a privacy-enhancing technology designed specifically to protect individuals when performing statistical analysis or training machine learning models. It works by introducing mathematically calibrated noise into datasets or query outputs so that the contribution of any single individual cannot be reliably determined.

Index

Pages in *italics* refer to figures and pages in **bold** refer to tables.

D

K

L

M

N

O

P

Q

R

S

T

U

V

W

Z

Online Test Bank

To help you study for your CDPSE Certified Data Privacy Solutions Engineer Study Guide, register to gain one year of FREE access after activation to the online interactive test bank—included with your purchase of this book!

To access our learning environment, simply visit www.wiley.com/go/sybextestprep, follow the instructions to register your book, and instantly gain one year of FREE access after activation to:

- Practice test questions, so you can practice in a timed and graded setting
- Flashcards
- A searchable glossary